NEW PRODUCT
MANAGEMENT

NEW PRODUCT MANAGEMENT

Eberhard E. Scheuing
St. John's University

Merrill Publishing Company
A BELL & HOWELL INFORMATION COMPANY
COLUMBUS   TORONTO   LONDON   MELBOURNE

Published by Merrill Publishing Company
A Bell & Howell Information Company
Columbus, Ohio 43216

This book was set in Garamond and Helvetica.

Administrative Editor: Pamela B. Kusma
Production Coordinator: Carol S. Sykes
Art Coordinator: Vincent A. Smith
Cover Designer: Brian Deep

Library of Congress Catalog Card Number: 88-62486
International Standard Book Number: 0-675-20922-6
Printed in the United States of America
    2   3   4   5   6   7   8   9 – 92   91   90   89

To Carol
in love and gratitude

PREFACE

Over the past two decades, the study of new product management strategies and practices has been gaining steadily in importance and sophistication. Pressures from customers, competitors, and shareholders emphasize the need for every firm to generate a steady stream of successful new products. As *Fortune* reported in its cover story of March 28, 1988, a company such as 3M stays ahead by introducing 200 new products a year. This requires creating a climate for innovation and establishing systematic, professional management of the new product function.

Goals of the Book

New Product Management is designed to acquaint students with the fundamental issues and approaches related to today's new product challenges. It can also serve as a useful supplementary text in introductory marketing courses, offering substance and depth on a vital and fascinating topic. Last, but certainly not least, *New Product Management* can be used as a helpful guide, reference, or handbook for marketing practitioners involved in new product activities.

This book provides an up-to-date, accurate, and concise overview of the process of new product management. Students will gain a comprehensive working knowledge of the concerns and techniques involved in creating and introducing new products in the marketplace, as well as in managing them throughout their market life.

Approach of This Book

New Product Management represents a highly readable, classroom-tested text that takes an evolutionary approach, discussing step by step the tasks and tools of modern new product management. It presents a balanced, realistic picture of the new product process, incorporating the latest research findings and current business practices. Many "real-life" examples underscore the principles presented in the text. End-of-chapter case histories were specifically written for the book. These cases enable the student to apply the concepts they have studied.

The student learns how to organize and plan for new products, becomes thoroughly acquainted with the steps and techniques involved in the evolutionary process, and learns how to design the proper introductory marketing mix. The student is also introduced to such special topics as managing the acceptance of new products, managing their product life cycle, and managing new products in service firms. Content material draws heavily on business publications, such as the *Wall Street Journal, Business Week,* and *Fortune,* and is illustrated by plentiful exhibits and tables.

In addition, Merrill has available a simulation, *Product Pursuit: New Product Planning Game,* by Agnes P. Olszewski and Janet Daugherty. This simulation enables students to learn more about new product management.

Acknowledgments

No textbook is ever written in a social or intellectual vacuum; rather, it is the outgrowth of a continuing exchange of ideas and experiences. In addition to providing their valuable insights, fourteen individuals have contributed case histories to the book. These contributions are gratefully acknowledged in each instance. For their kind encouragement and support, I would also like to thank Earl L. Bailey of The Conference Board, Gerald Griffin of the Norton Agency, my friend Eugene M. Johnson of the University of Rhode Island, and my dynamic chairperson, Herb Katzenstein.

For their thoughtful and helpful suggestions, which contributed significantly to the improvement of the manuscript, I owe a debt of gratitude to the following reviewers: Richard H. Behrman, Meredith College; Jim Brock, Montana State University; Peter S. Carusone, Wright State University; Robert W. Cook, West Virginia University; Neil Ford, University of Wisconsin-Madison; A. H. Kizilbash, Northern Illinois University; Tridib Mazumdar, Virginia Polytechnic Institute & State University; James U. McNeal, Texas A & M University; Heikki J. Rinne, Brigham Young University; Cathie H. Tinney, St. Louis University; and Richard A. Wozniak, Northeastern Illinois University.

Inasmuch as this book is an attempt to engage in an ongoing dialog with current and future marketing executives and academic colleagues, readers' comments, inquiries, and suggestions would be greatly appreciated.

Eberhard E. Scheuing

CONTENTS

NEW PRODUCT
MANAGEMENT

PART ONE

The Job of New Product Management

*I*n a high-level economy the continuous development and introduction of innovations become the fuel of growth for both individual companies and the economy as a whole. In the long run, a steady flow of new products is needed for firms and industries to survive and prosper under the onslaught of technological and market change. Respondents to a survey by Booz, Allen & Hamilton, Inc., anticipated the contribution of new products over the next five years to represent fully one-third of their corporate profits.[1]

Many markets are characterized by a rapid turnover of products. In a speech before the annual New Products Conference sponsored by the American Marketing Association, Herb Baum, the president of Campbell Soup Company, stated that about 6,000 new products would enter the marketplace in 1987 and 80 percent would fail. "Only 4% of all new products reach the $20 million sales level, and a mere .5% bring in $100 million," according to Baum.[2] In light of this report, the estimate that 80 percent of today's products will be gone in ten years, while 80 percent of the products sold then will have been introduced in the meantime, appears entirely credible. In a Conference Board survey, 35 percent of the respondents reported that "their companies get at least half of their revenues from products that were not in production ten years ago."[3]

The need for new products largely arises from the behavior patterns of consumers. "A *Better Homes & Gardens* survey reflected that 44% of consumers purchased a new product in the past 10 days," Baum said.[4] Beside their desire for newness, consumers' problems, needs, wants, expectations, attitudes, preferences, and values are forever changing. This is due to higher educational and income levels, changes in employment patterns, altered life-styles, increased leisure time, and easy availability of credit, to name but a few factors. Marketing research, therefore, must serve as an early warning system, detecting shifts in

1

consumer purchasing behavior. This will enable marketers to stay in tune with the marketplace and meet these changes with suitable new products.

Although Booz, Allen & Hamilton quotes a 65 percent success rate among its survey respondents, many innovations fail in the marketplace.[5] This lack of acceptance can be caused by the following:

- Inadequate product performance
- Buyer indifference or confusion
- Aggressive competitive tactics
- Inept marketing effort
- Rapidly changing technology
- Insufficient dealer support

But a firm that launches an unsuccessful product and simply blames unfavorable circumstances may be taking it too easy on itself. Coca-Cola totally misread the market in its introduction of New Coke. Violent market reaction forced the company to reverse itself and reintroduce the original formula under the name Classic Coke. But the same company was enormously successful in its worldwide introduction of Diet Coke, known overseas as Coca-Cola Light. Individual companies experience different success rates in new product introduction. Some firms are simply less sophisticated than others in understanding buyer behavior and are less careful in planning and executing new product programs. In these businesses the tremendous waste of new product effort and money can be significantly reduced by better knowledge and management of new product processes.[6]

New product management, then, provides ample opportunity and challenge for able, ambitious individuals. It bears the crucial responsibility of ensuring the uninterrupted output of new products. To shed some light on this substantial task, Chapter 1 highlights the role that products play in a firm's marketing effort. This requires a definition of the nature of a product, followed by a discussion of what constitutes a new product. The chapter concludes with a review of the different categories of new products available to the resourceful new product manager.

Chapter 2 is devoted to new product planning. Beginning with the new product management cycle, the entire planning process is analyzed in chronological order, including an overview of strategic options. The third chapter examines the organizational framework and tools. Clearly, for continuity of effort and output, proper organizational provisions must be made. A number of alternative structures are available, which may even be used in combination with each other. The structural new product organization must be complemented by an appropriate process organization that maps out and coordinates the many activities involved in new product evolution.

NOTES

1. See Booz, Allen & Hamilton, Inc., *New Products Management for the 1980s* (New York: Booz, Allen & Hamilton, Inc., 1982), 4.
2. "Most New Products Start with a Bang, End up as a Bomb," *Marketing News,* 27 March 1987, 36.
3. Michael G. Duerr, *The Commercial Development of New Products* (New York: The Conference Board, 1986), 3.
4. "Most New Products Start with a Bang," 36.
5. See Booz, Allen & Hamilton, *New Products Management,* 7.
6. Ibid., 6f.

CHAPTER 1

The Nature of New Product Management

Marketing attempts to produce satisfactory and mutually beneficial exchanges with a chosen target group.[1] Managing this function means identifying and seizing opportunities as well as coping with a variety of environmental challenges and threats. As a vital part of marketing management, *product management* can be described as the analyzing, planning, implementing, and controlling of product-related marketing activities. Although product management deals with both established and new products, this text concentrates on new product management.

New product management

- Concerns itself with the analysis and evaluation of new product opportunities and challenges.
- Involves planning a firm's new product effort on a continuous basis to ensure survival and steady growth in the long run.
- Needs appropriate structural and process organization for smooth functioning.
- Directs the evolutionary process leading from idea to launch of an innovative item.
- Means continuous monitoring and evaluation of environmental changes and their consequences.

New product management, therefore, is an exciting, challenging task that requires dedicated people with a variety of abilities and skills. Because it also tends to involve long hours, it is often a job for young, energetic, enthusiastic individuals who are eager to prove themselves. Many product managers are in their late twenties or early thirties. They typically manage a given brand for an average of two years and then move up to greater responsibilities or on to other firms. Product managers are not specialists in one area of marketing but, rather, are generalists who are equally comfortable with marketing research and advertising planning, product development, and field selling.

Successful new product management depends on a thorough understanding of the role of products in a firm's marketing effort. This, in turn, presupposes a careful and thoughtful definition of what constitutes a product. Only after the term *product* has been defined adequately does it become meaningful to explore the characteristics of *new* products. The final section of this chapter addresses the ways in which a product can be new.

The Role of Products in a Firm's Marketing Effort

The production and/or distribution of products has always been at the heart of business enterprises. Firms offer products to the public and generate revenues through their sale. But the role of products in marketing efforts differs dramatically among companies, depending on the prevailing management philosophy.

Under the old concept of marketing, a producer designs, develops, manufactures, and markets a product in isolation from the ultimate consumer. In this view the emphasis is clearly placed on the product, not the consumer. Figure 1–1 illustrates the fact that in such a one-way relationship the producer must use promotional pressure to get the consumer to buy something that may be neither needed nor wanted.

A company practicing the old concept of marketing is engineering and production oriented, and its product offering is technology driven. This type of company tends to offer a product in the marketplace merely because that product is technologically feasible and represents an advance over prior alternatives. Market factors usually are not considered. Mamiya's electronic still imaging—akin to still photographs on an electronic medium, such as videotape—is an example of such a product for which there is no discernible demand. Panasonic offers a television receiver with a screen size of 1.5 inches (measured diagonally), mainly to demonstrate its technological prowess. In a similar vein AT&T has had picturephones available for more than a quarter century but has not found a profitable way of marketing them.[2]

This risky hit-or-miss approach succeeds only in the absence of serious competition or in the presence of significant shortages. Figure 1–2 demonstrates this kind of situation, which can be called a sellers' market because the sellers have the upper hand and determine what is happening in the marketplace. When there was a steel shortage in the United States, steel makers decided what type of steel to sell to whom at which prices. Under such conditions, products will be bought, even if they do not fit buyer needs exactly. Buyers simply have no choice.

However, as the supply expands because of unfulfilled demand, the balance of power in the marketplace shifts from a sellers' market to a buyers' market. As

FIGURE 1–1
The Old Concept of Marketing

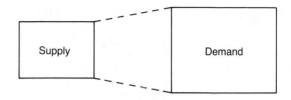

FIGURE 1–2
Sellers' Market

shown in Figure 1–3, the buyers' market means that undersupply has changed to oversupply, and supplier market dominance has been replaced by competitive pressure. The sudden onslaught of vigorous competition for the buyer's dollar forces a new attitude toward marketing and hence the role that products play. Instead of being ignored, the wants, needs, and problems of consumers are now carefully investigated.

In fact, marketing research is an essential part of the new concept of marketing, which aims to provide satisfaction to chosen target groups. This fundamental reorientation of the marketing relationship between producer and consumer is illustrated in Figure 1–4 by means of a circle that places the consumer at both the beginning and the end of the marketing process. By addressing need gaps or inadequately solved problems, the product now provides need or want satisfaction or a problem solution.

Companies adhering to the old concept of marketing attempt to create markets for products—the products are given while demand must be created. In contrast, followers of the new concept of marketing try to create products for markets—demand exists, so products must be shaped to satisfy it. The old concept emphasizes the seller's needs and focuses on the product, whereas the new concept highlights the buyer's needs and concentrates on the consumer as the key to success.

Enlightened managers fine-tune their firms' marketing efforts by carefully researching their markets to determine market capacity, volume, and resistance. *Market capacity* is the total potential demand for a product, preferably measured in terms of units. This figure, which is also called market potential, represents the maximum that can be sold in a given market by an entire industry. It is determined by the number of people in this market who are both able and willing to buy.

Market volume, on the other hand, is the total actual sales volume of the entire industry in this market. As shown in Figure 1–5, it constitutes the realized

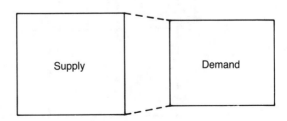

FIGURE 1–3
Buyers' Market

FIGURE 1–4
The New Concept of Marketing

portion of the market capacity, or the share of the total potential demand that has been successfully converted into actual sales. The ratio of market volume to market capacity thus could be considered the rate of market penetration and could be used as a measure for the degree of market maturity. This ratio is very low when a new product category is launched and approaches 100 percent when a market becomes saturated.

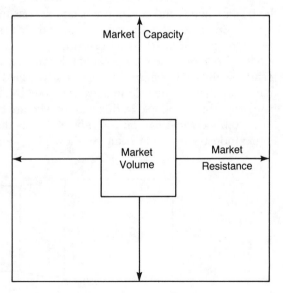

FIGURE 1–5
Market Assessment

Accordingly, the entire demand for a revolutionary product that is creating a completely new market—the electric car, for example—is initially of a potential nature. Because no purchases have as yet been transacted, the market volume is zero. The subsequent growth in market volume is better understood if one considers the changes in market resistance occurring over time. *Market resistance* can be viewed as the unwillingness of potential buyers to purchase the products of a specific company. It occurs in two versions, primary and secondary. Primary market resistance is encountered when a new market is being created. The risk associated with the purchase of a completely unknown product is extremely high, and very few buyers are willing to take a chance at this point. *Primary demand,* or the generic demand, for any product in this new category has not yet been generated. The pioneering firm thus must overcome resistance against change and newness in general when it attempts to create a new market.

As the innovation becomes better known and increases in popularity, market volume grows while primary market resistance dwindles steadily. Buyers become better acquainted with competitive offerings, brand loyalty develops, and secondary market resistance builds up. This secondary market resistance is due to the emergence of *selective demand,* which represents the demand for specific competing brands. Secondary market resistance may be even harder to overcome through increased promotional efforts than primary resistance. At this point consumers have become familiar with the product category and will change their brand affiliation only if given a good reason to do so. When the market volume finally approaches market capacity, saturation makes further penetration very expensive.

Although a major factor, the product nevertheless does not stand as the sole pillar of a company's marketing effort. Rather, it works in conjunction with the other elements of the firm's marketing mix—namely, price, promotion, and distribution. Every product needs a supportive relationship with these other components of the *marketing mix*—the marketer's tool kit—to succeed. A good product that is priced too high or too low will fail because buyers will perceive it as being overpriced or of poor quality. And, contrary to the old adage "if you build a better mousetrap, the world will beat a path to your door," no product will sell itself; it needs promotional support. Finally, a product cannot be bought if it is not available because of improper distribution.

The product is thus at the very core of the marketing mix. A firm with a superior product and a fine-tuned marketing mix can succeed superbly. Depending on how well they are designed, the other elements of the marketing mix can add to or detract from the impact of the product itself and therefore make it more or less salable.

Defining the Product

The concept of a product is more elusive than it first appears. Under the old concept of marketing, a product was viewed as a specific combination of physical and chemical characteristics—in other words, a material thing. This emphasis on tangible aspects, however, prevented marketers from creatively understanding and responding to consumer needs and wants.

Brand names, prices, and services associated with tangible items differentiate products in the consumer's mind. Viewing a *product* as a combination of tangible and intangible attributes therefore is essential. Intangible aspects are an integral part of what the customer is buying. In fact, it may be just these intangibles that set an otherwise undistinguished *parity* item apart from the competition and imbue it with a special value, thus creating a *differential advantage*. Because of a strong promotional effort, Clorox has long been the leading household bleach even though competing products are functionally identical and often less expensive. Heublein markets three vodkas: Smirnoff, Relska, and Popov. Although essentially the same from the physical point of view, the three products are differentiated in the buyer's mind through different prices, packaging, branding, and advertising.

As illustrated in Figure 1–6, the term *product* covers both services and goods. Whether a product is considered a service or a good depends on the tangible components' share of its total value. If less than half of a product's price is accounted for by tangible elements, it is called a *service*. On the other hand, if more than 50 percent of a product's market value consists of tangible characteristics, it is referred to as a *good*.

The term *product* thus describes a complex bundle of tangible *and* intangible benefits that a business offers to the marketplace. Indeed, what a customer buys is typically not a tangible item at all. Rather, the buyer acquires anticipated want satisfaction or an expected problem solution. Charles Revson, the legendary founder of Revlon, said, "In the factory, we make cosmetics; in the store, we sell hope." And Theodore Levitt, professor of marketing at Harvard University, has pointed out that "industrial purchasing agents do not buy quarter inch drills; they buy quarter inch holes."

The benefit-bundle perspective relates closely to the three-layer concept of a product, which is shown in Figure 1–7.[3] At the heart of any product offering is its *core benefit*—the key benefit consumers expect to derive from its consumption. For example, the core benefit that a toothpaste buyer desires is healthy teeth, and an airline passenger seeks quick transportation from one point to another. Core benefits are undifferentiated and generic and thus can be obtained from most competitors in a market.

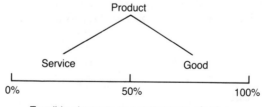

Tangible elements as a percentage of value

FIGURE 1–6
Product Continuum

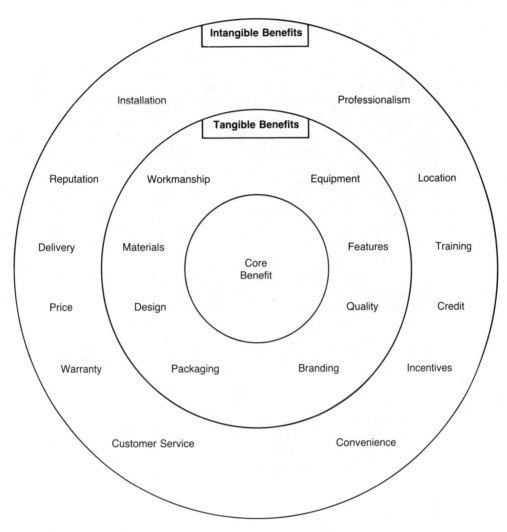

FIGURE 1–7
Three-Layer Product Concept

The core benefit is delivered to customers by means of the two surrounding layers of tangible and intangible benefits. The *tangible benefits* consist of the materials and parts used in making the physical item, its features, design, and workmanship. Particularly in a service enterprise, the tangible benefits also may include the design and appearance of the facility, uniforms, and equipment. Hertz, for instance, replaces its car rental fleet every year to provide the latest models. Quality, too, is becoming an increasingly powerful competitive tool.[4] Consumers look for quality in the products they buy and are often willing to pay a premium for it. The quality of Japanese-made products has given them a strong foothold in many U.S. markets. Similarly, branding and packaging can make a substantial difference in a consumer's perception of a product. When Toro introduced a snowblower under an unknown name, consumers hesitated to buy. The company then decided to market it under the name Toro and built it into a substantial success.

The third layer is composed of *intangible benefits* that make a difference to buyers and thus serve to differentiate further the product in their minds. As Figure 1–7 demonstrates, the list of intangibles can include the reputation of the firm and the professionalism of its people. The name Kodak, for example, is so strong that the firm is even making inroads in Japan. Delivery, installation, and training are key elements in IBM's enormously successful approach to doing business. Especially for service firms, facility location is of vital concern. McDonald's, for instance, conducts extensive studies of traffic flow patterns before selecting a site for a new outlet.

Convenience of product or facility access and use is another important consideration. Easy-to-open beverage containers and automated teller machines offer this benefit. Price, credit, and incentives often go hand in hand. Car manufacturers' finance subsidiaries have long been vital marketing tools, and rebates have become popular in more recent years. In the airline industry, frequent-flier plans have mushroomed to the point where every major airline must offer or participate in such a program. Warranty and customer service round out the picture. Perhaps L. L. Bean will serve as an appropriate example here. Its unlimited warranty and round-the-clock customer service have made this mail-order firm a legend in its business and have contributed to spectacular growth.

Products are the building blocks of a company's offering in the marketplace. A *product* is an individual unit offered for sale, in the form of either a good or a service. Examples of products are a Chevrolet Camaro and a one-year certificate of deposit. A *product line* is a group of related products that serve the same purpose in slightly different ways. All entries in a product line are variations of the same basic product concept. As a market matures, the number of products in a product line expands. Examples of product lines are sports cars and certificates of deposit. A *product category* is composed of all the products competing with each other in a market. Examples of product categories are passenger cars and savings instruments. Passenger cars include sports cars, sedans, station wagons, and vans. Savings instruments include certificates of deposit and savings accounts.

A *product mix* is the combination of products that a company offers for sale. As illustrated in Figure 1–8, a product mix can be described in terms of its two dimensions. The horizontal dimension of *width* refers to the number of product lines offered. The vertical dimension of *depth* reflects the number of products in each line. These products can be made by the company in its own plants (this is called the "make" option in the make–buy decision) or bought from an outside source and resold under the company's name ("buy"). Increasingly, American firms choose to buy products overseas, restricting themselves to designing and marketing.[5]

Having thus explored the meaning of the term *product,* it is now appropriate to investigate the circumstances under which a product can be considered new. As will become evident, this is primarily a matter of buyer perception and behavior.

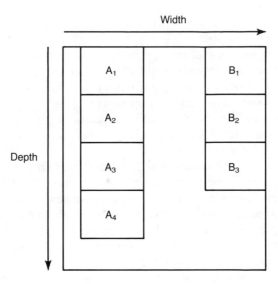

FIGURE 1–8
Product Mix Dimensions

Characteristics of New Products

A *new product* is a product that is *perceived* as new by an individual. Often, this also means that it is new to a specific company.[6] But the operational definition remains focused on buyer perception. Whatever makes a difference to prospects renders a product new in their eyes. This difference could be a name change, a package change, a reformulation, a repositioning, an altered price, or a new channel of distribution.

Warner-Lambert has repositioned Trident sugarless gum as a cavity preventive and Listerine mouthwash as a fighter of plaque and gum disease. It also converted the antihistamine Benadryl from a prescription drug to an over-the-counter product—a move that more than quadrupled sales in two years.[7] Aseptic packaging of fruit juices has eliminated the need for refrigeration and made it easier to carry them along in lunchboxes. Reformulating and repackaging food products for preparation in microwave ovens has given the food industry a welcome boost.[8]

The emphasis placed on buyer perception in the definition of a new product has two important consequences. First, a product does not have to be new in the objective sense that it has never been available before. It only must be perceived as new and different. As a case in point, mopeds were popular in Europe for a quarter century before they were viewed as new products by American prospects. Moxie represents less than 1 percent of soft drink sales in the United States and has remained unknown to most consumers. When presented with it, consumers perceive it as a new product, even though it has been marketed in this country for more than a century.

Second, a product that is objectively new is not new to the marketplace unless it is so perceived. When the newness of a product has not been adequately communicated, consumers have no reason to try it, and it fails. Jergens had long been the leading brand of hand lotion in the United States. Then the company introduced a significant innovation called Jergens Extra Dry. This product has a creamy consistency as opposed to the more liquid established product. But consumers did not realize the difference, and the product lingered. In contrast, Chesebrough-Pond's introduced a similar product, Vaseline Intensive Care, which now dominates the hand lotion market.[9]

An *innovation,* in turn, is an *idea* perceived as new by an individual.[10] A new product, then, is simply the manifestation of the underlying innovative idea. This explains why companies must spread new ideas rather than new products. Apple had to educate consumers and educators about the nature and merits of personal computing before it could sell significant numbers of its products. This company single-handedly created the market for personal computers through an aggressive educational effort that slowly gained acceptance for this revolutionary concept.

Creating a new market means educating consumers to respond to a new idea and then supplying the appropriate product. Once a new concept has been accepted, selling the product becomes much easier. An innovative product is perceived by prospects to differ sufficiently from existing alternatives so that they will consider trying it. The extent of this difference from previously available choices can be called the *degree of newness.* Based on the amount of change required in buyer behavior, three levels of innovation can be distinguished: continuous, dynamically continuous, and discontinuous.[11]

Continuous innovations do not require any change in consumption behavior and are therefore most readily accepted by consumers. They offer variety or the excitement of newness without disrupting established behavior patterns. To put it another way, the same function is being performed in the same way. Because it is easy to effect and relatively risk free, this type of innovation is by far the most frequent. A new flavor, color, or size may be added to an existing lineup of products, or an additional feature or performance improvement may be incorporated into an already available product. Colgate-Palmolive introduced a lemon-lime version of its Palmolive dishwashing liquid, and Procter & Gamble launched Mountain Spring Dawn dishwashing detergent, a new scent.

Dynamically continuous innovations serve an established function with a new technology. Consumers have to change their behavior to a new, more convenient way of performing the same task. The attraction of advanced technology, however, often is counteracted by a higher price tag. An example is the evolution from manual to electric typewriter and then to word processing workstation. Unless the advantages of such innovations outweigh the higher price and the need to learn new skills, primary market resistance will occur. Of course, if the new technology is less expensive or significantly more convenient, it will be accepted much more readily. Microwave popcorn is extremely popular because of its ease and speed of preparation, in spite of its substantially higher price.

If dynamically continuous innovations are sometimes resisted because of their behavioral and cost implications, *discontinuous innovations* may encounter outright hostility. They are disruptive and require the consumer to establish completely new behavior patterns. Discontinuous innovations are quite rare and occur only a few times during a lifetime. They involve the use of a new technology to serve functions not previously performed. If widely accepted and employed, they can transform the lives of many people. The personal computer, with its many possibilities, represents such an event. Life-styles and work patterns have been changing in its wake. Personal data can be stored, called up, and processed; distant data banks can be accessed for a fee; and shopping and banking at home are already available in various locations. The personal computer has also enabled the decentralization of workplaces. "Telecommuters" work in their homes and communicate with their employers via telecommunications links.[12]

Types of New Products

Products can be new in a number of ways. Basically, however, the different categories of new products involve either technological or marketing changes. *Technological changes* refer to instances when existing products are altered or entirely different products are added. *Marketing changes,* on the other hand, mean offering products in a different way or to different markets; that is, the marketing effort is either intensified or extended.

Booz, Allen & Hamilton uses a different scheme in its classification of new products. As shown in Figure 1–9, the two dimensions of its new product matrix are newness to company and newness to market. The circles indicate the location of its six new product categories on the matrix, list their names or descriptions, and report their frequency among the survey respondents. Although the concepts discussed on the following pages do not match the Booz, Allen & Hamilton categories exactly, they have been included in Figure 1–9, enclosed in boxes, for easier comparison.

The additional profits gained by the same amount of effort tend to be higher for new products and new markets. Many American companies, therefore, prefer to develop and introduce innovations rather than trying harder to sell more present products to present markets. Growth opportunities, however risky they may be, are simply greater in new markets. Existing markets frequently have reached the point where total demand no longer grows. In such a situation, a firm can obtain higher sales volume at the expense of competitors only by spending heavily to gain additional market share. Sales efforts in established markets, consequently, often are directed at stabilizing market share, whereas new products are sought and new markets entered in pursuit of growth objectives.

Modification

Developing and introducing radical innovations rarely are possible or promising. Rather, relatively modest product changes often suffice to rekindle sales. *Modification* involves altering one or more features of an existing product. To make the change

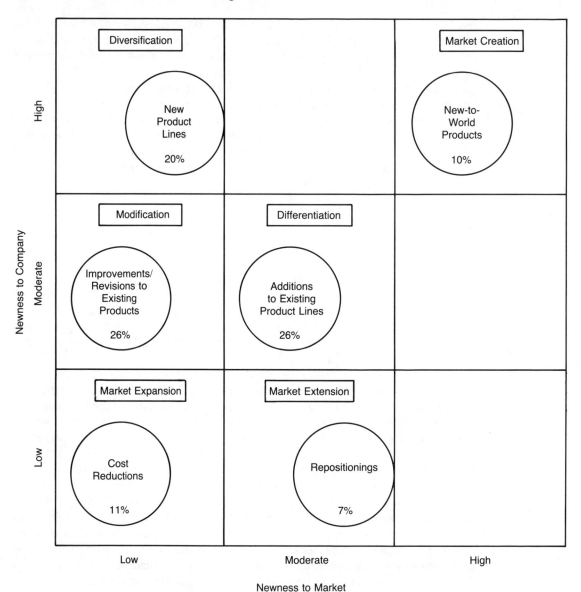

FIGURE 1–9
New Product Categories (*Source:*   Adapted with permission from Booz, Allen & Hamilton, Inc., *New Products Management for the 1980s* [New York: Booz, Allen & Hamilton, Inc., 1982], 9.)

more obvious, it often is external; that is, the product design is altered. The previous model is then discontinued, and the new model is marketed in its place.

A simple, useful test helps distinguish this approach from other types of technological innovation. One need only look at both the number of product lines and the number of products before and after the change was made. If both numbers remain unchanged, modification has occurred. It means keeping products up-to-date and maintaining the momentum of a product line by replacing and updating aging models. Publishers use this approach by publishing new editions of popular textbooks every two to three years.

Modification is common in the garment industry, where a new fashion trend frequently is based on minor differences compared to previous designs. In the automobile business, too, technological obsolescence occurs too slowly, so psychological factors are used to create an artificial aging process. Fashions and car models are altered annually or even more frequently because the natural buying rhythm would be too slow for continuous high-level production.

Modification is not restricted to change in exterior design or appearance ("cosmetic" changes). It can be executed just as well in the form of technological improvements in a product's performance characteristics. This is often the case for groceries or drugs, for which product appearance is fairly irrelevant but noticeable performance improvements can make a difference.

Whether minor or significant, internal or external, modification always means that only the altered product is now offered for sale and the former model no longer is available. If both the old and new models are offered simultaneously, an innovation is not a modification but a differentiation. Among technological innovations, modification is by far the most frequent type. It satisfies both the consumers' desire for the excitement of newness and their somewhat paradoxical need to buy familiar items.

For a seller, this approach is also quite attractive because it constitutes a low-risk route to ensuring stable growth. The company already has established a "consumer franchise" or following for the product that is being updated. No significant investment in new, unproven technology is required, and the short-term payoff, though relatively modest, is fairly certain. Without modification, buyer interest would likely wane. With modification, the same function is being served with the same technology, which means that a continuous innovation has occurred.

Figure 1–10 illustrates the product mix impact of the three types of technological innovation for a company offering two product lines, A and B, with four and three products, respectively. In the case of modification, product A_4, by an alteration

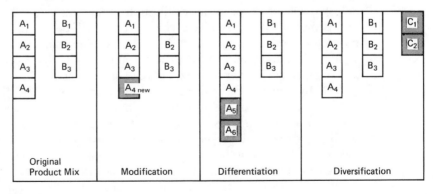

FIGURE 1–10
Categories of New Products: Technological Changes

of some feature, is converted into product A_{4new}. It is evident that the numbers of both products and product lines remain the same. In the Booz, Allen & Hamilton scheme shown in Figure 1–9, such improvements and revisions to existing products represent a low degree of newness to the market but a moderate degree of newness to the company.

Differentiation

In a growing market where the numbers of buyers, competitors, and products steadily increase, it becomes necessary to offer more variety. *Differentiation* expands existing product lines by offering additional versions of the basic product concept. The number of product lines remains unchanged while the number of products (variations) within existing lines increases. The established products are not phased out but rather are enhanced by additional products that offer variations in size, flavor, color, design, or features. J. C. Penney originally introduced its Fox shirt as a short-sleeved knit shirt in solid colors. This line was subsequently expanded to include woven shirts, which enabled stripes and plaids to enter the picture.

As market volume in a product category approaches market capacity, sellers tend to compete by responding to the unique needs of particular buyer groups. This results in an increase in the number of products offered. In fact, as a market matures, increased choice through product differentiation (or line extension, as it often is called) becomes a major competitive tool. As can be seen in Figure 1–9, Booz, Allen & Hamilton describes this approach as additions to existing product lines. Its respondents reported that more than a quarter of their new product introductions fell into this category. Figure 1–10 demonstrates differentiation by adding products A_5 and A_6 to product line A.

Diversification

In today's tough, competitive climate, astute managers pursue the objectives of growth and stability simultaneously. Growth without stability remains highly vulnerable and may lead to failure. The fate of several companies in the personal computer industry (Osborne, for instance) illustrates this principle. Stability without growth means merely staying in place. This becomes self-defeating in a growing market because it produces a loss in market share. As a stagnant giant, General Motors has steadily lost market share in the domestic car market. Only the combination of growth and stability can help ensure the future of an enterprise.

In their pursuit of these objectives, managers realize that growth becomes more difficult as markets mature. Secondary market resistance increases as the volume of a market moves toward capacity. Many markets in the United States are at the point where total market volume increases very slowly, if at all. Individual firms then can grow only at the expense of competitors. Established products, therefore, rarely can guarantee continued growth or stability. New ways constantly must be found to ensure the survival and future of a business. Diversification offers a potential solution to this challenge.

Diversification is the strategy of a company's growth through entering new businesses. This may involve adding new product lines. In Figure 1–10 this is demonstrated by adding product line C in the form of products C_1 and C_2. As can be seen, the numbers of both product lines and products increase. Here, only the addition of different products for other applications represents diversification. In contrast, adding variations of the same basic product concept, which will compete in the same overall market, is differentiation. Instead of deepening the product mix, diversification as shown here broadens the offering. Philip Morris bought Miller Brewing Company and later General Foods to broaden its presence in grocery stores and reduce its dependence on the tobacco business. R. J. Reynolds made a similar move by buying Nabisco Brands.

As a new product category, diversification straddles the fence between technological and marketing changes. Offering new products in new product lines involves a technological change. But it also often means selling to a new group of customers and thus represents a marketing change. Booz, Allen & Hamilton shows "new product lines" as scoring low on the newness to market scale if a company enters established markets but high in terms of newness to the company as it adds new product lines to its mix of businesses.

Market Creation

Occasionally an enterprising company leaps boldly into the unknown and instead of entering an existing market attempts to build one from scratch. *Market creation* occurs when a firm introduces a revolutionary product that attracts sustained interest and thus creates a completely new market. In the Booz, Allen & Hamilton matrix (Figure 1–9), the "new-to-the-world products" occupy a location that combines high ratings on both scales. Such products are completely new not only to the company but also to potential buyers and may even qualify as discontinuous innovations.

Market creation is a risky undertaking, a courageous gamble that the radically new product will catch on and become a growth opportunity. Market creation also straddles the fence between technological and marketing changes as it incorporates both new products and new markets. It even could be considered an extreme form of diversification because it involves entry into nonexisting markets with products not previously available from any source. It is classified here as a marketing change, however, because the marketing challenge of creating a new market from ground zero is likely to be enormous. Primary market resistance will be substantial because prospects must establish totally new behavior patterns. The cost and uncertainty of such radical change discourage all but a hardy flock of daredevils from buying at this early stage of the game. The lone marketer of the innovative product needs a great deal of conviction and staying power to overcome massive resistance and pursue primary demand creation with missionary zeal.

But the innovative product's rewards can be sizable. The original firm in a market faces no competition. It may well establish a lasting leadership position in this emerging market. And it may reap substantial profits from its efforts before competitors erode its lead. Apple created the personal computer market, driven by the abilities and convictions of its founders, Steve Wozniak and Steven Jobs. Although it attracted many entrepreneurs to this industry, its leadership was seriously challenged only when IBM decided to enter this field.

Figure 1–11 shows the three types of *marketing* changes that represent new product categories. Starting with the current sales volume of a firm in existing markets, market creation means new sales from new markets and thus a broadening of its base. By moving away from its established products and markets, the company may be hedging its bets and building a new base for the future. That is certainly what AMF did when it entered leisure equipment businesses to move away from its original machine tool business.

Market Expansion

A far less radical marketing change involves obtaining more sales from existing markets. *Market expansion* means marketing current products to current markets in new ways. This can be done in the form of a new advertising campaign, a new package, a new price, or a new distribution channel. Nissan developed a new advertising campaign to give its cars a more distinctive image.[13] Quaker State offered its motor oil in translucent plastic containers with pouring spouts. Best-selling books are routinely offered in paperback versions for mass-market appeal. Electronic publishing is a new form of information distribution by means of computer terminals.

Because a firm often has a substantial stake in its current markets, working them for more yield makes a great deal of sense. It may suggest, for instance, more varied usage. Arm & Hammer Baking Soda has been promoted as a refrigerator

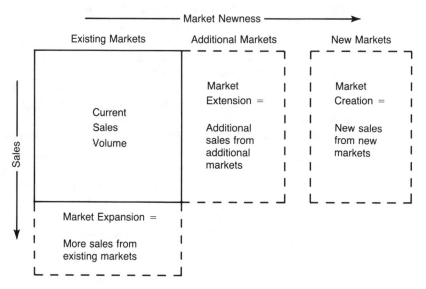

FIGURE 1–11
Categories of New Products: Marketing Changes

deodorant and a drain cleaner. Not every increased effort in existing markets, however, can be considered a new product. New stimuli must be presented and new approaches used. A manufacturer that formerly sold its products through appliance dealers and now decides to supply department stores has created innovations. But only marketing changes that make a difference to buyers can be considered market expansion.

Branding previously unbranded items can give them a quality image. Perdue chickens, Indian River grapefruit, Sunkist oranges, and Chiquita bananas are examples of this approach. Challenged by Datril, Tylenol cut its price and became a best-selling analgesic. A new advertising theme may kindle interest by promoting a more meaningful benefit. Procter & Gamble changed its advertising for Pampers from offering convenience to mothers to emphasizing babies' dryness and happiness.[14] Latching on to a consumer trend can also give a product new momentum. Perrier mineral water was promoted as a natural product during a period of concern for health. Sales also benefited from the decision to expand distribution from health food stores to supermarkets. In the Booz, Allen & Hamilton scheme (Figure 1–9), market expansion is most closely associated with "cost reductions."

Market Extension

When market volume for a product category approaches its peak, market expansion efforts no longer produce the desired results because competition has become too fierce. A company then must find and develop new markets. As Figure 1–11 illustrates, *market extension* means entering additional markets with current products to obtain additional sales from new users.

Additional markets can be found, for instance, in existing sales territories in the form of different target groups. Or a company can extend its geographic coverage to the international scene by exporting domestic products. Culligan extended the market for its water softeners by entering the European market. And a company can extend its markets by promoting new applications for existing products. This was done for Arm & Hammer Baking Soda by suggesting its use as a refrigerator deodorant and drain cleaner.

Market expansion deepens a firm's penetration of its present markets. Market extension broadens its customer base to include new groups. The initial cost of market extension tends to be higher than for market expansion in markets that still have room to grow. The risk is also higher because the company enters unfamiliar territory.

Market extension frequently is accomplished through repositioning mature brands.[15] In the Booz, Allen & Hamilton scheme, such a move represents a low degree of newness to the company but a moderate level of newness to the market. *Repositioning* means reshaping buyers' perception of an existing product to appeal to additional market segments. This is done by suggesting new characteristics or uses. Procter & Gamble scored impressive sales gains after promoting Ivory soap for adult use.[16] Johnson & Johnson did the same with its Baby Shampoo and promoted its Baby Oil as a skin softener, makeup remover, and bathwater softener.

SUMMARY

New product management is a vital part of any firm's marketing effort. It involves the strategic management of product-related marketing activities and provides a challenging opportunity for dedicated people. As markets evolved to more intense competition, many firms changed their marketing efforts to be customer focused. They realized that as market volume approached market capacity, market resistance would grow and a better understanding of buyer needs would be required.

Today's marketers are well aware that a product represents a combination of tangible and intangible attributes. These can be visualized in the form of a three-layer concept that surrounds a core benefit with bundles of tangible and intangible benefits. Taken together, they offer a problem solution or want satisfaction. Individual products are grouped into product lines. These, in turn, form a firm's product mix, which can be described in terms of its width and depth.

A new product does not have to be new in an objective sense; rather, it merely has to be perceived as new by the target group. Conversely, a new product that is not perceived as such is likely to fail. Innovations are ideas perceived as new. Continuous innovations do not require a change in behavior. Dynamically continuous innovations involve adaptation, say, to a new technology. And discontinuous innovations prompt new behavior patterns.

New products derive from either technological or marketing changes. Booz, Allen & Hamilton bases its distinction on a newness to market–newness to company matrix. Modification means altering features of existing products. Differentiation offers more variety in existing product lines. Diversification adds new product lines. Market creation occurs when a firm creates a new market and industry by introducing a revolutionary product. Market expansion looks for more sales from existing markets. Market extension represents additional sales from additional markets.

As might be expected, these six categories of new products are often used in combination to achieve steady growth in a fast-changing environment. Modification or differentiation can be employed in connection with expansion or extension efforts. Diversification attempts to extend a company's business into additional markets. Several new product categories can thus be used at the same time, even in the same market. In an all-out effort, an automobile manufacturer may modify current models, offer increased selection, diversify into additional product lines, create a new market for electric cars, expand the market through selective rebates, and appeal to new buyer groups through repositioning familiar models.

NOTES

1. See "AMA Board Approves New Marketing Definition," *Marketing News,* 1 March 1985, 1.
2. Berman and Evans disagree with this perspective and foresee a shift from a "market pull model" to a "technology push model." See Barry Berman and Joel R. Evans, "Marketing Warfare: A Scenario for the Next Ten Years," *Review of Business,* Summer 1984, 7.
3. Compare Philip Kotler, *Marketing Management,* 6th ed. (Englewood Cliffs, NJ: Prentice-Hall, 1988), 446.

4. See Kenneth H. Bacon, "Higher Quality Helps Boost U.S. Products," *Wall Street Journal,* 11 Jan. 1988.

5. This trend was decried in "The Hollow Corporation," *Business Week,* Special Report, 3 March 1986, 56–85.

6. See *Management of the New Product Function* (New York: Association of National Advertisers, 1980), 3.

7. See Laurie Baum, "A Powerful Tonic for Warner-Lambert," *Business Week,* 30 Nov. 1987, 146.

8. See Mary J. Pitzer, "Hey, Ma, What's in the Microwave?" *Business Week,* 30 Nov. 1987, 68, 70.

9. See Al Ries and Jack Trout, *Positioning: The Battle for Your Mind* (New York: McGraw-Hill, 1981), 141.

10. See Everett M. Rogers, *Diffusion of Innovations,* 3rd ed. (New York: Free Press, 1983), 11.

11. See Henry Assael, *Consumer Behavior and Marketing Action,* 3rd ed. (Boston: Kent Publishing Co., 1987), 448–449.

12. See "It's Rush Hour for 'Telecommuting,'" *Business Week,* 23 Jan. 1984, 99. But the results of this arrangement have been largely disappointing. Accordingly, most such experimental programs have been scaled back or eliminated. See Clare Ansberry, "When Employees Work at Home, Management Problems Often Arise," *Wall Street Journal,* 20 April 1987.

13. See Ronald Alsop, "What's a Nissan? New TV Ads Give Car Brand a Personality," *Wall Street Journal,* 15 Oct. 1987.

14. See Bill Abrams and Janet Guyon, "Ten Ways to Restore Vitality to Old, Worn-Out Products," *Wall Street Journal,* 18 Feb. 1982.

15. See Eugene J. Cafarelli, *Developing New Products and Repositioning Mature Brands* (New York: John Wiley & Sons, 1980), 221ff.

16. See Abrams and Guyon, "Ten Ways to Restore Vitality," 31.

CASE STUDY

SUPERIOR BINDER COMPANY

Superior Binder Company is a manufacturer of loose-leaf binders, index tabs, and presentation kits for businesses and other organizations. Established in 1929, the company has grown to $18 million in sales and has slightly more than 200 employees. The company's main plant is located in Summit, New Jersey, and smaller plants are located in Hartford, Connecticut, and Baltimore, Maryland. Superior sells its products through its own sales representatives in the northeastern and Middle Atlantic states. It employs a total of twenty-two salespeople, who report to four district sales managers located in New York City, Boston, Washington, D.C., and Richmond, Virginia.

Product Strategy

Superior's major product line consists of a broad range of custom binders and presentation materials in a variety of forms and materials. Superior's management takes pride in its ability to produce large and small orders to meet specific customers' requests. Artwork, printing, color, size, type of materials, and special features (such as a pocket for a salesperson's business card) are the major ways that a binder is customized. In addition to customized binders, which represent approximately 70 percent of Superior's sales, customized sales presentation kits, display folders, index tabs, and similar items account for 10 percent of sales.

An additional 10 percent of sales come from stock binders. These are binders produced in a few standard sizes and colors. Although stock binders have been produced primarily for the consumer market, which Superior has not entered, they are becoming more popular with industrial and commercial buyers. Stock binders, indexes, and related products can be mass-produced at lower

costs and inventoried. As a result, they can be sold at lower prices, and customers' orders can be filled immediately.

In addition to its traditional product lines, Superior has begun manufacturing computer software packaging. Sales of these products, which are almost entirely customized, have increased rapidly and now account for 10 percent of Superior's sales. However, if Superior wishes to become a major factor in the software market, it must expand its production and marketing capabilities and its product line in this area.

Market Analysis

As with most products, the market for binders and related products can be divided into three major segments: industry and commerce, consumers, and government (see Exhibit 1–A). Superior has concentrated on industrial and government buyers

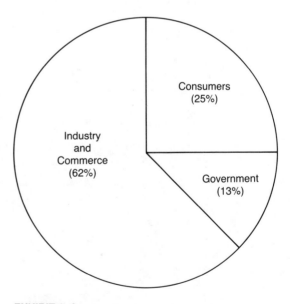

EXHIBIT 1–A
Segmentation of the Binder Market

This case was prepared for instructional purposes by Eugene M. Johnson, Professor of Marketing, University of Rhode Island, Kingston. Although based on an actual business situation, names, places, and other data have been disguised.

and has not made a serious attempt to sell to consumers.

A detailed analysis of the government market reveals that state and local education agencies and other state and local government agencies buy most of the binders. The federal government purchases only a small portion of the total number of binders sold in the United States. Government purchases are shown in Exhibit 1–B.

EXHIBIT 1–B
Government Purchases of Binders

	Percentage of U.S. Total
State and local education agencies	6.0
Other state and local agencies	5.3
Nondefense federal purchases	1.4
Federal defense purchases	0.5

Major industrial purchasers of binders and related products are shown in Exhibit 1–C. The banking industry purchases one-third of all the binders bought in the United States. Other major purchasers of binders and related products are wholesale traders, business services, insurance companies, and medical services.

Government agencies and industrial buyers purchase binders and similar products for a wide variety of uses. These include training, sales manuals, operations manuals, presentation folders, and so forth. Although many buyers still purchase customized binders and presentation materials, stock binders are becoming more popular because of their lower cost and greater flexibility.

EXHIBIT 1–C
Major End Users of Binders by Industry

	Percentage of U.S. Total
Banking	33.2
Wholesale trade	4.1
Business services (including advertising agencies)	3.4
Insurance	2.1
Medical services	2.0
Real estate	1.2
Utilities	1.2
Printers and publishers	1.1
Communications	1.0
Professional services	0.9

Production Factors

In recent years the binder industry has been relatively profitable. According to a trade association report, plant gross profit margins are approximately 31 percent compared to 25 percent for the U.S. manufacturing average. Rising material and labor costs, however, have put pressure on firms to increase productivity. Many binder manufacturers have accomplished this through automating their production. They have simultaneously shifted their product line toward more standardized products.

Superior has also invested in new equipment. This will make the firm more competitive on large orders. The majority of Superior's orders, however, continue to be for relatively small quantities of customized binders. These orders cannot be mass-produced on the newer, more productive equipment. Further, if the firm decides to go after a larger share of the software packaging market, it must invest in more specialized equipment.

Product Strategy Issues

Bob Allen has just assumed the recently created position of marketing manager. Bob was one of Superior's leading salespersons for the past seven years and completed an M.B.A. in marketing at the state university's evening division six months ago. In his position as the company's first marketing manager, Bob reports to Frank Martinelli, vice president of sales.

Bob knows that one of his major tasks is to develop a product strategy for Superior. As he begins to think about the options, a number of ideas and concerns emerge.

"The ability to produce high-volume orders efficiently and to manufacture smaller, highly customized orders is a real competitive advantage. However, we need to emphasize this more in our sales presentations and other promotional messages. We also need to point out our special expertise in the design and production of a broad range of custom binders and presentation materials in a variety of forms and materials.

"On the other hand, in certain regional markets and for some end users, stock binders are becoming more popular. We need to keep abreast of the demand for stock binders and search for other products that can be produced and sold as stock items. This would expand the breadth of our product line and also provide production efficiencies.

"Although I feel that Superior's basic product strategy should be to concentrate on improving and enhancing our existing product line, we also should consider new product ideas. In particular, if we want to be a more significant factor in the software market, we must expand our capabilities.

Perhaps we should hire someone from the software industry as a product manager for this area.

"We should put more emphasis on developing and selling diploma covers and similar products that can be produced efficiently with our new equipment. We also should explore the development and stocking of a line of laminated folders. Finally, there may be market potential for a limited line of high-quality correspondence folders and highly customized presentation kits."

Discussion Questions

1. Evaluate Superior's current product strategy.
2. Should Superior develop more stock products, or should it continue with its emphasis on customized products?
3. Should Superior go after a larger share of the computer software packaging market?
4. What should be Bob Allen's next step?

CHAPTER 2

New Product Planning

New products are the lifeline to a company's future. Managing them successfully requires careful planning. But planning is useless unless it proceeds from a solid base of facts, thoroughly analyzed to provide insights into actual past and likely future patterns. Of course, any new product plan is only as good as its execution. Tight control must, therefore, be exercised during the implementation phase to ensure plan adherence.

New product planning is an intricate cyclical process that leads from analysis to action. It involves an in-depth examination of the company's strengths and weaknesses as compared to market challenges and opportunities. This review may well result in organizational changes or a restructuring of the product mix. Management can then set new product objectives. These have traditionally been quantitative, such as in the form of required sales revenue levels. In recent years, however, many firms have been paying increasing attention to qualitative issues, such as reducing risk and applying new technologies.

The new product objectives are then translated into strategies. The array of options includes market segmentation, positioning and repositioning, and diversification. Tactical decisions fill in the operational details, spelling out the marketing mix for the product launch phase. Once approved, the new product plan is put into action. To make sure that the new product stays on its preassigned course, its progress is carefully monitored. Deviations between planned and actual results are investigated and corrected.

The New Product Management Cycle

As Figure 2–1 illustrates, new product management consists of several activities that occur cyclically. This process can be called the *new product management cycle*. Any

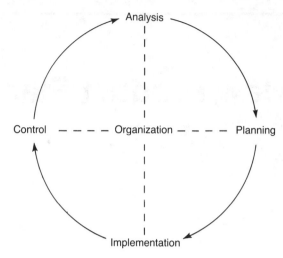

FIGURE 2–1
The New Product Management Cycle

firm's new product effort must be based on a comprehensive analysis of relevant information. A strong foundation on facts enables the development of plans that can give new directions to a company. Proper implementation requires a control system that reports exceptions to the planned course and thus permits timely corrections. The fifth and final ingredient in the process is organization of people and activities. The person who bears the responsibility for new product activities in a firm will be referred to in this book as the *product manager,* regardless of the specific organizational setup chosen.

In performing the analytical function, product managers must build and effectively use appropriate data bases. To assess an innovation's chances of success, they need up-to-date information, which can be gained from secondary and primary data. *Secondary data* are already in existence because they have been collected for a different purpose. *Primary data* are generated specifically for the new product task at hand.

Secondary data can be obtained from internal sources, such as billing records. They are also available from external sources, including trade associations, trade publications, government publications, and marketing research firms that sell such data on a subscription basis. The Food Marketing Institute, the magazine *Progressive Grocer,* the *U.S. Industrial Outlook,* and retail sales data supplied by A. C. Nielsen Company are examples of such outside sources. Primary data for new products are collected internally among company employees and externally in the marketplace, usually in the form of focus group sessions and/or surveys. They are the subject of project-specific marketing research studies. Primary and secondary data then are combined for better insight.

To become actionable information, however, data must be processed, compared, and interpreted. Properly used, information can be a powerful tool, enabling a product manager to identify and seize a market opportunity before the competition does. The need for a competitive edge emphasizes the importance of timely, accurate, and complete information about the market.

New product planning builds on this constantly evolving base of information and insight. As the environment changes, so must a firm's new product effort. *New product planning* means managing a company's future business. Based on analysis and forecasts, product managers anticipate future events and trends and design appropriate responses. The resulting new product plan must be integrated into the overall corporate planning system.

The responsibility of product managers does not end with designing new product plans. They must also implement them. This involves ensuring the following:

- Raw materials and packaging arrive on time.
- Production stays on schedule.
- The new product is shipped on time.
- Promotional materials are sent to retailers.
- Shelves are stocked.
- Advertisements appear in the media as planned.
- Displays are set up properly.

When Taster's Choice freeze-dried coffee was launched in upstate New York, the entire brand management team was assembled on location. Having first won over Nestlé's sales force through an aggressive internal selling effort, the team members were on hand to assist the salespeople in every conceivable way. They helped in the selling effort to retailers, stocked shelves, and monitored advertising in a hands-on, all-out team effort to make the new brand succeed.

The New Product Planning Process

The process of new product planning occurs in several stages that become sections of the new product plan. Figure 2–2 shows the sequence of stages and their cyclical nature. The process begins with a review of past and current sales patterns and environmental developments. It continues with a candid assessment of the firm's strengths and weaknesses, as well as a systematic look at possible future directions. Moving from factual analysis to creative speculation, astute product managers examine their basic new product options at this point. Through careful identification of problems and opportunities, they lay the groundwork for mapping the future course of action.

Before new product objectives can be formulated, however, corporate and marketing objectives have to be taken into account. *New product objectives* are the

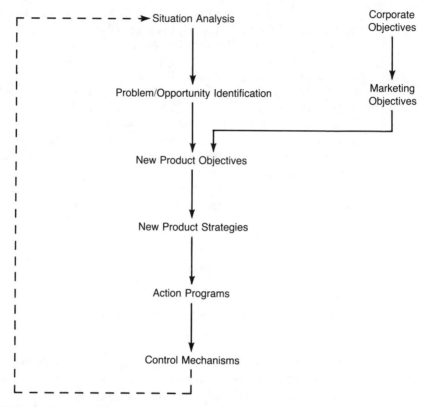

FIGURE 2–2
The New Product Planning Process

targets that a firm's new product effort attempts to reach during the planning period. They, in turn, drive the *new product strategies,* which represent the basic thrust of this effort. The resulting *action programs* describe the tactical or operational details of the marketing mix. To ensure compliance in plan implementation, control mechanisms must be put in place. They help close the new product planning loop by feeding back data to situation analysis.

New product planning means thinking ahead and preparing for anticipated challenges and opportunities. This approach produces a number of important benefits:

1. Thinking ahead means being prepared to counter emerging threats with swift defensive moves and seize opportunities aggressively the very moment that they present themselves, that is, before competitors move in and diminish the firm's chance of success.
2. Proactively managing market events instead of passively permitting them to occur and affect the company's business results in better coordination of the company's

various functional units. Concerted effort is a prerequisite for a successful new product program.

3. The performance standards contained in a new product plan enable comparative analysis of actual results and thus the determination of the extent of plan realization.

4. New product planning heightens management's sensitivity and responsiveness to environmental changes and their relevance to the company's business.

5. A new product plan is a powerful means of communication, clearly conveying to everyone concerned the objectives to be pursued and the tools to be used, simultaneously fostering a spirit of commitment to an important common cause.

To deliver these benefits, new product planning must be smoothly integrated into the overall corporate planning system. Figure 2–3 illustrates this vital relationship. It demonstrates that new product planning receives and uses market informa-

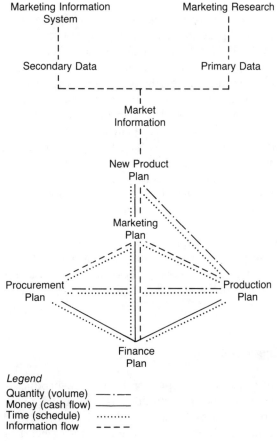

FIGURE 2–3
New Product Planning in the Corporate Planning Context

tion inputs from two principal formal sources. It obtains secondary data on a steady basis from the marketing information system and primary data on a project-by-project basis from marketing research. Based on these inputs and in tune with corporate objectives, a new product plan is developed. This plan now must be coordinated with the major components of the corporate planning system, in other words, the key functional plans. As an initial step, the new product plan is integrated into the marketing plan. Coordination then occurs first through the exchange of information. Second, it involves fine-tuning of cash flows, namely, funds for start-up expenses and revenue projections. Third, the timing must be synchronized for smooth execution and maximum effect. Quantity coordination, on the other hand, is likely to be effected directly between product and production management. Production, in turn, will have to check with the purchasing department to determine whether the materials, components, and supplies can be obtained in time. But the core interaction occurs between the marketing and finance plans. After all, the entire new product planning effort becomes an exercise in futility unless adequate up-front funding can be made available.

New product plans typically follow a fairly standardized format. An outline for a new product plan accordingly is presented in Figure 2–4 in annotated form. The plan begins by objectively reporting facts about the past developments and current conditions in the relevant market. This historical reflection provides the necessary background and forms the basis for projection and goal-oriented action. The following section aims to identify specific present challenges and opportunities as they relate to the company's particular strengths and weaknesses.

From these early analytic and prognostic sections emerges the statement of new product objectives. Based on assumptions and projections about future environmental parameters, new product objectives usually are stated quantitatively. These quantitative new product objectives, however, often are supplemented by qualitative considerations. Decisions then must be made about the new product strategies that will be employed in pursuing these objectives. After an overall approach has been chosen, the strategy to be applied to each element of the marketing mix must be determined. Translating these latter strategies into actionable form is the task of the subsequent action programs. But any new product plan is only as good as its enforcement. Review and control procedures must be established to monitor and to ensure plan adherence.

New Product Objectives

Once the analytical portion of the new product plan has been completed, and the challenges and opportunities have been identified clearly, product management can turn to the formulation of new product objectives. Because the objectives determine the plan's direction, they are at the very heart of new product planning. Without objectives, the new product effort would be rudderless, drifting aimlessly in the rough seas of environmental change and competitive aggressiveness.

This points out the need to account for external and internal constraints when setting new product objectives. Even though the objectives should be ambitious and challenging, they also should be realistic and achievable. Accordingly, assumptions must be made and forecasts developed concerning future environmental conditions and trends likely to affect the new product effort. These projections then govern the formulation of new product objectives.

Most companies express these objectives in very specific *quantitative* terms. They may strive to achieve certain volume objectives, for instance, such as a certain number of cases sold in the first year of a new liqueur. This way of stating new product objectives has the distinct advantage of being unaffected by price changes that may become necessary during product introduction. It is, however, more difficult to administer in a multiproduct situation where quantities of different products do not compare or add up easily.

It is easier, therefore, to use revenue objectives that spell out target dollars for the planning period. Price adjustments are then automatically reflected, and sales of different products can be added without difficulty. Alternately, a firm may choose to target a certain market share. This approach is very popular because

- A certain minimum market share generally is necessary for a new brand to be viable—in the cigarette industry this minimum is pegged at 0.4 percent.
- A sizable market share produces cost savings from mass production.
- High market share means high profitability.
- High market share means market leadership.

The final quantitative new product objective is profit or return on investment. In computing new product profits, assumptions must be made during the analytical phase about future prices, costs, and operating levels. Because of heavy up-front expenses for research and development, advertising, and distribution, new products typically do not begin to earn a profit for several years after their introduction.

In addition to quantitative new product objectives, product management may pursue *qualitative* objectives. These can include risk distribution, antitrust defusion, technology application, seasonal or cyclical compensation, or community responsibility. Risk distribution suggests entering other markets to avoid placing "all eggs in one basket." Antitrust defusion means discouraging regulators by entering unrelated fields. Mobil bought Marcor, the parent of Montgomery Ward, to avoid government scrutiny for expanding in the oil industry. To apply new technology and maintain its leadership position, Boeing has had a tradition of continuously developing new aircraft. Competing with McDonnell Douglas and Airbus Industrie, it designs fuel-efficient aircraft in anticipation of commercial airlines' future needs.[1] Mamiya's electronic still-imaging system, another example of cutting edge technology, seems to be ahead of its time but may find a market in the future.

A firm's new product effort also may be guided by a desire to compensate for seasonal or cyclical fluctuations in its current business. Nurseries and swimming pool installers often offer Christmas decorations during the slow winter months. General Electric compensates for cyclical variations in its appliance business by

FIGURE 2–4

Outline of a New Product Plan (*Source:*   Adapted with permission from Eberhard E. Scheuing, "Marketing Planning for Small Businesses," *Better Business* [Jan./Feb./March 1984], 15–16.)

I. *Situation Analysis*

A factual report on where the company stands in terms of its product offering, its competition, and its market, combined with a review of the historic trends that led up to this situation. This section should be kept strictly objective and should not contain any interpretation.

A. The Market
   1. Description of the product category, its history, and significance in its industry
   2. Sales and market share trends of major competitive brands
   3. Identification of the category's stage in the product life cycle
   4. Examination of the market's potential for growth during the planning period

B. The Buyers
   1. Determination of the role players in the buying process and their relative importance
   2. Purchasing motives, considerations, and habits, including time, place, frequency, and quantity
   3. Buyer knowledge of and attitudes toward the company's products vs. competitive entries regarding quality, service, price, styling, and packaging
   4. Usage and consumption habits: who, when, where, why, how, how often, how much

C. The Product
   1. History of the firm's products from conception to date
   2. Current composition of the product mix: quality levels, available models and options, prices
   3. Competitive rankings in both laboratory tests and market surveys
   4. Ongoing product research, both inside and outside the firm, and expected technological improvements

D. Performance Record
   1. Review of the company's sales history
   2. Examination of its market share trend
   3. Analysis of production and marketing costs
   4. Profit history

II. *Identification of Problems and Opportunities*

Based on the facts presented in section I, product management pinpoints the firm's unique strengths and weaknesses. These are matched with the challenges to be conquered during the planning period and with the opportunities that invite new product action.

A. Marketing Problems
   1. Product-related problems
      a. Shift in buyer preferences regarding design or functional characteristics
      b. Performance weaknesses in comparison to competitive offerings
      c. Government warnings or bans on ingredients

        d. Technological obsolescence
   2. Marketing mix problems
        a. Changes in distribution or buying patterns
        b. Intensified price competition
        c. Ineffective promotional approach
        d. Declining profitability

B. Marketing Opportunities
   1. Revitalization of lagging sales through product modification
   2. Deepening of the product mix and thus enlargement of buyer selection through product differentiation
   3. Broadening of the product mix and thus distribution of risk through diversification into additional businesses
   4. Taking a bold step forward and possibly redirecting the entire company by creating a new market from ground zero
   5. Attempting greater penetration of present markets by intensifying marketing efforts in the form of market expansion
   6. Repositioning existing products or introducing them in additional markets in a market extension effort

III. *Statement of New Product Objectives*
Given the comprehensive factual evaluation of the company's situation in section I and the interpretation of current marketing challenges and opportunities in section II, product management is now in a position to develop the objectives that will guide its new product effort. For these objectives to be realistic and achievable, however, assumptions and projections about environmental conditions and trends during the planning horizon must be formulated first.

A. Assumptions and Projections about Future Conditions
   1. Economic assumptions
        a. Trends of business cycle and industry output
        b. Consumer and capital spending
        c. Interest rates
        d. Inflation
   2. Technological assumptions
        a. Availability and quality of materials
        b. Cost reductions from technological advances
        c. Intensity of research and development efforts
        d. Likelihood of technological breakthroughs
   3. Sociopolitical assumptions
        a. Changes in age structure and geographic distribution of the population
        b. Shifts in values, needs, and behavior patterns of buyers
        c. Fate of pending legislation
        d. Regulatory climate

B. New Product Objectives
   1. Quantitative objectives
        a. Sales volume objectives
        b. Sales revenue objectives
        c. Market share objectives
        d. Profit or return on investment objectives

(continued)

FIGURE 2–4 *continued*

     2. Qualitative objectives
       a. Risk distribution
       b. Antitrust defusion
       c. Technology application
       d. Season/cyclical compensation
       e. Community responsibility

IV. *New Product Strategies*

New product objectives serve as targets to strive for and points of comparison for evaluating actual results. New product strategies are the basic approaches chosen in their pursuit.

  A. Overall New Product Strategy
     1. Product mix definition
       a. Broad and shallow
       b. Narrow and deep
     2. Market segmentation
       a. Demographic segmentation
       b. Geographic segmentation
       c. Psychographic segmentation
       d. Benefit segmentation
     3. Positioning
       a. Positioning a new entry
       b. Repositioning an established brand
     4. Diversification
       a. Horizontal diversification
       b. Vertical diversification
       c. Lateral diversification

  B. Functional New Product Strategies
     1. Product strategy
     2. Pricing strategy
     3. Distribution strategy
     4. Promotion strategy

V. *Action Programs*

To make the new product strategies operational, they must be translated into detailed action steps: who, when, where, what, how much. Responsibilities must be assigned, schedules set, budgets determined, and milestones identified.

  A. Product Action Program

  B. Pricing Action Program

  C. Distribution Action Program

  D. Promotion Action Program

VI. *Control Mechanisms*

Although section V completes the design phase of the new product plan, it must now be decided how its execution will be monitored. Prior to implementation, procedures have to be developed for both review (comparing actual and planned figures) and control (plan revision or corrective action).

A. Reporting Rules
  1. Feedback mechanism
     a. Timing
     b. Responsibility
     c. Content
     d. Form of presentation
  2. Processing of actual data backflow
     a. Schedule
     b. Types of analyses
     c. Exception reporting
B. Review and Control Procedures
  1. Review schedule and pattern
  2. Policy on plan revisions
  3. Corrective action

---

offering a broad array of financial services. A sense of community responsibility, finally, can cause a firm to develop and market products that otherwise may be unattractive. Such could be the case for telephones for the handicapped, research on cures for rare diseases, or soybean-based high-protein beverages for Third World countries suffering from malnutrition.

A variety of quantitative and/or qualitative objectives thus can direct a company's new product planning activity. Formulated in challenging, achievable form, they govern the choice of new product strategies used in their pursuit.

New Product Strategies

Most product managers now formulate specific new product strategies to control the process of *new product evolution* that continues with idea generation and leads to the ultimate market introduction of a new product. A Booz, Allen & Hamilton survey found that 77 percent of the responding firms incorporated this step in their new product processes. They use it to "identify the strategic business requirements that new products should satisfy. The requirements, which can be both market and company driven, determine the roles to be played by new products."[2] These potential roles are presented in Table 2–1, together with their response frequencies. The report goes on to state that "industrial goods companies are more likely to have developed their most successful new products to satisfy technological objectives, while consumer nondurable companies are more likely to have developed their most successful new products to satisfy market requirements."[3]

Just as the strategic roles of new products are affected by the nature of an industry, so do they, in turn, often shape the new product categories chosen. Companies, for instance, develop new-to-the-world products to maintain a position as a product innovator or exploit technology in a new way. Many firms launch additions to existing lines or revisions of existing products to defend market share positions.[4]

TABLE 2-1
Strategic Role of Most Successful New Product

Classification	Role	Frequency (%)
Externally driven	Defend market share position	45
	Establish foothold in new market	38
	Preempt market segment	34
Internally driven	Maintain position as product innovator	47
	Exploit technology in new way	28
	Capitalize on distribution strengths	26
	Provide a cash generator	14
	Use excess or off-season capacity	7

Source: Adapted with permission from Booz, Allen & Hamilton, Inc., *New Products Management for the 1980s,* p. 11. Copyright © 1982 by Booz, Allen & Hamilton, Inc., New York.

As these comments indicate, *new product strategies* are a firm's means to achieve and maintain a competitive advantage. They represent basic thrusts, giving broad outlines for courses of action. Their selection depends largely on market conditions and opportunities but also the company's own strengths and weaknesses. After all, *"strategic planning* is the managerial process of developing and maintaining a viable fit between the organization's *objectives* and *resources,* and its changing *market opportunities.*"[5] It is evident, then, that "a well-formulated new products strategy matches market opportunities with internal capabilities."[6] In fact, the two most important factors contributing to the success of new products are product fit with market needs (88 percent of responses) and product fit with internal functional strengths (62 percent).[7]

Important considerations in new product strategy selection are the degree of market maturity and thus its rate of growth and competitive intensity.[8] Once chosen, the strategy drives the entire new product process. "Thus it provides focus for generating ideas and concepts, serves as a cost-effective prescreening mechanism, and establishes precise criteria for evaluating the product's success."[9]

Resourceful product managers can choose from a menu of new product strategy options that includes portfolio management, market segmentation, positioning, and diversification. These alternative new product strategies differ somewhat in their applicability and limitations. In mature markets, however, where growth has slowed and competition intensified, they are likely to be applied aggressively. Where circumstances warrant, they can be used in combination with each other.

Portfolio Management

The term *portfolio* is often used to describe a company's mix of businesses. Within this context, however, the expression *portfolio management* will be used to refer to a set of decisions shaping the composition of a firm's product offering or product mix. Under the new marketing concept, portfolio management is market driven, that is, it is based on market opportunities and needs. It involves decisions concerning what the firm wants to be to whom. Such decisions can fundamentally restructure an entire enterprise and substantially affect its nature and fate. American Can, for instance, defined its business as financial services, sold off its packaging operations, and renamed itself Primerica.

Portfolio management requires a careful and thorough review of a company's current offering to determine what should be culled, what should be updated or repositioned, and what should be added. The answers to these questions depend on market opportunities and management philosophy. Before decisions on individual products can be made, the dimensions of the product mix must be outlined.

A narrow product mix, as illustrated in Figure 2–5(a), is composed of a small number of product lines. This situation mirrors management's decision to specialize. Richard D. Irwin is a publisher that specializes in college textbooks in business and economics. Specialized companies are in a position to offer a larger choice and often better quality in their area than firms that are active in many product areas. And they may be very successful in this strategy of market niching[10] if they can avoid attracting larger, more aggressive competitors.

A company's ability to meet competition can be enhanced by concentration on a few product lines, which can even lead to a dominant position in a chosen market segment. But this approach is risky because the business depends heavily on a limited market and its changes over time. New developments in this market to which management does not adjust fast enough can endanger the profitability and even the survival of the company. Both Bulova and Timex offered deep selections of watches. Both ignored the arrival of Texas Instruments and other outsiders in the form of digital watches, considering such timepieces a passing fad. Both lost significant amounts of business and had to start offering digital watches, too.

The problem of dependence on a limited market can be overcome by the addition of new product lines via diversification, which broadens a firm's offering. A broad product mix includes many product lines and thus usually offers only a limited selection in each line. Figure 2–5(b) portrays this situation. While both product mixes shown are composed of forty products, the first mix is narrow and deep, but the second mix is broad and shallow.

Both companies are vulnerable. Company A is likely to hold a strong position in the part of the market that it caters to. But it can be eliminated quickly if customer preferences shift or if well-heeled, aggressive competitors enter the picture. Firm B, instead of being all things to all people, may end up being nothing to nobody because its choice remains too limited to entice members of the various target groups into buying. Woolworth's is such a store that continues to linger with limited growth prospects.

It appears appropriate for both firms to review their portfolios. In the first firm, product management might want to hedge its bets through diversification into additional product lines. The second company should discuss shrinking the width of its product mix and adding products vertically for more selection. Portfolio management constantly attempts to improve the efficiency, market position, and success of a company by concentrating on profitable lines while balancing risk and capturing growth opportunities.

A_1	B_1	C_1	D_1
A_2	B_2	C_2	D_2
A_3	B_3	C_3	D_3
A_4	B_4	C_4	D_4
A_5	B_5	C_5	D_5
A_6	B_6	C_6	D_6
A_7	B_7	C_7	D_7
A_8	B_8	C_8	
A_9	B_9	C_9	
A_{10}	B_{10}	C_{10}	
A_{11}		C_{11}	
A_{12}			

(a) Specialized Product Mix (Narrow, Deep)

A_1	B_1	C_1	D_1	E_1	F_1	G_1	H_1	I_1	K_1
A_2	B_2	C_2	D_2	E_2	F_2	G_2	H_2	I_2	K_2
A_3	B_3	C_3	D_3		F_3	G_3	H_3	I_3	K_3
A_4		C_4	D_4		F_4	G_4	H_4		K_4
A_5			D_5		F_5		H_5		

(b) Multifaceted Product Mix (Broad, Shallow)

FIGURE 2–5
Comparison of Product Mixes

Market Segmentation

A strategy of *market segmentation* means breaking down the market for a product category into smaller segments to better identify and satisfy the needs of these groups. This becomes necessary in mature markets where buyers have become more knowledgeable and demanding and competitors offer more choice. Market segmentation means offering different products and marketing mixes to the various segments in the marketplace.

To understand the role of market segmentation in new product management, it is necessary to relate this strategy to the product life cycle. The *product life cycle* is the sales pattern for a product category over time. As will be discussed in detail in Chapter 15, the cycle begins with market creation or the introduction of a new-to-the-world product in the marketplace. A period of rapid growth follows. As the growth rate slows down, the market matures and eventually reaches its sales peak. During the saturation stage, sales remain fairly stable, although competition is fierce. Ultimately, market volume is likely to decline steadily as the product is superseded and displaced by a more advanced substitute. This pattern is shown in Figure 2–6.

As a new market is being created, the pioneering firm is well advised to follow an *undifferentiated strategy.* The marketing task at this point consists of generating primary demand by educating consumers to a new way of doing something. Consequently, the company should present one type of product uniformly and powerfully to create sufficient interest for the market to take off. Instead of highlighting the differences among potential buyers, product management looks for the largest common denominator, trying to appeal to the largest possible number of people.[11] This approach helps to contain cost while concentrating buyer interest. If a company were to introduce picturephones to the consumer market, for example, it would be unwise to offer them initially in different screen sizes, decorator colors, and black and white versus color transmission. Such a broad initial selection would dramatically increase cost and confuse consumers.

As market volume grows, product management may want to husband its resources and temporarily specialize on serving the needs of one or a few groups in the market. A *concentrated strategy* is characterized by such a precise orientation toward specific submarkets. Rather than assuming an insignificant position in the overall market, the company tries a niching approach, aiming to become a leader in one or more segments. The marketing efficiency and image of a firm can benefit from such concentration. But it also becomes vulnerable to demand shifts that hurt its narrow base.

As the market matures, it requires more comprehensive coverage. In a *differentiated strategy,* a company caters to the entire market by using different products and marketing mixes for its various segments. The firm wants to be identified with the entire product category and expects brand loyalty even as needs

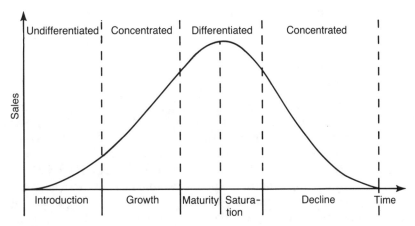

FIGURE 2–6
Market Segmentation during the Product Life Cycle

change. To attract and hold business in fiercely competitive mature markets, many consumer goods manufacturers use a differentiated strategy by offering different brands at different prices, sometimes even through different channels of distribution. Most food manufacturers sell under their own brands but also supply retailers under private labels. General Motors provides car buyers with a broad range of vehicles for every taste and pocketbook.

A company that markets to one segment and then introduces a new product aimed at another segment of the same market must worry about a potential *cannibalization effect.* This term refers to the possibility that the new entry will siphon customers off from the established brand. Ideally, this effect would be minimal because the new brand should draw buyers from other brands in its segment rather than the company's established brand in another segment. When Colgate-Palmolive introduced Ultra-Brite toothpaste, the new brand did not cannibalize Colgate toothpaste significantly. Instead, it acquired most of its buyers in the tooth-brightener segment of the market, as intended.

Markets can be segmented on a geographic, demographic, psychographic, or behavioral basis.[12] For a variety of reasons, geographic segmentation or regional marketing of new products has become very popular lately. Tastes and preferences differ regionally throughout the United States.[13] Differences in buying behavior can be measured for units as small as 340 households.[14] And catering to regional differences is profitable.[15] Demographic segmentation uses socioeconomic characteristics, such as age, sex, income, and education, to break down a market. Easy availability of data from government statistics makes this a popular approach. The results have been mixed. A soft drink "just for girls," called Like, failed; hair-coloring products for men are successful.[16] Psychographic segmentation is based on life-styles. Charlie perfume from Revlon has been successful by appealing to young career women on the go. And General Foods introduced Cycle canned dog food based on a comprehensive psychographic study of dog owners.[17] Among the behavioral variables, usage rate is important. Single-serving containers of food products sell well, both to singles and families with staggered eating patterns. Benefit segmentation emphasizes expected benefits. Concern about plaque has resulted in Tartar Control Crest toothpaste.

Positioning

The third major new product strategy is *positioning.* This term refers to an approach that attempts to place a company's product in a desirable location on the buyer's perceptual map. For every product category that they buy, consumers compare, judge, and select from competing products in a process that can be illustrated through a system of coordinates called a perceptual map. The relative positions or locations of competing brands in such a two-dimensional model can be identified by asking consumers to rate the different products according to a number of attributes. As the respondents express the strength of their feelings regarding these characteristics, average scores are entered in the diagram, which then shows comparative product ratings on the key factors determining buyer choice.

A brand's position on a perceptual map is the result of three types of influences:

1. The company's total effort, including its marketing mix
2. Environmental influences, including competitive efforts, and actions of government agencies
3. Buyers' own perceptual processes, including internal influences on them

And it is indeed in the mind of the buyer where competitors battle: "Positioning is what you do to the mind of the prospect. That is, you position the product in the mind of the prospect."[18] It is, therefore, of utmost importance for product management to position its product in such a way as to compare favorably with competing brands.[19] This means that management should not only strive for competitive distinctiveness but also aim to match buyers' perception of an ideal product in this category.

To determine a desirable position for a prospective new product, product management must first ask buyers to rate currently available products on a number of relevant attributes. The average ratings for each brand are then entered in a diagram where the two most important buying considerations form the two axes. Figure 2–7 presents a hypothetical perceptual map of the detergent market based on the two dimensions of gentleness and cleaning power.

Because sales, market share, and profit information is not available, graph (a) does not indicate the relative success of each of the ten brands in this hypothetical market. What becomes evident, however, is the fact that in the minds of the respondents the competing brands possess widely differing characteristics. Brand C, for instance, is seen as being gentle on the fabric but somewhat average in cleaning power. This product might be Ivory Snow. Brand G, on the other hand, is seen as a very powerful detergent with somewhat moderate gentleness. This product could be Bold 3. The graph also shows which brands compete most directly with each other in the eyes of buyers. For example, F competes with G but not with A.

While Figure 2–7(a) reveals important competitive information, it represents only the first stage of positioning analysis. To facilitate decision making on strategic positioning, buyers' ideal points also have to be entered into the picture. Each ideal point represents an individual buyer's preferred kind of product as expressed by desired scores on the two graph dimensions. In the second stage, therefore, each individual ideal point is entered into the picture, making it a scatter diagram. The result of this stage is illustrated in Figure 2–7(b). Because individual preferences tend to be similar for different buyer groups or segments in the market, six clusters can be identified.

Cluster 1 finds a detergent with relatively little cleaning power acceptable, provided that it is reasonably gentle. It is made up of senior citizens who do not soil their clothes. Cluster 2 has baby laundry to do and is most concerned with a detergent's or soap's gentleness to the skin. Cluster 3 is the smallest and is satisfied with moderate levels of cleaning and gentleness. Cluster 4 is the largest group in the market, searching for the best of everything. Clusters 5 and 6 are composed of blue-collar workers with heavily soiled clothes who are mostly concerned about cleaning power and do not worry much about gentleness to heavy-duty fabrics.

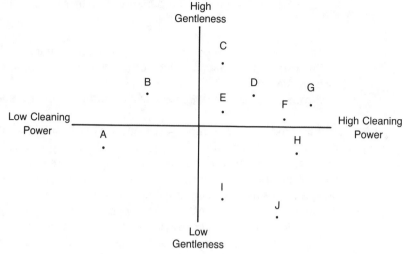

(a) Actual Positions of Competing Brands

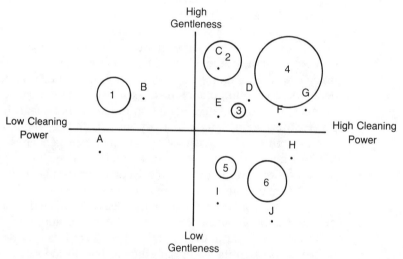

(b) Distribution of Ideal Point Clusters

FIGURE 2–7
Perceptual Map of Detergent Market

Figure 2–7(b) clearly reveals significant opportunities. Only cluster 2 currently is adequately served by brand C. All other ideal point clusters are only peripherally served by existing brands. Sizable market opportunities or need gaps are available for astute product managers to exploit under these circumstances. This can be achieved in either of two ways:

1. Introducing a new brand in a desirable location on the perceptual map, or
2. Repositioning an existing brand by moving its location on the map in a more desirable direction

Significant opportunities are beckoning in the centers of clusters 1, 4, and 6. They can best be addressed by new brands that are given an appropriate position through product and package design as well as advertising. Several existing brands, however, could benefit from repositioning. Brands B and D offer more cleaning power than clusters 1 and 3 require, respectively. Perhaps these two clusters could be educated to this higher level of performance through advertising. Brands G and J would require reformulation and heavy advertising to move convincingly into clusters 4 and 6.

Detecting market gaps and positioning opportunities for new entries has become an increasingly popular and important pursuit for many companies. Chrysler Corporation, for one, conducts periodic surveys asking "owners of different makes to rank their autos on a scale of one to 10 for such qualities as 'youthfulness,' 'luxury' and 'practicality.' The answers are then worked into a mathematical score for each model and plotted on a graph that shows broad criteria for evaluating customer appeal."[20] An example of a perceptual map of the automobile market resulting from this endeavor is shown in Figure 2–8. Chrysler also uses the perceptual mapping technique for plotting individual models and identifying ideal point opportunities. It then attempts to direct a new product at an unoccupied position through changes in styling, price, or advertising.[21]

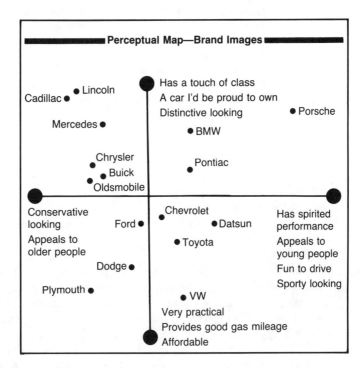

FIGURE 2–8
The Automobile Market (*Source:* Reproduced with permission from John Koten, "Car Makers Use 'Image' Map as Tool to Position Products," *Wall Street Journal,* 22 March 1984)

Positioning analysis is a useful tool for highlighting and exploiting new product opportunities by positioning innovations in clusters with substantial unsatisfied potential. But the perceptual mapping technique has another important application. It is equally powerful in identifying the locations of a company's current products and assessing their appropriateness in terms of ideal point clusters. Because these clusters shift over time, current product positions may have to be adjusted. This task is called *repositioning*. It means rekindling the sales volume of an established brand by altering its perception in the minds of customers. But such a move requires careful prior investigation: "When a mature brand is not faring well, a research program should be undertaken to identify, develop, and evaluate a basic repositioning to gain a stronger share level within the product category."[22]

Such a program might consist of five stages:

1. An exploratory qualitative stage involving focus group sessions and benefit probe tests to provide input for the quantitative research that follows.
2. A major quantitative study from which a strategic positioning will be developed and which will serve as the source for generating specific concepts.
3. Another quantitative stage with small and large scale testing to evaluate the absolute trial potential for alternative concepts, culminating in a final, highly appealing concept.
4. A quantitative stage using in-home use and sales wave type tests to evaluate the specific product varieties developed to ascertain product to concept fit, maximize product acceptance, and provide an estimate of potential ongoing volume for the product.
5. The final stage involves small scale advertising communication/persuasion tests (if the results of Stage 4 prove favorable to market introduction), undertaken to evaluate alternative executions for the product. These would determine if the executions effectively translate each concept in terms of desired benefits/imagery as well as overall appeal.[23]

The benefit probe, in particular, attempts to discover desired benefits that help to create a distinctive image and enhance sales potential. As the new concept evolves, it must be refined and successfully translated into product form. Because advertising plays a key role in creating the new image, advertising research is used to find the best execution.

Besides shifts in consumer preferences, repositioning can be triggered by aggressive competitors that enter a brand's comfort zone and reduce its distinctiveness.[24] Such me-too products can seriously undermine a brand's uniqueness and create confusion in the minds of buyers. In the face of such a challenge, product management can either reposition its own brand or try to reposition the competition by emphasizing the weaknesses of competing brands in the form of comparative advertising.[25] This approach was used by McDonald's and Burger King in the "battle of the burgers."

In repositioning its own brand, a company can first suggest more frequent or varied usage to current users.[26] The objective of this approach is to have loyal buyers see the product in a new light, adding excitement to a familiar item. For food items, new recipes can be proposed, such as using Duncan Hines cake mixes for making desserts. For infrequently used products, regular application can be proposed, such as periodic Quaker State oil changes for car engines.

A second approach attempts to attract new users. Johnson & Johnson attracted new buyers to its baby care products by appealing to the adult market. Third, a company can reposition a brand by promoting new uses. This was done successfully by Du Pont for nylon, which was originally developed for use in parachutes but subsequently was expanded to applications in hosiery, tire cord, and carpet yarns.

Although repositioning does not necessarily require physical changes in product design, it is often helpful if buyers can detect a product change caused by a reformulation.[27] New packaging will also reinforce the new positioning.[28] Where appropriate, pricing or distribution changes may support a repositioning effort.

Diversification

The final new product strategy is *diversification,* which involves entering new businesses by adding new product lines and/or markets in the pursuit of growth. As a departure from past ways of doing business, it bears both greater risks and greater rewards than portfolio management, market segmentation, and positioning. Ultimately, it is a move that most businesses must take to survive and prosper in a rapidly changing environment where traditional markets decline and new markets grow.

A number of reasons can cause a company to diversify. It may seek to compensate for seasonal fluctuations in its business by entering product lines with different seasonal patterns. Some garment manufacturers, for instance, alternate between the production of lingerie and swimwear. A firm also may want to use participation in overseas markets to balance changes in the U.S. business cycle. Ford Motor Company was generating impressive profits overseas when its U.S. operations were running deeply in the red. Global geographic diversification thus makes sense from a risk-balancing viewpoint.

A manufacturer may want to broaden its sales base, as the production of generic cigarettes by Liggett & Myers illustrates. Or it may sell unused capacity to outsiders. Aerospace companies offer other firms the use of their computer facilities. McAuto, the data processing subsidiary of McDonnell Douglas, even expanded to the point of buying other businesses in its field.

The emergence of new markets can also encourage diversification. Time Inc. diversified aggressively into cable television. Some firms diversify to avoid antitrust suits in their current businesses. Mobil, however, lived to regret its acquisition of Marcor, the parent company of Montgomery Ward, as this retailer continued to pile up huge losses. This particular experience notwithstanding, diversification can help a company improve its operating results without giving up its established base.

Diversification can be carried out as horizontal, vertical, or lateral diversification. In the case of *horizontal diversification,* a company enters a related business on the same level of production or distribution. The firm adds different product lines for other applications to its current product mix. The old and new businesses are related, however, either in terms of their technology or their distribution. A technological relationship exists if the same equipment is used to produce the new line, for instance, a women's outerwear firm adding children's clothes. A distributive relationship is used, on the other hand, if the old and new products move through the same channels, regardless of their technologies. Procter & Gamble uses this approach in marketing a broad product mix, ranging from detergents to beverages and from paper goods to toothpastes, through grocery stores. In both instances, a company using horizontal diversification builds on an existing strength.

Vertical diversification adds preceding or subsequent stages of production or distribution to a firm's established business. Such a move is driven by the desire to gain more control and achieve higher profits. A garment manufacturer like Benetton may acquire a textile mill or open up retail stores. Sears produces some of the appliances it sells. *Lateral diversification,* finally, means entering unrelated businesses. Both General Electric and Sears, Roebuck and Company have acquired financial services firms.[29]

New Product Tactics

Once product management has set new product objectives and has chosen the new product strategies to be employed in their pursuit, these broad guidelines must be translated into operational form. Essentially, a series of tactical decisions must be made that spell out the day-to-day activities to be undertaken in new product marketing. In other words, product management must formulate the new product's marketing mix.

The critical choices that must be made here include the following:

- What mix of new products to introduce
- What their features should be
- How to package the new entries
- What brand names to use
- What to charge for them
- How to distribute them
- What to spend on advertising and sales promotion
- How to sell them

All of these decisions are necessarily related to and dependent on each other. For example, the selection of a particular channel of distribution affects packaging, pricing, promotion, and all the other elements of the introductory marketing mix. The decision to mass market a new line of cosmetic products through drugstores and grocery stores means inexpensive packaging suited for self-service selection, moderate prices, and advertising in mass media.

Tactical decisions must be spelled out in considerable detail to represent a true action program. Deciding on the introductory marketing mix is time-consuming but crucial to the success of a new product. Because of this importance, an entire section of this book, namely, part three, is devoted to an in-depth discussion of the introductory marketing program.

New Product Program Implementation and Control

With the new product plan in place, responsibilities assigned, schedules set, and budgets authorized, nothing should stand in the way of program implementation. The new product, fully developed and tested, can now be launched in the marketplace. And timeliness is of the essence. Every day lost in implementing a fully operational plan increases the possibility of competitors beating the company to the marketplace with their own new products. Market conditions often change rapidly, making it essential to seize opportunities as quickly as possible.

Implementation of a new product program means carrying out the planned activities at the proper times. Product management must oversee and direct program implementation, making sure that it stays on target. This requires the use of review and control procedures.

No matter how well conceived it is, any new product plan is only as good as its implementation. To ensure that the actual results match the planned outcomes, product management must keep tabs on the program's progress. This monitoring task involves periodic reviews. If they reveal discrepancies between actual and planned results, the reasons for the observed differences must be explored. These reasons can be either controllable or uncontrollable. Controllable or internal reasons mean that the actual new product achievements fell short of the planned level because of inadequate effort. Uncontrollable or external reasons for discrepancies are caused by changes in the environment that have occurred since plan approval. They may make it impossible to achieve plan targets with the approved resources.

But merely identifying the reasons for discrepancies between planned and actual results is not enough. Product management is responsible for making things happen, not explaining why they did not happen. Controllable reasons require decisive corrective action, for instance, overtime in the plant or a special sales contest. Uncontrollable reasons, on the other hand, usually mean revising the plan to adjust to the changed circumstances in the marketplace. For instance, if a competitor has launched a new product, the timetable for a company's own introduction may have to be shortened and initial sales projections reduced to more moderate levels.

New product control is the process by which product management ensures that new product performance goals are met or adjusted. Many companies employ several criteria in this process to avoid being misled by chance variations in any single measure. The most popular new product performance criteria are share of market, profit contribution, sales volume, and return on investment, followed by payback period, internal rate of return, and net present value.[30] It is no accident that all of these performance measures are financial or, for that matter, quantitative in nature. For a new product to be successful, it simply must produce solid, bottom-line results. Only then can qualitative objectives come into play as additional considerations.

SUMMARY

The new product management cycle is an action model for product management in the pursuit of its new product responsibilities. It begins with the analysis of past and present market data and the forecasting of future conditions. Based on this input, product management formulates a new product plan as a blueprint for action. On approval, the plan is implemented under its supervision. To ensure plan adherence, product management engages in a continuous process of monitoring and adjustment. This control feature closes the loop of the new product management cycle. The fifth ingredient of the cycle is new product organization, the framework that drives and structures all new product activities.

New product planning is a major component of the new product management cycle, but it is also a key element in a company's corporate planning system. Based on market information from different sources, it spells out how the company intends to grow during the planning period. The new product plan, in turn, is part of the more comprehensive marketing plan, which must be coordinated with the other component plans of the corporate planning system in a number of ways. The new product planning process itself consists of the formulation of objectives, the selection of appropriate strategies and tactics, and the design of review and control procedures.

Every new product process needs to be driven by quantitative, measurable objectives. These may be supplemented by qualitative objectives. Resourceful product managers can choose from a number of new product strategies in their pursuit of these objectives. They include portfolio management, market segmentation, positioning, and diversification. Portfolio management addresses itself to the composition of a firm's product offering in the marketplace. Market segmentation means identifying subgroups in the market and designing new products to meet their unique needs. Positioning means placing a new product in a desirable location on the buyer's perceptual map. And diversification involves entering a new business, which could be achieved in a horizontal, vertical, or lateral direction. New product tactics flesh out the broad outlines of the strategies chosen with operational details. Their implementation is monitored and adjusted in the control process.

NOTES

1. See Katherine M. Hafner, "Bright Smiles, Sweaty Palms," *Business Week,* 1 Feb. 1988, 22–23.
2. Booz, Allen & Hamilton, 10.
3. Ibid., 11.
4. See ibid.
5. Philip Kotler, *Marketing Management,* 6th ed. (Englewood Cliffs, NJ: Prentice-Hall, 1988), 33.
6. Thomas D. Kuczmarski and Steven J. Silver, "Strategy: The Key to Successful New Product Development," *Management Review* (July 1982) 27.
7. See Booz, Allen & Hamilton, *New Products Management,* 16.

8. See Earl L. Bailey, ed., *Product-Line Strategies* (New York: The Conference Board, 1982), 11f.
9. See Kuczmarski and Silver, "Strategy: The Key to Successful New Product Development," 26f.
10. See Kotler, *Marketing Management,* 342.
11. See ibid., 302.
12. See ibid., 287.
13. See Alix M. Freedman, "National Firms Find That Selling to Local Tastes Is Costly, Complex," *Wall Street Journal,* 9 Feb. 1987.
14. See Betsy Morris, "Placing Products: Marketing Firm Slices U.S. into 240,000 Parts to Spur Clients' Sales," *Wall Street Journal,* 3 Nov. 1986.
15. See Christine Dugas, "Marketing's New Look," *Business Week,* 26 Jan. 1987, 64–69, and Dwight J. Shelton, "Regional Marketing Works and Is Here to Stay," *Marketing News,* 6 Nov. 1987, 1, 25.
16. See Ronald Alsop, "For More Men, Old Gray Hair Ain't What It Appears to Be," *Wall Street Journal,* 30 July 1987.
17. See Leon G. Schiffman and Leslie Lazar Kanuk, *Consumer Behavior,* 3rd ed. (Englewood Cliffs, NJ: Prentice-Hall, 1987), 154–157.
18. Al Ries and Jack Trout, *Positioning: The Battle for Your Mind* (New York: McGraw-Hill, 1981), 3.
19. See Subhash C. Jain, *Marketing Planning & Strategy* (Cincinnati: South-Western Publishing Co., 1981), 257.
20. John Koten, "Car Makers Use 'Image' Map as Tool to Position Products," *Wall Street Journal,* 22 March 1984.
21. See ibid.
22. "Research Methodology Detailed for Repositioning Mature Brands," *Marketing News,* 24 June 1983, 11.
23. Ibid. Reprinted with permission.
24. See Jain, *Marketing Planning & Strategy,* 262.
25. See Ries and Trout, *Positioning: The Battle for Your Mind,* 77ff.
26. See Jain, *Marketing Planning & Strategy,* 263ff.
27. See Eugene J. Cafarelli, *Developing New Products and Repositioning Mature Brands* (New York: John Wiley & Sons, 1980), 221.
28. See Lorna Opatow, "Packaging Is Most Effective When It Works in Harmony with the Positioning of a Brand," *Marketing News,* 3 Feb. 1984, 3, and "Repositioned Buitoni Foods Tests Marketing Campaign in N.Y., Eyes National Distribution," *Marketing News,* 30 Oct. 1981, 1, 8.
29. See "The New Sears: Unable to Grow in Retailing, It Turns to Financial Services," *Business Week,* 16 Nov. 1981, and Robert F. Gurnee, Vice President and Corporate Treasurer, Sears, Roebuck and Company, "Revolution in the Financial Services Industry," remarks delivered at the 23rd Annual Business Conference of St. John's University, New York, 5 April 1984.
30. See Booz, Allen & Hamilton, *New Products Management, for the 1980s,* 11.

CASE STUDY

MASON LOCK

The Mason Lock Manufacturing Company produces locksets in Brooklyn, New York, in a factory that employs about 150 people. In its current form, it was organized in 1934 by Ralph Mason and his son Henry. The firm prospered and grew over the years, but the heirs were not interested in the business and sold it to Harry and Ted Hart, another father-and-son team.

At the time of the sale, Mason Lock was earning about 5 percent net before taxes on a sales volume of $14 million. All sales are generated through the efforts of eighteen manufacturer's representatives operating in territories east of the Mississippi River. Mason's strongest sales territory is the New York metropolitan area.

Industry and Market Composition

Mason Lock is a member of the builders' hardware manufacturing industry (SIC 3429). The 1977 industry census indicated that the industry consisted of eighteen U.S. firms. Although this number has remained rather constant over the years, the census does not specify how much of the industry's product originates overseas. By the same token, it is unclear how much is imported by other firms that are not classified as manufacturers. Total industry sales in 1984 amounted to about $2.5 billion.

The lock-manufacturing sector of the industry is fairly concentrated:

- Three New England manufacturers control about 14 percent of the market
- Two Midwestern firms have about a 20 percent share each
- Two West Coast companies hold a combined share of 25 percent
- Two New York producers together account for about 2 percent of industry sales

---

This case was prepared for instructional purposes by Martin R. Schlissel, Professor of Marketing, St. John's University, New York, New York. Although based on an actual business situation, names, places, and other data have been disguised.

All of these firms compete nationwide or, as in Mason's case, over a large regional area. A few smaller producers that serve local markets complete the industry.

The major source of demand is new construction. The replacement market is small because locksets last for decades. The market consists of three major segments, with each segment requiring a somewhat different product and/or exhibiting different buying behavior. These segments are residential, private nonresidential (commercial), and public works (government). Of these, the residential segment is by far the largest, representing almost half of all new construction. Exhibit 2–A presents detailed statistics on the composition and evolution of the construction market.

Although new construction is projected to be at an all-time high in 1987, declining or leveling trends are evident in all segments. Within the largest subsegment, single-family residential construction, there is a further trend toward larger and more expensive housing units (see Exhibit 2–B).

In an effort to keep costs down, new home builders who are the lockset buyers for the residential segment have generally been buying standardized, lightweight, rather simply engineered locksets. They almost invariably buy from wholesalers of builders' hardware. On the other hand, the architects and engineers who design commercial and public works buildings usually specify heavy-duty locksets, sometimes of a special design. Specialized wholesalers, called contract hardware wholesalers, submit bids on individual, large construction projects. Builders or government agencies are rarely sold to on a direct basis by manufacturers.

The federal government plays an unusual role. Although its actual purchases are rather limited, its design needs influence industry design policies. Government bids usually specify a particular design option that has been previously approved by government engineers. Most lockset manufacturers, therefore, design their products so that they meet one or more government design specifications (specs). This enables wholesalers interested in bidding on a government job to quote their products. At the same

EXHIBIT 2–A
Value of New Construction Put in Place
(in billions of 1982 dollars except as noted)

								Percent Change	
Type of Construction	1977	1982	1983	1984	1985	1986[1]	1987[2]	1985–86	1986–87
Total New Construction	294.3	244.4	272.0	308.0	324.9	340.6	343.2	4.8	0.8
Residential	149.1	85.4	123.1	146.1	146.3	161.4	167.1	10	4
Single family	100.2	41.5	70.2	80.6	79.4	89.7	95.1	13	6
Multifamily	16.9	16.2	22.9	27.8	27.5	28.3	26.1	3	−8
Home improvement	32.0	27.7	30.0	37.6	39.4	43.3	45.9	10	6
Private Nonresidential	87.0	108.1	98.5	109.0	121.6	117.4	112.9	−3	−4
Manufacturing facilities	12.2	17.3	12.4	12.9	14.2	12.8	14.1	−10	10
Office	8.4	23.0	20.0	23.9	28.3	26.3	22.4	−7	−15
Hotels & motels	1.5	4.1	5.0	6.2	6.6	6.9	6.5	4	−5
Other commercial	15.1	14.2	14.5	20.4	25.2	25.2	24.7	0	−2
Religious	1.7	1.5	1.7	2.0	2.2	2.3	2.3	4	0
Educational	1.1	1.5	1.5	1.5	1.7	1.9	2.0	10	5
Hospital & institutional	5.2	5.9	6.3	5.8	5.0	4.9	4.8	−2	−2
Misc. buildings	1.9	1.7	1.8	2.3	2.4	2.3	2.3	−4	0
Telephone & telegraph	6.3	7.1	6.3	6.8	7.0	7.5	7.9	7	5
Railroads	2.0	2.6	3.0	3.4	3.4	3.1	3.2	−8	2
Electric utilities	17.1	18.3	17.4	14.8	15.4	14.2	12.8	−8	−10
Gas utilities	3.8	5.5	3.7	4.2	5.3	5.4	5.5	2	2
Petroleum pipelines	1.8	0.4	0.5	0.3	0.3	0.3	0.3	0	10
Farm structures	7.0	3.7	3.1	2.6	2.1	1.9	1.7	−10	−10
Misc. structures	1.7	1.3	1.5	1.9	2.5	2.5	2.5	0	3
Public Works	58.2	50.9	50.3	52.9	57.0	61.8	63.2	8	2
Housing & redevelopment .....`...	1.5	1.7	1.7	1.5	1.4	1.3	1.3	−5	0
Federal industrial	1.3	1.6	1.7	1.7	1.8	1.7	1.6	−5	−6
Educational	8.7	5.9	5.2	5.1	6.0	6.6	6.9	10	5
Hospital	2.8	2.0	2.0	1.9	1.8	1.8	1.8	0	−2
Other public buildings	5.8	5.8	6.1	6.3	7.2	8.1	8.4	12	4
Highways	14.3	13.4	14.4	16.0	17.5	18.9	19.5	8	3
Military facilities	2.2	2.2	2.5	2.7	2.9	3.1	3.0	7	−4
Conservation & development	5.8	5.0	4.8	4.5	4.8	4.4	4.5	−8	2
Sewer systems	8.0	5.5	5.3	6.1	6.9	7.8	8.0	13	3
Water supplies	2.7	2.9	2.1	2.6	2.6	3.1	3.3	20	5
Misc. public structures	5.3	4.9	4.6	4.5	4.1	4.9	4.9	20	3

[1]Estimated.
[2]Forecast
Source: U.S. Industrial Outlook 1987—Construction, p. 1–1.

time, residential and commercial builders are influenced in their assessment of a lockset's quality by their knowledge of which spec it meets, if any. With their emphasis on strength and durability, the specs insist on steel, brass, bronze, and even cast iron materials in locksets.

Mason's Product Mix

To be a full-line supplier, a lockset manufacturer must provide a set for each possible door function. A residential product mix, therefore, would include entry, passage, bedroom, bathroom, and closet door

EXHIBIT 2–B
Number of Housing Starts and Major Determinants of Housing Demand, 1978–87

| Year | Total Housing Starts (millions of lots) | Average Annual Effective Interest Rates on Conventional Mortgages of 25 Years with 75 Percent Loan-to-price Ratios (percent) | Prices for New Single-Family Houses | | Population[2] (millions) | | Households (millions) | Per capita Disposable Personal Income (1982 dollars) |
			Median Sales Price ($000)	Price Index of New One-Family Houses Sold Excluding Lot Value (1982–100)[1]	Total	25–44 Years		
1978	2.0	9.7	55.7	70.4	222.1	59.2	76.0	9.735
1979	1.8	11.3	62.9	80.1	224.6	61.2	77.3	9.829
1980	1.3	14.0	64.6	88.8	225.7	62.6	80.8	9.722
1981	1.1	16.7	63.9	97.0	228.0	64.7	82.4	9.769
1982	1.1	16.6	69.3	100.0	230.3	66.8	83.5	9.725
1983	1.7	13.3	75.3	102.6	232.6	68.9	83.9	9.930
1984	1.7	13.1	79.9	106.2	234.8	70.9	85.4	10.421
1985	1.7	11.9	84.3	108.4	237.0	72.9	86.8	10.563
1986[3]	1.8	10.4	90.0	115.0	239.3	74.8	88.6	10.800
1987[4]	1.8	9.9	—	—	241.6	76.5	90.0	—

[1]The price index is intended to measure changes over time in the sales price of homes which are the same with regard to ten important characteristics including floor area, location, construction features, amenities, etc.
[2]The 1978 and 1979 estimates are based on the 1970 population Census; the data for 1980–87 are based on the 1980 Census and Bureau of Census projections.
[3]Estimated
[4]Forecast
Source: U.S. Industrial Outlook 1987—Construction, p. 1–4.

locksets. A product of contemporary design usually consists of two parts—a latch section and a knob section. The two sections are assembled together on the door after two holes have been drilled to accommodate the parts.

A lightweight residential set may be made of cast aluminum or zinc die cast because of their very low cost of manufacture. But these materials cannot long endure hard, regular use. Their injudicious use has cost builders a great deal of time and money in service and replacement expenses. Although steel sets are about twice as costly to make, they do not function smoothly or quietly and are adversely affected by dampness.

A fine working lockset is a cylindrical design. It contains more working parts, but they are all enclosed in the housing, which keeps out dust and dampness, and uses lubricants to maintain a long and service-free working life.

Some lockset manufacturers also offer mortise locks. Old-fashioned looking, they are large, flat, and bulky and usually are made of cast iron with some bronze parts. These sets are very strong and

consequently are used in situations where great strength is needed and protection must be maximized. Mortise sets are costly to install because of the large cutout that must be carefully drilled through the narrow stile of the door without marking the door's surfaces. However, mortise sets can be made attractive by hanging accompanying decorative escutcheons around the doorknobs. In present-day residential construction, mortise sets might be installed in front doors of large, expensive colonial-style homes. Commercial builders usually install these large, heavy sets in store doors, office doors, and building entrances.

During the 1950s housing boom, Mason was one of the largest volume producers of die-cast, through-the-door locksets. Its main buyers were large-volume builders of low-priced tract homes, whose primary concern was to keep costs low. But the firm's sales volume decreased sharply from its one-time peak of $25 million when steel sets were introduced. In the 1960s, Mason dropped the die-cast sets from its mix and began manufacturing steel sets in all finishes while continuing to make nonworking parts of zinc material. By this time, however, industry leaders were producing cylindrical locksets. After a few years, even the low-end manufacturers upgraded their offerings by adding cylindrical sets.

In addition to its full-function line of steel residential locksets, Mason's product mix today also includes an entry mortise lock with a cast-iron case and a half-dozen different decorative escutcheons and one store door escutcheon.

Looking Ahead

Concerned about Mason's unsatisfactory performance record, the owners, Harry and Ted, hold a review session. "I must say, Ted, I was a bit surprised by the poor construction forecast, but construction is a cyclical industry. It should improve again in the near future, although not much in the New York City area, I'm afraid. There is not much open land left. How about putting your brand-new business degree to work? Tell me where we should go from here."

"Well, Dad, I really wonder sometimes whether it was such a smart move for us to buy this business. But, no kidding, I think we can make a go of it if we make some strategic changes. We should begin by finding out what we have to do to make our steel locksets conform to government specs. It might cost us some money to make a few tools and dies, but we have to do something to move this business into the 1990s."

Discussion Questions

1. What do you think of Ted's suggestion as to how to begin to move Mason Lock into the 1990s? Would you recommend a different procedure to the Harts?
2. What problems do you think the Harts face?
3. What should be the first step toward solving these problems?
4. What do you think should be the major elements of Mason Lock's strategic program?

CHAPTER 3

New Product Organization

Because new products are a company's lifeblood, their genesis should not be left to chance. Rather, organizational provisions must be made to guarantee the proper attention to the new product task at the appropriate levels within a company. The organization also must ensure a steady flow of marketable new products that become available at critical points in a company's history. The responsibility for product innovation must be clearly defined and assigned, and a system for the planning and control of the evolutionary process must be developed.

New product organization refers to the logical structuring, coordination, and control of all job functions and activities involved in new product programs. Reporting and working relationships must be established, authority and responsibilities specified, tasks outlines, methods decided on, and checkpoints put in place. The success of a firm's new product effort depends heavily on a thorough understanding of the new product process by all concerned, an agreement on objectives and priorities, and the smooth interplay of all organizational units. In principle, all functional areas of a company are potential contributors to new product success.

Organization for product innovation can be subdivided into two major types according to the elements being structured. *Structural organization* organizes people and their working relationships, which is otherwise known as the "chain of command." Although reorganizations do occur, these relationships and responsibilities tend to be fairly static over time. The structural organization is usually illustrated in the form of an organization chart, which shows position titles.

Process organization, on the other hand, deals with structuring new product activities for logical sequencing and optimum execution. This type of organization is dynamic and must remain flexible to accommodate adjustments. To facilitate comprehension and control, process organization is usually shown in the form of a flow diagram. This kind of graph outlines the sequence in which the activities are to be performed, the time intervals allotted to them, and their relationships with each other. Figure 3–1 highlights the differences between the two types of new product organization.

New product organization is necessary for a firm to provide continuity and economy of effort as well as maximum impact. It introduces accountability and performance orientation into what might otherwise be a haphazard series of events. And it uses logic where emotions might otherwise prevail. By injecting order into potential chaos, new product organization makes a significant contribution to new product management.

Structural Organization

In every firm there is a definite need for a specific individual to be in charge of the new product management function. Such a focal point is required (1) to make sure that somebody feels responsible to make new products happen, and (2) to enable people with new product ideas to present them to a clearly identified person for due consideration.

The individual responsible for new product management in a given firm generally will occupy one of the following four positions: new product director, product manager, chairperson of a committee, or head of a task force or team. Table 3–1 summarizes the characteristics of these structural organization alternatives. The exhibit clarifies that the unit controlling new product activities can be built in different ways into a company's organization. The selection of one solution over another depends largely on the firm's resources and objectives.

The New Product Department

Because of their exclusive dedication to new products, new product departments have enjoyed considerable popularity in recent years. Typically reporting to a top executive, they are usually classified as high-level staff functions. In a recent survey

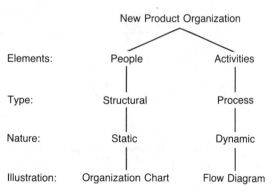

FIGURE 3–1
Organizing for New Products

TABLE 3–1
Structural Organization Alternatives

Organization Form	Nature	Focus
New product department	Permanent, full-time	New products
Product manager	Permanent, full-time	Established and new products
New product committee	Permanent, part-time	Stage of evolutionary process
Task force	Temporary, full-time	One new product

by The Conference Board, 76 percent of the respondents stated that in their companies the new product development function reports to a person with the job title of executive vice president and above.[1]

This fact is highlighted in Figure 3–2, which shows the new product department reporting to the executive vice president. This arrangement is very effective because it enables the new product department to coordinate the participation of the different line departments in the firm's new product effort. If the new product department had instead been assigned to report to the vice president, marketing, it would have had to emphasize a marketing perspective to new products. It also would have suffered from a lower organizational status and the resulting loss of influence.

New product departments usually employ just a few people. It is not their job to perform new product activities. Rather, they are to ensure that designated groups do the work assigned to them on schedule and within budget. Department members also interface with the research and development and marketing depart-

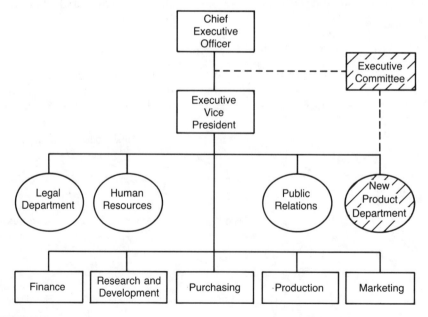

FIGURE 3–2
The New Product Department as a High-Level Staff Function

ments regularly on ongoing projects. They may further negotiate license agreements with patent owners or even the acquisition of entire companies possessing a certain technology.

Every new product department must initiate, coordinate, and control a continuous series of new product processes. And it must oversee the execution of the individual tasks. Essentially, it has to ensure that new products come about and are launched at a steady pace.

Toward this end a new product department acts basically as a new product planner. It analyzes relevant data, identifies challenges and opportunities, and sets new product objectives. Its moment of glory comes in the formulation of new product strategies, which then must be translated into tactics. Its role ends, though, with the successful introduction of a new product, which is then transferred to a line function. To carry out this broad mission, a new product department should be staffed with high-caliber personnel who are free from day-to-day operating responsibilities for current products and devote all their talents to building the company's future. This involves collecting and processing a broad range of new product ideas and ensuring that they move on schedule and within budget through the evolutionary stages and functional departments.

The Product Manager System

Product managers have been variously described as "little marketing managers, entrepreneurs, information centers, influence agents, integrators, little general managers, product planning and development analysts, boundary spanners," and " 'little presidents.' "[2] Their responsibilities can range from managing a product line with $2 million in annual sales, for instance, a line of industrial cleaning products, to controlling a single brand representing $500 million in sales revenues, such as Crown Royal Scotch at Seagram's.

The term *product management* was first applied in the late 1920s by Procter & Gamble on its Camay soap. This form of new product organization is used in multiproduct firms to give individual products or product lines the care and attention they need to prosper in highly competitive environments. Without product managers, they might well wither and die because no one would feel responsible for them. Product managers serve as "product champions," as relentless advocates and spokespersons, extolling a product's virtues and gaining recognition and support for it.

After more than sixty years, the product manager concept is alive and well because of the level of personal commitment and involvement that it elicits. Other than the chief marketing officer's job, product management is the only area that requires a marketing generalist. This is so because product managers are responsible for every facet and aspect of marketing related to their assigned products. And product managers are very dedicated, hardworking people because their careers are directly linked with the success of their products. Lee Iacocca was the product manager for the Ford Mustang and later moved on to become the president of the Ford Motor Company. John Smale, the former product manager for Crest toothpaste, became chief executive officer of Procter & Gamble. Product managers who are associated with product failures, however, often find their careers stalled.

Depending on their realm of responsibility, four types of product managers can be distinguished:

- Established products only
- Established and new products within a product line
- New products only
- Particular new products only

The first type is exclusively concerned with the management of an established product or product line. It is this type's responsibility to design and implement plans that will help defend and strengthen the brand's market share and leadership position.[3] This undivided attention is due to the importance of the brand to the firm's overall performance. Tide detergent and Crown Royal Scotch whisky represent substantial contributors to the sales revenues and profits of Procter & Gamble and Seagram's, respectively. This fact alone qualifies them and other products like them for the special care of an experienced and dedicated product manager. This manager will initiate and manage updates of the brand, ranging from packaging redesign to product reformulation.[4] Since its introduction in 1947, Tide detergent has been reformulated about fifty times. A few years ago a liquid version of this leading detergent was introduced to fend off challenges from the growing liquid subcategory and participate in its expansion.

Probably the most frequent type of product manager is fully in charge of a given product line. These managers shoulder the burden of innovation in addition to managing the established products within their line. This means being responsible for the periodic evaluation of current products, including decisions about their deletion, as well as the timely initiation of evolutionary processes leading to profitable additions to the line. These product managers must develop long-range strategies as well as annual marketing plans for their product lines. They must continually interpret market data to spot trends and identify emerging challenges. And they must work closely with both internal departments and external agencies to ensure steady growth of their part of the business. In their roles as communicators, coordinators, and controllers, these product managers relate as follows to other relevant units:

Division Management
- Keep informed about market conditions and product performance
- Obtain approval for strategy, plan, and budget
- Achieve authorization for innovations

Advertising and Sales Promotion
- Communicate promotion objectives and needs
- Jointly develop promotion plan for product line
- Coordinate execution of promotion plan

Marketing Research
- Identify information needs, both one-time and continuous
- Cooperate in problem formulation, project design, and execution
- Assist in interpreting and formatting findings

Packaging
- Specify packaging requirements
- Initiate and coordinate package development projects
- Review packaging changes and the results of packaging research

Sales
- Visit field and call on accounts with salespeople on a regular basis
- Inform and train sales force members in intricacies of new products
- Win sales management's support for own product line in competition with other product managers

Production
- Review product requirements for production management and staff
- Assist in identifying and eliminating product quality and delivery problems
- Solicit favorable scheduling and anticipate supply disruptions

Purchasing
- Outline material needs for planning period with sufficient lead time
- Value-analyze product functions to consider material substitutions
- Examine opportunities for product redesign as prompted by new materials or technologies

Research and Development
- Communicate desired product characteristics
- Monitor project progress
- Analyze test results and initiate product modifications

Accounting
- Prepare annual budget request
- Request cost and profitability studies for current and new products
- Propose consideration of price adjustment to meet competitive challenge

Advertising Agency
- Establish advertising objectives
- Select copy platform and execution approach
- Consider media schedule and composition of media mix

Although these forms of interaction with the various other units of a firm are typical for product management, other contacts occur from time to time as appropriate. Because of a growing tide of lawsuits, all promotional materials, including advertisements and packages, must be cleared with the legal department. The legal department would insist on proper warnings, support for claims made, and written statements about product use from endorsing celebrities. Free publicity may be obtained with the help of the public relations department. Outside consultants and marketing research agencies complete the picture of a busy product manager interfacing with a variety of internal and external resources to enhance the success of a specific product line.

The third type is a product manager who is only concerned with the development and introduction of new products. Unburdened by any responsibilities for the management of established products, this type concentrates exclusively on generating and launching a steady flow of new products. Juggling a variety of projects at various stages of evolution, this kind of product manager relies heavily on creativity and persuasiveness. After having successfully guided an innovation through its internal evolution and its introduction in the marketplace, this manager turns over the responsibility for its daily management to the appropriate line manager. Used only in combination with managers of established brands, this type of manager nonetheless suffers from two inherent problems. First, this individual may feel deprived of reaping the fruits of the new product effort by having to turn the innovation over to someone else. Second, it is difficult to transfer the new product manager's accumulated knowledge and insight concerning the new product to another person.

A project manager, finally, takes charge of a specific new product project from the beginning, serving as its guardian throughout the evolutionary process. This approach can be found in the automobile and food industries, where new projects can consume considerable amounts of time and money. Because of full-time involvement with the project, the project manager may, however, lack objectivity in evaluating the innovation and its chances of commercial success.

Some companies are troubled by the strong focus on products that characterizes the product manager system. These firms use instead an alternative called *market management*. Whereas product managers essentially become product specialists, market managers concentrate on understanding, predicting, and serving the unique needs of the firm's various markets. Such an arrangement makes a great deal of sense if a company serves highly diverse, complex markets with distinctly different need and behavior patterns that require in-depth familiarity with customer operations. It can also help allay fears that a product management organization would become too technology driven. Market management creates market-centered organizations that are market driven. Figure 3–3 illustrates the differences between the two approaches for a company serving three distinct markets (for instance, retailers, institutions, and export) with four different product lines (for example, food products, cleaning products, paper products, and beverages).

As Figure 3–3 shows, a product management organization focuses on the separate product lines. The product manager for product line A markets it to all of the company's markets. Although fully acquainted with their respective products, the product line specialists may not fully appreciate the differences among the three markets. Market managers, on the other hand, specialize in the intricacies of individual markets. The market manager for market 1 draws on all four product lines to assemble a product mix that is uniquely suited to fit the needs of this market.

Some products may have to be modified to adapt to special market conditions. As a potential drawback, market managers may lack adequate product knowledge. Some companies therefore have chosen to combine a market management organization with a product management structure into a hybrid form called a *matrix organization*. Du Pont has done this by matching product managers for rayon, acetate, nylon, Orlon, and Dacron with market managers for menswear, womenswear, home furnishings, and industrial markets.[5]

Of the three approaches, product management is by far the most frequent. Its major strength lies in its product champions. While giving them a great deal of responsibility, however, companies often fail to grant them appropriate authority. This conflict between broad-ranging tasks and limited decision-making power is high-

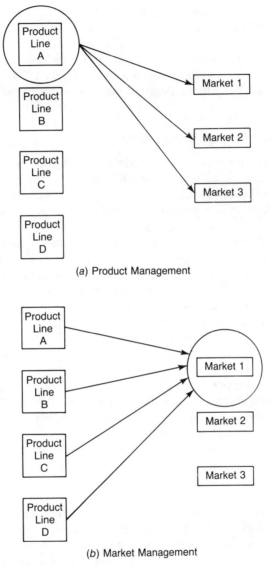

(a) Product Management

(b) Market Management

FIGURE 3–3
Product and Market Management

lighted by the fact that product managers have very few people reporting to them—usually just a secretary and an assistant product manager. Thus, to accomplish anything, they must rely on their persuasiveness. They must convince their superiors that their plans and proposals are sound and deserve to be approved. And they must win the support and cooperation of their peers, such as sales, advertising, and marketing research managers. A company's sales force typically sells its entire product mix, and has only a limited interest in promoting a given product manager's products. Because they have no direct authority over its members, product managers must "sell" the sales organization on the merits of selling particular products. This need to obtain the cooperation and support of many other units of a company to make a product line succeed can be viewed as a key strength of the product management system. It fosters a spirit of internal competition for resources that bodes well for the line's external competitiveness in the marketplace.

New Product Committees

It can be reasonably argued that new product project authorization decisions should always be made by a committee and never by any individual alone, not even a firm's chief executive officer. Too much depends on the wisdom of these decisions to leave them to one person's judgment. Thus, a high-level committee, made up of the company's senior executives—its chief executive officer, executive vice president, and the vice presidents heading the line departments—is usually formed to make these crucial decisions that allocate resources and chart the future path of the firm. This group is usually referred to as the *executive committee*. Figure 3–2 shows such an executive committee and its role in the new product process. Day-to-day tactical new product issues are the responsibility of the new product department. Key strategic decisions, however, are made by the executive committee at critical points in the new product process.

In contrast to the executive committee, *new product committees* specialize in certain aspects of the new product process. They are a permanent part of the organization, staffed by representatives from all affected line departments who assume this task in addition to their regular duties. New product committees are used to communicate, advise, screen, coordinate, and make decisions.[6] They can be formed with charters limited to any stage of the new product process, but most frequently they are used to screen and evaluate new product proposals. They also may have authority to provide seed money to develop ideas further or conduct marketing research.

New product committees often work under the direction and with the support of the new product department. Like other groups, they can suffer from an inability to reach agreement, infighting, or dominance by a strong personality or department. Where they are used creatively and sincerely, however, and not just as a means of compromise, better decisions will result. A variety of backgrounds, experiences, insights, and viewpoints will be reflected in the outcome of their deliberations. And the participating departments will support the committees' decisions because they were involved in making them.

Task Forces

A *task force* combines entrepreneurial spirit—often personified by an enthusiastic leader—with the effects of a pool of highly talented and strongly motivated people working toward a common objective. Assembled on a full-time, though temporary, basis by bringing together key representatives from the various line departments involved, this elite group is given the specific task to develop and introduce a new product or even new business of great significance to the firm. The task force method can be distinguished from the three other forms of new product organization as follows:

- It is the only form that is temporary in nature; it will be disbanded on project completion.
- Compared to a new product department, which is responsible for a steady flow of innovations, it is a group of people working on the evolution of a single product concept.
- Although it may be headed by a project manager, it always employs the team approach instead of the one-person product manager system.
- In contrast to new product committees, it is neither restricted to a single phase of the new product process nor concerned with a variety of proposals, but rather it deals with only one idea through all the stages of evolution.

Because of its importance for a company's future, a task force may bypass regular channels and report directly to top management. A number of advantages can be cited for the task force approach:

- It creates "a situation where the challenge can engender enthusiastic commitment and increase the odds for success through the interaction of innovative thinking with entrepreneurial drive."[7] At 3M, the Statement of Corporate Management Principles states that "the first principle is the promotion of entrepreneurship and insistence upon freedom in the workplace to pursue innovative ideas."[8] An example of the successful application of this principle was Art Fry's invention of Post-it Notes, which was based on proprietary technology and became an attractive business for 3M.[9]
- It permits circumventing constraints on creativity and bureaucratic red tape delays in gaining approval.
- It enables significant productivity increases as well as advances in technology and business methods through "charged-up small-within-big teams."[10] IBM was able to introduce its first personal computer within two years of making a commitment to this product category by creating a "skunkworks" team with an open budget and freedom from red tape in a former warehouse in Boca Raton, Florida.
- It provides "concentrated effort on a specific development mission, without distractions from current operations or other new-product responsibilities."[11]

On the other hand, the task force method also has some serious disadvantages:

- Although it conceptually involves a joining of forces and talents of a select group of highly capable employees from different departments, in reality it often encounters the very real "problem of how to find qualified individuals of demonstrable competence, and then persuade them to accept posts that may be regarded by some as a high-risk diversion from their main career paths."[12]

- Line departments will want to retain the very key personnel that task forces seek to attract.
- Because of their intense involvement, task force members are likely to lack the critical distance to objectively evaluate the project and "kill" it if it lacks viability.[13]
- A genuine transfer-of-knowledge problem will occur if on project completion the new product is transferred to an operating unit and the task force that guided its evolution is disbanded. The people charged with the management of the product on an ongoing basis will have considerable difficulty absorbing the insights and experiences gained by the task force's members during the project. Some companies solve this problem by converting the task force into a line unit and using its members in the continued management of their product.

Although they possess similar characteristics, project groups and venture teams are sometimes distinguished from task forces. Venture teams in particular are usually corporate-level undertakings of a long-term strategic nature. They are formed to get a company into new businesses and perhaps even lay the foundation for a complete restructuring of its operations. For this reason, venture teams usually enjoy high-level status and appropriate funding. Colgate-Palmolive even created a separate subsidiary as its vehicle for venturing into new businesses.

Choosing the Right Setup

Which organizational form or combination is ideal for a specific company's new product effort depends on a number of factors: its objectives and current structure, its financial strength and market situation, as well as its human resources. A firm with a functional marketing organization will probably do well to institute a new product department for the purpose of initiating, coordinating, and controlling new product programs. A company with a product-based structure, on the other hand, may want to rely on new product committees.

The various types of new product organization are not mutually exclusive but can be combined in a manner most suitable for the conditions prevailing in a particular firm.[14] Such a combination can increase the effectiveness of the innovative effort considerably. In the final analysis the crucial factor in the selection of a structural new product organization is the way in which the basic organizational alternatives are coordinated for maximum efficiency and profitability. To attain this goal there should be at least one individual at the top-management level who lends personal support to new products and has sufficient authority to ensure the success of new product programs. Directly or through some intermediary unit, the new product department, product managers, new product committees, task forces, or a combination of them will report to this individual.

The appropriateness of a company's new product organization can be judged based on its clarity and ease of administration as well as its ability to make things happen. The success of any new product program, regardless of its inherent merits, depends to a considerable degree on the effectiveness of its organizational setup. The latter, in turn, hinges on the proper allocation of authority and responsibility as well as on the entrepreneurial spirit and personal involvement of the individuals involved.

Process Organization

As the preceding discussion indicated, it is essential to position the new product organization clearly and effectively within the management structure of a firm. The second major organizational task for product managers is then to ensure the smooth execution of the many activities involved in bringing an innovation to market. In every new product process, they must organize, coordinate, and supervise complex sets of activities. In addressing this challenge, they can use a tool for process organization and planning called PERT (program evaluation and review technique).

This technique is useful for first-time or one-time tasks, such as new product evolution. It organizes a large number of activities into a logical sequence that permits completion of a new product project in the shortest possible time. Firms use PERT to schedule and budget resources and communicate performance expectations to everyone involved. This technique is designed to keep the product manager informed about the project's actual progress and to help ensure its completion on time and within budget.

With PERT, the activities involved in a new product project are illustrated in the form of a network diagram that shows the relationships among the various activities. Every PERT diagram consists of two types of components, namely events and activities. An *event* is a point in time at which an activity begins or ends. An *activity* is the physical or mental work performed between two events. Activities can be consecutive, which means that they follow each other and thus depend on each other. Or they can be concurrent in nature, in which case they occur at the same time, independently of each other. The purpose of PERT in new product organization is to schedule as many activities as possible concurrently to shorten the duration of the project and expedite the launching of the new product.

Each PERT diagram features only one starting event and one event that completes the project. Many consecutive and concurrent activities in several departments connect these points. A series of sequential activities leading from the starting point to the completion point is called a *path*. The longest sequence of this kind, known as the *critical path,* determines the duration of the entire project. It needs particular management attention because any delay on this path will postpone the completion of the project as a whole.

Process organization via PERT is conducted in three stages:

1. Estimating—developing likely time frames for the various activities and paths
2. Planning—making decisions about schedules and budgets
3. Controlling—monitoring progress and taking corrective action where necessary

The network diagram for a new product project is first drawn up in the estimating stage. The logic of PERT forces a careful review of this initial scheme to see if some of the consecutive activities could be rescheduled concurrently to compress the project's duration. After the diagram has been finalized, three separate estimates are developed for each activity, namely, an optimistic, most likely, and pessimistic estimate. The three estimates are then averaged with the help of a weighted formula to determine the expected time consumption of an activity. After the expected times for each path have been added up, the critical path can be identified.

During the second stage of PERT, management uses its judgment to convert estimates into schedules. In the process the estimated figures may be adjusted somewhat. At the same time the responsibility for completing specific activities on time is assigned to identified individuals. While the project is in progress, scheduled and actual times are compared continuously. Any delays that endanger timely project completion cause prompt corrective action, such as overtime. Even if schedule slippages occur, PERT thus facilitates intervention during a project and on-time completion.

SUMMARY

Because it means creating something different, introducing change and deviating from past practices, any new product effort is likely to fail unless the proper organizational framework is set up. Organization is the logical, efficient, and effective structuring of elements. It must address itself to both the static structural relationships between people and the dynamic sets of activities involved in the new product process. Organizing for new products means positioning the new product function in a company's organization chart *and* designing a program for effective new product evolution and control.

Regarding a firm's structural new product organization, four basic choices are available: the new product department, the product manager system, new product committees, and task forces. A new product department is a high-level staff unit that is responsible for generating and introducing a steady flow of new products. A product manager is a marketing generalist who manages the entire marketing effort for a particular product or product line. Product managers may be responsible for established and/or new products. While the executive committee has the ultimate new product decision-making authority, new product committees specialize in a phase of the new product process, for instance, idea screening and evaluation. Task forces are teams formed to manage a specific new product project all the way to market introduction. These different approaches can be combined to best suit the needs and conditions of a particular firm.

In the area of organizing new product activities, one of the most dramatic and useful developments has been the availability of PERT. New product management has been quick to adopt this powerful tool for planning and controlling new product projects. The PERT method demands a detailed, logical breakdown and planning of the individual activities involved in a specific project. It is applied in three stages:

estimating, scheduling, and controlling. With the help of a network diagram, the progress and status of the project is continually reflected, enabling timely corrective action if it veers off course.

NOTES

1. See Michael G. Duerr, *The Commercial Development of New Products* (New York: The Conference Board, 1986), 55.
2. Carl McDaniel and David A. Gray, "The Product Manager," *California Management Review* (Fall 1980): 87, and C. Merle Crawford, *New Products Management* (Homewood, IL: Irwin, 1983), 173.
3. See Al Ries and Jack Trout, *Marketing Warfare* (New York: McGraw-Hill, 1986), 31–36, and Philip Kotler, *Marketing Management,* 6th ed. (Englewood Cliffs, NJ: Prentice-Hall, 1988), 319–330.
4. This must be done with great care so as not to discourage loyal buyers while trying to attract new ones. See Leon G. Schiffman and Leslie Lazar Kanuk, *Consumer Behavior,* 3rd ed. (Englewood Cliffs, NJ: Prentice-Hall, 1987), 178–180.
5. See Kotler, *Marketing Management,* 714–715. For a similar matrix at Glidden's Industrial Coatings unit, see also Michael G. Duerr, *Commercial Development of New Products,* 38.
6. See David S. Hopkins, *Options in New-Product Organization* (New York: The Conference Board, 1974), 45–47.
7. Ibid., 34.
8. Lester C. Krogh, "Can the Entrepreneurial Spirit Exist within a Large Company?" paper delivered at the 1984 Research & Development Conference of The Conference Board, New York, 25 April 1984, 1.
9. For a description of this fascinating case history see Gifford Pinchot, III, *Intrapreneuring: Why You Don't Have to Leave the Corporation to Become an Entrepreneur* (New York: Harper & Row, 1985), 137–142.
10. See Thomas J. Peters, "A Skunkworks Tale," *Best of Business* (Spring 1984): 86–87.
11. See Hopkins, *Options in New-Product Organization,* 34.
12. Ibid., 35.
13. See Barry M. Staw and Jerry Ross, "Knowing When to Pull the Plug," *Harvard Business Review* (March–April 1987): 68–74.
14. See Booz, Allen & Hamilton, Inc., *New Products Management for the 1980s* (New York: Booz, Allen & Hamilton, Inc., 1982), 13.

CASE STUDY

WINDS OF CHANGE

It was Neil H. McElroy, a young advertising manager, who persuaded Procter & Gamble's top brass to institute the brand manager system some six decades ago. Although resisted at first, the idea soon caught on. Individual brands were managed aggressively as competitive businesses with control over manufacturing and sales. To this day, brand managers are dynamic, young people who thrive on the "up or out" challenge of their jobs. Says Frank Baynham, a former brand manager for P&G's Folgers decaffeinated coffee: "You spend 12 or 18 months on a brand, and the goal is to get your stripes and bolt" to a bigger brand or a post as associate advertising manager supervising several noncompeting brands.

This linkage between brand performance and personal career drives the system. The job involves hard work and high pressure. But the sky is the limit. John Smale is a case in point. Like McElroy, he worked his way up to chairman and chief executive of the consumer products giant from the ranks of brand management. Starting as assistant brand manager of Gleem toothpaste, he propelled himself to stardom as brand manager of Crest. His stroke of genius was the first-ever endorsement of a dentifrice by the American Dental Association, which made his brand the market leader.

The level of personal commitment and involvement often is all-consuming. For four years, Bruce Miller spent most of his waking moments thinking about his brand, Crisco. "My whole life was grease," he says. He developed marketing and advertising strategies, planned sales promotions, and coordinated package design. And he carefully watched his competitors' moves, especially those of his colleague managing P&G's Puritan brand. "We thought of ourselves as the hub of the wheel," he continues. "We didn't have much contact with manufacturing or purchasing. We'd go to research and ask for something and they'd say, 'That's impossible.'

We'd say, 'Do it anyway.' " After thorough marketing research, P&G would then introduce a superior product with great fanfare and military precision, exercising its enormous marketing muscle and expertise.

Cracks in the System

But the old system is beginning to show its age and a number of ailments. The limitations of unbridled brand management became evident with the introduction of Pringle's reconstituted potato chips. Despite warnings about product cost, taste, and texture and armed only with results from a single test market, the brand and advertising managers won approval for new chips plants. Although P&G never abandoned the product, it was gravely disappointed with its performance and had to retrench for some time.

The dominance of marketing executives proved detrimental in other ways, too. P&G's large research staff often could not obtain support even for major technological breakthroughs. Olestra—the cholesterol- and calorie-free fat substitute for which P&G is currently seeking government approval—languished in labs for more than two decades because of the company's "rigid organizational structure," charges Hercules Segalas, an analyst at Drexel Burnham Lambert, Inc., and a former P&G engineer. While researchers hailed Olestra as a dietary breakthrough that promises to take the fat out of the richest foods, marketers kept insisting that P&G was in the business of "selling products, not ingredients," Segalas says.

There are other reasons for questioning the adequacy of the traditional brand manager system at P&G. Mired in slow-growth markets, P&G suffered its first annual profit decline in thirty-two years in 1985. It also experienced losses in market share in its core businesses, namely, diapers, detergents, and toothpastes. Faster-moving competitors managed to beat the company to the marketplace. While P&G was still testing refastenable tabs on Pampers diapers, Kimberly-Clark introduced refastenable

This case was adapted from Jolie Solomon and Carol Hymowitz, "Team Strategy: P&G Makes Changes in the Way It Develops and Sells Its Products," *Wall Street Journal*, 11 Aug. 1987. Helpful suggestions were received from Irving Fitterman, Assistant Professor of Marketing, St. John's University, New York, New York.

Huggies and quickly captured a large portion of the market.

Retailers, too, have become more independent, thanks to electronic purchase-tracking systems. No longer dependent on manufacturers' surveys, they are less susceptible to the brand managers' rhetoric and pressure and rely more on early sales results. Retail buyers also place greater emphasis on regional tastes and preferences of their increasingly demanding clienteles. Brand management worked well during an era characterized by housewives who were brand-loyal. Today's consumer market is considerably more differentiated and fickle, prominently including single households, working couples, and the elderly, among others.

Discussion Questions

1. Should P&G continue its traditional brand management system unaltered? Why, or why not?
2. Should the company emphasize cooperation instead of internal competition?
3. If you feel that change is needed, should P&G move to a market management, matrix (combination product and market management), or team approach? Explain your reasoning.
4. Because many top managers of P&G come from the brand management ranks, what effect will the new approach you are recommending have on the career paths of young executives? On the company?

PART TWO

The Evolution of New Products

F or their survival and growth, business firms depend on sufficient demand for their products. To create, satisfy, or increase demand, they must continually develop and introduce new products. The intricate and time-consuming internal process that produces these innovations is called *new product evolution.* It consists of a series of steps that lead from opportunity identification to the market introduction of a new product.

New product evolution is the internal genesis of a new product. It is described here as a process that consists of three major stages, which, in turn, are broken down into twelve steps. Significantly, every evolutionary process is triggered by initiating forces. These are environmental events and developments that can create problems or opportunities for the firm. Product management must be sensitive to their relevance and potential impact. This presence and interpretation of initiating forces constitutes the first stage, called *initiative.*

The second major stage of *decision making* is at the very heart of the evolutionary process. It consists of ten steps that include generating, screening, and evaluating new product ideas, turning them into products, and testing these products in the marketplace. Because of their importance to the success of new products, these steps are described and discussed in considerable detail in the six chapters forming part two of this book. The third and final stage of the evolutionary process is labeled *commercialization.* It represents the introduction of the new product in the marketplace. Because choosing the right introductory marketing program is crucial to the success of this effort, part three is devoted to outlining choices and selection criteria.

CHAPTER 4

Initiating the Evolutionary Process

The nature, intensity, and extent of a company's efforts to generate and introduce new products vary widely, depending on industry conditions, management priorities, and performance record. Despite this diversity, a definite chronological pattern of the evolutionary process emerges. This pattern will be presented in this chapter and elaborated on in the following chapters.

At each step of the evolutionary process, complex decisions must be made. Although their structure and procedure are comparable to other marketing decisions, their content typically differs in at least two crucial ways: It involves a greater degree of uncertainty and a larger potential impact on a company's business than most decisions related to established products.

To succeed under such conditions, product managers must be particularly sensitive to environmental changes and their likely consequences for the firm. Whether internally initiated or externally driven, change is inevitable. But it must be channeled in a planned fashion. New product objectives help give direction to change that will be beneficial to the company.

A Model of the Evolutionary Process

New products result from a slow and deliberate process whose duration is all but unpredictable. The evolution of new products is an internal process that must wind its way through the intricacies of a firm's organizational structure. A model of its stages and steps is presented in Figure 4–1.

While "in 1968, on average, 58 new product ideas were considered for every successful new product, today only seven ideas are required to generate one successful new product."[1] This significantly reduced number is due to many firms'

I. Initiative
   1. Initiating forces
   2. Identification of problem or opportunity

II. Decision Making
   1. Definition of new product objectives and criteria
   2. Start of comprehensive marketing research program
   3. Analysis of market and company data
   4. New product strategy formulation
   5. Idea generation
   6. Screening
   7. Business analysis
   8. Development
   9. Market testing
   10. Finalization of marketing program and initial production

III. Commercialization

FIGURE 4–1
Stages and Steps of New Product Evolution

increasing technological and marketing sophistication, which gives better focus to their new product effort. Different types of industries, however, tend to allocate the total time spent on new product processes (from screening to commercialization) differently. Manufacturers of industrial goods place particular emphasis on engineering or development (Figure 4–1, stage II, 8), spending 47 percent of total new product time on this step. Producers of consumer nondurables devote only 30 percent of new product time to development, whereas consumer-durable companies allocate 36 percent. In contrast, consumer-oriented marketers place more emphasis on commercialization (Figure 4–1, stage III; an average of about 27 percent) as compared to industrial goods marketers (18 percent). From 1968 to 1981, the percentage of new product expenditures resulting in successful products increased from 30 to 54 percent.[2]

As Figure 4–1 indicates, a new product process is set in motion by the *initiative* stage, during which initiating forces are recognized and pinpointed. Astute product managers monitor environmental developments and assess their relevance to the company's continued success. A variety of internal and external stimuli can serve as initiating forces, setting a new product process in motion. But these events, trends, or facts will only produce a timely response if a product manager is aware of them and judges their significance correctly. Every relevant environmental occurrence translates into a problem or opportunity for a firm that may well warrant a new product response.

At the heart of new product evolution is the second stage, called *decision making*. Indeed, the entire new product process could be viewed as a complex single decision-making process, which, in turn, consists of many contributing decisions at all levels of a company's organization. The ten steps composing this stage involve a broad range of tactical detail decisions, which together will determine the fate of the innovation and possibly that of the company.

The stage begins with the *definition* of new product objectives and criteria. This set of decisions specifies the desired outcomes of the new product effort. It also highlights the scales that will be used to measure actual performance against the objectives. Step 2 marks the beginning of a comprehensive *marketing research* program that accompanies the entire new product process. It generates marketing information that enables product managers to make better decisions. An *analysis* of early findings reveals market gaps and opportunities that are then matched with the firm's strengths in a creative search for new product concepts.

Next comes the formulation of the new product *strategy* that will govern this particular evolutionary process. The purpose of this vital step is to identify the strategic business requirements that the prospective innovation is intended to satisfy. These requirements, which can be either externally or internally driven, map out the role that the new product will be expected to play within the firm. Potential strategic roles for new products are reported in Figure 2–5. As stated there, the nature of an industry bears a great deal of influence in determining which role is chosen for a specific new product effort. Formulating a clear and precise new product strategy early on in the new products game is probably the most significant single improvement made in new product management in recent years. And the impact of this improvement is being felt in the form of lower cost and higher success rates.

Only against this carefully crafted background and with this in-depth preparation can idea generation become truly beneficial and meaningful. As the single most creative step of the process, *idea generation* is guided by the motto "the more, the merrier." Whether existing ideas are collected from various sources or new ones generated in a number of different ways, the purpose of this step is to outline the gamut of potential courses of action.

The ideas emerging from idea generation then are subjected to a first scrutiny during the immediately following screening step. *Screening* is a quick and somewhat superficial analysis aimed at separating the wheat from the chaff. Its purpose is to determine which ideas look sufficiently promising to merit more detailed study. Because this is primarily a first sorting procedure to identify ideas that deserve a closer look, neither a lot of money nor a lot of time should be spent at this point.

Business analysis represents a much more thorough investigation of those ideas that survived the screening step. Because it is designed to yield recommendations to top management as to whether or not to approve the ideas in question as development projects, their business prospects must be examined very carefully. Toward this end, they must be fleshed out as full-fledged concepts and tested with consumers. Where screening examined feasibility and profitability, business analysis develops and reviews complete *impact statements*. These statements explore how the company's operations, image, finances, and human resources would be impacted if a given proposal were adopted. Clearly, the end of the business analysis step constitutes a major go/no go decision point in new product evolution because it involves the commitment of substantial human, financial, and physical resources for possibly extended periods of time.

Because of this significance, the early steps of new product evolution have received increasing management attention lately. Successful companies "conduct more analyses early in the process and focus their idea and concept generation. And they conduct more rigorous screening and evaluation of the ideas generated."[3] This up-front rigor squeezes a lot of waste from later steps in the process and thus increases both the effectiveness and the efficiency of the dollars spent.

Development is the most time-consuming and also a potentially very expensive step. It involves transforming specifications on paper as written by idea generators and molded by marketing research into tangible products that can be manufactured on a production line. This means designing blueprints in the research and development department, building models and prototypes, and laboratory testing them under extreme conditions. From this step emerge fully functioning products that have the engineers' approval and are ready to be sold.

Before that can happen, however, they must undergo at least two types of market testing. *Product testing* determines whether the new product performs satisfactorily in the hands of the consumer and whether the consumer prefers it to competitive offerings. The outcome of this type of testing enables final product improvements. But it does not ensure the salability of the innovation. This latter concern is addressed by *test marketing,* where the new product is offered for sale in a number of select test markets. The results of test marketing permit final adjustments in the introductory marketing program before the full-scale launch. Initial production to "fill the pipeline" to the marketplace then completes the core stage of new product evolution.

The third and final stage of this process brings the high point toward which every prior step has been building: the full-scale market introduction of the new product. This *commercialization* may be subdivided into an initial regional introduction because of limited capacity, followed by a nationwide rollout as capacity expands. Although this stage constitutes the culmination of the entire new product process leading up to it, it also marks the beginning of the product life cycle, which represents the sales pattern of the new product throughout its market life. Although new product evolution is essentially an internal process leading from the recognition of the need to act to the market readiness of a new product, the product life cycle describes the subsequent phases of the innovation's life in the competitive market environment.

Initiating Forces

New product initiatives result from a confluence of two elements: initiating forces and the responsiveness of at least one individual within an organization to these forces. A multiplicity of external and internal factors can act as triggers setting off a new product process. *External factors* are events or developments in the company's environment that affect the outcome of its marketing effort. The environment is by definition outside the direct control of product management. It is also forever changing, as a matter of fact at a steadily accelerating pace. Because product management possesses only very limited influence over the environment, the most frequent and usually most meaningful strategic response is *adaptation* of the firm's marketing program. This adaptation often involves a new product process.

Environmental occurrences become *initiating forces* when product management judges them to be relevant to the company's business and responds to them with evolutionary processes. But these processes can also be set in motion by internal factors that surface within the company's own organization. Either way, a great deal of judgment is involved in determining what a particular event or trend or fact means to the firm's future sales and whether an innovative effort is indicated. In and of themselves, neither external nor internal factors initiate evolutionary processes; their significance must be recognized by product managers, who set evolutionary processes in motion.

In a rapidly changing environment, early symptoms of possible negative trends must be watched and analyzed as carefully as indications of potential new marketing opportunities. A company with a well-functioning early warning system has an indisputable edge over the competition and may well be or become the industry leader. Forecasting thus plays a vital role in the evolutionary process by predicting alternative future environmental conditions together with their associated probabilities of occurrence. Innumerable methods are available for this purpose, but all are subject to certain limitations.[4] Although of considerable benefit to product planning, none have been or ever will be able to eliminate the entrepreneurial risk of the product manager completely.

In new product planning a distinction is often made between forecasts and assumptions. *Forecasts* are projections of future conditions and results, usually based on a continuation of past trends and patterns that often are simply extended into the future. *Assumptions,* on the other hand, use a broader perspective. They take a wide variety of developments into account that are likely to shape different parts of the environment. Assumptions describe the projected future economic, technological, and social environments and should be updated regularly as new information becomes available.

Product managers use forecasting to predict the relevant future environment of the firm. The level of interest in an early prognosis of long-term changes and the eagerness to foresee the "world of tomorrow" have increased significantly over the years and spawned a number of visionary books.[5] Progress-minded product managers reflect this growing corporate concern with the future by realizing that marketers must anticipate changes in purchasing and consumption habits as well as in life-styles and technologies and develop new products to satisfy tomorrow's demand. Companies at the cutting edge of these developments will have strong positions in the markets of the future.

Polaroid Corporation is one company that is betting on the growth of electronic imaging. This is "a process that takes bits of information from a computer and converts them into a picture."[6] According to Sheldon Buckler, the company's director of technical and industrial photography, " 'electronics is absolutely essential' to the future of the industry and of Polaroid."[7] Consequently, the company has invested heavily in this endeavor.

About a dozen firms have taken this technology and applied it in the form of computer-aided design (CAD) to the practice of medicine. "Doctors can now manipulate three-dimensional color images of complex bone fractures or tumors tucked deep in the brain. Since these images can be cut apart and put back together on the computer screen, a surgeon can simulate an operation before performing it."[8] CAD systems can even be used to "custom-design and manufacture artificial bone for sections of the skull."[9]

In their search for new drugs, some researchers have turned—with some success—to undersea organisms. "Scientists have focused on creatures that secrete special chemicals to ward off predators or to capture dinner."[10] The ongoing investigation has produced some early results. "Arthritis patients, for example, may get relief from a potent poison that sea sponges use to protect themselves. The blood of the horseshoe crab contains a protein that may provide a more sensitive test for anemia. And human tests are under way on a possible anticancer drug derived from tiny ocean dwellers known as sea squirts."[11]

The Economic Environment

The first part of the environment that product managers need to monitor is the economic environment. It consists of the three "Cs" of customers, consumers, and competitors. *Customers* are intermediate buyers, such as wholesalers or retailers, that buy for resale. *Consumers,* in contrast, are ultimate buyers who buy for personal consumption. *Competitors* may provide food for thought by developing new processes or introducing new products. It makes good business sense to examine competitive offerings promptly and closely. They can provide inspiration for imitative products or even improvements. Competitive withdrawal from or entry into certain markets can also initiate new product processes.

Customers can trigger new product evolution both directly and indirectly. Direct influence is at work when they suggest or request specific innovations. European department stores routinely present manufacturers with samples and ask for similar designs. Sears has its own design staff and designs its own products, at times, after carefully researching available models. Sears, too, asked Armstrong Tire to design a high-performance tire specifically and exclusively for its automotive outlets. Indirectly, a change in merchandising or location policy can open up new opportunities for suppliers.[12]

Consumers affect product management mostly in an indirect way by changing their needs, values, and behavior patterns. Some consumers, though, actively offer unsolicited suggestions to companies, many of which have, for legal reasons, adopted strict policies to reject them. Others will only examine them after receiving a signed waiver or examine only patented ideas.[13] Mostly, however, consumers do not take the initiative in contacting a firm and suggesting new product ideas. Rather, it is left to product management to reach out and survey consumers to explore their preferences and problems.

Changes in the age structure and geographic distribution of the U.S. population can have profound effects on marketing opportunities. The median age of the population has passed thirty and will reach thirty-five by the turn of the century. Baby boomers have moved into middle age, the share of teenagers has been declining, and the share of senior citizens is increasing steadily. This shift has decreased the traditional strong base of the soft drink industry among teenagers. Accordingly, industry leaders have successfully positioned a variety of new offerings toward the upscale, health-conscious adult market. Diet Coke became Coca-Cola's most successful new product introduction ever. Even an upstart company like New York Seltzer has been able to ride this wave with great success.

As young people with limited means form households, soaring mortgage costs and house prices shut them out of the established housing market. Innovative responses have included affordable stripped-down, no-frills houses and variable-rate mortgages. As consumers manage their finances more carefully, factory outlets and home equity loans have blossomed. Generic products, however, by and large have not fulfilled their original promise. Touted as a way to cut grocery shopping bills for inflation-weary consumers, their no-frills packaging and bland quality failed to attract a substantial following. Notable exceptions are paper products and generic cigarettes. To combat the success of these two categories, manufacturers of well-known, high-priced national brands have introduced competing budget-priced brands. Procter & Gamble, for instance, introduced Banner toilet paper in competition with Charmin, and Kimberly Clark introduced Hi Dri paper towels in competition with Kleenex paper towels.

The home environment, too, has been changing under the impact of the computer revolution. As prices have softened as a result of competitive pressure, personal computers have become quite affordable, and they incorporate advanced technology. Today's personal computers have advanced graphics capabilities and can be used for interactive learning. Sophisticated software permits them to serve as word-processing centers, bookkeeping systems, and home entertainment media. Combined with push-button telephones and television screens, personal computers can access and use vast, distant data banks. They also permit home banking and home shopping. Personal computers also can be used to monitor and control personal budgets or appliances.

The Technological Environment

The technological environment, with its steady advances and occasional breakthroughs, is a constant source of new product initiatives. Although it is dangerous for a company to be strictly technology driven and offer a product simply because it is technologically feasible, great marketing stimulation and sales success can emanate from technological progress.[14] On the other hand, of course, imminent next-generation products can stifle sales of current items. Technological progress can thus be a double-edged sword. Industry leaders like IBM and AT&T have always managed technological change carefully so as not to disturb their current business and their large installed base, adopting a go-slow policy and making change gradual and evolutionary rather than revolutionary. In a fiercely competitive environment, however, even they have been forced to move more quickly. The pace of change in the personal computer industry, for instance, has become so rapid that products tend to be outdated by the time they hit the market. This has led to great buyer confusion and an industry shakeout.

The impact of *computers* is probably the most pervasive technological development to affect life in the United States. It has permitted twenty-four-hour electronic banking through automated teller machines as well as instantaneous electronic funds transfer by means of debit cards with precoded magnetic strips. This provides hope for America's bankers, who are drowning in a flood of daily checks and are advocating a shift to a cashless and even checkless society.

Another cutting-edge technology whose full impact is still emerging involves the use of lasers. These bundled parallel-light beams achieve such high temperature and energy levels that they can cut or fuse human cells, metal, or other substances on impact. Among their many applications, lasers are used in foot surgery and compact disc players. And they have revolutionized telecommunications, where high-frequency pulsing of laser beams over high-grade optical glass fiber strands can simultaneously increase message capacity and decrease cost.

With the advances in space technology, factories in space stations have become a genuine possibility. The conditions of absolute vacuum and lack of gravity allow for remarkable improvements in the production of highly sensitive equipment, growing of crystals, and the manufacture of other high value-added items.

Gene splicing and bioengineering involve a new technology that holds great promise but is only now beginning to move into industrial production. Most significant research is still being done in relatively small firms without adequate resources to exploit their discoveries. Pharmaceutical companies invest in them to keep their options open and obtain licenses for marketable products.[15] A recent breakthrough was the approval of Genentech's Activase, a heart drug (blood clot dissolver), by the Food and Drug Administration. What made this event even more unusual was the fact that this biotechnology firm will be marketing the new gene-spliced drug itself rather than through licensing arrangements.[16]

Changing Life-Styles

Tomorrow's conditions and life-styles will necessarily differ from today's. Consumers will ask for more choice and more special features, and they will be more demanding but also more inclined to spend money. In buyers' markets, sellers will depend even more on their ability to read market needs correctly. Distribution channels and buying rhythms are undergoing important changes. Many items previously sold only in drugstores are now sold routinely by supermarkets and other mass distribution outlets or vitamin specialists, such as General Nutrition Centers. Probably more books are sold outside bookstores than through them. One company that is successfully bucking this trend is Bookstop. This thirteen-unit Texas bookstore chain bases its success on large stores (each outlet is four times as large as the average competitive store), long hours (open at least twelve hours a day, 362 days a year), giant selection, low prices, and its devotion to service.[17]

Affluent, busy consumers, particularly in dual-earner households, are increasingly taking to the convenience of armchair shopping, thus giving the direct-mail marketing industry a boost. L. L. Bean, for example, has virtually exploded in recent years into a company with more than $500 million in sales, employing more than 800 telemarketing operators during the Christmas season. Factory outlets have been congregating in malls, attracting sizable crowds from sizable distances. Major garment manufacturers sell more than 50 percent of their output at off-price, either through factory-owned stores or off-price retailers, such as Marshall's. Grocery stores are growing larger, some, like Edward's, in the form of warehouse clubs. Leading grocery chains are upgrading their merchandise mix, installing bakeries, fresh-flower departments, and deli counters, giving their stores a facelift, and introducing more leading brand names. Even previously unbranded merchandise, such as fruit and vegetables, increasingly is being branded.[18]

Pressed for time and tired after a full day of work, consumers increasingly reach for the convenience of microwave foods. But appearance and taste are still a problem in many cases.[19] Responding to changes in consumer preferences, fast-food chains have been moving from a pastel-colored plastic environment to greenhouse and brass effects.[20] They have also introduced chicken dishes because of concern over red meat, and salads or salad bars for the health conscious. Because of rising repair costs and changing technologies, consumers make replacement purchases of durable goods earlier.[21]

Competitive Strategy

A change in a competitor's marketing mix can lead to different reactions, depending on the market situation, the firm's financial strength, and management's willingness to take risks. Management may, for instance, adopt an attitude that chooses to ignore a competitive move as unimportant and without merit. Bulova and Timex paid little attention when Pulsar introduced the first electronic digital watch at a price of $2,500, shrugging it off as a passing fad. When this product category started to take off, the leaders were consequently electronics companies like Texas Instruments, not mechanical watch companies. The watch companies' efforts to catch up were belated, setting them back in the competitive race.

When Hanes introduced L'eggs pantyhose, sold in egg-shaped containers through freestanding displays in supermarkets, the whole industry was aghast. Hanes had violated the traditional practice of selling women's hosiery through department stores in cardboard packages. But the idea caught on, making hosiery an impulse item. Today, a substantial portion of sales in this category moves through mass distribution outlets.

Another possible strategy would be to adapt the marketing mix for the company's existing products, for instance, by reducing prices. This well may work, provided that the competitive innovation does not possess a differential advantage. But it could also backfire, cheapening a product's image and antagonizing current buyers.

Still another philosophy takes a "wait and see" approach, waiting for the first signs of success and then copying a new product. It involves a deliberate decision to let other firms do the innovating while standing by as a spectator instead of taking the lead. Both product and market development costs thus are borne by the pioneering firm. The would-be imitator acts as a mere observer until it becomes clear that the new idea has caught on and demand is taking off. At this point the imitator joins the fray at considerably less risk and expense.

Internal Forces

Internal initiating forces are dominated by two departments: research and development (known as R&D) and marketing. As technological know-how increases and new materials, methods, and products become available, manufacturers must invest large amounts of money in R&D to keep pace with technological progress. In fact, in 1987, $123 billion was spent in the United States on R&D, with government and industry splitting the tab about evenly. Nonetheless, the U.S. share of worldwide R&D spending has declined steadily over the past two decades (from 70 to 55 percent of the total spent by the United States, Japan, West Germany, Great Britain, and France), with Japan taking up the slack (from 8 to 21 percent).[22]

Even the largest industrial corporations in the United States have found keeping up with the technology race a difficult challenge to meet and thus have joined forces with domestic or international competitors. AT&T and IBM, together with other American chip makers, helped launch Sematech, a semiconductor research consortium, and are each contributing hundreds of millions of dollars worth of technology. All American car makers have teamed up with Japanese firms to develop new products in joint ventures. Whether they go it alone or jointly, however, American companies are rediscovering R&D as the key to future success and are investing more heavily in it. Merck, a high-flying pharmaceutical company, attributes its phenomenal success to hefty investments and a strong corporate commitment to R&D. Monsanto, too, is betting a great deal on it, hoping that high-technology products will emerge that can become growth businesses in the 1990s.[23]

Thousands of inventions are made each year in all parts of the world. Many of them are being patented by one or more national patent offices. A *patent* is a legal document (issued in the United States by the U.S. Patent Office) that grants a patent holder (usually the inventor, sometimes the employer) the right to the exclusive use of a specified invention for a limited period of time (in the United States, seventeen years). The United States alone issues about 1,700 patents per week or about 90,000 patents a year, of which anywhere from one-quarter to one-half are granted to foreigners. Nonetheless, "U.S. researchers get more patents than the rest of the world combined."[24]

It is of great importance for every company to keep up with the latest developments in its field. This can be done by studying appropriate publications, attending seminars and conferences, and checking with scientific research laboratories. Mead Data Central sells a data base that subscribers can scan electronically for new patents in their field. The National Technical Information Service, an agency of the U.S. government, keeps government-owned inventions (the U.S. government is the world's largest patent holder with tens of thousands of patents) and research reports on file and makes information available for a nominal fee.

A company's own R&D department may well turn out ideas or products that have good market chances. It may engage in basic research and/or product development. *Basic research* aims to discover new technologies, methods, or materials but *not* products. Its payoff is uncertain and unpredictable, and its results lack immediate applicability and marketability. United States spending for basic research amounted to about $15 billion in 1987 or 12.2 percent of the $123 billion total. Of this amount, corporations contributed approximately one-fifth.[25]

When basic research succeeds, it produces a technological breakthrough that advances the state of the art and may even warrant a Nobel Prize. "Since World War II, 127 American scientists have won the Nobel Prize, compared with 98 Europeans and five Japanese."[26] Seven of these Nobel Prizes have gone to Bell Labs scientists, more than to any other industrial institution in the world.[27]

A long-range program of basic research can be called laboratory oriented because its key figure is the scientist-inventor. A great deal of faith and patience are required of senior management to continue funding such an effort. After all, the area of research is only vaguely defined, and substantial resources are absorbed long before the salability of any end product can be ensured. But the payoffs can be substantial. Bell Labs, where historically only 10 percent of human and financial resources were invested in basic research, has over the years "produced the transistor, the laser, the solar cell, and the first communications satellite, as well as sound motion pictures, [and] the science of radio astronomy."[28]

Product development, on the other hand, is aimed at commercial applicability and salability, converting research outcomes into marketable products. Striving for short-term profits, its risk is limited by marketing research. Consequently, the product manager becomes the dominant figure, reducing the engineer's role to meeting target market specifications. The costs of such a program are often reasonable, and its rewards are attractive. As the example of Bell Labs underscores, laboratory-oriented basic research and market-oriented product development can coexist and complement each other well.

The other major internal source of new product initiatives is the marketing area itself. Declining sales volume, shrinking market share, or decreasing advertising effectiveness signal the need for new marketing impulses. Another negative aspect can be a firm's dependence on just a few large accounts or a limited number of products because suppliers or products may be displaced quickly. Du Pont's introduction of Lycra, a synthetic elastomer fiber, killed the market for natural rubber for elastic fabrics within two years.

Besides product management itself, a firm's sales organization is in constant touch with the market, observing competitive moves, reading customer desires, and learning about emerging technologies. It can and should serve as a prime mover, initiating new product processes to seize opportunities and counter threats. Marketing research is often called on to offer recommendations for action. The advertising function can provide useful and creative information and ideas. For instance, the concept of Cycle dog food—different formulations for the various stages in the canine life cycle (puppy, adult, overweight, and old dog)—was suggested by General Foods' advertising agency and proved tremendously successful.

Innovative processes may also be the outgrowth of top management's strategic growth mindedness. Sometimes a company enters new areas because investing its profits in its old product lines is not as profitable and promising as joining young, rapidly growing markets. Having examined its product/business mix by means of a growth matrix and other analytical tools, senior management may well conclude that a major redirection of the corporate thrust is advisable.[29] This may involve divestiture or acquisition of entire units or both. In contrast, the new direction may be accomplished by starting up and building a complete division from scratch. Whether minor or major, many new product processes are started by a decision on the part of senior management.

In addition to research and development, marketing, and the executive suite, any other employee of a company might suggest a useful idea that deserves further consideration. Analytical and creative people can be found in every department and at every level from assembly line worker to middle manager. Some firms conduct occasional or even periodic contests to stimulate creative thinking, offering monetary rewards. Others use formal suggestion systems to encourage a steady flow of suggestions, some of which may turn out to be very profitable for the company.[30] A traditionally neglected source such as production line workers can become a powerful resource if properly tapped, for example, in the form of quality circles. Purchasing problems may also propel the development of new or different products. If materials or components for current products are not available in the necessary quantities or become too expensive, these products may be reformulated. To retain and strengthen a firm's competitiveness, value analysis is often used in determining whether an existing product's functions can be performed satisfactorily at a lower cost, such as by substitution of a less expensive material or design modification.[31] Conversely, new materials, components, or technologies can be presented to purchasing managers by current or prospective vendors. Their mere availability often will trigger thought processes that lead to new and better products.

In sum, there is a wealth of external and internal forces of a general or specific nature that can initiate processes of new product evolution. These processes will not come to pass, however, unless someone within the firm identifies and responds to pertinent forces.

Sensitivity to Environmental Changes

The secret, or art, of successful product management lies in the early detection of marketing problems and opportunities and their conscious, deliberate solution or exploitation. To accomplish this, product managers must be sensitive to initiating forces. Only if relevant environmental influences are taken into account can product strategy remain up-to-date and profitable. Because every company depends on its environment, constant monitoring is a must. This task is very much part of a product manager's job. Its execution can be divided into six steps:

1. Keep a tab on broad trends appearing in the environment.
2. Determine the relevance of an environmental trend.
3. Study the impact of an environmental trend on a product and/or market.

4. Forecast the direction of an environmental trend into the future.
5. Analyze the momentum of the product and/or market business in the face of the environmental trend.
6. Study the new opportunities that an environmental trend appears to provide.[32]

In a sense, product managers must set up an early warning system to identify emerging changes at their outset. *Environmental scanning* serves as such an exception-reporting system by systematically and periodically reviewing significant differences in environmental parameters. What is significant to a company's business, however, remains frequently a matter of personal judgment. This means that inevitably a very personal quality of successful product managers enters into the picture: the ability to assess correctly both the relevance and significance of environmental developments to the company's business. This unique characteristic can be referred to as *vision*. Together with planning ability and persuasiveness, vision differentiates successful product managers from unsuccessful ones as well as successful companies from unsuccessful ones.

Vision involves the creative interpretation of facts, attuned even to undercurrents that are not visible on the surface. This can come only from frequent immersion in the turbulent waters of competition. To succeed, product managers cannot be desk-bound people. Rather, they must spend a great deal of their time in the field, traveling with salespeople, talking to customers, and experiencing competition firsthand. Only in this way will they develop and maintain a proper sense of perspective. As a matter of fact, most employers will require prior sales experience on the part of would-be product managers. When they hire persons directly out of college, employers will typically ask assistant brand managers to first serve a tour of duty in their sales force of at least six months. There is simply no substitute for personal frontline experience. Even the best product management information system cannot replace experience but rather supplements, amplifies, and updates it.

Accordingly, as useful and important as it is, environmental scanning and monitoring will only truly serve its purpose if it is used and interpreted by sensitive, imaginative individuals. Initiating forces that will affect a company's sales unless proper action is taken do not initiate any evolutionary processes. People do, in particular product managers. Only if at least one individual within an organization realizes what certain environmental changes mean to a company's future and correctly identifies the resultant problem or opportunity can an adequate organizational response be formulated. Sensitivity to environmental changes is thus one of the foremost qualities of successful product managers.

Giving Direction to the New Product Effort

After an initiating force has been properly recognized and the need for an organizational response identified, it becomes essential to begin the decision-making portion of the evolutionary process promptly. This requires the initial step of defining new product objectives and criteria. As outlined in Chapter 2, a variety of quantitative and/or qualitative objectives can govern the evolutionary effort. In addition to survival, every business firm pursues the prime objective of growth, the attainment of which generally is measured via sales volume, market share, and/or profit. Although established products may provide a measure of stability for some time to come, growth in its various forms usually will come from new products.

Because the substance and outcome of an evolutionary process are derived directly from its objectives, new product objectives must be chosen with considerable care. Their selection must take into account both market conditions and company resources. The market conditions include the level of actual and potential demand and its projected growth pattern, the stage of the product life cycle and degree of market maturity, and the intensity of competition from domestic and overseas sources. The company resource component means that new product initiatives tend to be most successful if they build on a firm's existing strengths either in terms of technological expertise and manufacturing capability or in terms of a distribution system that can carry additional products to the same target audiences.[33] New product objectives also should be challenging but realistic. If they are to contribute to the future growth of the company, a certain element of risk is inevitable in new product ventures. New product objectives should require an exceptional team effort for their achievement, rather than setting routine, easily attainable targets. But product managers must be careful not to set their sights too high so as not to discourage those involved through a lack of realism.

After the new product objectives have been chosen, they must be made operational by means of shorter-term, specific, quantitative goals or criteria. *Criteria* are instruments of measurement and comparison. Insofar as they are quantitative in nature, they are objectively measurable and thus permit comparative choices and precise performance evaluation at any point in the game.

By identifying specific objectives for a given new product process and translating them into operational criteria, product management gives direction to the new product effort and governs its entire execution. It has responded to the initiating forces by setting in motion the decision-making process that is at the heart of new product evolution. To facilitate the subsequent examination of new product ideas, the product manager now should develop a checklist for new product ideas, such as the one presented in Figure 4–2.

Finance

Additional investment required
Length of payback period
Return on investment
Projected sales volume and market share
Amount of risk involved

Research and Development

Technological know-how available
Amount of time needed for development
Competitive distinctiveness
Uniqueness of product features and benefits
Availability and extent of patent protection
Potential for expanding range of applications
Environmental safety
Performance under stress conditions

Production

Production know-how available
Projected production cost
Make or buy
Ease of procuring materials and components needed
Availability of trained labor
Production and storage facilities and equipment needed
Use of excess capacity

Marketing

Compatibility with current product mix
Compatibility with company image and distribution channels
Salability to present customers
Government regulations and approval required
State of the economy
Market trends
Degree and nature of competition
Number of potential new buyers
Adequacy of present sales force
Projected length of product life cycle
Price and quality level
Advertising budget needed
Ability to provide adequate customer service
Extent of diversification from established business
Anticipated positioning

FIGURE 4–2
Checklist for New Product Ideas

SUMMARY

Processes of new product evolution do not start by chance. They must be set in motion in a first stage called initiative. A multitude of initiating forces can serve as triggers. They can be broadly grouped into market, technological, and company factors.

A firm must continuously project and anticipate its relevant future environment to improve its chances for survival and growth through anticipatory adaptation. Many of these developments are clearly foreseeable because they are based on technology that is already available today and only needs widespread consumer acceptance and use.

Powerful influences on tomorrow's product scene can be expected from shifts in the geographic, age, income, educational, and occupational distribution of the national and world populations. Domestic and foreign competitors, through their market actions, stimulate new product processes. Customer suggestions can have a similar impact. Finally, the firm's own research and development and marketing departments as well as other internal sources can serve as initiating forces resulting in new product evolution.

But all these stimuli will have no effect on the company's decision making unless they are perceived, evaluated, and acted on by responsible and responsive product managers. It is a prime task of product management to be alert to external and internal challenges and opportunities as they emerge. Only if they are identified and assessed correctly can appropriate action be forthcoming. Great reliance thus is placed on marketing research to provide the necessary factual input to complement the product manager's market knowledge and intuition.

To arrive at meaningful and successful new product decisions, product management must determine the objectives and criteria that will be applied to the evaluation of possible alternative courses of action. Only if specific goals are known from the very beginning can optimum new product decisions be achieved.

NOTES

1. Booz, Allen & Hamilton, Inc., *New Products Management for the 1980s* (New York: Booz, Allen & Hamilton, Inc., 1982), 14.
2. Ibid., 15.
3. Ibid., 12.
4. See Yoram Wind, "A Framework for Classifying New-Product Forecasting Models," *New-Product Forecasting,* 3–42, edited by Yoram Wind, Vijay Mahajan, and Richard N. Cardozo (Lexington, MA: D. C. Heath & Co., 1981).
5. See, for instance, Alvin Toffler, *The Third Wave* (New York: William Morrow & Co., 1980), and John Naisbitt, *Megatrends* (New York: Warner Books, 1984).
6. Theresa Engstrom, "Polaroid Pegs Its Future on Electronics," *Wall Street Journal,* 16 Aug. 1984.
7. Ibid.

8. Brian Dumaine, "Designer Bones," *Fortune,* 18 Feb. 1985, 109–110.
9. Ibid., 110.
10. James P. Miller, "Search for New Drugs Focuses on Organisms under the Sea," *Wall Street Journal,* 24 July 1987.
11. Ibid.
12. See "Grand Union: Jimmy Goldsmith's Maverick Plan to Restore Profitability," *Business Week,* 14 May 1984, 188ff.
13. See Gerald G. Udell and Del I. Hawkins, "Corporate Policies and Procedures for Evaluating Unsolicited Product Ideas," *Research Management* (Nov. 1978), 24ff.
14. See Barry Berman and Joel R. Evans, "Marketing Warfare: A Scenario for the Next Ten Years," *Review of Business* (Summer 1984): 5–8.
15. See Toffler, *The Third Wave,* 162ff.
16. See Joan O'C. Hamilton, "Birth of a Blockbuster: How Genentech Delivered the Goods," *Business Week,* 30 Nov. 1987, 138–142.
17. See "Supermarket Format Propels Bookstop," *Chain Store Age,* Dec. 1987, 57–60.
18. See Eleanor Johnson Tracy, "Here Come Brand-Name Fruit and Veggies," *Fortune,* 18 Feb. 1985, 105.
19. See Alix M. Freedman, "Space-Age Savor: Flavor Specialists Strive for Better Microwave Foods," *Wall Street Journal,* 29 July 1987.
20. See Trish Hall, "At Fast-Food Restaurants, Plastic Is Out, and Marble, Brass and Greenhouses Are In," *Wall Street Journal,* 3 Dec. 1985.
21. See "Life in the Electronic Playpen," *Time,* 28 May 1984, 70–71.
22. See Stuart Gannes, "The Good News about U.S. R&D," *Fortune,* 1 Feb. 1988, 49.
23. See Kenneth Labich, "Monsanto's Brave New World," *Fortune,* 30 April 1984, 57ff.
24. Gannes, "Good News about U.S. R&D," 49.
25. Ibid., 49.
26. Ibid.
27. See Gene Bylinsky, "The New Look at America's Top Lab," *Fortune,* 1 Feb. 1988, 61.
28. Ibid.
29. See, for instance, Labich, "Monsanto's Brave New World," 57ff; "Changing a Corporate Culture—Can Johnson & Johnson Go from Band-Aids to High-Tech?" *Business Week,* 14 May 1984, 130ff.; and "R.J. Reynolds: The Consumer Is King Again," *Business Week,* 4 June 1984.
30. See E. Patrick McGuire, *Generating New-Product Ideas* (New York: The Conference Board, 1972), 21ff.
31. See Eberhard E. Scheuing, *Purchasing Management* (Englewood Cliffs, NJ: Prentice-Hall, 1989), 232–234.
32. Adapted from Subhash C. Jain, *Marketing Planning & Strategy* (Cincinnati: South-Western Publishing Co., 1981), 84ff.
33. Booz, Allen & Hamilton found "product fit with internal functional strengths" to be the second most important factor contributing to new product success (63 percent of responses). See Booz, Allen & Hamilton, *New Products Management,* 16. Similarly, The Conference Board survey listed "new business closely related to old" as the third most important factor (70 percent of responses) associated with new product success. See Michael G. Duerr, *The Commercial Development of New Products* (New York: The Conference Board, 1986), 13.

CASE STUDY

SMOKE SIGNALS

Nonsmokers appear to be winning the war, "and the estimated 55 million Americans who smoke are beginning to look like an endangered species."[1] Headlines like "No Smoking Sweeps America," and commentary like "Smokers are fast becoming outcasts—both socially and legally"[2] tell the story eloquently.

On December 16, 1986, the U.S. Department of Health and Human Services issued its most severe warning ever about the dangers of smoking for the 185 million Americans who are nonsmokers. Not only did Surgeon General Koop spell out the risks borne by nonsmokers via passive or involuntary smoking (environmental tobacco smoke) but he called for a variety of measures to protect the public health. As quoted in the *New York Times* on December 17, 1986, this outspoken physician and government official, in referring to the need to eliminate or severely limit smoking at the workplace, called for "further restrictions at the Federal, state and local level." In turn, he is "sensing a groundswell in government agencies as well as in Congress to move forward on this issue." His sharply worded conclusion followed an equally critical report on smoking issued in November 1986 by the National Academy of Sciences.

Trying to Stem the Tide

The Tobacco Institute, the industry lobby organization, had anticipated this attack. In early December 1986, it issued a statement that charged Dr. Koop with making inaccurate public statements about passive smoking as well as pressuring scientists who did not truly share his antismoking views. The industry also claimed that today's atmosphere contains so many pollutants that it is virtually impossible to trace the exact impact of tobacco smoke on an individual's health.

This case was contributed by Alfred C. Holden, Associate Professor of Marketing, St. John's University, New York, New York.

In mid-July 1987, the House of Representatives voted to ban cigarette smoking on domestic airline flights of less than two hours. Representatives from tobacco-growing districts noted that the 198 to 193 vote for this amendment to the transportation spending bill was anything but decisive. Moreover, the Reagan administration considers the House version of the transportation spending bill too costly and threatens to veto it. The Senate, too, may well vote to reject such a controversial amendment. Meanwhile, the Tobacco Institute reports that further study of passive smoking must be undertaken before conclusions can be drawn.

In view of rising national budget deficits and intense efforts to find sources of additional revenues, it is not surprising that the tobacco industry is worried. When an American smoker puts down at least $1.25 to buy a pack of cigarettes, taxes make up 32 cents of the price. Of that amount, 16 cents represent federal excise tax. When the latter was raised by 8 cents (to 16 cents) in 1983, cigarette unit sales fell by 5 percent, the worst single drop in two decades. In mid-1987 a Congressional coalition concerned about budget balance and health issues proposed at 16-cent increase or another doubling of the federal excise tax for enactment in fiscal year 1988.

As the Pressure Mounts . . .

Product liability suits and corporate restraints or bans on smoking at the workplace are two additional challenges confronting the tobacco industry. Survivors of deceased heavy smokers have brought hundreds of lawsuits against cigarette manufacturers, which have had to spend rapidly growing sums of money to defend themselves in court. To date, courts have ruled that the warnings printed on cigarette packages are adequate and that manufacturers are consequently not liable for the harm caused by the voluntary consumption of their products. But a look at the asbestos industry indicates that it may take only one successful lawsuit to open the tide gate to severe financial stress for the entire tobacco industry.

Meanwhile, the antismoking movement is gathering momentum. A 1986 survey by the Bureau of National Affairs found smoking controls in place in 36 percent of U.S. companies and smoking bans under consideration by 21 percent. In addition, nineteen states and many municipalities regulate workplace smoking. Curiously, there is very little resistance by smokers to smoking bans. In fact, 90 percent of smokers claim a desire to quit smoking and actually welcome corporate restrictions and support programs. There is a new sense of urgency among corporate executives to establish and enforce smoking policies because of "disability, negligence, and workers' compensation cases that nonsmokers have won against their employers."[3]

The Tobacco Institute has tried to cope with this onslaught by doubling its staff over the last decade. It not only fights the liability claims of nonsmokers but also assists smokers in combating private and public sector restrictions.

Case Notes

1. Gregg Levoy, "Up in Smoke," *American Way,* 1 Oct. 1987, 48.
2. For further information on the "no-smoking" movement, see the special report in *Business Week,* 27 July 1987, 40–52. For a different perspective on the issues involved in this matter, see Daniel Seligman, "Don't Bet against Cigarette Makers," *Fortune,* 17 Aug. 1987, 70–77.
3. Levoy, "Up in Smoke," 48.

Discussion Questions

1. In view of the developments described in the case study, how do you assess the situation and outlook for the cigarette industry?
2. What are the implications of your assessment for new product strategy in cigarette companies?
3. Do you think the industry's defensive activities will be successful in the long run?
4. What new products could bring new growth to cigarette companies? Specifically, what do you think of the introduction of a "smokeless cigarette" as reported in the business press?

CHAPTER 5

Generating New Product Ideas

Idea generation, processing, and evaluation increasingly are governed by economic considerations. In most industries, development and production technology are so advanced today that technological problems or challenges generally have been or can be solved. This transfers the burden of identifying which avenue to take and directing the design and engineering effort to product management. Triggered by initiating forces and controlled by new product objectives, the evolutionary process thus moves next toward exploring market needs and wants and pinpointing substantive opportunity areas that align closely with the stated objectives. This procedure is necessary because in most markets the consumer ultimately determines the fate of individual products and entire companies. But it is inappropriate to engage in a one-shot activity in the form of a single survey of a target audience, supply the results to product management, and never follow up. Rather, it is essential to conduct marketing research for new products as an ongoing dialog, a creative interchange between the company and the marketplace.

A Comprehensive Marketing Research Program

Ideally, evolutionary marketing research involves a systematic program of sequential steps designed to research various aspects of consumer behavior and guide the evolution of appropriate, promising products. The steps involved in such a program are outlined in Figure 5–1. The comprehensive marketing research program to facilitate new product evolution is illustrated as a series of concentric circles.

    The two parties in this vital dialog are the producer (which may be producing durable or nondurable consumer products, industrial goods, or services) and the consumer (which may be an individual, a household, or an organization). The

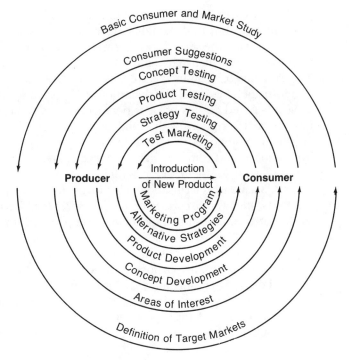

FIGURE 5–1
Comprehensive Marketing Research Program (*Source:* Adapted with permission from Eberhard E. Scheuing, "An Integrated Consumer Research Program to Facilitate and Evaluate Innovations," in Eberhard E. Scheuing, ed., *Meeting the Marketing Challenge* [New York: St. John's University, 1970], p. 8)

product manager acts as the personification of the producer, aiming to identify and satisfy the needs and desires of the consumer. The upper half of each circle represents a marketing research step, eliciting specific input or feedback from the consumer to the producer. The lower half of each circle reflects the actions that the producer takes in preparation for or in response to a particular round of marketing research. As becomes evident, the program is designed to provide successive focusing of the new product effort, proceeding from the vague and broad market opportunity identification to the specific and narrow definition of the new product and its marketing program. The program is time-consuming and expensive, but it substantially reduces risk and increases certainty of product management in a new venture.

The program begins with the definition of target markets. In essence, this means that the company's management must decide what it wants to be to whom. In other words it must examine the company's *raison d'être,* that is, its particular strength and uniqueness. From this soul-searching emanates a *mission statement* that defines what business the company is in. This business definition should not be formulated in terms of currently available products or technologies. Such an approach would tend to put blinders on management's perspective and may ultimately doom a company by making it cling to meanwhile obsolete technologies and outdated products when only progressive adaptation could ensure survival. Instead, the nature of a company's business should be defined in terms of *functions* to be performed, in terms of *needs* to be served, or in terms of *problems* to be solved. Railroad companies then would view themselves more broadly as being in the transportation business, and telephone companies would consider themselves to be in the telecommunications or information business. The definition of target markets in a particular new product project is based on this broader perspective of a company's business mission. This involves a description of the kind of people and the type of need that the firm proposes to serve. Such a description, as developed by a product manager in a hypothetical food company, may, for instance, read, "prepared single-serving meals of high quality for diet-conscious middle-aged adults."

Such early clarification helps focus the marketing research effort. Its initial step consists of a *basic consumer and market study.* This is a broad-based benchmark study that establishes the information base on which the remainder of the program will be built. The basic consumer study portion is designed to provide an in-depth analysis of the motivations, attitudes, needs, problems, wants, and habits of the relevant consumers. Its purpose is to explore who buys and consumes what, when, where, how, in what quantities, and how often. By investigating influences on these behavior patterns, product management can learn about the forces that shape the current and potential future markets.

Questions to be answered at this point include the following:

- Factors influencing brand selection or rejection in the present market
- Satisfactions and dissatisfactions resulting from currently available products
- Sources of product information for consumers and their relative importance
- Consumer sensitivity to different price levels
- Demographic and life-style characteristics of buyers

One of the most difficult but also potentially most rewarding tasks at this point is the detection of hidden problems, needs, or wants. These need gaps often are unknown to the consumers themselves but might provide profitable avenues for product innovation. Ingenuity and intuition accordingly are essential qualities of a resourceful marketing researcher in this crucial initial round if the outcome is to represent a major departure from existing ways of serving the target groups.

Toward this end, exploratory research tools such as projective techniques and focus group sessions prove particularly valuable. *Projective techniques* present respondents with deliberately ambiguous stimuli in the form of words or pictures and ask for their interpretation or completion. Seemingly talking about the person in the picture or story, interviewees nonetheless project their own feelings into their answers, unaware about the fact that they are really talking about themselves. The range of projective techniques includes word association, sentence completion, story completion, picture association, picture completion, picture story, and depth interviewing.

Word association presents respondents with a series of words, asking them to state what comes to their minds when hearing them. This technique is also most useful in testing potential new brand names and what they mean to consumers. A belated study discovered, for instance, that the word "Edsel" meant diesel and truck to potential buyers but did not create positive associations for a new passenger car. The Ford Motor Company learned from this mistake and subsequently chose the name "Mustang" for a new sports car.

Sentence completion requires respondents to complete a series of incomplete sentences. Story completion asks the consumer to complete a half-told story. Picture association looks for an interpretation of what is shown in a picture. Picture completion uses a cartoon-type format, suggesting that the viewer fill in the answer to a statement made in the picture in the empty balloon. Picture story involves the interviewee in developing a story about a picture. And depth interviewing means unstructured, one-on-one probing in the form of a conversation.

Focus groups are casual roundtable discussions with groups of relevant consumers in a relaxed setting. The discussion is guided by a trained moderator whose job is to keep the conversation going and focus it on the crucial issues. Focus group interviews can be used to detect need gaps and product-related problems experienced by the target market. The sessions are taped for subsequent analysis. Their results offer valuable information for guiding the design and execution of later marketing research steps.

To gain a better understanding of its target market, the food company mentioned previously conducts a number of focus group sessions in various parts of the country. The results of its basic consumer study indicate a growing calorie-consciousness among members of the target audience. Appetite appeal is of prime importance, whereas price or cost is a secondary consideration for this affluent group.

Basic market data are often readily available from published sources or commercial data suppliers that sell them on a subscription basis. Industry information can be obtained from trade journals, trade associations, or industry surveys. Monitoring and tracking these reports and secondary data over several periods allow product management to acquaint itself with the trends in the marketplace and shifts in demand patterns as they evolve over time.

The food company can obtain demographic data on target market characteristics and spending patterns from the U.S. Commerce Department or The Conference Board. It can buy retail food store sales data from A. C. Nielsen Company. And it can study articles and data in such trade publications as *Supermarket News* or the *Progressive Grocer.* The Food Marketing Institute also may be of assistance.

From the broad-based benchmark study emerge opportunities in the form of unmet needs or problems. Consumers may be dissatisfied with available choices, or market trends may reveal promising market segments or *niches* to those alert and creative enough to spot them.[1] Product management then must prioritize the different opportunities according to their degree of attractiveness. This early assessment will be somewhat crude because the information base is still somewhat limited. Nonetheless, product managers choose areas of interest based on preliminary profit projections, anticipated market capacity, threat of competitive entry, and other pertinent considerations.

With so little to go on, it would be a grave mistake to turn the matter over to the research and development (R&D) department for further action. More specific input is needed from consumers in the form of product suggestions. Of course, consumer suggestions for new products are usually not very well thought out. Offered on the spur of the moment, these ideas must be sorted out and subjected to screening. If they survive this first scrutiny, they are fleshed out and exploded into full-fledged product concepts. A *product concept* is a description of a potential product, highlighting its purpose and essential features. But converting ideas into concepts makes sense only if the questions of feasibility and profitability have been answered affirmatively.

The concepts thus developed, sometimes accompanied by drawings or package mock-ups, are then again presented to a sample of potential buyers. The purpose of this step, called *concept testing,* is to eliminate from further consideration new product concepts that do not hold any real promise. Presented with several alternative concepts, participants are asked to rank them in their order of preference. Researchers also aim to identify the characteristics of people who respond favorably to a given concept.

But simply picking one of several competing concepts is not enough. Researchers additionally must probe for desired product features. At this point, adding, deleting, or altering product features is still very easy because the product does not yet exist in tangible form. Concept testing thus is aimed at formulating detailed product specifications that tell engineering precisely what the market wants. This approach is an outgrowth of the new concept of marketing; the old concept left scientists self-guided, without any marketplace input.

Its research up to this point leads the food company to conclude that there is an attractive and largely untapped market for frozen, fully cooked single-serving gourmet dinners with carefully controlled calorie counts. The dinners should have high visual and taste appeal, be made of high-quality ingredients, be microwaveable, offer a variety of fancy dishes, and be packaged distinctively.

By now, enough information has been assembled from both external and internal sources to conduct a thorough *business analysis* and present findings and recommendations to management. Authorized projects then are assigned to R&D personnel for *product development.* This involves translating product specifications into tangible, marketable products. The results of their efforts, fully laboratory tested and technically mature products, then would appear to be ready for national distribution. Crucial information is still missing, however, before this risky decision can be made. Consumer reaction to the actual product must be investigated, marketing mix elements must be tested, and trial sales results should be evaluated before the launch decision is made.

Continuing the dialog, consumers next are asked to try the product and report their experiences. *Product testing* focuses on tangible product attributes rather than implied psychological attributes. Its findings will reveal whether the product is perceived as being different from and better than those presently available. Where appropriate, the new product is accompanied by the established product that it is intended to attack. The two products usually are presented without brand identification to determine whether the new entry can stand on its own merits.

This phase of research aims to determine performance and preference. Does the new product perform satisfactorily in the hands of the consumer? Although the product already has met performance specifications in the laboratory, consumer satisfaction is essential because it governs repurchasing. Consumers are also asked to indicate which of the two products they prefer. Three outcomes are possible. The test product may be perceived as being superior to the established brand. Such an advantage should be exploited in its advertising. Second, the new product may be rated equal to its counterpart. That makes it a "parity" or "me-too" product, which must then be differentiated through creative advertising. The final possibility—that the innovation is viewed as being inferior to the alternative choice—typically means abandonment of the project because redesign and retesting are likely to prove too costly.

It would be a serious mistake, however, to assume that an innovation that successfully passes a product test is assured of success in the marketplace. People might like a new product but still not buy it for a variety of reasons, for example, price. Product testing is a necessary but still insufficient prerequisite for commercial success. It is certainly safe to assume that a product will fail in the marketplace if it fails product testing. But the opposite is not true. Time and again, new products have brought raves from consumers in product tests, only to fail during subsequent market introduction. Pillsbury developed a preflavored baked bean product and invited consumers to taste it in their test kitchen. The new product was very well received during these taste tests but failed nonetheless in the marketplace. It turned out that consumers prefer to buy a bland product and add their own flavoring. A satisfactory physical item is consequently not enough. It must be supported by a strong marketing program.

The marketing program is examined in detail during the *strategy testing* round of marketing research. Having determined the most desirable product and/or product features and having made the improvements that the results of product testing suggested, product management freezes the design of the product and triggers initial production. But the success of an innovation not only depends on its physical excellence. It is also affected by the product's presentation. The product's name, advertising, packaging, and distribution establish expectations in consumers' minds that set the stage for acceptance or rejection. The strategy-testing module of the research program is, therefore, designed to facilitate optimum presentation of the new product in the relevant market segments.

Of course, product management would be unlikely to let an innovation evolve to this point and then ask itself how to introduce it. Rather, in a joint effort with the company's marketing research and advertising agencies, it has been formulating alternative strategic approaches that could be employed to introduce the innovation. These strategies translate into alternative marketing mixes and include different names, packages, advertising campaigns, and distribution channels.

Media habits and store patronage patterns as well as the specific criteria to be used in evaluating the persuasiveness of an advertising theme will have been established in the course of previous steps of the research effort. Therefore, instead of applying arbitrary or mechanical considerations, such as conscious recall or message registration, the criteria employed are based on the knowledge of what impels purchase among the particular target group in question.

As part of the research design, respondents will be asked to indicate where they would most likely shop for this kind of product and how they would feel about a novel distribution scheme being considered. They also will be exposed to actual examples of alternative proposed names and executions of advertising and packaging, reacting to specific rather than abstract ideas. Brand names and advertising messages are assessed regarding such obvious functions as memorability but, more importantly, also regarding the degree to which what they say or mean fits the needs for which the product was designed and thus suggests a positive image. A major value of this phase of the program is that it permits the exploration of creative ideas before they are committed to the marketplace. The research therefore will contribute to, instead of simply testing, the creative function. The techniques used may range from word association in branding studies to split run or split cable in copy research.

Split-run copy testing exposes a part of the readership of a given print medium (newspaper or magazine) to a test advertisement for the product, while the rest of the audience receives an alternative advertisement in the same issue of the same publication. This experimental design ensures that no factors other than the variation in advertising execution affect the outcome of the research. After an appropriate time interval, matched samples of the two reader groups are interviewed concerning recall, recognition, and other relevant aspects of the two advertisements. The results typically only reflect the relative merits of the two copy designs, without suggesting improvements or indicating the absolute sales volume to be expected.

In the *split-cable method,* television commercials are substituted in a similar manner within the framework of a cable television system. Instead of connecting all subscribers within a community to a single master cable line, two major coaxial cable lines are strung throughout the community. This enables alternating hookups, in effect splitting the subscribers into two groups without their knowledge. Assignment of a given subscriber to a cable line is carefully planned to produce comparable groups. Special electronic gear permits simultaneous exposure of the two groups to two different commercials for the same product on the same channel, with all other influences such as media exposure, store and brand availability, and even weather remaining the same. A company interested in comparing the relative pull of two commercials will measure attitudes and behavior both before and after the test by means of interviews and purchase diaries. Repeated exposure is necessary over a period of at least six weeks to establish meaningful differences. Exposing viewers in a natural setting and measuring actual behavior changes will clearly determine which of the two commercials is more effective.

On completion of strategy testing, product management knows which name, package, advertising campaign, and distribution pattern look the most promising. From these elements it can thus assemble the *introductory marketing program.* While the individual marketing mix components have been evaluated separately, however, their combination still must be tested to see whether they work in concert to achieve the new product objectives. Combined testing is particularly necessary because substantial sums of money and the company's reputation are at stake. Although absolute certainty is impossible to attain, a sensitive and well-designed test marketing effort offers a high probability of reliably predicting the ultimate acceptance and profitability levels of a new product. As the "acid test" to determine whether the product sells in an authentic sales environment, *test marketing* serves as a last checkpoint to help prevent marketing mistakes.

This last step of the comprehensive marketing research program is designed to assist in the final go/no go decision and to help put the finishing touches on the marketing program. It has two specific goals: to project sales results at varying input levels (e.g., price, advertising spending) and to enable a final decision on whether the product can be marketed profitably on an expanded basis. Additionally, test marketing permits the company to further sharpen its marketing tools by identifying those customers who in fact purchase the product, pinpointing the rewards that consumers find in the product, and developing an understanding of the role that the product plays in the consumer's usage habits.

A market test is costly and time-consuming because it must, if it is to be a valid predictor, be an accurate miniature model of the planned full-scale presentation. It requires considerable investment in product manufacturing, packaging, advertising, sales promotion, and distribution. General Foods, for instance, had to build a $5 million plant merely to manufacture a sufficient supply of Cycle canned dog food for test marketing.

Because substantial expenses are incurred, test marketing should be used only for new products that have passed every other examination of consumer acceptance. It is simply too dangerous and too expensive an instrument to be used for "beating around the bush." Instead, product management should by now be able to forecast market test results with a high level of accuracy and employ this experimental method only to confirm its projections.

Test markets must be chosen with care to be truly representative of national patterns relevant to the product in question. The number of test markets employed will depend on the number of variations within the marketing mix that are deemed worthy of investigation. For example, if three different price levels are being seriously entertained, at least three cities will be required. Similarly, if two package designs look equally promising, a minimum of two test areas is needed. Of course, only one variable should be altered at a time, and two or more markets per variant are clearly preferable.

As has been indicated, the market test must simulate the actual presentation of the product that will ultimately occur on the national level. To provide a meaningful indication of market response, it is vital that the test be continued for a period of time long enough to fully examine the influence of novelty effects and to identify atypical patterns in consumer reaction. Some products, for instance, take off rapidly but subsequently decline at a comparable rate. Others start slowly but build secure and continuing loyalty. The test marketing must be continued long enough so that such patterns can be clearly identified.

Continuing test marketing beyond the time span necessary to discern purchasing patterns, however, can prove dangerous. Many times competitors have stepped in, copied the innovation, and successfully introduced it to the national market while the originating firm was still preoccupied with its market test. Nestlé, for instance, read the test market results for General Foods' innovative freeze-dried coffee Maxim (which anyone can buy from such marketing research houses as the A. C. Nielsen Company) with great interest. The company moved swiftly in developing and launching its own freeze-dried coffee under the name of Taster's Choice. This product became a success from the outset and continues to outsell Maxim by a significant margin.

Sales results alone, however, do not adequately indicate market success. Sales figures must be supplemented by feedback from the consumer in the form of interviews and/or purchase information.

Successful test marketing completes the comprehensive marketing research program, giving the innovation final clearance for full-scale marketing. This means national introduction, using the marketing program that worked so well during the market test. The program was presented here as a continuous sequence in an effort to facilitate the understanding of the role that marketing research plays in new product evolution. In actuality, though, the research phases are intimately interwoven with the other steps of the evolutionary process and will thus be treated in more detail in Chapters 6 through 9.

Idea Generation and Collection

After product management has formulated new product objectives and begun a comprehensive marketing research program, it can proceed to deal with the new product challenge creatively and aggressively. *Idea generation,* the creation and gathering of innovative ideas, is at the very heart of the new product process. New products spring from creative ideas. Without unique ideas to set it apart from the pack, a firm cannot move ahead of the rest of its industry. It is thus the quality of the idea generation process and the effort devoted to it that can make for a competitive edge in a rapidly changing environment. Any products emerging from the new product process can only be as good as the ideas produced at its outset.

Accordingly, the time and effort invested at this early stage pay off handsomely in later stages. Changes in competition, demographic trends, life-styles, and technologies are some of the influences triggering idea generation.[2] Idea generation is most successful in companies whose management actively creates an organizational climate that encourages innovation. This is easier said than done. Large organizations are prone to becoming very bureaucratic, stifling individual initiative with endless red tape. When individuals fear the derailing of their careers if ventures do not pay off, they will try to play it safe and tread familiar and well-worn paths. It takes courage to welcome failure as a learning experience and as the price of success, effectively making managers entrepreneurs rather than administrators.[3]

Fostering this entrepreneurial spirit sometimes requires cutting a unit loose from the constraints of the organizational mainstream and allowing it to operate as a freewheeling "skunkworks," as IBM demonstrated in the case of its personal computer.[4] Removing inhibitors to daring moves in new directions is a crucial prerequisite to idea generation that is to break the shackles of the past.[5]

In addition to creating the proper organizational climate, however, one of the foremost ingredients in successful idea generation is *creativity*. This term refers to the ability to solve problems with novel approaches. It requires thinking that is unconventional, irreverent, and unrestrained. Creativity is the hallmark of small businesses in the United States. Their lack of resources and constraints encourages innovative solutions. And creative people often possess a degree of sensitivity and insight that others lack. They can get right to the heart of a problem, suggesting approaches that are not encumbered by traditional notions. They should be given the funds and freedom to create if a firm and its buyers are to benefit from their talents.

Companies need bold, imaginative thinking if they want to break the mold of tradition and conquer new frontiers. Generating new product ideas is a creative task that they sometimes choose to conduct as a team effort. The members of such a *search team* may be recruited from any level or functional area because their main qualification is creativity. Many managers are not qualified for this task, because their analytical way of thinking inhibits the creative process.

Outside consultants, specialists from marketing research or advertising agencies, and distributor or user panels, on the other hand, often serve as valuable resources. Since distributors and users are interested in new products and influence their success in the marketplace, many firms have established advisory groups with representatives from these customer categories. A major manufacturer of sporting-goods equipment uses panels of minor league coaches in this capacity.[6]

Preferably, an idea generation team reports directly to top management in a staff relationship. This kind of organizational setup guarantees independence and immediate access to the center of decision making. Such a search team should be composed of people who display imaginativeness, audacity, and open-mindedness. Its participants should be freed from their line responsibilities during its sessions because frequent interruptions make creative team work impossible. Some companies take the members of an idea generation team to a resort hotel for three days of creative sessions, sports activities, and fun. This provides a relaxed, unstructured environment away from the pressures of the office, enabling them to concentrate on the task at hand and release their creative abilities.

When using creative teams, top management should not exert time pressure because novel ideas cannot be planned, programmed, or organized. Any limitations concerning an idea's usefulness, economy, success chances, feasibility, and profitability inhibit the creative process and have no place in it. Creativity operates most successfully if it is uninhibited and receives thoughtful consideration. If a company is not producing a steady flow of creative ideas, this could be due to the fact that it did not hire the right people, discourages innovative thinking, or did not establish clear guidelines for generating, submitting, and processing creative ideas.

Sources of New Product Ideas

As companies try to identify and tap various sources of new product ideas, they discover that many of them originate from within and that marketing and R&D top the list as the most prolific sources. Table 5–1 presents the results from a recent study by The Conference Board. It shows that 62 percent of the responses indicated internal sources of new product ideas, whereas 38 percent listed external sources. Only three of the 179 companies involved checked a single source; most tap into a variety of sources (more than four on average). The combination of marketing and R&D labs produced 41 percent of the responses. Together, these two internal sources were considered most important by 59 percent of the firms indicating such a ranking. The leading external source are customers, with 17 percent of all responses. They

TABLE 5–1

Sources of New Product Ideas (base 179 companies; multiple responses)

Sources	Responses No.	%	Most Important No.	%
Internal sources				
Marketing	157		33	
Research and		41		59
development labs	154		41	
Employee suggestions	66		3	
New product				
committees	50		4	
Corporate planning	42		2	
Total	469	62	83	66
External sources				
Customers	130	17	36	29
Acquisitions	59		4	
Consultants	48		1	
Inventors	43		2	
Advertising agency	8			
Total	288	38	43	34
Total, all sources	757	100	126	100

Source: Reprinted with permission from Michael G. Duerr, *The Commercial Development of New Products* (New York: The Conference Board, 1986), 21.

are considered most important by 29 percent of the respondents giving such a ranking. The low number for advertising agency participation may not be truly representative for their role, because only 11 of the 179 firms produce food, tobacco, and consumer products whereas the remainder are essentially industrial goods manufacturers. Notably, competitors were omitted as potential sources for new product ideas.

Internal Sources. The new product ideas that come from marketing personnel usually involve the modification of existing products or the extension of current product lines. Their way of thinking is market driven. They are constantly scanning and monitoring the market and thus are tuned in to changes in buyers' needs, wants, or behavior patterns as well as modifications in competitive offerings. This is particularly true of salespeople, who can feed frontline information back to product management.

At Toledo Scale, salespeople reported two problems from the field. The label printers in their food store prepackaging scales used mechanical slugs that had to be changed manually. A separate label with the scanner bar code had to be applied to the package. According to the salespeople, store personnel wanted electronic memory printers and wanted the scanning code placed on the same label. An engineer and a marketer formed a team that visited customers to develop exact specifications. With management support and proper funding, this effort eventually resulted in a successful new scale.[7]

Engineers and scientists in the R&D labs, on the other hand, tend to be technology driven. Inherently analytical, systematic, and creative, they may, however, become fascinated by the feasibility of a new product without regard for its commercial viability. To overcome this potential danger of isolation from the marketplace, many firms pool their marketing and technological talents in an effort at cross-fertilization of ideas. Because an idea ultimately must be both technically feasible and profitably salable, top management should encourage interaction between these two functions and encourage regular meetings. Some market knowledge on the part of engineers and some technical familiarity on the part of marketers leads to sounder new product ideas. Dow Chemical routinely invites a customer's top-level technical people for meetings with its own research scientists to promote close contact with the market.[8]

Employee suggestions from any employee of a company can potentially contribute valuable ideas. Hundreds of firms have established employee suggestion programs, reporting very rewarding results from encouraging employee creativity through incentive systems.[9] Strategic planners—often in the form of senior managers rather than specialized staff units, which have been largely disbanded—also can be a good source of ideas. In contrast to the market and technical orientations of marketing and R&D, they have a future-orientation. They determine the direction in which the market and thus the company will be headed and can stimulate thinking accordingly.

Another starting point for internal idea generation could be to take a careful look at the company's existing products and product lines. Examining their features and benefits may lead to improvements. One such method is *value analysis,* which essentially asks whether the same function can be performed for less money. It may accomplish this purpose by substituting a less expensive material or revamping the manufacturing process.

A final internal source of new product ideas may come from the by-products of a current manufacturing process that typically must be disposed of at some expense to the firm. An increasing number of firms are trying to turn the sale of these incidental items for previously unthought-of applications into profitable sidelines.[10] Iowa Beef Processors, the big meat packer, manages to sell the fat, hides, bone, glands, and even gallstones from the cattle it processes.[11]

This kind of approach makes sense from an ecological standpoint, too, as it is becoming more and more difficult to find environmentally safe and inexpensive ways of disposing of manufacturing by-products. If a company can recycle them and open up a secondary market in the process, it can earn income from such by-products rather than expend funds on them.[12]

External Sources.　Although many firms would prefer to generate new product ideas internally, they might overlook some very attractive opportunities by limiting their search effort in this manner. A veritable treasure trove of ideas awaits resourceful product managers who look outside their firms for inspiration. Among the more frequently used external sources are suppliers, customers, competitors, consultants and agencies, inventors and patents, and universities.

Suppliers can be valuable idea sources if they "possess technical expertise which permits them to suggest changes that result in new products for companies to which they sell."[13] Many companies actively solicit this kind of input in the form of vendor clinics where competing vendors are familiarized with the company's products and operations and encouraged to suggest cost-saving moves.[14] Others leave this kind of initiative up to their suppliers.[15] Forever competing to obtain or increase their share of a company's business, vendors have every reason to propose product modifications that enhance their sales potential. "For example, plastic and fiberglass suppliers provided General Motors with considerable help in the design of the Pontiac Fiero, which involved plastic and fiberglass panels attached to a metal space frame."[16]

Customers include here both intermediate buyers (namely, distributors, wholesalers, and retailers) and ultimate buyers (consumers and in certain instances manufacturers). Intermediate buyers can provide feedback from the marketplace or present suggestions or requests of their own. They also can supply competitive product information that may prove helpful. Ultimate buyers or consumers, on the other hand, constitute the "horse's mouth" because their reaction ultimately determines a new product's success. Paying close attention to their needs and desires makes good sense and can pay off handsomely.

Customer input can be obtained in various ways. It can come in the form of unsolicited suggestions, which must be handled with great care because of their potential legal ramifications, prompting some firms to avoid them altogether. A Colorado businessman, for instance, claims that he originally suggested the idea for 3M's Post-it Notes to the company in 1971 and was rejected. The company, in turn, traces its introduction of the product to the relentless championship of an employee, Art Fry, who originated the idea on his own in 1974 while singing in a church choir.[17] One study examined the reactions of 166 companies to 35 unsolicited ideas. Only one-third of the firms responded in a legally sound fashion by requesting a signed waiver, stating that they will only look at patented ideas, or flatly rejecting any ideas from outsiders. The remainder reacted in legally dangerous ways, namely, giving no response or evaluating the proposals.[18]

NBC receives more than 250,000 suggestions, ideas, and questions per year and devotes an entire department to their review. One consumer suggested to Ben & Jerry's Homemade an ice cream named Cherry Garcia in honor of the lead guitarist of the Grateful Dead. It became the company's third-best-selling brand.[19]

Rather than relying on random inputs from the marketplace, a company may want to actively solicit customer suggestions. This can be done in the form of focus group sessions, which are likely to produce a variety of ideas. An electrical equipment manufacturer invited a select group of customers to a weekend retreat where they provided original and promising ideas.[20] Fisher Controls Company asked its sales representatives in North America and Europe to assemble groups of innovative customers. Members of its development team then met with these groups to discuss a new generation of control room instruments. After several rounds of discussion throughout the design process, the new products were introduced with great success.[21]

Increasingly, companies are employing user advisory panels that serve as sounding boards for concept generation and refinement. But innovative users may go a step further and actually develop, rather than merely suggest, new products. One-third of the software that IBM leases for large- and medium-sized computers was designed by customers. Pillsbury's annual Bake-Offs have produced several user-developed products. The majority of new process machines used by the semiconductor industry were developed by users.[22] Companies can benefit by identifying such new product sources and obtaining the necessary rights.

On a larger scale, surveys can be conducted to elicit problem statements that can be translated into innovative ideas. Less frequently used but often quite meaningful is observation of customers as they go about their daily business.

But the potentially most fruitful external source of new product ideas are competitors, both domestic and international. They are, after all, in the same business, going after the same customers. This is not to advocate industrial espionage or any other illegal or unethical means of acquiring competitive information. But there are numerous ways in which competitive intelligence can be gathered. One of them is shopping abroad. In a West German supermarket, executives of Minnetonka found toothpaste in a pump dispenser. They contacted its manufacturer and introduced the first such product in the United States.[23]

Domestically, competitive intelligence can be gathered in one or more of the following ways:

- "Hanging out" at favorite watering holes, for instance, in Silicon Valley, and just listening to conversations that may inadvertently reveal proprietary information (Having dinner at a seafood restaurant, the marketing vice president of a portable computer company overheard a conversation about a new computer that Hewlett-Packard would introduce two months later—a fact that helped him in his competitive planning.[24])
- Hiring a firm specializing in competitive monitoring
- Subscribing to specialized data bases
- Buying specialized industry reports (from Frost & Sullivan) or specialized newsletters (e.g., *New Product News* from Dancer, Fitzgerald, Sample)
- Checking classified help-wanted ads for information on competitors' intentions, strategies, and planned products
- Analyzing labor contracts and other competitive details revealed in the business press
- Studying aerial photographs
- Obtaining information filed with government agencies under the Freedom of Information Act
- Reviewing competitive product and promotional literature
- Reading annual reports and quarterly reports to stockholders (An issue of *Quaker Quarterly* contained a lengthy article, "The Serpentine Path to New Product Success," that described in considerable detail the evolution of Quaker Chewy Granola Bars.)
- Counting tractor-trailers leaving competitors' loading bays

- Engaging in *reverse engineering,* that is, obtaining samples of new competitive products and taking them apart to examine their composition and construction.[25]

Quite a number of other tactics are used. Many, however, cannot be endorsed because of their questionable legitimacy.

Some consulting firms even have developed specialized seminars training managers in competitive intelligence-gathering practices. A popular tool for learning what the competition is doing is attending trade fairs where competitors and their wares are assembled under one roof. One manager of a mature division reports getting ideas for new industrial products from his annual visits to the Chicago hardware show.[26] Product pick-up services obtain samples of new competitive products in test market stores. A licensing arrangement with a domestic or overseas competitor gives ready access to competitive technological know-how and shortens the time to market introduction.

After General Foods invented soft-moist dog foods and received a patent, Quaker Oats negotiated a license and began offering KenL-Burgers in competition with Gainesburgers. Upjohn, a major pharmaceutical manufacturer, entered into a license agreement with Booth Chemical Company of Great Britain to make and market in the United States an ibuprofen product (a nonaspirin headache remedy). It received a nonexclusive license with the express provision that the licensor could enter the market itself. Although Upjohn marketed the drug under the trade name Motrin, Booth later entered the market with an identical product under the name Rufen, vigorously competing with its own licensee.

Well-managed companies also require their salespeople to routinely file competitive activity reports whenever they spot a new product or special promotion. Trade publications typically carry new product news. "Most manufacturers announce their new products to the trade in these publications, either via advertisements or in editorial copy."[27] Leading marketing research agencies offer consumer goods marketers an opportunity to subscribe to commercial services that report on new product introductions and test marketing results.

Whatever the means for acquiring information about new competitive products, this knowledge may spark different reactions. A company may simply do nothing, judging the event irrelevant to its business. This kind of complacency may prove dangerous because it gives attackers time to get established in the marketplace.[28] American watchmakers' reaction to digital watches showed this pattern. A wait-and-see attitude, however, may be quite appropriate because many new products fail in the marketplace. Although Procter & Gamble has not declared Pringles reconstituted potato chips a failure and withdrawn it from the market, its sales have been disappointing. Competitors, accordingly, have not rushed into the market with me-too products but rather have emphasized the fact that they sell real potato chips.

A frequent response is *imitation,* matching a successful innovation with a parity product. Competitors quickly jumped on the bandwagon created by Reynolds' introduction of Brown-In-Bags, plastic bags for preparing turkeys or roasts. This can be a sensible approach if the originating firm is unable to fill the rapidly expanding demand. It is also usually a low-risk and low-cost strategy.

A third possible avenue is to introduce an improved version of a competitive product. Benefiting from the competitor's development work at a lower cost, a follower may be able to bring out a better product, perhaps even at a lower price. Procter & Gamble did not invent disposable diapers but significantly improved their performance characteristics in its first market entry called Pampers.

Other potential sources of new product ideas include outside consultants as well as advertising and marketing research agencies. Consultants may be hired to identify market opportunities. Advertising agencies often view themselves as marketing advisors to their clients. They research the market and put their creative talent to work in developing new product concepts. The concept for General Foods' Cycle dog food—different formulations for the different stages of a dog's life cycle—came from an advertising agency. Marketing research agencies, in the course of doing custom research for a company, may suggest new products to fit identified problems or need gaps.

Inventors also can be a fertile source of new product ideas. Tens of thousands of them lack the resources to capitalize on their inventions. For legal reasons, it is best to deal with inventors only after they have obtained a patent or at least signed a disclosure waiver form. But even locating the right inventor can be a difficult task because many of them lead a quiet life and work on their ideas at home in their spare time.

Some inventors take the initiative and contact firms that they believe might be interested in their invention. Others exhibit their innovations at patent expositions, waiting for visitors to express an interest. Patent brokers or patent attorneys may act as go-betweens, bringing the two parties together. Occasionally, the brokers or attorneys get into the act themselves, acquiring the rights to an invention and capitalizing on them, typically through resale or licensing, rarely through manufacture and marketing. Regularly perusing the *Official Gazette* to check out the 1,700 or so patents granted weekly in the United States also can yield clues to promising ideas.

In addition to seeking out individual inventors, idea-hungry firms can turn to licensors to obtain rights to innovations. Large manufacturers possess plenty of "surplus technology"—ideas that do not fit their mainstream mission or do not satisfy their minimum sales revenue requirements. Some companies, such as General Electric, have organized systematic programs to market unused ideas to outsiders. In addition to obtaining down payments and royalty fees, licensors also may benefit from cross-licensing clauses that let them share in improvements made by their licensees. Licensees, in turn, often acquire more than just rights. They also may get advice, drawings, prototypes, equipment, and parts.

The U.S. government, as the owner of more than 30,000 patents, has established a clearinghouse for technical information in the form of the National Technical Information Service. For a nominal fee this agency makes available the latest government-sponsored research reports and patent information. Commercial laboratories conduct new product development work under contract. Research support for universities may grant corporate sponsors certain rights to the outcome. One of the most comprehensive of such arrangements has been entered into by Monsanto and

Washington University Medical School in St. Louis. Monsanto scientists work in the university labs and vice versa. Monsanto makes substantial grants to the school. The university receives the patents, but Monsanto has the right to obtain exclusive licenses to all patents that it wants to commercialize.[29]

Finally, a company should keep abreast of current developments in its fields of interest by scanning scientific journals and attending seminars, workshops, conventions, and conferences. The list of potential idea sources is long and varied and limited only by the imagination and sensitivity of the product managers involved.

Techniques for Idea Generation

One of the most popular idea generation techniques is and remains *brainstorming.* A group is assembled, given a basic direction, exposed to relevant facts and trends, and encouraged to let its collective fantasy run wild. A leader keeps the discussion from veering into irrelevant matters but should refrain from imposing personal views or pronouncing judgment. Participants are encouraged to contribute ideas freely, regardless of their apparent feasibility or profitability. It is crucial to the success of such a session that the group be kept small and that no proposal be ridiculed or rejected. It is best to hold brainstorming sessions away from company premises and have them run by disinterested, skilled outsiders.[30]

The cross-fertilization of ideas resulting from such intense interaction could lead to an outstanding suggestion that might not have come about without the effect of group dynamics. Emphasis should be placed on the quantity rather than the quality and depth of the ideas presented. For maximum creativity, tone and mood should be relaxed, free-flowing, and fun.

Brainstorming often concentrates on suggesting problem solutions. *Reverse brainstorming* takes the opposite tack by trying to identify potential problems that could occur with existing or proposed products. The objective is to debug a product or product concept before real problems arise. This approach makes a great deal of sense as a preventive measure at a time when product liability is being interpreted by courts ever more strictly and broadly.[31]

Direct group interaction can, however, suffer from such problems as the discussion being dominated by a strong-willed individual or the conversation drifting off into irrelevant subjects. The *delphi technique* attempts to overcome these problems by using only written exchanges. Participants state their thoughts in writing, which are then circulated for comment. Responding to these comments, the writers may revise their positions. Successive rounds of written interchange ideally will produce thoughtful consensus. This approach, however, is quite cumbersome, requires highly articulate and motivated individuals, and lacks the spontaneity of live interchanges.

In *attribute listing,* a new product that a firm would like to develop or an existing product that it would like to improve is broken down into its attributes. These attributes then are analyzed to see if they could be modified with a view toward cost reduction or performance improvement. *Morphological analysis* and *forced relationships* are similar methods, looking at performance characteristics to effect ideas for product refinement.

SUMMARY

New product processes benefit greatly from a comprehensive marketing research program that establishes and maintains a dialog with the marketplace. Such a program helps product management to sharpen the focus of product development and the introductory marketing mix on buyer needs and desires and thus make them more successful.

After defining the target markets to be served, the program moves to a basic consumer and market study. This is a broad-based benchmark study that examines buying and consumption patterns as well as competitive and distribution trends. From this background study will emerge one or more areas of interest to the company. In attempting to seize selected opportunities, the company will need to generate ideas, some of which will be solicited in the form of suggestions from target consumers.

These suggestions, pooled with other ideas, are refined into a few key concepts, which are then subjected to concept testing. This research phase explores not only which of several concepts finds the most favor with consumers but it also aims to identify desired features. The products that are subsequently developed then are tested for performance and preference in the product testing round of research. Alternative strategies concerning price, branding, packaging, and advertising are examined separately during strategy testing. The winning approaches are assembled into an introductory marketing program, which is subjected to test marketing in a limited number of cities. If it succeeds, the new product is launched full scale.

During the decision-making stage of the process of new product evolution, idea generation assumes a key role. Actually, this step involves both generating ideas internally and collecting them from external sources. Internal idea sources are dominated by marketing and R&D. Although they would seem to be at opposite ends, a close working relationship between them would serve a business best. Ideas also can come from employee suggestions, specialized search committees, managers, value analysis, and by-products of the manufacturing process.

In terms of external sources, suppliers can provide valuable inputs that often are solicited in the form of vendor clinics. Customers are a logical resource, because they will decide the fate of a new product on its introduction. Care must be taken, though, with unsolicited customer ideas because of potential legal ramifications. Some companies conduct focus group sessions with selected customer groups. Others employ user advisory panels on a continuing basis. In some instances users actually will develop new products instead of merely suggesting them.

A powerful source of new product ideas are competitors, which can be tapped through competitive intelligence in a number of legitimate ways. These include trade press announcements, trade fair attendance, and licensing from both domestic and overseas competitors. A company can respond to competitive new product introductions by doing nothing, imitating the product, or improving on it. Other external sources are consultants, advertising and marketing research agencies, inventors, patents, and universities.

The creative techniques used for idea generation include brainstorming, reverse brainstorming, the delphi technique, and attribute listing. Brainstorming is a freewheeling creative group session, whereas reverse brainstorming tries to anticipate and prevent problems. The delphi technique uses written exchanges, and attribute listing attempts to modify product attributes.

NOTES

1. See Philip Kotler, *Marketing Management,* 6th ed. (Englewood Cliffs, NJ: Prentice-Hall, 1988), 342–343.
2. See Richard N. Foster, *Innovation: The Attacker's Advantage* (New York: Summit Books, 1986), and Peter F. Drucker, *Innovation and Entrepreneurship* (New York: Harper & Row, 1986), 30–140.
3. See Michael G. Duerr, *The Commercial Development of New Products* (New York: The Conference Board, 1986), 13–19. See also Thomas J. Peters and Robert H. Waterman, Jr., *In Search of Excellence* (New York: Harper & Row, 1982), 193, and Gifford Pinchot, III, *Intrapreneuring: Why You Don't Have to Leave the Corporation to Become an Entrepreneur* (New York: Harper & Row, 1985), 224–229.
4. See Thomas J. Peters, "A Skunkworks Tale." *Best of Business* (Spring 1984): 86–87.
5. See E. Patrick McGuire, *Generating New-Product Ideas* (New York: The Conference Board, 1972), 6.
6. See Robert G. Cooper, *Winning at New Products* (Reading, MA: Addison-Wesley Publishing Co., 1986), 72.
7. See Duerr, *Commercial Development of New Products,* 22.
8. See ibid., 24.
9. See McGuire, *Generating New-Product Ideas,* 22, and Cooper, *Winning at New Products,* 85–86.
10. See McGuire, *Generating New-Product Ideas,* 26.
11. See Robert A. Fox, "Putting Marketing on a 'Business' Basis," presentation to 1982 Marketing Conference, sponsored by The Conference Board, New York, 20 Oct. 1982, 16.
12. See Tom Stundza, "Scrap Scrapes against the Environment," *Purchasing,* 9 April 1987, 64A4–64A11.
13. McGuire, *Generating New-Product Ideas,* 30.
14. See Eberhard E. Scheuing, *Purchasing Management* (Englewood Cliffs, NJ: Prentice-Hall, 1989), 225.
15. See Gregory Stricharchuk, "Smokestack Industries Adopt Sophisticated Sales Approach," *Wall Street Journal,* 15 March 1984.
16. Cooper, *Winning at New Products,* 79.
17. See Bill Abrams, "Minnesota Mining and Manufacturing Co.," *Wall Street Journal,* 9 June 1983, and Pinchot, *Intrapreneuring,* 137–142.
18. See C. Merle Crawford, "Unsolicited New Product Ideas: Handle with Care," *Research Management* (Jan. 1975): 22. See also C. Merle Crawford, *New Products Management,* 2nd ed. (Homewood, IL: Irwin, 1987), 164–169.
19. See Tananarive Due, "We the People Speak: Give Us Square Kix, Flying Beauty Parlors," *Wall Street Journal,* 14 Sept. 1987.
20. See Cooper, *Winning at New Products,* 72.
21. See Duerr, *Commercial Development of New Products,* 23.
22. See Eric von Hippel, "Get New Products from Customers," *Harvard Business Review* (March–April 1982): 117–118.

23. See Ronald Alsop, "U.S. Concerns Seek Inspiration for Products from Overseas," *Wall Street Journal,* 3 Jan. 1985.
24. See Erik Larson, "Many Top Secrets in the Silicon Valley Are Spilled at Tables," *Wall Street Journal,* 29 June 1984.
25. See Steven Flax, "How to Snoop on Your Competitors," *Fortune,* 14 May 1984, 28ff.
26. See Cooper, *Winning at New Products,* 76.
27. Ibid.
28. See Al Ries and Jack Trout, *Marketing Warfare* (New York: McGraw-Hill, 1986), 58–66. See also Foster, especially chapters 1 and 5 to 8.
29. See Duerr, *Commercial Development of New Products,* 26.
30. See Frederick D. Buggie, *New Product Development Strategies* (New York: AMACOM, 1981), 85. See also Duerr, *Commercial Development of New Products,* 27–28.
31. See McGuire, *Generating New-Product Ideas,* 18.

CASE STUDY

LEARNING FROM THE COMPETITION

For the past two decades, the fortunes of the U.S. automobile industry have been rather volatile. In 1980 and 1981, the "Big Three" automakers—General Motors, Ford, and Chrysler—suffered combined losses of $7 billion. In contrast, in 1983, 1984, and 1985, their combined net income was $24 billion. Challenged by intensifying competition, both from imported and domestically produced vehicles (a growing number of them made by foreign manufacturers in their American plants), they chose to streamline operations, upgrade facilities, and design new automobiles. They also paid more attention to quality, one area where the reputation of foreign-made vehicles clearly surpassed their domestic rivals. And for good reason. As *Business Week* reported (June 8, 1987): "As many as one-quarter of all factory hands don't produce anything—they just rework things that were not done right the first time." Specifically, General Motors took the following measures:

• Closed aging plants, trimmed its work force, and reduced its inventories.
• Undertook a $40 billion, seven-year effort to automate its plants and redesign its cars.
• Bought Electronic Data Systems Corporation in 1984 for $2.5 billion to help develop a computer network and control robots.
• Initiated the $5 billion Saturn project aimed at efficient domestic small car production.
• Teamed up with Toyota for joint production at its Fremont, California, plant.

The results to date have been most disappointing. Automation has not trimmed cost and

This case was contributed by Janet R. DiLorenzo-Aiss, Instructor in Marketing, St. John's University, New York, New York. It was based on the following articles: Kevin Tottis, "Auto Makers Look for Ideas in Rivals' Cars," *Wall Street Journal*, 20 July 1982, 29; Jerry Flint, "Best Car Wins," *Forbes*, 27 Jan. 1986, 73–77; William J. Hampton and James R. Norman, "General Motors: What Went Wrong," *Business Week*, 16 March 1987, 102–110; Otis Port, "The Push for Quality," *Business Week*, 8 June 1987, 130–135; "Copycat Stuff? Hardly!" *Business Week*, 14 Sept. 1987, 112; James B. Treece, "Can Ford Stay on Top?" *Business Week*, 28 Sept. 1987, 78–86; and Alex Taylor III, "Who's Ahead in the World Auto War," *Fortune*, 9 Nov. 1987, 74–88.

raised quality as expected. In fact, the little automated Fremont plant under Japanese management turns out some of the highest quality GM cars. The redesign efforts produced look-alike cars, and newly designed automobiles such as the Chevrolet Beretta did not catch on. The Saturn project is years from fruition, if it will ever bear fruit.

Chrysler, after facing bankruptcy, executed a dramatic turnaround. It not only lowered its breakeven point significantly, the company also managed to gain buyer confidence with unprecedented warranties and capture their imagination by bringing back convertibles and pioneering mini-vans.

But what and how has Ford done during recent years? While Chrysler's fortune improved, General Motors' market share and profits declined steadily. In 1986 Ford earned $3.3 billion on $62.7 billion in sales as compared to GM's $2.9 billion profit on revenues of $102.8 billion. In the first half of 1987, Ford's income of $2.9 billion exceeded the combined earnings of GM and Chrysler. Under dynamic new leadership, Ford achieved this remarkable feat through rigorous cost cutting, unswerving commitment to quality, and innovative styling. How was the company able to achieve success in new product introduction where GM failed? It listened to its customers and competitors, the two prime external sources of new product guidance.

Competitive Intelligence

Where GM once dominated the U.S. automobile market, the market's composition has changed so dramatically that by now the "best car wins"—in the words of Louis Lataif, sales vice president at Ford. This fact has given Ford an incentive to succeed by providing outstanding cars. It placed strong emphasis on quality, calling it "Job 1," as well as innovative styling. Ideas for new cars come in part from its research and development centers as well as from its engineering units. Because this kind of creative approach is costly and time-consuming, the company also taps strategically into other sources of new product ideas. This includes customer input generated through marketing research.

Increasingly, however, Ford Motor Company has been relying on product improvement ideas that were unwittingly supplied by its competitors. In a process known as reverse engineering, the company systematically and painstakingly disassembles competitive cars, carefully examining and cataloging each of their 30,000 or so parts. The purpose of this exercise is to uncover ideas that might benefit Ford's own design and engineering efforts.

Working with a small staff of crack mechanics at the company's research center in Dearborn, Michigan, Robert Camron serves as its chief dissector, or pathologist. Although he has bought and taken apart competitors' cars for thirty years, he feels that his job has never been more important to his employer than today. According to Stuart M. Frey, Ford's vice president of engineering and planning, his company is looking for innovations that help its products work better and save money.

To stay on top of competitive new car introductions, Robert Camron studies trade magazines for announcements, attends auto shows, and keeps in touch with suppliers. When new cars are introduced, he buys them from local dealers and takes them apart bolt by bolt in a process that can take up to two weeks. When he discovers an intriguing innovation, he puts it through a demanding torture test to determine how well it holds up in the long run. When he is satisfied that an innovation represents a solid improvement, he recommends it to Ford's management for incorporation in future cars.

Because General Motors and Chrysler operate similar reverse engineering labs, they learn about Ford's innovations in the same way. Ironically, this can lead to competitors improving on each other's advances and then unintentionally sharing this information. Understandably, though, the companies take great care not to infringe on each other's patents. At times they find it useful, however, to barter patent rights. Clearly—and without resorting to any sinister industrial espionage tactics—in the automotive business, competitors can and do learn from each other.

Generating Winning Ideas

This fact was particularly evident in the design and successful introduction of Ford's Taurus. The company began this effort by assembling a highly qualified team of stylists, engineers, and manufacturing specialists. Their mission was simply to conceive an outstanding car. Leaving no stone unturned, the team learned from assembly line workers, customers, and competitors. It looked at more than fifty competitive cars in the prospective vehicle's class category of four-door, midsize cars. It asked consumers for "best in class" characteristics exemplified by rival entries from all over the world. These characteristics included such details as the effort required to turn the steering wheel and the ease of resetting the clock.

The team then selected about a dozen cars (most of them foreign) for thorough dissection. The strip search identified no less than 400 features for the Taurus wish list. They ranged from improved lumbar support systems to increased engine part accessibility. Systematically addressing all of them, the team claims to have matched or exceeded the competition on 90 percent of the features. In implementing the innovative design, the company gave production workers unprecedented authority to stop the line if they felt that quality was unacceptable. Consequently, the car's introduction was delayed several months while quality problems were being solved. The Team Taurus approach became a model for subsequent new car projects.

Discussion Questions

1. What do you think of Ford's reverse engineering activities? Are they beneficial to the company and the industry as a whole?
2. Evaluate Ford Motor Company's approach to new product idea generation as illustrated by Team Taurus.
3. Should companies engage in competitive intelligence? Why, or why not?
4. What other sources of new product ideas could and/or should be used by Ford Motor Company?

CHAPTER 6

Screening New Product Ideas

The motto of the idea generation stage was "the more, the merrier." To ensure that no promising idea would be overlooked, a comprehensive and wide-ranging effort was undertaken to tap into the broadest possible gamut of idea sources and collect their relevant ideas. In addition, various internal and external sources were used to generate new product ideas from scratch. This substantial effort was governed by the consideration that the outcome of the evolutionary process can only be as good as its input in the form of new product ideas. The result of this phase was a pool of ideas of varying degrees of complexity, sophistication, and refinement.

For a number of reasons, not all of these ideas are worthy of corporate attention, funding, and pursuit. They may not be feasible from a technical point of view, they may not be profitable, they may not offer sufficient volume potential, they may not be compatible with the company's mission and image, and so on. Given the company's overall, marketing, and product objectives as well as internal and external constraints, only a very small number of ideas can and deserve to be turned into marketable products. These ideas must be identified and distilled from the accumulated pool through a process of successive elimination.

It may appear paradoxical at first sight that idea generation is driven by the desire to come up with as many ideas as possible whereas subsequent stages are characterized by an almost missionary zeal aimed at eliminating as many new product ideas as possible. The logical link between these seemingly contradictory pursuits, however, is quite simple. Collecting and generating a large number of innovative ideas presents management with an opportunity to reconsider its business and examine a variety of potential new growth directions. Rather than frivolously pursuing many of them simultaneously without adequate commitment and support, however, subsequent stages are designed to single out high-potential growth opportunities, which are then addressed with resources and dedication sufficient to make them happen. It is the concentration of human, financial, and physical resources toward a few promising ventures that makes a rigid selection process a logical consequence of a broad-based idea generation effort.

The first of these review steps is called *screening*. It involves the initial sorting out of the competing ideas according to their relative merits. For one reason or another, the majority of the ideas will be rejected at this point. Surviving ideas, however, are not yet home, free and clear. Rather, they are subjected to further, more intense scrutiny before resource commitment is made with the blessing of top management. It could be said, therefore, that the purpose of screening is to identify and select candidate ideas for more thorough examination. In the "New Products World Series," screening constitutes the elimination games and the survivors represent the semifinalists from which the winner will be chosen.

But because it must be carried out expeditiously and efficiently, screening is subject to potential problems. It may variously result in the rejection of a good idea or the failure to screen out poor ideas. These very real dangers can and should be minimized systematically.

A number of alternative screening tools are available to the resourceful product manager. They range from graphic techniques to quantitative approaches, in each case ensuring that a variety of aspects are considered in this preliminary review instead of relying on subjective intuition. Whichever approach is chosen, the result of a well-executed screening program are a few select ideas holding considerable promise and well worthy of further investigation.

The Need for a Preliminary Review of New Product Ideas

Where the idea generation stage was creative, the screening stage is analytical. Idea generation is freewheeling and supportive, screening rigid and critical. The two stages, though sequential, differ significantly in their thrust and nature. Accordingly, different talents are needed. Idea generators build, screeners dissect. It takes a sharp, detached, analytical mind to do a good job of screening. Accordingly, the two tasks cannot and should not be handled by the same people. It makes little sense to ask the same person to create a new product idea and then proceed to judge its economic merits objectively. Having conceived it, the individual is bound to be biased in favor of its implementation. To have a proper system of checks and balances, screening must be conducted by employees who were not involved in idea creation and collection and thus have no ax to grind. Also, it takes different mind-sets to execute the two types of assignments. Creativity requires fantasy and enthusiasm; analysis, objectivity and detachment.

Having produced and gathered a large number of new product ideas in the preceding stage that are all potentially competing for management attention and corporate resources, product management in the screening phase faces the challenge of separating the wheat from the chaff economically. It is simply not economically justifiable to examine all proposed ideas thoroughly. If fifty or more ideas are suggested, not every one can meaningfully be subjected to concept testing, a technical feasibility study, sales forecasting, and other projected impact measurements. It would be a dissipation and waste of corporate resources to look carefully into all of them. This is why screening must precede business analysis. It is charged with assessing the relative merits of the competing ideas as they present themselves at this early stage. And it has to do so without causing substantial expenditures in time and money, at the same time safeguarding the company against the potential consequences of poor judgment. It must operate under time pressure and budget constraints, substituting educated managerial guesses for the collection and interpretation of factual data.

Notwithstanding these constraints, screening aims to direct corporate resources toward the most promising suggestions by identifying high-potential candidates for further investigation. This helps to prioritize prospective pursuits in a preliminary fashion and prevent wanton waste of time, money, and talent. But the possible dangers involved in this activity are substantial. Poor judgment at this point can set a process in motion that ultimately results in failure or leads to the rejection of an idea with considerable merit. These potential problems will be examined next, together with ways of combating them.

Dangers in New Product Idea Screening

Decision making means risk taking. Screening new product ideas inevitably incurs the risk of incorrect assessment of an embryonic idea's chance to succeed in the marketplace—if and when it is turned into a marketable product some time down the road. For discontinuous innovations, this becomes a highly speculative exercise because they represent pioneering ventures into uncharted territory. The challenge of projection under such circumstances might be akin to predicting whether a newborn will become president of the United States. It takes a great deal of imagination, intuition, and vision on the part of the screeners to recognize the potential of such ideas and pass them on to the next stage for more intense scrutiny.

Most new product ideas, however, represent far less radical departures from past avenues. This makes it considerably easier to project their likelihood of success. Because many new product ideas constitute modifications of existing products, there is a track record available that facilitates projections and limits the risk of incorrect assessment. Nonetheless, whether ideas are radically or moderately different from current products, risk is always inherent in new product efforts. There can be no change, no growth, no future without risk. It is an integral part of the challenge and opportunity of product management. Accordingly, it cannot and should not be eliminated. After all, hand in hand with risk goes reward. Risk is not only institutional, it is also a personal phenomenon. If an idea succeeds, the product manager associated with it will also succeed. If it fails, its product manager may suffer a setback.

Risk spells growth, and growth spells risk. The greater the risk, the greater the potential opportunity or, for that matter, the greater the potential penalty. Some managements will shrink from what they consider to be taking chances and will prefer tried and true paths of a more conservative nature, possibly miring a company further in declining businesses. Other managers, typically heading smaller firms, will embrace what they view as attractive growth opportunities, fully cognizant of the possible price tag if things do not work out as anticipated.

Although risk is inherent in all business decisions, it is particularly great in new product efforts. At the screening stage, this risk manifests itself in two ways: Good ideas may incorrectly be rejected and poor ideas may be allowed to proceed.[1] Ideally, all judgments made at this point would prove to be correct. But that would require the foresight of an oracle and the wisdom of a Solomon; and because they are not in abundant supply, errors in judgment are bound to occur.

The potentially more severe of the two types of errors consists of the mistaken rejection of a good idea. How could this happen? If an idea is good, why wouldn't it be happily accepted and rapidly moved along? Some of the best ideas that end up profoundly affecting our lives have a habit of masquerading as long shots or as eccentric pursuits without commerical value. Alexander Graham Bell's telephone was rejected by Western Union. Westinghouse declined the opportunity to manufacture fluorescent light bulbs under a license. IBM and Eastman Kodak were not interested in Chester Carlson's copying machine. From 1939 to 1944, he was turned down by no less than twenty firms. Tiny Haloid Corporation of Rochester, New York, finally recognized the immense potential, eventually transforming itself into mighty Xerox.[2] Business history abounds with examples of innovative employees who, unable to get their employers to accept and implement their ideas, leave their jobs and start firms of their own, which often become very successful. A recent example is Steve Chen, who left Cray Research and is receiving IBM's backing in designing and building supercomputers.[3]

Good ideas are rejected at the screening stage for either of two reasons: inadequate information or management's reluctance to assume substantial risk in a new product venture. The more innovative an idea is, the more it differs from established ways of doing business, the more speculative its outlook becomes, and the less solid, factual information is available. Often it is simply impossible to determine beforehand what the market reaction will be to a novel idea. When Sharp introduced the first electronic calculator at $400, it was a relatively bulky gadget for office use. No one could foresee then that a decade later wallet-size versions would retail for less than $10, become disposable, and be widely used by students and shoppers. Similarly, when Pulsar introduced the first digital watch at $2,500, the industry dismissed it as a fad for the affluent and gave no consideration to jumping on the bandwagon. A decade later, digital watches had substantially affected the timepiece market and were selling for less than $10, again rendering them disposable items.

When such revolutionary ideas come along, marketing research finds it difficult to project price and demand levels at the time of eventual introduction of the resulting product. This is so because prospective buyers experience problems when asked to envision what they will do at that point, having little basis in their own experience for meaningfully predicting their likely buying behavior. This scarcity of hard facts about events several years into the future leaves the pursuit of such ideas a gamble that many managements are unwilling to take.

But even if the market and profit data are reasonably solid, management's reluctant attitude about risk taking may squelch the prospects for a truly innovative concept. If the numbers look good but the "downside" risk is substantial because of heavy up-front research and development and introductory marketing expenditures, management may shrink from making the necessary commitment. After all, saying

"No" to a new idea generally seems the safer route to take, ostensibly protecting jobs and corporate assets against exotic risks. It certainly appears to be a better approach than putting one's job on the line for a concept whose potential is totally unproven. Thus the more an innovative idea diverges from a company's current entries, the greater its likelihood of rejection in the screening stage. This could mean a painful loss to the firm, postponing or preventing as it does the company's entry into a possibly very lucrative market.

The other screening danger—allowing poor ideas to proceed further through the evolutionary process—is potentially somewhat less serious, although it can result in considerable waste. The problem is less severe because subsequent stages—hopefully, the business analysis phase—should pinpoint the idea's lack of merit and eliminate it from further consideration. Letting an idea slip through that should have been rejected outright does not reflect very favorably on the company's screening procedure. This stage is supposed to screen out ideas without apparent merit so that only worthy ideas receive closer attention in the succeeding stages. If faulty methodology permits a sizable number of poor ideas to proceed beyond screening and tie up corporate resources unjustifiably, then this important preliminary review phase has failed to accomplish its purpose and has turned dysfunctional and counterproductive. Of course, poor new product ideas that erroneously were not rejected at the screening stage have by no means been accepted and approved for development and introduction. But the scary possibility exists that they will continue to elude the checkpoints and selection mechanisms in the new product system and thus will end up being introduced in the marketplace, only to fail miserably, costing the company not only money but also damage to its reputation.

So both dangers in new product idea screening—rejecting good ideas and passing poor ones—are serious and should be minimized systematically. A first safeguard against screening pitfalls is never to let the same person generate and screen an idea; objectivity is bound to suffer and talents will prove inadequate for mastering both tasks well. A second way to ensure the integrity of the screening phase is to assign it to a committee rather than a single individual. Several minds and diverse backgrounds are better than one for examining the ramifications of an innovative idea. It is best to compose such a committee of representatives of the various functional areas, that is, product management, sales management, engineering, production, purchasing, and accounting or finance. By drawing all major units of the company into the picture and receiving their input, one simultaneously overcomes the "not-invented-here" syndrome and ensures critical support for the surviving ideas. The breadth of experience and support represented by a screening committee that is constituted as described previously is needed to do justice to new concepts and to compensate for personal bias.

A third safeguard consists of keeping a file of rejected ideas and periodically reviewing them. In this manner no idea is ever permanently eliminated from further consideration. Rather, it is reconsidered regularly to see if changes in technology, availability of materials, or market conditions have altered its chances of success. Although screening pitfalls cannot be avoided altogether because solid information can be scarce so early in the game and human judgment is involved, they can be minimized systematically by applying the preceding methods, thus reducing them to manageable proportions.

Tools for Screening Innovative Ideas

Every company must create an idea-filtering system suited for its unique objectives, needs, and conditions that guarantees thoroughness and economy. Slipshod evaluations will come back to haunt management, but the expenditures for screening itself must stay within reasonable bounds. An in-depth business and economic analysis of every innovative idea causes unnecessary expenditures in time, money, and human resources. Screening thus misses its purpose if it becomes too detailed and time-consuming. Screening should be a quick selection of promising ideas from the assembled pool to facilitate the concentrated application of resources to the best proposals in the subsequent stages.

To discard the majority of ideas for lack of merit and single out the semifinalists in any kind of systematic fashion requires a framework for decision making. Such a framework is supplied by a checklist or its quantitative equivalent, consisting of different criteria by which the characteristics and outlook of the various suggestions will be judged. Ideas that score well on such an instrument are passed on to the business analysis stage for more intense scrutiny while the remainder are deleted from further consideration at this point.

Two screening mechanisms—quite different in their approaches—are discussed here. Other screening tools are available in the literature. However, they tend to fall largely within the two categories represented in the following discussion and mainly constitute variants of their basic concepts.[4] The first of these screening tools is a graphic technique entitled *the new product profile chart*. A useful device for determining a potential product's impact on the company's situation, this idea evaluation chart is illustrated in Figure 6–1.

In this approach to new product idea screening, a total of twenty-six criteria are applied to an innovative suggestion to estimate the consequences of its potential development and market introduction for four crucial functional areas of the firm: finance, production and engineering, research and development, and marketing. At the outset, certain key figures must be estimated and entered in the box in the upper right-hand corner labeled "product." They include forecasts of annual sales, price, annual earnings (before taxes), and total capital investment. As presented in Figure 6–1, the chart refers and applies to large chemical companies. It can, however, be readily modified for companies of any size or industry. Although the framework of criteria listed is applicable to most businesses and will require significant alterations only for service enterprises, the meaning of the four possible scores must be adjusted to reflect the specific circumstances of each firm using it, thus making it a company-specific chart that cannot be used without change by another organization.

To return to the explanation of how to use this screening device, the box in the upper right-hand corner expresses estimated annual sales in pounds. This is common in the chemical industry, whereas other industries employ different volume measurements (e.g., tons or cases) or even revenue dollars. This estimate refers neither to total market demand (also known as market capacity or market potential) nor to projected first-year sales. Rather, this estimate asks for a sustainable sales level for the company in this commodity, in other words, its expected sales potential (which is expected market share × market potential). "Price" refers to the average achievable net price over the foreseeable future. "Annual earnings" from this pro-

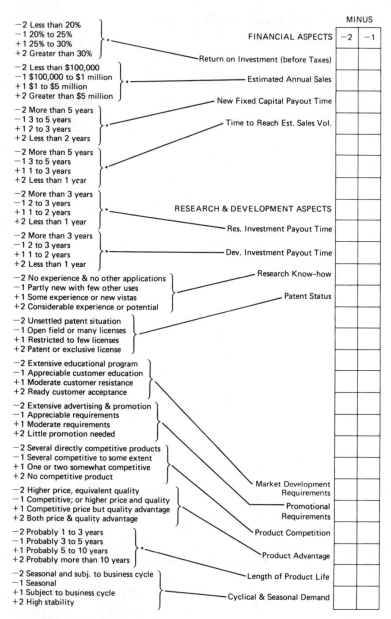

FIGURE 6–1

New Product Profile Chart (*Source:*   Reprinted with permission from John S. Harris, "The New Product Profile Chart: Selecting and Appraising New Projects," *Chemical and Engineering News* 39 [17 April 1961])

PLUS

+1	+2

PRODUCT:

Est. Annual Sales _____ lbs.

Price: $ _____

Annual Earnings: $ _____
(before taxes)

Total Capital Investment: $_____

PRODUCTION & ENGINEERING ASPECTS

Required Corporate Size

- −2 Can be made by any bucket operator
- −1 Most companies could compete
- +1 Average or larger sized companies
- +2 Only a very large company

Raw Materials

- −2 Limited supply or suppliers
- −1 Limited availability inside company
- +1 Readily available from outside sources
- +2 Readily available inside company

Equipment

- −2 New plant needed
- −1 Mostly new equipment
- +1 Some new equipment
- +2 Present idle plant useable

Process Familiarity

- −2 New process—no other application
- −1 Partly new—few other uses
- +1 Familiar process—some other uses
- +2 Routine process or promising other uses

MARKETING & PRODUCT ASPECTS

Similarity to Present Product Lines

- −2 Entirely new type
- −1 Somewhat different
- +1 Only slighty different
- +2 Fits perfectly

Effect on Present Products

- −2 Will replace directly
- −1 Decrease other sales somewhat
- +1 Slight effect
- +2 Increase other product sales

Marketability to Present Customers

- −2 Entirely different customers
- −1 Some present customers
- +1 Mostly present customers
- +2 All present customers

Number of Potential Customers

Suitability of Present Sales Force

- −2 More than 500
- −1 Less than 5; or 100 to 500
- +1 5 to 10; or 50 to 100
- +2 10 to 50

Market Stability

- −2 Entire new group needed
- −1 Some additions necessary
- +1 Few additions necessary
- +2 No changes necessary

Market Trend

- −2 Volatile market, frequent price cuts
- −1 Unsteady market
- +1 Fairly firm market
- +2 Highly stable market

Technical Service

- −2 Decreasing market
- −1 Static, mature market
- +1 Growing market
- +2 New potential market

- −2 Extensive service required
- −1 Moderate service requirements
- +1 Slight service requirements
- +2 Negligible service required

spective new product asks for the (before taxes) profit contribution anticipated from this contemplated venture. This figure is computed by deducting projected product-related cost (including depreciation on any additional investment) from the fore-casted sales revenues (price × volume expectations). The "total capital investment" is the additional investment, if any, in productive capacity required to produce this product.

Based on this preliminary input, the screener now proceeds to rate the idea according to each of the twenty-six criteria listed. Each criterion can receive a score ranging from −2 to +2. These scores can be generically interpreted to mean the following:

$$-2 \quad \text{very undesirable}$$
$$-1 \quad \text{moderately undesirable}$$
$$+1 \quad \text{moderately desirable}$$
$$+2 \quad \text{very desirable}$$

Deliberately, there is no central score of zero (0). Including a zero score often results in a noncommittal, indecisive score that distorts the results unnecessarily. As it is designed, the chart forces a choice—at least moderately—in the positive or negative direction. Where such a choice cannot meaningfully be made, omitting a rating on the criterion in question signals lack of adequate information.

For a rating of plus/minus 1, the screener shades a single square. Ratings of 2 in either direction involve shading both squares on the appropriate side of the dividing line. This ensures visual continuity and maximum impact. As indicated previously, this graphic technique is intended for visual inspection, not for numbers crunching. No overall score therefore is determined that would permit in a single combined number a comparison with alternative proposals. Another factor to consider when evaluating this screening tool is the fact that the criteria are not weighted according to their relative significance. This makes it appear as if they were all of equal importance—hardly a correct impression. What the individual scores mean and how strongly they advocate passing or rejection remains somewhat unclear. Surely it would be foolish to net out the positive and negative scores and recommend passing if the result is positive, and vice versa.

Nonetheless, the technique is very useful and powerful because it permits a synoptic consideration of many aspects and can simplify complex comparisons. This can be seen from Figure 6–2, which demonstrates the application of the new product profile chart by using a case example. Stage I pictures a new chemical product during the initial phase of applied research. It is evident that there are some information gaps that cannot be filled at this time. Stage II reflects a second evaluation after the start of process research. The outlook has become very good. Even though an unavoidable by-product was detected, preliminary tests suggest that it can be sold profitably. Most of the gaps have filled in on the plus side. In stage III, however, the picture has definitely changed in the negative direction. Further research on the by-product determined that it cannot be sold, thus making the financial prospects for the entire project look very gloomy. The price of the main product would have to be increased, thereby prolonging the period of time necessary to reach the estimated

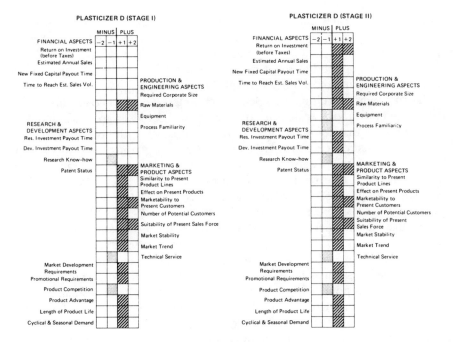

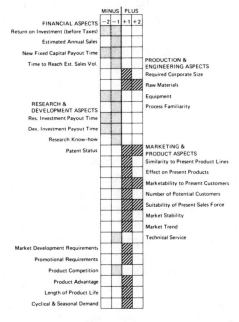

FIGURE 6–2

Applying the New Product Profile Chart: A Case Example (*Source:* Reprinted with permission from John S. Harris, "The New Product Profile Chart: Selecting and Appraising New Projects," *Chemical and Engineering News* 39 [17 April 1961])

sales volume. Other findings indicate the necessity of a new plant. The main product, therefore, cannot be produced and sold at a profit unless some application for the by-product can be found. As this case example vividly illustrates, the new product profile chart can be applied to the same idea repeatedly as it moves through the evolutionary process and more information becomes known.

Another kind of preliminary selection tool is less detailed and for this reason easier to use. When a rating scale is used, the new product ideas are evaluated with the help of a matrix that combines spheres of performance with product idea compatibility values. This approach entails the quantification of qualitative considerations to enable a comparison of many ideas on the basis of their overall ratings. The underlying concept is to capitalize on a company's existing strengths in selecting candidate ideas. All proposed ideas are examined as to their degree of fit with these strengths and passed or rejected accordingly.

Product management can build a company-specific rating model by first engaging in a thorough soul-searching process to determine the nature and extent of the firm's competitive advantage. Perfect candor and a sincere attempt at objectivity are absolutely essential here. Independent outsiders could prove a valuable source of input at this point. Having identified the sources of the firm's marketplace edge, they must be combined into a list. This list may well contain both functional and nonfunctional areas of strength—labeled "spheres of performance" in Table 6–1. But it deliberately omits any areas of weakness and may therefore prove to be an incomplete listing of the firm's operating units. The next step is to assign relative weights to the performance spheres and enter them in column A. Because the total competitive advantage is derived from the company's resources and their use, the relative weights constitute the contributions to the overall competitive edge made by each of the areas listed. "The greater the competitive advantage the company has in a specific sphere, the greater would be the assigned weight, since it would be more significant in relation to over-all company success."[5] Because they represent shares of the overall competitive advantage, the relative weights always must add up to 1.0 (or 100 percent).

This part of the rating framework is company specific and thus remains unchanged, regardless of the ideas being screened. It would only be modified if the composition of the firm's market strength changed. Section B of the screening matrix, in contrast, is idea specific and reflects how compatible each idea is with each performance sphere. Possible values range from 0 (incompatible) to 1 (perfect fit). These "product compatibility values" are idea-impact coefficients that express the compatibility of proposed ideas with the particular characteristics of the individual spheres. Ideas that stray far afield from a firm's traditional business receive low scores, whereas ideas that build on existing strengths achieve high compatibility values. As a result, tried and true paths tend to be welcomed while boldly innovative moves would be out of favor. The outcome could be complacent mediocrity, concentrating on low-risk, low-growth mature businesses and neglecting high-risk, high opportunity ventures.

Next, the product compatibility values are multiplied with the respective relative weights to produce weighted values. The latter not only reflect an idea's fit with a given area but simultaneously the area's importance in the overall competitive

TABLE 6–1
Screening Matrix*

Sphere of Performance	(A) Relative Weight	(B) Product Compatibility Values											(C) A × B
		0	.1	.2	.3	.4	.5	.6	.7	.8	.9	1.0	
Company personality and goodwill	.20							X					.120
Marketing	.20										X		.180
Research and development	.20								X				.140
Personnel	.15							X					.090
Finance	.10										X		.090
Production	.05									X			.040
Location and facilities	.05				X								.015
Purchasing and supply	.05										X		.045
Total	1.00												.720

*Rating scale: 0–.40, poor; .41–.75, fair: .76–1.0, good. Present minimum acceptance rate: .70.
(*Source:* Reprinted with permission from Barry M. Richman, "A Rating Scale for Product Innovation," *Business Horizons* [Summer 1962]: 37–44)

context. These products, listed in column C, then are added to compute a single composite rating to indicate the idea's relative merit. A low overall score would lead to immediate rejection, whereas a high total rating pinpoints a very attractive idea. Accordingly, depending on a company's current minimum acceptance rate, a given total score would mean either further investigation or deletion of more detailed analysis of the proposed idea.

Table 6–1, however, not only illustrates the methodological framework of the screening matrix, it also presents a case example of the application of this technique. In this instance, a large manufacturer of photographic equipment is examining the idea of marketing batteries. To make a meaningful decision, product management uses the screening matrix shown in Table 6–1 to determine the degree of desirability of the product idea as well as its compatibility with the company's situation in the various areas of performance.

The firm possesses a distinct competitive advantage in the area of marketing because it commands a well-known name and a worldwide distribution and service network. The firm is also a leader in the research and development field, famous for its engineering know-how and the reliability and convenience of its models. Because the company has been able to develop pride among its employees and a reputation for dependable, durable, and high-quality products, this nonoperational sphere like the two previously mentioned functional areas is assigned a weight of .20 (or 20 percent) as an indication of its great importance for the overall success of the firm. A slight competitive edge exists regarding the company's management personnel because of sophisticated selection, training, and compensation policies. The remaining spheres of influence are not characterized by any substantial superiority of the company. This fact is reflected in lower relative weights.

How does the new idea of marketing batteries fit into the framework of these area characteristics? Because the same distribution channels and promotional strategies can be applied, the innovation matches perfectly with the current marketing program. The know-how of the firm's research and development scientists in combination with expert outside consultants also permits an optimistic prognosis for this sphere, even considering the fact that in all probability patent protection for this product will be impossible to obtain. The necessary labor and executive personnel are available, although additional training will be required. No significant difficulties are expected in attempting to provide the financial resources required for the development and introduction of the product. Production as well as purchasing do not pose any problems, either. The low rating on "location and facilities" results from the necessity to acquire new facilities in a new location because existing plants are ill-equipped to manufacture this kind of product. A product compatibility score of .6 in the field of company personality and goodwill indicates problems encountered in matching batteries with the image of a firm that is well established in the photographic equipment business. A marked negative impact is, however, not foreseen, because the company is known for its aggressiveness and reliability.

Multiplication of the weights with the compatibility values leads to the scores shown in the last column of Table 6–1. The sum of these products represents the overall idea fit, in this case .72. Because the company uses a cutoff rate of .70 for new product proposals, this innovation will be investigated further.

SUMMARY

Having generated a rich pool of ideas in the idea generation step of the evolutionary process, a company faces the task of whittling it down to a manageable size in a first round of processing. To avoid overlooking any potentially rewarding pursuit, the governing rule of idea generation had to be to develop as many ideas as possible from a variety of sources. But during the screening step, product management must master the challenge of essentially sorting all ideas into two categories—promising ideas that will be investigated further and ideas that do not seem to possess sufficient merit to be examined in more detail.

The purpose of screening is to serve as a first, preliminary filter that eliminates from further consideration ideas that are not feasible and/or profitable. In-depth business and economic analyses of all new product ideas would be impractical and wasteful in terms of time, money, and personnel. Screening enables a company to concentrate its analytical efforts on a few select ideas. But it must be done economically and efficiently. Screening misses its purpose if it becomes too detailed or time-consuming.

If the procedure is too fast and superficial, however, it may result in one of two potentially serious mistakes: promising ideas may mistakenly be rejected, or products doomed to failure may erroneously slip through the screen. Every company therefore must create an idea-screening framework that is simultaneously opportunity sensitive and cost-efficient. Its purpose is not so much rejection of unworthy ideas but rather the identification of high-potential ideas.

Toward this end, product management can employ either graphic or numerical screening devices. A new product profile chart requires product managers to rate new product ideas on a four-point scale according to twenty-six criteria. The ratings are shown in graphic form. A screening matrix, on the other hand, measures how well a new idea capitalizes on a firm's existing strengths. Whatever tool is used, only a limited number of top-rated ideas move on to business analysis for more comprehensive scrutiny.

NOTES

1. See Roger A. More, "Risk Factors in Accepted and Rejected New Industrial Products," *Industrial Marketing Management,* (Nov. 1982): 9–15.
2. See "Invention Rejected 20 Times: Copier Revolutionized Work," *Sunday Freeman,* 29 Sept. 1985, 53.
3. See Geoff Lewis, "Big Changes at Big Blue," *Business Week,* 15 Feb. 1988, 93.
4. See, for instance, Yoram J. Wind, *Product Policy: Concepts, Methods, and Strategy* (Reading, MA: Addison-Wesley Publishing Co., 1982), 306ff.; Robert G. Cooper, *Winning at New Products* (Reading, MA: Addison-Wesley Publishing Co., 1986), 95–121; and Michael G. Duerr, *The Commercial Development of New Products* (New York: The Conference Board, 1986), 29–36.
5. Barry M. Richman, "A Rating Scale for Product Innovation," *Business Horizons* (Summer 1962): 39.

CASE STUDY

RESTING COMFORTABLY

Joan Fabioli feels that dynamic innovation is overdue in the staid and unimaginative bedding market. Her responsibilities at Stecker's, a major department store chain, include managing the bedding department—an area in which her company has a substantial interest and presence. She meets with Phil Singer, the firm's marketing research manager, to discuss her need for an opportunity assessment of the bedding market. After talking to several marketing research suppliers, they award the contract to the Design to Market Group, which has designated Doug Miller as the project director. They chose the group because of its ability to translate research findings into concepts, designs, and prototypes for a new kind of bedding comfort.

Doug and his team swing into action. They collect and analyze secondary data about the bedding market. Trained moderators conduct several focus group sessions with carefully screened consumers in different locations across the country. And Design to Market Group interviews 1,500 consumers in the form of shopping mall intercepts in strategically selected cities. The results provide a clear picture of the current situation and outline desired characteristics of prospective innovations.

The Current Bedding Market

In 1986, bedding sales at retail amounted to about $2.6 billion. The market is dominated by three manufacturers and a retailer—Sealy, Serta, and Simmons and Sears—which between them control 60 percent of the market. Bedding is a very profitable category, which explains Joan's interest in expanding Stecker's share and assuming a leadership posture in this market. Most bedding is sold through furniture stores, but department stores hold 35 percent of sales.

One manufacturer's recent study found that the vast majority of mattress customers are women

in the 18- to 40-year-old bracket. They buy primarily at four points in their life cycles: when they move, when they marry, when their children outgrow their cribs, and when they leave home.

Unlike water heaters and car batteries, mattresses are usually not emergency purchases. Consumers can choose when to buy and are often triggered into buying by sales prices. According to the study, most buyers consider mattresses big-ticket items and purchase them the same way they purchase refrigerators. Some three-quarters of all buyers reported having made their last bedding purchase in a furniture or department store. In contrast, only 10 percent had bought bedding in bedding specialty shops or warehouse showrooms, although 18 percent intended to go there in the future.

Shoppers experience difficulty identifying differences among competing sets of bedding. So they place great emphasis on the ticking (the cover fabric). Consumers want the ticking to be fancy, rating mattress quality by the choice of cover material. Over the last thirty years, the old striped cotton ticking has been displaced by fancy damasks or jacquards as well as printed and quilted materials. Size preferences are shifting, too. A home furnishings publication's survey found that 42 percent of the respondents now own double beds, 24 percent queen size, and 22 percent king size. If they were to buy new bedding, however, only 24 percent of those who currently own double beds would pick that size again; 35 percent wanted queen size, and 29 percent would shift to king size.

Bedding demand is price-elastic. Two-thirds of bedding sales are made on price break. And branding is a crucial decision-making variable. In the manufacturer's survey, 82 percent of the respondents reported that brand name was the major factor in buying decisions when shopping for bedding. Most consumers feel unable to evaluate adequately the performance of bedding before purchasing. Thus the reputations of the manufacturer and retailer become key decision-making criteria. Having a reputation for quality is essential for expensive products like bedding that are bought infrequently.

This case was contributed by George Maggiore, Director of Marketing Research, The Brooklyn Union Gas Co., Brooklyn, NY.

And only a few brand names have good name recognition among consumers.

In bedding, as in many consumer markets, a solid brand name is the result of a long-term process that involves direct product experience, word-of-mouth, promotion, and public relations exposure. Continuous, heavy promotion "legitimizes" a product or company. Consumers think that a heavily promoted brand must be good. And in many cases, this becomes a spiral of strength: As promotion increases, so does market share, which, in turn, supports more promotion. Leading brands therefore continue to increase their market shares at the expense of lesser brands.

Bedding may be the most heavily promoted of all furniture products. Sealy spends $4.5 million, Simmons $4.2 million, and Sears $2.5 million on bedding promotion. National advertising in magazines and on television builds image and brand share. Newspaper advertising for bedding announces special sales.

Many Americans' notion of proper sleeping equipment refers to the following:

A mattress constructed with innersprings and padding on both sides, featuring handles for turning and vents on the sidewalls

A boxspring (foundation) that combines with the mattress as a set into a standard 14-inch thick structure

This perspective is shaped by primary experiences at home, the advertising by mattress makers, and the product offering in retail stores.

Time to Take a New Look?

But change may be on the horizon. Waterbeds and futons have made inroads into the traditional bedding market, suggesting that it may be time to revisit established notions and examine what consumers really want from a bedding product. Under Doug's able leadership, the research team discovers five problem areas that may be converted into opportunities for innovative bedding concepts:

1. Comfort: The psychological problem of how good the bed feels. Discomfort should not interfere with sleep.
2. Support: The physiological problem of averting damage to the user's body.
3. Durability: The mechanical problem of degradation of the structure through use.
4. Bedmaking: The operational problem of maintaining the product in use.
5. Space: The environmental problem of locating, carrying, and converting the structure.

The study included a heavy emphasis on benefit identification and analysis to facilitate concept development and testing. Selected relevant research findings follow.

Consumers were asked to consider a list of twenty-four mattress characteristics and rate them relative to their importance in mattress selection. Comfort (76 percent) and proper body support led the list, followed by guarantee/warranty (66 percent), shape retention (65 percent), firmness (62 percent), and value for the money (59 percent). Firmness is equated with alleviation of back problems, not with sound or comfortable sleep.

When asked what constitutes a "top-quality" mattress, brand name (40 percent) was the bellwether of quality, trailed by firmness (23 percent) and durability (18 percent). Innerspring mattresses are preferred 9:1 over foam mattresses. This may be due to a lack of familiarity with the improvements that have been made in recent years in foam mattress performance characteristics.

Respondents expressed positive purchase interest for the top five benefit statements derived from earlier qualitative research as follows:

• A mattress that is strong, firm, and always springs back (79 percent)
• A mattress that prevents one sleeper from rolling into the other (68 percent)
• A mattress that does not transmit vibration between sleepers (67 percent)
• A mattress that allows better air flow and breathability (65 percent)
• A mattress whose correct firmness is prescribed by your body weight and height (56 percent)

But the potential consumer market incidence for mattress purchase is very limited. Less than one-third of the respondents expects to purchase a mattress within the next two years (30 percent).

Any innovative bedding concepts must take these factors into account. In a market where consumer attitudes have been strongly influenced by a few heavily promoted brands, new entries must incorporate traditional consumer beliefs about bedding, offer relevant additional benefits, and stay within the pricing and promotional context of the market.

Doug presents these findings to Joan and Phil, stating that technology is available for innovative bedding designs and that there is room for innovation in this market.

Discussion Questions

1. What steps should Joan take next in her effort to develop and implement an innovative bedding concept?
2. What consumer problems or benefits should Stecker's new bedding product address?
3. In your opinion, what should be the product characteristics and features?
4. Who would constitute the target market for this new product?
5. What positioning would you recommend for it?

CHAPTER 7

Evaluating New Product Ideas

After the first sorting of ideas has taken place in the screening stage, only a limited number of proposals will have survived this initial hurdle. In its 1968 study, Booz, Allen & Hamilton reported a dramatic reduction, from fifty-eight to about thirteen ideas, in the screening phase—a rejection rate of approximately three-quarters of the ideas originally generated. With a reported starting pool of only seven ideas in the 1980s, only minor reductions by one or two ideas can be achieved during screening, making the current value of this stage somewhat questionable.[1]

The ideas that have not been rejected in the screening stage can be considered the semifinalists. To the screeners, they looked attractive and promising enough to warrant further, more thorough examination. This is the purpose of *business analysis*, the phase of new product evolution immediately following screening. It could be described as a comprehensive study of the probable impact of a proposed new product on a firm's operations. Expanding the information base through marketing research and internal intelligence gathering, the consequences of adopting the idea and converting it into a product are spelled out in considerably more detail than before.

This kind of care and thoroughness is made possible by the fact that because of prior screening only few ideas have advanced to this point. The attention lavished on them could not meaningfully be given to a large number of ideas. On the other hand, a comprehensive analysis of each surviving idea is absolutely necessary because top management will be called on at the end of this stage to make a critical go/no go decision. The premier purpose of business analysis is to come up with recommendations to top management on whether or not to approve a particular idea as a development project.

The end of the business analysis stage thus represents a crucial juncture in the evolutionary process. Every stage and step before this point could be called mental in nature, essentially a triggered process of search for direction in the new product effort. Now the matter becomes quite serious. Depending on the scale of the undertaking, corporate or divisional resources would have to be committed, possibly to a substantial extent. This is also the reason why top management, usually in the form of the executive committee, has to step in rather than leaving this decision to product management.

To move from raw idea to full-fledged business recommendation requires a great deal of effort on the part of many people. First, an idea must be "fleshed out" and transformed into a product concept by pinpointing the prospective product's basic purpose and identifying its key characteristics. This more comprehensive description of a potential product then should be presented to members of the target market for their reaction. This is the *concept test,* which aims to discover whether the concept is viable and appeals to prospects. It also helps to select the most promising concept from several alternatives. Concept testing also sharpens eventual product design by probing for desired product features, turning this wish list into product specifications.

Provided a concept generates a positive market response, the likely repercussions of its implementation and introduction in product form are studied next. To borrow a term from ecological analysis, the firm has to develop an *impact statement* that describes the probable impact of the concept on capacity utilization, employment, image, sales, profit, and a variety of other aspects. In other words, what needs to be examined is how well the concept fits with each functional area and how strongly its adoption will affect each area, either adversely or positively.

Based on projections of price and demand levels, break-even quantities are determined for different marketing mixes and compared with their respective expected volumes. If the results of such break-even analysis are disappointing, product managers can engage in strategic alteration of the break-even point by changing the configuration of the revenue and cost curves. Only if a proper comfort level is reached and the required investment produces sufficient rewards will the concept advance into the finals.

Presuming that a concept has successfully passed these tests of external and internal viability, the next issue to be resolved is whether the firm should produce the item itself or farm out its production to an outside source. Because this make or buy decision can affect the acceptability of a concept, the decision may already have figured prominently in the earlier step of impact statement development. Using outside sources, particularly international sources, can add a whole new dimension to business analysis of new product concepts.

The ultimate purpose of the business analysis stage, however, is to present recommendations to top management as to which of the proposed concepts should be approved as development projects. Predevelopment analysis now has been completed, and the executive committee must decide whether to authorize funding for specific projects or terminate their pursuit. Resources are committed, and the direction of the ensuing effort has been set.

Formulating and Testing New Product Concepts

As stated previously, what emerges from screening are raw ideas that have survived a first review based on the fairly limited information available at the time. They hold sufficient promise, though, to warrant further, more thorough investigation. Toward that end, however, these ideas must be thought out more carefully and expressed in more substantive, testable form. In other words, the surviving ideas must be transformed into *product concepts,* which are essentially descriptions of envisioned products and their features as well as any anticipated variants such as different flavors or sizes.

When evolving an idea into a product concept, product management first must ask itself what problem or need the product is intended to solve.[2] Second, it must define how the product proposes to address the need or problem. And third, it must spell out the relevant features that the product is intended to possess. Ideally, the suggested product will offer a solution to a problem or satisfy a need that has remained unsolved or is being satisfied inadequately. Or perhaps a general solution exists, but the one being proposed is more specific and thus helps in segmenting the market.

Implicitly or explicitly, the problem definition will contain a definition of the target market, that is, the customer group that the product is intended for. The concept statement ultimately must be presented to the target group for testing purposes. Having set the stage by means of the problem definition, the second component of the statement describes the nature of the problem solution. To be appealing and compete favorably with available alternatives, this solution should take an innovative approach or at least contain some novel aspect that prospects are likely to perceive as significant.

The third component of the concept statement offers details concerning the relevant characteristics of the new product. These may relate to the composition of the product, its size, capacity, speed, or other operational features. Of course, the statement should contain only features that make the proposed problem solution or need satisfaction more believable and attractive. Extraneous, irrelevant aspects would only detract from and dilute the impact of the concept. Preferably, some of the features would be unique; at the least, they should be distinctive and important. And these features must translate into benefits that the prospective buyers are likely to consider worthwhile and significant.

Typically containing both verbal and visual elements, a concept statement will usually read like an advertisement. It describes and praises the innovation in several paragraphs of text and in an accompanying drawing or mock-up. The drawing, showing how the product is used, should be kept simple. Unnecessary detail is likely to distract from the core message and should be avoided. The purpose of the drawing is to support and illustrate the text, not to assume a life of its own. A mock-up, used more rarely, is an empty package that permits an interviewee to physically handle the "product."

Figures 7–1 and 7–2 present examples of new product concept statements. They show how a combination of descriptive and persuasive copy and simple drawings can be used to introduce a new concept to a group of potential buyers. Figure 7–1 deals with Counter Lite, an easy-to-install fluorescent lighting fixture for use over kitchen countertops. Figure 7–2 refers to Video Meeting, a high-tech video teleconferencing service for local telephone company business customers.

New Product Concept Testing

After the proper care has been given to the formulation of new product concepts by building the original raw ideas up to operational descriptions, their acceptability must be examined through discussions with representatives of the target market. Such *concept testing* represents qualitative research that is exploratory in nature. Generating numbers is hardly crucial at this point. Rather, the thrust of marketing research is to pinpoint needs and desires, feelings and attitudes, in order to refine and streamline the concept or discard it for lack of a positive response.

The purposes of concept testing are fivefold:

1. Select the strongest concepts from a pool of alternatives.
2. Eliminate weak concepts that find little favor with the target market.
3. Identify key consumer concerns and evaluation criteria in the product category.
4. Determine desired product features.
5. Pinpoint proper product positioning.

The first and second purposes coincide in the sense that they serve to narrow the field further and concentrate resources on the most promising avenues. Thus the selection process clearly continues, and survival of the screening stage does not represent an automatic ticket to development. Intention-to-buy scales or simple preference rankings can be used for this sorting task.

An intention-to-buy instrument asks a consumer to indicate on a scale from 1 to 5 the intensity of current feelings about the concept, envisioning it as a product that is readily available in the marketplace. An example of such a scale is presented in Figure 7–3. Although an intention-to-buy measure is quite preliminary and hypothetical at this point, because the product exists only as an unrefined concept, experience has shown that only concepts that achieve a rating of 1 or 2 ultimately stand a chance to succeed in the competitive game. This early indicator, therefore, has considerable validity in predicting future buyer behavior.

Preference rankings simply ask the respondents which of the six or seven concepts that are typically evaluated in concept testing they like best, second best, and so on. Concepts that consistently rank at the bottom of the list are discarded.

The third function of concept testing—identifying key consumer concerns and evaluation criteria in the product category—provides an essential learning experience for product management in becoming acquainted with a new field of endeavor. One of the things management has to learn is how consumers think and

Preparing a meal on the kitchen counter can be an eye-straining experience. Daylight from windows may not reach adequately. And ceiling lamps are often too far away, possibly behind a person's back, to offer sufficient light for cutting vegetables or meat on countertops.

That is the reason why Counter Lite was created. It provides convenient, efficient lighting for kitchen work surfaces. And it is safe and economical to use.

Counter Lite is a self-contained fluorescent lighting fixture that is 20″ long, 2 1/2″ high, and 3 1/2″ wide. You can easily install it yourself by gluing or attaching it to the bottom of an overhead cabinet.

Counter Lite offers even light distribution and saves energy: the 20-watt bulb included in the package does the work of a 60-watt incandescent bulb! The fixture comes with its own cord and switch. All you need to do is attach it and plug it in.

Counter Lite—easy to buy and easy to use. Saves you money, too—in purchase, installation, and operation. And it gives your eyes new comfort!

FIGURE 7–1
New Product Concept Statement for Counter Lite

In today's business world, many companies have facilities in multiple locations. They may be regionally clustered or spread out across the United States. Managers assigned to these facilities often have a need to meet and discuss important issues. But traveling for this purpose can be expensive and time-consuming.

That is the reason why Video Meeting was developed. It is a service from your local telephone company that enables you to confer live over short or long distances. From specially equipped rooms at different facilities, your managers can discuss their mutual concerns directly with each other. They can relax in comfortable settings that you create according to your firm's specific needs.

Video Meeting eliminates the time and cost of travel. You gain productive time by keeping your managers where they belong. But they still benefit from their colleagues' and superiors' insights and experiences by conferring with them via Video Meeting. Using this service, they can see each other in living color and talk freely without using telephone sets.

Video Meeting is fast, effective, and moderately priced. It gives you all the benefits of meeting in person without the drawbacks of travel time and expenses.

FIGURE 7–2
New Product Concept Statement for Video Meeting (see opposite)

FIGURE 7–3
Intention-to-Buy Scale

1 Definitely will buy the product
2 Probably will buy the product
3 Undecided—may or may not buy
4 Probably will not buy the product
5 Definitely will not buy the product

talk about such products. Technical language may pass by the consumer completely and thus frustrate rather than inform. An "aperture control adjuster" on a prospective camera may simply be a "red button" in the consumer's mind.

Although this kind of response reflects on the language that consumers would use to describe the product, in a broader sense their entire frame of mind relating to the concept must be explored. Product management needs to gain insight into the perception, perspective, and viewpoint of consumers. Management needs to learn whether such products are considered essentials or luxuries and whether their purchases are utilitarian or emotional in nature. It must investigate attitudes as well as purchase and usage patterns. And it must probe for important attributes that affect consumer product choice. These product attributes provide the evaluation criteria that consumers use in choosing between alternative products and point to the benefits that they expect to derive from the use of the product.

This discussion leads to the next purpose of concept testing: to determine desired product features. Whereas the concept statement contains feature and benefit

Meeting Room A

Meeting Room B

descriptions, concept testing examines their desirability. In essence, consumers will be invited to design or redesign the product based on the broad outline contained in the concept statement. They will be asked which of the features should remain, which should be added, and which should be dropped to bring the concept more in line with consumer needs and desires. Reconfiguring the product at this point is inexpensive because no money has been spent yet on product development.

The final outcome of concept testing is an outline for proper product positioning. Having explored the dimensions of the consumers' "perceptual map," product management can identify competitive positions and place the new product in an attractive location as defined by the desired feature combination. This will help greatly in the design of communications efforts related to the innovation. It may also influence the formulation and design of the product itself, as well as its package.

Using Focus Groups in Concept Testing.   The technique used most frequently in conducting concept testing is the *focus group interview*.[3] A versatile qualitative tool, the focus group interview involves the simultaneous interviewing of a small group of potential buyers of the product. A session usually is conducted as a casual roundtable discussion with six to ten participants. A meeting of less than six participants prevents a true discussion; more than ten mean that some will not contribute. Experience has shown the range of six to ten to be ideal for getting input from every attendee.

Recruits for a group session should be chosen from the product's target market, and they must possess relevant experience (e.g., own and use a product in the category) to be able to talk intelligently about the product. The selection of recruits is facilitated by employing a *screening questionnaire,* a brief list of questions designed to determine whether the individual qualifies as a prospective participant. The questions check for recent product experience but add other categories to distract from the true thrust of the research. In this way, one avoids "presensitizing" the subjects, that is, giving them time to think about the topic and come to the session with preconceived notions and premeditated answers. To assemble meaningful groups, the screening questionnaire also includes some demographic information. The questionnaire can be administered either over the phone or in person, such as by intercepting persons shopping in a mall. In either event, the questionnaire should be kept very brief and used only to qualify recruits, not to extract any substantive information on the topic at hand.

To entice recruits to attend interview sessions, they usually are offered an inducement, in the form of a meal or an amount of cash. Even then, some who have agreed to come will fail to materialize. It is good practice, therefore, to overinvite, that is, get twelve to fourteen acceptances. This allows for several "no-shows" and still enables a discussion to take place.

The setting for this discussion should be relaxed and casual, to encourage a free and uninhibited flow of information. It is therefore better to hold such meetings in hotel conference rooms or even specially designed, centrally located facilities that can be rented from marketing research organizations. Such facilities have the advantage of being equipped with recording devices and special mirrors that permit observation from an adjoining room by interested employees of the sponsoring firm.

If not already built in, high-sensitivity microphones should be placed in several locations on the table so that the entire session can be voice taped and no comment is lost. It would be even better to videotape the interview. This would enable careful observation and interpretation of facial expressions, gestures, and body language, in addition to the spoken words. An operator may be needed for the equipment because a session can run anywhere from one to two hours. Name cards should be placed at the seats and refreshments made available.

The key figure in a focus group session is the *moderator,* who introduces the topic and leads the discussion. This person is assisted by a *moderator's guide,* which can be described as a list of questions or issues to be covered during the session. The guide is structured into topical areas to facilitate orientation and provide a logical framework for the discussion. In concept testing, the moderator uses *concept boards* as props, which are simply enlarged versions of the concept statements and drawings or mock-ups. An easel also might be helpful to list key statements made by the participants.

A session gets under way with an introductory statement by the moderator. The moderator will introduce him- or herself and explain the purpose of the gathering as well as the "rules of the game." Everyone is encouraged to speak up at any time and speak freely because there are no right or wrong answers. The use of the recording equipment is explained, highlighting the need to speak one at a time. During the "ice-breaker" or "warm-up" part of the interview, the moderator goes around the table, asking simple factual questions of each participant, such as name, occupation, residence, and product ownership.

During the main portion of the session, the different concepts are presented and discussed one at a time with the help of the concept boards. In conducting this portion, moderators are well advised to follow the guidelines presented in Figure 7–4. These dos and don'ts are based on experience and thus can save a novice moderator from a great deal of grief and aggravation. The moderator must remain flexible throughout the interview, adapting to new circumstances and concerns as they evolve.

Dos	*Don'ts*
Keep discussion on topic.	Don't mention company or brand name.
Cover all questions, though not necessarily in sequence.	Don't permit excursions or verbal battles.
	Don't let anyone dominate the discussion.
Involve all participants.	Don't let more than one person talk at a time.
Play "devil's advocate," if none present.	
Pursue worthwhile ideas of participants.	Don't let an unclear answer stand.

FIGURE 7–4
Guidelines for Focus Group Moderators (*Source:* Reprinted with permission from Eberhard E. Scheuing, "Focus Group Interviews—A Hot Line to Your Customers," in *Marketing Update* [New York: Alexander-Norton Publishers, 1977], p. 3)

The moderator also should probe for more detail when an unanticipated line of thinking emerges. And it takes diplomacy to keep the discussion on topic.

The rewards of focus group sessions can be substantial. These sessions can help fulfill all five purposes of concept testing listed previously. After reviewing concept statements and their visual aspects one by one, participants will be asked to rank them in their order of preference. They also will be called on to indicate the intensity of their intention to buy and to identify the features that they find desirable. This assists in determining market response to the alternative concepts. Two to three focus group sessions will typically suffice in exploring a pool of six or seven concepts. Beyond that, the answers become redundant. And going for the numbers would be dangerous with this technique. Being qualitative in nature, a focus group session is not intended to produce frequency distributions. So head counting becomes a perilous temptation: three out of ten people in a group agreeing on a topic does not mean that 30 percent of the target market hold this opinion. Focus group results are not projectable, because the samples are too small and the participants were not selected at random.

Developing Impact Statements

Concept testing stands at the beginning of business analysis for a good reason: Concepts that do not find a strong, favorable market response are simply not viable. They will never "fly" as products. And technical feasibility becomes irrelevant if a product cannot be sold. So market reaction must be explored before any further internal analysis can meaningfully occur. Those concepts that do well in concept testing, however, are next examined for their likely impact on the firm's current operations.

The impact statements thus developed attempt to measure the probable repercussions of a concept's implementation and introduction in the form of a product. This is done to determine the degree of fit that a concept has with each functional area, as well as the nature and extent of the effect that it will have on each area. Toward this end, the impact analysis framework presented in Figure 7–5 may be used. This exhibit is itself based on the new idea checklist in Figure 4–2 and represents an adaption of this list for the purpose of impact analysis.

In the financial area the essential question is: How will this product affect our financial results over its projected life? Also, what additional investment is required, and how can it be funded? When it comes to research and development, the foremost concern is technical feasibility. If a product cannot be made, it becomes irrelevant that a strong market demand exists and the financial aspects are attractive. Time, talent, and funding needed to convert the concept into a product must be examined carefully. And the likely outcome of all this effort must be projected in terms of the distinctiveness and benefits of the product.

As a company reviews the in-house availability of the requisite production talent and skills, the possible learning curve involved, and the cost of internal production, inevitably the issue arises whether it would be better to farm out production.

(This make or buy decision is discussed more thoroughly in a later section of this chapter.) Purchasing concerns also must be addressed here. Many firms make the mistake of ignoring lead times required for tooling and securing an adequate supply of materials and components for the product and its packaging. They learn, to their regret, that such nonchalance can cost them dearly in lost production time and missed deadlines. Rethinking the product or its package may well be required if materials shortages or unacceptable lead times block the original plan of action. Different materials may have to be substituted or the product reconfigured.

Another line of inquiry is concerned with facilities and equipment needed for the product, both for its production and storage. If current facilities are adequate in terms of available capacity and relationship to the state of the art, no problem exists. If new and/or additional equipment is needed, however, lead times may measure in years and thus interfere with plans for the innovation's introduction. Some relief might be obtained in the used equipment market. An extreme act would be to buy a company in the field primarily for the purpose of obtaining its equipment. But some form of joint venture or contract manufacture may offer a solution.

The marketing area, finally, is represented by a host of questions. They begin with an examination of how well the new product fits in with and enhances the current product mix. Does it simply add depth in the form of a line extension, or does it open up a new dimension by adding a new and promising product line? Is it consistent with the basic makeup of the existing product mix? Are there valuable synergies between the company's present business and the new venture? Does the new product render existing components of the product mix obsolete? And how would it affect the corporate image? Does it fit nicely or will a separate brand identity have to be created?

A case in point illustrates this issue. When Ralston-Purina decided to enter the frozen entree business, it faced a problem. Long known throughout the land as the premier feeder of farm animals and house pets, the company could hardly capitalize on its well-known name to introduce a line of gourmet foods. Marketing both pet foods and gourmet dinners was incompatible in the prospect's mind. Never one to hide its corporate identity altogether, Ralston-Purina chose the name "Checkerboard Restaurant" for its new line—a reference to its corporate symbol, or logo, the red and white checkerboard that has adorned farm feed stores for generations. The venture failed nonetheless for lack of management expertise in a fast-growing but highly competitive market.

Another example underscores the point further. American Machine & Foundry Company had long been in the machine tool business when it began its foray into recreational equipment. Its original name would hardly fit with or enhance an array of products ranging from skis to tennis rackets. Because of the highly lucrative nature of these new products, coupled with the decline in its traditional business, the company changed its name to the meaningless acronym AMF Inc. Similar name changes have occurred in other corporations as they expanded into new lines. Corn Products Company altered its name to CPC International and Columbia Broadcasting System adopted its initials, CBS Inc., when their corporate families grew to include many new fields unrelated to their original names (such as records and publishing in the case of CBS).

Finance

Additional investment required
Length of payback period
Impact on cash position and liquidity
Impact on debt/equity ratio
Impact on cash flow
Impact on sales volume and market share
Impact on profitability—short term
Impact on profitability—long term
Amount of risk involved

Research and Development

Technological know-how available
Need for new engineering expertise
Amount of time needed for product development
Amount of funding needed for product development
Expected degree of competitive distinctiveness
Uniqueness of product features and benefits
Product performance under stress conditions
Potential for expanding range of applications
Availability and extent of patent protection
Environmental impact

Production

Production know-how available
Projected production cost—direct and indirect

FIGURE 7–5
Impact Analysis Framework

A whole complex onto themselves are questions related to a new product's salability to the existing customer base. If the new product addresses the same target market as the current product mix, the present distribution channels and sales organization probably will prove appropriate. If, however, an entirely separate customer group must be acquired and developed, current channels may well be inadequate. To develop and service separate distribution channels for the new product would likely require a new and separate sales organization. This move alone could become very costly and time-consuming unless the new product promised to grow into an entire lucrative line. Otherwise, some other solution, such as using manufacturer's representatives or piggybacking on some other manufacturer's sales organization, would have to be found. If the innovation requires repair and maintenance service, its impact on the existing customer service operation also would have to be examined.

Environmental aspects, such as government regulations, market conditions, and consumer purchasing and consumption behavior, also must be taken into ac-

Ease of procuring materials and components needed
Availability of trained labor
Need for new skills and personnel
Production and storage facilities and equipment needed
Need for new facilities and equipment
Impact on capacity utilization rate—short term and long term

Marketing

Impact on current product mix—width, depth, consistency, salability
Impact on company image
Compatibility with existing distribution channels
Need to develop and maintain separate distribution channels
Salability to present customer base
Need to acquire and develop new customers
Number of potential new buyers
Need for separate sales organization
Government regulations and approval required
Degree and nature of competition—moderate or intense, familiar or
    unfamiliar, domestic or foreign
Projected length of product life cycle
Current life cycle stage of product category
Projected price and quality level
Advertising and sales promotion budget needed
Sales budget required
Impact on customer service operation
Extent of diversification from established business
Anticipated positioning

FIGURE 7–5
continued

count. This is where the basic market and consumer study that was conducted at the outset of the evolutionary process comes into play. It will give insights into the degree and nature of competition as well as the product life cycle characteristics facing the new entry. Price and quality level also can be set in the context of competitive offerings. Given the product features and benefits desired by consumers in concept testing, the innovation's positioning can be strategically formulated. The final concern is the required spending level for personal selling on the one hand and advertising and sales promotion on the other.

Break-Even Analysis

A crucial element in the evaluation of a new product proposal is the determination of the minimum sales volume necessary to cover cost. This quantity is called the *break-even quantity* because it reflects the point where revenues equal costs, that is, where the company breaks even on the new venture. The method employed in computing the break-even quantity is referred to as *break-even analysis.*

The break-even quantity could be considered the profit threshold—the golden gate to profits generated by the innovation. If an additional unit is produced and sold beyond this point, a profit is earned by the new product. The profit increases in linear fashion the more additional units are sold beyond the break-even point. This is so because a "scissor effect" occurs in that the total cost and revenue curves, having intersected at the break-even point, continue to diverge farther and farther from each other. Of course, this process does not go on forever. Eventually, total cost curves up and ultimately intersects the revenue curve once more, producing a second break-even point. Beyond this point, increasing losses are generated because of mounting cost caused by overtime pay, spot purchases of materials, and machine breakdowns. Within the relevant range, however, profits increase steadily for every additional unit sold beyond the break-even quantity.

At times, though, the break-even point of an otherwise very attractive product proves discomfortingly high. This may be due to substantial expenditures for new equipment, relatively high material and labor costs, and/or somewhat moderate revenue expectations. Either way, break-even quantities are not cast in concrete. They can, and perhaps should, be altered by managerial decisions. This process of deliberate modification of revenue and/or cost curves to reduce the break-even point can be referred to as break-even management. Before its tools and implications can be discussed, however, a brief review of break-even analysis is in order.

Determining the Break-Even Quantity

The most basic equation in business reads

$$Profit = Revenue - Cost$$

or, expressed symbolically

$$Z = R - C$$

Because there is no profit or loss present at the break-even point, this formula can be transformed into the *break-even definition* as follows:

$$R = C$$

The break-even quantity, however, at which this condition occurs requires for its computation the splitting of individual cost categories into their fixed and variable components. *Fixed cost* is a type of cost that is unrelated to production volume and remains unchanged regardless of the output level. *Variable cost,* on the other hand, varies directly with production volume, starting at zero at shutdown and increasing proportionately with every additional unit produced. The two main elements of variable cost are direct material and direct labor costs.

Taking this basic distinction into account, the *break-even formula* reads as

$$Q_B = \frac{F}{p - v}$$

or

$$\text{Break-even quantity} = \frac{\text{Total fixed cost}}{\text{Unit contribution}}$$

In all the equations, capital letters symbolize total product-related levels, and small letters refer to unit-level amounts. For instance, F means total product-related fixed cost, whereas p represents price per unit and v stands for unit-variable cost.

The expression *unit contribution* (to fixed cost and profit) refers to the residual value arrived at after the (avoidable) out-of-pocket variable cost per unit has been paid off out of the price achieved for a unit. This remainder can then be used first to pay for the product-related fixed cost—which is incurred anyway, regardless of whether or not the product is produced—and then generate a profit. The break-even formula thus specifies the number of units at which the sum of the unit contributions pays for the total product-related fixed cost so that both fixed and variable costs are covered and no profit or loss exists. Because this is the profit threshold, a lower quantity would mean a loss and a higher number would translate into a profit.

After the break-even quantity has been determined for a given marketing mix, it must be compared with the volume that product management expects to sell under these conditions. This sales forecast in units is called the expected quantity, or Q_E. If the expected quantity is smaller than the break-even quantity, the firm would realize a loss from adopting the respective marketing mix. Only if it is substantially larger than Q_B should product management consider employing the appropriate marketing mix. Where a new product is related to an existing line, its sales projection can be based on that line's track record. Otherwise, the expected volume will be determined by a combination of marketing research information and managerial judgment.

A Case Example of Break-Even Analysis.   The application of break-even analysis in the evaluation of new product proposals is best illustrated by using a case example.[4] This example will show that marketing mix decisions, among others, strongly influence the break-even volume. The number of alternative marketing mixes that can be considered for potential adoption is limited only by product management's imagination and the company's ability and willingness to generate (especially sales estimates) and process data (manual vs. computer processing).

A proposed innovation may, for instance, require an additional investment of $60,000. With an estimated economic life span of five years and a straight-line decrease in value (salvage value at the end of five years = $0), this amount results in a fixed annual depreciation cost of $12,000. Top management assigns the product a share of general overhead amounting to $26,000 per year. The variable cost per unit is determined at $10. For both advertising budgets and distribution cost allowances, two alternative spending levels of $10,000 and $50,000, respectively, are being considered. The price per unit will be set at either $16 or $24.

Given these inputs, the various break-even volumes now can be computed by adapting the break-even formula to this particular situation as follows:

$$Q_B = \frac{F}{p - v} = \frac{I + O + A + D}{p - v}$$

where Q_B = break-even quantity, that is, the quantity required to be sold at a given price to cover the product's total cost

I = annual depreciation of the additional investment necessary for the production of the innovation

O = the proposal's assigned share of general overhead

A = alternative advertising budgets

D = alternative distribution cost allowances

p = alternative prices

v = variable cost per unit

Because the first two components of the fixed cost remain unchanged for all marketing mixes and the variable cost per unit does not fluctuate, the equation can be modified as follows:

$$Q_B = \frac{\$38,000 + A + D}{p - \$10}$$

With depreciation, share of overhead, and variable cost per unit being constant, the break-even quantity necessary to cover cost is solely a function of the marketing mix. The latter in this case is represented by the interplay of the price of the proposed innovation and its advertising and distribution expenditures. The eight combinations possible under the preceding constraints are shown in Table 7–1.

The columns of Table 7–1 should be read as follows: The first column simply gives a consecutive identification number to each of the eight alternative marketing mixes being considered. The second through fourth columns, labeled p, A, and D, reflect two alternative levels each for price, advertising, and distribution cost. If the particular combination of advertising and distribution expenditures is added to the $38,000 identified in the preceding equation, the fixed cost contained in the fifth column is arrived at. The break-even quantity is derived by inserting the fixed cost and the price into the equation. The next column reflects the demand estimates as developed by product management based on available marketing research information.

The last three columns are conditional on the realization of the expected quantity. Total cost is computed as the sum of total fixed cost and total variable cost. In equation form, this can be expressed as follows:

$$C = F + (v \times Q_E)$$

TABLE 7–1
Break-Even Analysis for a New Product Proposal

Marketing Mix No.	Price, p ($)	Advertising Budget, A ($)	Distribution Budget, D ($)	Total Fixed Cost, F ($)	Break-Even Quantity, Q_B	Expected Quantity, Q_E	If Q_E Materializes		
							Total Cost, C ($)	Total Revenue, R ($)	Profit/ (Loss), Z ($)
1	16	10,000	10,000	58,000	9,667	12,400	182,000	198,400	16,400
2	16	10,000	50,000	98,000	16,333	18,500	283,000	296,000	13,000
3	16	50,000	10,000	98,000	16,333	15,100	249,000	241,600	(7,400)
4	16	50,000	50,000	138,000	23,000	22,600	364,000	361,600	(2,400)
5	24	10,000	10,000	58,000	4,143	5,500	113,000	132,000	19,000
6	24	10,000	50,000	98,000	7,000	8,200	180,000	196,800	16,800
7	24	50,000	10,000	98,000	7,000	6,700	165,000	160,800	(4,200)
8	24	50,000	50,000	138,000	9,857	10,000	238,000	240,000	2,000

Total revenue is the product of price and expected quantity:

$$R = p \times Q_E$$

Profit or loss is the difference between revenue and cost, but it also could be expressed as unit contribution times the difference between the expected and break-even quantities:

$$Z = R - C = (p - v)(Q_E - Q_B)$$

Which of the alternative marketing mixes should be chosen depends on product management's philosophy. If it strives for volume or market share, it probably will adopt mix 2, which produces both the largest expected quantity and the highest revenue (mix 4, though characterized by higher numbers, is not a contender because it results in a loss). If profit is the main consideration, mix 5 looks the most attractive. It combines the highest profit with the lowest cost by charging a relatively high price while keeping advertising and distribution expenses at very modest levels. Such a strategy may be appropriate for a radical innovation that meets with enthusiastic consumer acceptance and thus virtually sells itself. Most innovations, needless to say, do not fall into this classification and accordingly require more generous support.

Four of the marketing mixes (mixes 1, 3, 5, and 7) from Table 7–1 have been selected in Figure 7–6 to enable a graphic comparison of the highest profits and losses. The revenue curves are identical for mixes 1 and 3 as well as for mixes 5 and 7, respectively. The total cost curves, on the other hand, are the same for mixes 1 and 5 as well as for mixes 3 and 7, respectively. It is dramatically evident that the higher price reduces the break-even volume to less than half of the original quantity and produces the highest profit at the expected level of demand if the austerity budget proposal is employed. Equally obvious is the fact that the budget combination of $50,000 for advertising and $10,000 for distribution results in losses at the two demand levels generated by the pricing alternatives under consideration.

Engaging in Break-Even Management

Occasionally, a marketing mix looks attractive, for a number of reasons, but its break-even quantity is too high. This could, for instance, be said to be the case for mixes 3 and 4 (see Table 7–1 and Figure 7–6). The price is modest, thus discouraging competition from entering, and volumes and accordingly imputed market shares are substantial, giving the company a solid base to work from and to generate profits. But the break-even quantities exceed the expected quantities in each case, resulting in losses and rendering these options inviable.

These two mixes are somewhat unusual, though, because a company's management rarely will bother to try turning around a loss situation if other attractive options are available. More typical candidate situations involve marketing mixes that result in expected volumes that do not significantly exceed the respective break-even quantities. This leaves a slim margin for error or a narrow comfort zone. Mix 2, for example, features a differential of only 2,167 units, or a mere 13 percent. Other than the extreme case of mix 8, which is priced high and too costly in comparison to its revenue potential, this is the slimmest of the margins produced by the profitable mixes. For mix 6, the differential is smaller yet (1,200 units) but the margin is slightly higher (17 percent). In view of the high price and the attendant vulnerability to competitive inroads of mix 6, its attractive profit nonetheless seems endangered.

Whatever the reason for discomfort, product management need not take break-even quantities as immovable. Rather, management can and should engage in *break-even management*—an active effort to strategically reduce the break-even point. Because the break-even point is affected by three variables, product management essentially has three tools at its disposal in attempting to alter the break-even quantity: increase revenue, reduce fixed cost, and/or reduce variable cost. These tools of prudent management can be employed either separately or in concert.

Increasing Revenue

Raising the price of the new product appears to be the "quick fix" for the break-even problem, increasing revenue in a hurry without much effort. Although this action may well work if kept within reason, product management must be aware of price elasticity. *Direct price elasticity* can be defined as the sensitivity of demand to price changes. The higher the price elasticity, the greater the impact of a price change on the expected volume. Elasticity will tend to be highest for products in the mature stage of their life cycle that lack competitive distinctiveness and are typically bought on price because of the easy availability of substitutes. In this event, raising the price to increase revenue is all but impossible, and lowering the price may increase volume but probably not revenue.

In contrast, if a new product is very distinctive and at least a dynamically continuous innovation, product management may enjoy a considerable amount of pricing flexibility. As a matter of fact, raising the product's price may actually increase its appeal to potential buyers. The demand for innovative quality products tends to be fairly inelastic, so an increase in price would not significantly lower demand and may even increase it because of the snob appeal of increased visibility.

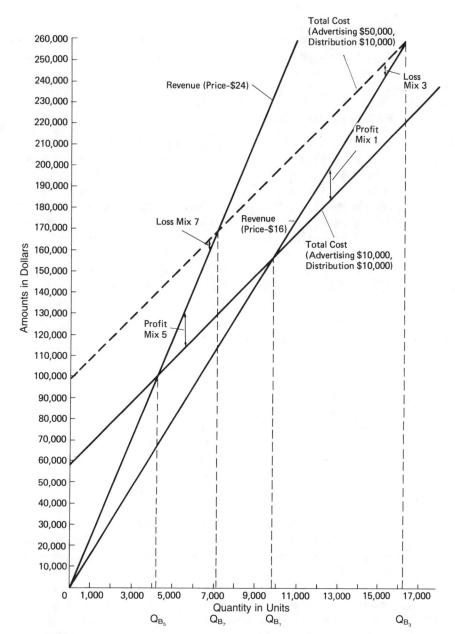

FIGURE 7–6
Break-Even Chart for Selected Marketing Mixes

Instead of raising the price uniformly and charging a single price for the new product, however, product management could consider a strategy of *price differentiation.* Provided that various market segments can be kept separate from each other, different prices would be charged to different segments in the marketplace. Where feasible, this invariably will increase revenue in that less price-conscious segments pay higher prices than under the single-price policy, whereas otherwise untapped groups enter the market at prices below the single-price level. Going from a single-price to a multiple-price approach is indeed a meaningful way to increase revenue if demand is price-elastic.

Reducing Fixed Cost

Another avenue to lowering the break-even quantity is to lower the product-related fixed cost. Where the cost category is discretionary, its level can be reduced by managerial decision. Budget levels for various components of the marketing mix, such as advertising, sales promotion, and personal selling, are among the discretionary categories. Furthermore, the allocation of overhead, including research and development cost, which often is made more or less arbitrarily, can be altered.

Among the more radical ways for bringing down fixed cost are the trimming of staff and the consolidation of production. As domestic and foreign competition have intensified in recent years, the management of many businesses has discovered that the "good old days" of growing sellers' markets—where there was room for bloated organizations and inefficient methods—are over. Instead, so the jargon goes, management has to run a "leaner and meaner" operation, "cutting out the fat" and getting the remaining employees to work harder and smarter. This may mean permanently removing management layers in a reorganization (middle management is the most frequent victim of this approach), offering inducements for early retirement, using attrition to shrink the work force by not replacing workers who leave, or closing offices and/or laying off clerical personnel.

A textbook example of such trimming and slimming is Chrysler, which, under the threat of bankruptcy and the stern leadership of Lee Iacocca, managed to lower its corporate break-even point dramatically. Other automobile manufacturers had similarly painful lessons to learn. Since the advent of deregulation, airlines, trucking firms, and telecommunications companies have been going through a comparable adjustment period. With the safety net of regulation removed, competition is making its impact felt, resulting in major cost-cutting and corporate restructuring programs. AT&T and its former operating companies, to cite but one example from a formerly regulated industry, offered generous inducements to encourage substantial numbers of employees to retire early and thus reduce excessive staffing levels by not replacing them. IBM, too, reduced its work force in this manner.[5]

Consolidation of production was mentioned as another tool in the war on fixed cost. Closing and/or selling off inefficient plants (possibly to employees, as has been the case for some steel plants) and concentrating production at fewer, more efficient facilities reduces fixed cost, frees up capital, and increases productivity. Del Monte closed twelve plants, including eight fruit and vegetable canneries, two distribution centers, and two can-manufacturing plants—without reducing its capacity. Consolidating all tomato processing in one facility made Del Monte a low-cost producer.[6]

Where an efficient plant exists but its fixed cost proves a burden, management may consider a sale-and-leaseback arrangement that releases working capital.

Computer-aided design (CAD) is a way to reduce the cost of product development. The ultimate move in the production area would be to buy rather than make the product, thus making many cost items variable that were formerly fixed.

Reducing Variable Cost

The final option in the break-even reduction effort is to lower the variable cost per unit, which can be achieved in a number of ways. Because variable cost consists primarily of direct material and direct labor costs, one way to lower it is to reduce waste. This can be achieved by using computer-aided manufacturing (CAM) techniques that maximize material yield and minimize scrap, for instance, in cutting. If the material received has a high level of defects, more stringent quality control requirements must be imposed on suppliers.[7] Practicing a company-wide commitment to quality can cut variable cost dramatically. "The typical factory invests a staggering 20% to 25% of its operating budget in finding and fixing mistakes."[8] Preventing quality problems through a zero-defects program simultaneously reduces cost and improves the salability of American-made products.[9]

Perhaps the new product, as it is conceived now, is overengineered so that it possesses more quality than is necessary to fulfill its purpose. Then lower-priced, lower-quality materials might be substituted. This could represent a significant savings because the material content of many products ranges to 50 or even 70 percent of its selling price. Even for the same material quality, shrewder purchasing can lower cost through economic order-quantity purchasing, competitive bidding, cooperative purchasing, overseas sourcing, and quantity discounts on annual blanket orders.

Again, the make or buy issue arises in that many products can be manufactured less expensively by outside vendors than in company-owned plants. Alternatively, the firm may consider moving at least part of the production process abroad to capitalize on low-cost labor, as many firms have done in the U.S.–Mexican border zone. Or they may engage in a joint venture to learn how to produce the product more cheaply at home. General Motors has entered into such an arrangement with Toyota Motor Corporation involving its previously shuttered plant in Fremont, California.

At the direct labor cost end, more and more companies have been bargaining for and receiving union contract concessions. They may involve givebacks—that is, reductions in labor cost, lower wages for newly hired workers, fewer job classifications, or cross-training for different jobs. Management may also consider building a plant at a new location and hiring nonunion labor.

Applying Break-Even Management

As stated earlier, the three tools of break-even management can be applied separately or in combination. Either way, they will move the break-even point to the left in the diagram and thus lower the break-even quantity. In so doing, they not only increase the comfort zone—the differential between break-even and expected quantity—but also the profit earned. Break-even management is therefore a most worthwhile exercise to engage in for those concepts that product management firmly believes in.

In the case example cited, the tools of break-even management can be used in many ways, too numerous to mention here. To pick out just two mixes for illustrative purposes, applications to mixes 3 and 4 will be discussed briefly. Both look like real losers at first sight, generating losses of $7,400 and $2,400, respectively. But they feature substantial volumes and market shares and might be turned around with little effort. Suppose, for instance, that the price could be raised to $18 with no loss in expected volume. With no other changes in mix 3, the break-even volume would drop to 12,250 units. This would mean a profit of $22,800, higher than for any other mix in the original table.

A simultaneous lowering of the fixed cost produces even more dramatic results. Suppose that the price in mix 4 is raised to $18 but the advertising and distribution budgets are cut to $40,000 each. This would reduce the fixed cost to $118,000. Even if this new combination lowers the expected volume to 21,000 units, the break-even point has been shrunk to 14,750 units and a profit of $50,000 emerges. If the variable cost per unit could also be lowered to $9, the profit would increase to $71,000—almost four times as high as the highest profit in the original table and a figure that hardly appeared possible at first sight.

The possibilities of break-even management are truly limitless in the evaluation of new product concepts. But their enthusiastic pursuit has to be tempered by cost/benefit considerations. What kind of effort does it take to achieve significant savings? Are the rewards achievable worth the effort? These are two key questions that have to govern break-even management for those concepts that product management believes hold great promise.

Make or Buy?

Repeatedly throughout this chapter the make or buy option has been briefly alluded to. It concerns the question whether a company should produce a new product in its own facilities ("make") or have it produced under contract by an outside source and resell it unaltered under its own name ("buy"). This, of course, presumes that a decision has been made to proceed with the innovation in the first place.

A case in point will illustrate the principle. Commercially prepared baby food was "invented" quite serendipitously by Daniel F. Gerber in 1927. One evening, his wife asked him to feed their daughter, who sat in happy anticipation in her high chair. Mrs. Gerber handed her husband a strainer with peas and left the kitchen. When she returned, Dan was frustrated, Sally screaming, and the kitchen a battlefield. The incident intrigued Dan, who reasoned that his frustration had to be shared by mothers all over the country. At the time, he happened to be running the Fremont Canning Company in Fremont, Michigan, with his father. The company canned vegetables for adult consumption and had experience in pureeing tomatoes. So he went to work on the challenge and introduced a first line of strained baby food products one year later. Eventually the firm changed its name to the Gerber Products Company and abandoned the adult market altogether. The name Gerber became virtually synonymous with baby food. For many years, the company used the slogan "Babies are our business—our only business" until a steady decline in the birth rate forced it to seek other ventures.

The point of the story is that Gerber decided to *make* the new baby food products in its own facilities. For a small, local company to undertake its first national advertising campaign and marketing program was an expensive and risky thing to do. But the Gerbers chose to go it alone and their gamble paid off handsomely. In contrast, the German baby formula producer Alete selected a much more cautious approach when it decided to enter the baby food arena. In 1956, with no commercially prepared baby food available in the German market, Alete sent a representative to the United States to study its baby food market, which by this time was almost thirty years old. His recommendation that Alete introduce baby food to the German market was accepted. To limit its risk, however, the company decided to enter the market with only two products (as opposed to Gerber's initial five) and have an outside manufacturer produce the initial supply under strict specifications and quality control procedures. Although this approach could have created a potential competitor, Alete did not want to invest in new plants until market volume justified such a move. As expected, market response was most favorable and the company soon shifted to in-house production.

General Foods built a $5 million plant just to test-market Cycle canned dog food. In contrast, Colgate-Palmolive continues to distribute Alpen cereal made by a British cereal manufacturer. The answer to the make or buy question varies from company to company, depending on its objectives and conditions. Zenith has its black and white television sets manufactured overseas under its name because it cannot make them at a competitive cost at home—a circumstance that severely impeded its ability to supply the market when it was hit by a West Coast dock strike.

Benefits and Drawbacks of Outside Sourcing

A number of factors advocate for or against outside sourcing. Cost and control are usually the overriding considerations. They typically work counter to each other: Lower cost favors outside sourcing, less control detracts from it. For one thing, buying from another manufacturer under what amounts to a *private branding* arangement (the supplying manufacturer places the buyer's brand on the product, not its own) eliminates the need to invest in new production facilities, the training of new workers, supervisory salaries, and related fixed costs. Even where existing facilities, personnel, and skills are adequate, "farming out" removes factory overhead and renders the entire production cost variable. This may serve to reduce both cost and risk.

A *cost* reduction would occur if the outside source could supply the product for less money than it could be produced internally. This may be the case if the vendor is further down the learning curve than the in-house facility and can thus produce the product in less time. Also, the supplier may employ nonunion labor or may be located abroad in a country with significantly lower labor cost. Lower energy cost could also be a factor for energy-intensive processes. But even if the cost per unit were identical from external and internal sources, there would still be a *risk* reduction since, as in Alete's case, no up-front investment for productive facilities would be required. Apart from the initial risk of market response to the product's introduction, the risk of ongoing operation is reduced to zero as the entire production cost has become variable. This translates into increased flexibility because the firm is not weighted down by the need to keep dedicated, possibly specialized, facilities and personnel occupied.

Where lower cost, reduced risk, and increased flexibility recommend out-side sourcing, *control* considerations can raise a strong argument against this practice. There is, first, the crucial issue of quality control, more important today than ever before. Quality, perhaps even more so than price, is a key reason why more and more American buyers have learned to prefer Japanese products to their U.S.–made counterparts. A good example is the passenger automobile market where Japanese makes have managed to capture a full quarter of all sales. Belatedly, this success has prompted American car makers to place renewed emphasis on quality, which Ford, for instance, claims is now its foremost concern. Control over product quality is necessarily more difficult if the product is supplied by an independent outside firm. It will typically require inspection control when the merchandise is received instead of permitting constant in-process control as is preached by statistical quality control specialists like W. Edwards Deming. Where a bid is priced very tightly, suppliers may well try to cut corners and will thus often require careful policing.

A second control issue concerns delivery and related services. It will, at times, be difficult to tell whether a vendor will meet the agreed-upon schedule— until it is too late. The damage to the buying firm's business can be incalculable. The third, and perhaps most important, control issue relates to the protection of trade secrets and industrial property rights, such as technical drawings, blueprints, specifications, product manuals, and the like. Farming out greatly increases the number of people who have access to this valuable information. They may leak it inadvertently, pass it on for compensation, or start their own businesses based on it. Worst of all, the buying firm may create a fierce competitor in the process. Having learned how to make the product, the supplier may decide to cancel the contract and enter the field itself. Polaroid, in contracting with Kodak to supply instant film, protected itself with an impenetrable wall of patents against this possibility. When major instant photography patents expired, however, Kodak promptly entered the market with its own version. A successful lawsuit by Polaroid subsequently forced Kodak to abandon this field altogether.

What the make or buy question ultimately comes down to is a cost/benefit analysis. Management has to determine and examine what the firm stands to gain and lose from outside sourcing. It may well gain a significant cost advantage but lose some control. In a compromise solution, it may decide to farm out various components to different suppliers and retain their assembly into the finished product. IBM chose this approach when it first developed its personal computer. Or it may set up production facilities in low-labor-cost countries that it either fully owns or co-owns in a joint venture format. Depending on the firm's objectives and concerns, there are many possible answers to the make or buy question.

A Critical Juncture

It is the principal function of the business analysis stage to advise management as to which concepts warrant being turned into development projects. Toward this end, the concepts are subjected to in-depth scrutiny in three respects: market, technological, and financial.

Market response is explored in concept testing that uses focus group interviews to find out which concepts are most appealing to consumers and what features they would like to see incorporated. *Technological analysis* tries to ascertain in discussions with research and development personnel whether it appears feasible to turn the product specifications that have emerged from concept testing into operational products. It also reviews the make or buy question from a technical perspective: Does the capability and capacity to produce this item currently exist within the firm? If not, does it make sense to create the necessary production capacity in-house, or would it be better to seek outside sources?

Financial analysis looks into the investment and cost aspects of the proposed new product. It investigates what kind of budget and time frame will be required for research and development. It also examines the additional investment necessary for new production equipment if the make option is chosen. And it computes the break-even point under different marketing mix configurations. Where appropriate, financial analysis may even engage in break-even management, strategically altering the location of the break-even point to make an innovation economically more viable. Break-even analysis as a method can even be applied to the make or buy question where it may well conclude that the costs of both alternatives equal each other at some point—the break-even point. Below this point, the buy option will likely involve lower cost, whereas the make option produces cost savings beyond the break-even point. This break-even quantity would then be compared to the expected volume, as discussed earlier. And break-even management applies here as a principle just as well.

Recommendations to top management then culminate the predevelopment analytical effort. It alone, as pointed out in Chapter 3, makes the crucial go/no go decisions at this critical juncture. All evolutionary activities up to this point can essentially be considered mental in nature. They basically involved the use of some human resources and a fairly limited level of expenditures. In its 1968 study, Booz, Allen & Hamilton measured the shares of the overall time and expenditures for successful new product introductions that were consumed by the stages of the evolutionary process. Significantly, it reported that on average some 10 percent of total expenditures and some 15 percent of the total time had cumulatively been incurred by the end of the business analysis stage.

This point represents a critical juncture because action must now begin. The luxury of analysis can only be afforded up to a point where it turns into paralysis.[10] Analysis is important and helpful, but it can become dysfunctional and counterproductive if it becomes excessive. It can neither replace managerial judgment nor eliminate risk. At the very least, analysis takes time, and time gives competition an opportunity to preempt the marketplace. So analysis should not be allowed to assume a life of its own, growing steadily and consuming continuously more money, time, and people. Rather, business analysis has to be conducted with clear funding, personnel, and time limits. Of course, these limits have to be adequate and reasonable or management would shortchange itself and the company.

Although creative thinking and analytical responsibilities will continue throughout the evolutionary process, a quantum leap takes place as the transition from business analysis to product development occurs. In essence, it is a discontinuous move from contemplation to action. Human, financial, and physical resources have to be committed, possibly at substantial levels and over extended periods of time. This by far transcends the realm of product management. It involves corporate priorities and resource allocations. This is why top management in the form of the executive committee enters into the evolutionary process in a rare appearance.

Before this ultimate decision-making body, product managers act as product champions—"individuals who believe so strongly in their ideas that they take it on themselves to damn the bureaucracy and maneuver their projects through the system and out to the customer."[11] In the fierce interdivisional competition for corporate resources, they have to plead their cases forcefully and come well prepared for detailed questioning. If they have not done their homework adequately and the documentation is not substantive enough, their proposals will at best be returned for further study and at worst shot down instantly and permanently. Only truly promising ventures will get the corporate nod of approval.

Of course, an executive go decision does not mean that the project is home free. Rather, an important hurdle has been cleared, and funding and support secured. Top management has to be kept informed about the status of the project through periodic progress reports and perhaps update briefings. But for now, with top management clearance, an idea-turned-concept has become a project ready to enter the product development phase and be transformed into a product.

SUMMARY

This chapter described the comprehensive business evaluation of those few ideas that survived the screening phase intact, having made a good initial impression. Commonly referred to as business analysis, this stage aims to determine which of these remaining ideas fit well in the total corporate context *and* promise to add sufficient sales and profits to justify the application of scarce corporate resources. The chapter began by clarifying that new product ideas actually have to be exploded into more elaborate product concepts in order to enable a thorough analysis of all their ramifications. New product concept testing begins this examination by researching market reaction to each innovative concept. Focus group interviews are used not only to have target group members select attractive concepts but also to have them specify desired benefits.

Once a concept has been tested and refined through concept testing, a long series of "what if" questions are asked. They try to determine the likely impact on the firm's operations of adopting the concept and developing it into a product. This impact analysis includes the projected cost of launching the product in the marketplace and covers the functional areas of finance, research and development, production, and marketing.

A crucial part of the comprehensive evaluation effort is break-even analysis. Its purpose is to determine the break-even quantity, that is, the number of units that have to be produced and sold in order to cover product-related cost and start earning a profit. Where this point proves to be unacceptably high for an otherwise very attractive product concept, break-even management can be used to improve the situation by either increasing revenue or reducing cost.

The question of make or buy concerns itself with the relative merits of internal sourcing versus external sourcing of the final product. Lower cost and less control are the two major issues related to outside sourcing. Depending on the relative importance of these benefits and drawbacks, the company will decide for or against this avenue.

The end of the business analysis stage represents a critical juncture. A decision has to be made by top management to accept or reject product management's project recommendation. If the product champions have their case well prepared, they may obtain the crucial go signal from the management committee. This clears the way for the provision of corporate resources and turns a new product proposal into a product development project.

NOTES

1. See Booz, Allen & Hamilton, Inc., *New Products Management for the 1980s* (New York: Booz, Allen & Hamilton, Inc., 1982), 14.
2. A good discussion of concept formulation can be found in Eugene J. Cafarelli, *Developing New Products and Repositioning Mature Brands* (New York: John Wiley & Sons, 1980), 90–91, 110–111.
3. This discussion of focus group interviews is based on Eberhard E. Scheuing, "Focus Group Interviews—A Hot Line to Your Customers," in *Marketing Update* (New York: Alexander-Norton Publishers, 1977).
4. This example was developed by the author based on Philip Kotler, *Marketing Management* (Englewood Cliffs, NJ: Prentice-Hall, 1967), 326–328.
5. See Aaron Bernstein, "How IBM Cut 16,200 Employees—Without an Ax," *Business Week,* 15 Feb. 1988, 98.
6. See Robert A. Fox, "Putting Marketing on a 'Business' Basis," presentation to 1982 Marketing Conference, sponsored by The Conference Board, New York, 20 Oct. 1982, 16.
7. See Ross H. Johnson and Richard T. Weber, *Buying Quality* (New York: Franklin Watts, 1985).
8. Otis Port, "The Push for Quality," *Business Week,* 8 June 1987, 132.
9. See Philip B. Crosby, *Quality Is Free* (New York: McGraw-Hill, 1979), and Kenneth H. Bacon, "Higher Quality Helps Boost U.S. Products," *Wall Street Journal,* 11 Jan. 1988.
10. See Thomas J. Peters and Robert H. Waterman, Jr., *In Search of Excellence* (New York: Warner Books, 1984), 31–54. In reporting on the characteristics of "excellent" American companies, the authors stress "a bias for action" as a major theme throughout their book.
11. Ibid., xvi.

CASE STUDY

BEAR ESSENTIALS

Bear Essentials is a small company that manufactures stuffed toy bears and their clothing accessories. The company was founded in 1975 by Jack Diamond at age thirty-nine. His personal involvement, combined with the efforts of its salespeople, have made the company well known throughout the East Coast region. In 1987, Bear Essentials reported sales of $14 million, reflecting an increase of 9 percent over 1986 and an average annual growth rate since its founding of about 16 percent. The company's plant is located in Peekskill, New York. It also owns a warehouse distribution center in Tampa, Florida. Bear Essentials currently employs 142 people, including 10 salespeople who report to regional managers in Boston, New York City, and Raleigh, North Carolina. Salespersons work on a commission of 5 percent of gross sales (minus returns) and receive a guaranteed minimum weekly draw.

Jack Diamond started his business by selling his bears to specialty shops in upstate New York where he was born and raised. He then expanded distribution by introducing the bears to department and discount stores on the East Coast. Bear Essentials' product mix consists of five sizes of teddy bears that can be dressed in various outfits that Bear Essentials produces. Clothing for the bears consists of boy or girl playclothes, casual wear clothes, and suits and dresses for "dress-up." For the Christmas season, Bear Essentials dresses the bears in a variety of red and green holiday clothing. A big seller is a pair of wedding bears, a set consisting of one bear wearing a tuxedo and the other a wedding gown. The wedding bears retail for $39.99; the other bears sell for $10.99 to $25.99, depending on their size. Changes of clothing for the bears can be purchased separately.

In recent years, the $12 billion toy industry has been experiencing difficulties. Declining popularity of a number of "hit" toys reduced industry profits by 70 percent in 1986. The major competitors

in the industry are Coleco Industries (Cabbage Patch Kids), Mattel (Masters of the Universe), Hasbro (Transformers), and Kenner Parker Toys (traditional toys and family board games). Hasbro is known as the foremost toy company in the world, boasting $1.2 billion in sales and profits of $99 million. Growing inventories forced price cuts and special promotions in 1986. Coleco and Mattel ended 1986 in the red and Hasbro suffered a decline in per share earnings for the first time in six years. The major trend for these large companies seems to be high-tech toys, mostly talking toys (Teddy Ruxpin, for instance). Technology has invaded the toy business with a vengeance. There are rumors that Coleco is planning and hoping for another blockbuster, namely, Cabbage Patch Kids that talk and sing and will retail for $100! Ohio Art, the company that invented Etch A Sketch in 1960, has survived in the toy business by avoiding the fads. In 1986, the company developed the Etch A Sketch Animator. Basically, it is an electronic version that plays back images in rapid succession, cartoon style. It is, however, one of the most expensive toys, retailing for $80.

Jack is worried because Bear Essentials has not expanded its offering in more than five years. The only changes made have been those relating to the clothing of the bears. He is aware that the toy industry as a whole has moved into high-tech toys and he feels that it is time for the firm to become more innovative. Looking for new ideas and eager to grow Bear Essentials, Jack recently hired Marty Randall to head the company's marketing department and spearhead its new product effort.

A New Concept

After careful investigation and examination of the current state of the toy industry, Marty Randall comes up with an idea that builds on the firm's expertise and reputation in toy bears. He meets with Jack Diamond and Ted Forsythe, the general sales manager, to discuss his thoughts. "In my opinion, it would be better for Bear Essentials not to enter the com-

This case was prepared by Meryl Schaffer, graduate research assistant at St. John's University, New York, New York, under the guidance of Joseph Chasin, Associate Professor of Marketing

petitive high-tech portion of the toy industry. Although adults may feel that these kinds of toys are pretty intriguing, most children lose interest in them very quickly and go back to playing with simple, basic toys. The manufacturer is often left with high inventory. Besides, high-tech toys are much more expensive to produce and our company has no experience making such toys." Marty feels that the firm is too small to run this kind of risk.

Instead, he has formulated a new product concept for Bear Essentials that is in keeping with its current product mix, namely, the concept of "Action Bears." Action Bears stand fourteen inches tall and feature strapped-on roller skates. The bears are made of plastic and are sturdy, not soft and cushy like most other bears. Because they are battery-powered, their arms and legs move and the skate wheels turn, enabling the bears to skate. They will be packaged in a strong box with a see-through cover. Children can play with the bears and use their imagination. The Action Bears wear sporty clothing, but additional outfits will be available. The bears are given some degree of uniqueness by embroidering individual names on their backs. "Children love animals, especially bears, that can do the things they would like to do. If the Action Bears on skates catch on, other Action Bears pedaling tricycles or driving cars can be introduced as well."

Marty continues: "Our overhead at Bear Essentials is quite modest. We have managed to increase productivity through the acquisition of very sophisticated automated machinery. Our current business will not suffer as we gear up for this new product." He adds: "I estimate our additional fixed costs to be about $150,000. Our cost to manufacture and market the Action Bears will then be about $7.50 per bear. Since I believe that we can sell them for $10.00 each, we will be earning a profit of about 33 percent per unit. The retailers, in turn, would sell the product for about $20, which is a reasonable price to pay for an action toy. We should do some research to determine how the consumer reacts to Action Bears."

Marty explains that a good toy is one that is attractive, interesting to children, well constructed, durable, safe, and good for children of various ages. Marty envisions annual sales exceeding 250,000 units. Marketing research can help determine if Action Bears fulfill the requirements for good toys and promise to be financially successful.

If Bear Essentials chooses to go ahead with Action Bears, the firm must act rather quickly. Marty presents a broad outline of the timetable. A hand-made prototype can be developed by the end of February. Marketing research can take place during March and April, with the results available in May. If the concept and prototype testing indicate the likelihood of success, the sales force can present the new product to customers in June for Christmas orders, which would have to be placed by August. Production would gear up with the goal of delivering the goods by late October or early November. Marty points out that the toy industry operates essentially on a two-month-a-year basis. Profits in this business are achieved mainly in December and January.

Jack is disappointed that in six months Marty has produced only one new product concept. But after thinking about Marty's arguments, he agrees that the firm has the ability to produce this item efficiently and at a relatively low cost per unit. He meets with the marketing research manager, Tom Lever, and explains the product concept to him, using the visual aids that Marty provided. He asks for a research project to determine the acceptability of the concept and its potential success in the marketplace.

A Proposed Marketing Research Program

Within two days, Tom meets again with Jack and presents him with an outline for a complete marketing research program. "The first step in the program will be focus group sessions in early March. From these groups, we should obtain first reactions to the Action Bear concept and perhaps gain ideas for additional concept variants." Tom further explains that the sessions will be conducted with parents of children five to nine years old. Randomly selected households in Essex County, New Jersey, will be contacted by telephone and screened for qualifications.

The recruited parents will be subdivided into two groups, according to income levels. The objective is to generate feedback from toy purchasers and measure their degree of price sensitivity. The group sessions will take place in a convenient location under the leadership of a trained moderator. The parents will first be shown the Action Bear concept on a presentation board to determine their reactions to the concept itself. Then they will be exposed to the actual prototype Action Bear on its roller skates and receive a demonstration of its performance characteristics. The total cost of the two focus group sessions is estimated at $6,000.

If the reaction of parents in the focus groups is positive, the second step of the research effort will be to watch children actually playing with the Action Bears. The children will be selected according to age and sex and grouped into sets of five. In a playroom, each group will be given an Action Bear, other bears produced by Bear Essentials, Fischer Price blocks, and Teddy Ruxpin with which to play. The play activities of the children will be observed by a child psychologist for seventy-five minutes through a two-way mirror and videotaped for later review. The cost of the five play groups, including videotaping, is estimated at $15,000.

If the results are favorable, a third step of the research project will be undertaken. It involves an in-home test in which prototype Action Bears are placed in 100 homes with children five to nine years old for one month in late March. Parents will be asked to comment on how the child reacts to and plays with the toy, and whether the child continues to show an interest in the toy over the course of the month. They will also be queried whether they would buy it for their children. Tom has learned that handmade prototypes will cost about $30 a piece. While they would be similar in appearance to mass-produced Action Bears, they would have to be made of different materials. The cost of this research phase is estimated at $5,000, including the cost of the prototype production.

A fourth and final step in the research program will be limited test marketing in late April. Tom points out that the results of this type of testing can be very ambiguous because it is small and of short duration. "One can really never be sure how a new product will sell until it is out on the shelves in key distribution areas." Fifteen Action Bears each will be placed in a total of nine stores in three cities with appropriate promotional support. Once again, handmade prototypes will be used. How the bears sell in April will serve as a reasonable indication of the level of sales during the ten off-months of the year. From these results, one might be able to project what Christmas sales could be. The cost of this step is estimated at $9,000, including the cost of manufacturing the prototypes.

Jack Diamond digests these details. The cost of the entire research project amounts to $35,000. While he realizes that this represents a substantial expenditure, he is also aware of the value of research and the insights that it can provide. It is often indicative of how well a new product will sell. He senses that Action Bears can be a hot item. But in the ever-changing toy industry, who can be sure?

Discussion Questions

1. What is your opinion of the Action Bears concept? How well does it fit with the current product mix of Bear Essentials?
2. Are all the stages outlined in the marketing research proposal necessary? Would you suggest other types of research? What specific information would you want to obtain from the different research phases?
3. If you were the focus group moderator, what areas of questioning would you explore?
4. If you were a parent in one of the focus groups, what strengths and deficiencies would you see in the Action Bears concept?

CHAPTER 8

Research and Development

After due authorization of a new product development project, the research and development department is called on to turn the concept into a salable reality. Product management hands over to the engineers and scientists market-based specifications as to what the ultimate product is supposed to look like and be able to do. But it continues the dialog and liaison to keep the developmental effort on target. As the product evolves, product management maintains contact with the marketplace to obtain feedback on the accuracy of product-market fit.

Surprisingly, small firms have a differential advantage when it comes to research and development. Economic logic would seem to suggest that their limited resources put them at a severe disadvantage and restrict them to copying the products of their larger competitors. Instead, their small size enables them to act and react quickly. Where they encounter difficulty is in capitalizing on their technical successes, turning them into economic successes as well. Large firms, in contrast, while slow in developing new technologies, may have more innovations available than they care to pursue themselves. In this event, they may license fully developed products to outsiders and assist in their implementation. A company can also avail itself of the option of contracting for research and development with an independent laboratory.

No matter where it is done, however, research and development is carried out in four distinct ways. *Basic research* is scientific research aimed at discovering new technologies. *Applied research* takes these new technologies and attempts to find useful applications for them. *Product development* goes one step farther and converts applications into marketable products. This means that the company has taken the important step from scientific exploration to commercial exploitation. The final type of research and development is called *product modification*. Occasionally also referred to as modification research, it involves changes in existing products, either cosmetic alterations or true functional improvements. These four categories are discussed in depth in a later section of this chapter.

A closer look at product development reveals that it moves through several stages, from an early conceptual phase to the ultimate release for full-scale production. In the process, several sequential cycles of design, construction, testing, and refinement occur. Ultimately, what works in prototype form has to be adapted for production line manufacture. And along the way, product management and technical personnel have to interact closely and continuously. Marketing and technical research have to work hand in hand in order to produce the best possible results and avoid snags that can doom a product. The product specifications formulated in the concept testing phase provide powerful guidance. Nonetheless, they may have to be updated and double-checked, especially if the product development process proves to be time-consuming or if some unexpected technology becomes available.

Determinants of Success in Research and Development

Research and development (R&D) is the technical, engineering, and/or scientific component of the evolutionary process. Its research element is more scientific in nature, aiming to discover new technologies and materials and exploring their range of applications. The development element is more commercially oriented and is directed at developing salable products. While some firms engage in pure research, it is the development element that is involved in all evolutionary processes. It encompasses the technical conceptualization and design of new products. It also includes the building and testing of models and prototypes. And it incorporates any refinement, redesign, or update of a product as well as ongoing cooperation with purchasing, production, and product management.

Available evidence indicates that carefully administered R&D programs can make significant contributions to the growth of a company's sales volume and profits and that their neglect spells doom. As a general rule, the higher a firm's R&D expenditures in relation to sales, the larger are its sales volume, profits, and future growth potential.[1] This generalization should be taken with a grain of salt, however. After all, it is not so much the quantity but rather the quality of the research effort that determines the outcome.

Small companies are not necessarily at an insurmountable disadvantage in the technology race, hampered by their limited resources. To the very contrary, they may enjoy a differential advantage because they are driven by an entrepreneurial spirit and the few members of the R&D team have less red tape and specialization to fight. Small companies can very well pioneer new products, often better than their larger competitors because the close working relationship within the management group offers more flexibility. Silicon Valley and the New England high-tech corridor are awash with examples of upstart firms that are defying the odds in developing highly innovative products. Because individual team members are often far more independent and influential than in a large firm and may in fact even own "a piece of the action," some small enterprises are able to attract capable, creative engineers who can achieve remarkable results, even on a modest budget.

An example underscores this point. A small company developed a process for duplicating a protective coating. With a grand total of fifty employees, it employed just two chemists on its research staff. During the course of one year, one of them spent part of his time on the project—at a total cost of $1,100. In comparison, it took a large firm with 20,000 employees, a 500-person protective coating division, and a development laboratory staff of fifty chemists and technicians eighteen months and $11,000 to do the same job.

How could this happen? Motivation is one likely explanation. In small companies, researchers have easy access to, and ready support from, top management. As a matter of fact, they may well be co-founders and co-owners of the enterprise. In any case, they are strongly and prominently involved in the affairs of the company on a daily basis and can clearly see the impact of their work. Members of an R&D unit in a large organization, on the other hand, may have to contend with a discouraging amount of bureaucratic red tape and diseconomies of scale. A second explanation may derive from specialization. In large organizations that employ thousands of people in research and development, specialization can become counterproductive and dysfunctional. Individuals who have been selected to make their expert contributions to their assigned pieces of the overall puzzle may lose sight of the "big picture," thus undermining the ability to fit all the pieces together smoothly. With the division of labor can come problems of communication, coordination, cooperation, and transfer of knowledge.

When creative, dynamic researchers become frustrated with the rejection of their inventive ideas by superiors who follow a different set of priorities, they may well leave the corporate environment and set up their own firms. Many computer companies have been started by IBM alumni, among them Gene Amdahl, who wanted to build large computers. Ingenuity alone, however, does not spell success—as Amdahl found out, flirting repeatedly with bankruptcy. And Osborne even ended up in bankruptcy court, in spite of an extremely popular portable computer. This goes to show that a good product does not sell itself but requires a good dose of staying power and marketing ability. Apple Computer acknowledged as much when it hired John Sculley, the former president and marketing whiz from Pepsi-Cola. Sculley proceeded to evict co-founder Steve Jobs and revive Apple's sagging fortunes.

Frequently, large companies are too sluggish to be truly innovative and daring, and their new product development cycles are far too long and slow to keep up with the competition. Many firms have realized this disadvantage and taken drastic steps to reduce it. In the early 1980s, it took Xerox an average of four to five years to develop and introduce a new copier. After laying off 17,000 people and cutting manufacturing costs by more than 50 percent, the company has slashed this time frame in half. But it needs to do more to meet Japanese competition head-on.[2] Conversely, IBM managed to bring out the original PC in one year by using the skunkworks approach. After folding the PC operation into its mainstream organization, the Personal System/2 arrived nearly two years late. Understandably, one of the major goals of the company's massive reorganization in 1988 was the achievement of speedier development cycles.[3]

While often being innovative, small companies have difficulty capitalizing on their inventions. Although corporate giants could readily afford to buy them, such moves have often backfired because entrepreneurial spirits leave. Instead, the two may join forces in a joint venture. The small firm provides the technology and the large partner the financing, thus preserving the motivation of key people in the small company and giving the large company the benefit of cutting edge technology. The small firm gains credibility, visibility, and access to a substantial resource pool, which enables it to concentrate on inventing. The large partner does what it does best, namely, produce the invention economically and market it aggressively through its nationwide or even worldwide presence and distribution network.

This kind of pattern has been characteristic of biotechnology firms, although typically not formally in a joint venture format. Major pharmaceutical companies have assumed minority equity positions (usually no more than 10 percent) in promising bioengineering firms like Biogen or Genentech, even on an international basis. In return for supplying capital and staying power through the critical early years when expenditures abound and revenues are virtually nonexistent, corporate equity partners normally receive first call on licensing arrangements for resulting new products. This arrangement permits the biotechnology firms to pursue their main interest of research while having access to an adequate capital base and obtaining a steady revenue stream.

Another relatively new and fairly promising form of joint effort is *cooperative research and development*. Here, several firms within an industry join forces, jointly financing and operating a research center that benefits all sponsoring companies. Usually set up in a research park that has close ties to nearby leading universities and often supported by substantial government incentives, such research centers are typically run on a not-for-profit basis to advance the state of the art. The results of a center's research and development efforts are available on equal terms to all participating firms.

Occasionally, the stakes in new product development become too high even for the biggest corporations in an industry. In 1984, Boeing conceived the 7J7, a fuel-efficient, medium-range, 150-seat airplane for the 1990s. Anticipating a development cost of $3 billion, Boeing invited Japanese manufacturers to assume a 25 percent equity partnership in the project. The Japanese firms enthusiastically agreed, eager to gain access to cutting-edge technology, and some 100 Japanese engineers moved to Seattle to work on the project. After spending $100 million on the 7J7 over a three-year period, however, Boeing abruptly reassigned two-thirds of the 900 employees working on the project and indefinitely delayed the introduction of the plane, perhaps because of the threat of a takeover by raider T. Boone Pickens.[4]

The scope of R&D can thus range all the way from an individual in dogged pursuit of an unusual idea, risking his or her own money, to giant multinational firms pooling resources because a given project would strain their separate capabilities. Even governments may become involved. As Japan prepares for a major participation in the worldwide computer market of the future, substantial government funds have been made available for industry efforts to develop artificial intelligence. With the possibilities spanning such a broad gamut, the question arises as to what factors determine success in R&D. This question is addressed in the following section.

Criteria of Research Success

Successful research and development is more likely to occur if a number of key factors are in place: objectives, intelligence, knowledge, creativity, organization, improvisation, communication, money, and time.

Objectives.   Without clearly stated objectives, no research effort can be expected to succeed. Within a system of management by objectives, corporate objectives translate into objectives of the R&D department and ultimately into project objectives. The project leader has to be thoroughly familiar with the applicable objectives and review periodically how well they are being met. Without objectives, the research effort would be rudderless and its success could not be measured and controlled adequately.

Intelligence and Knowledge.   It is also a truism that research requires intelligence—a person's ability to think logically and analytically and to understand and dissect a problem thoroughly and comprehensively. Intelligence without knowledge, however, is of little use. Research scientists must be familiar with the body of knowledge in their particular field and must keep up with the latest developments, methods, and findings—a formidable task, as it has been estimated that technological knowledge doubles every ten years and many fields, such as semiconductor technology, evolve very rapidly. Scientific journals, seminars, and conventions are just some of the means for this continuing professional education for researchers, designed to meet the challenges of tomorrow. Without this ongoing effort to keep themselves informed about the state of the art, researchers would fall hopelessly behind and would have to reinvent the wheel over and over again in a most wasteful fashion that could also result in patent litigation because of alleged infringement on existing patents.

Creativity.   Knowledge, in turn, has to be complemented by an individual's ability to generate innovative thoughts. Creativity in the form of original ideas is the mark of a good researcher. It can become a crucial element in a firm's attempt to distinguish itself from its competitors and gain an edge over the competition. Only products and processes that are distinctive and different enough from currently available alternatives are patentable. Without the uniqueness and potential leadership that spring from creativity, a company is likely to become an also-ran.

Research Organization versus Improvisation.   The fifth component of research and development success is organization. This aspect involves planning and budgeting, scheduling and coordinating, assigning authority and responsibility, and directing and controlling. Organization of research activities and efforts further means supervision that calls for a unique combination of skills, namely, scientific knowledge and leadership ability. This combination is apparently present in Arno A. Penzias, the Nobel Prize–winning astrophysicist who heads the research effort at AT&T Bell Laboratories.[5]

In contrast to Penzias's ebullient nature, however, many scientists are introverted intellectuals who detest any responsibility for managing others and instead prefer to work by themselves, unaffected by funding constraints and deadlines. Creativity, they say, is unpredictable, and problems will often occur that need to be conquered. For these reasons, they object to being pinned down to cost estimates and project completion dates.

Organization of the R&D function is necessary to establish working relationships and ensure project completion within a predetermined time frame. Without organization, chaos would result, individual efforts would not be coordinated and synchronized, and specialization and teamwork would be impossible. Organization ensures clear cooperation, steady progress, and timely evaluation. It possesses built-in checkpoints and triggers corrective action when a project veers out of control. It thus acts as an invaluable tool in the execution of a project.

Improvisation.   Not all situations, however, can be provided for in manuals, policies, guidelines, rules, and formal relationships or flow diagrams. Unanticipated conditions, opportunities, and challenges may require improvised responses. Thus improvisation takes over where organization leaves off. It helps fill in the gaps and cope with new and one-time situations. Whereas organization deals with repetitive tasks and stable structures, improvisation is concerned with keeping the creative atmosphere flexible and adaptive, finding prompt solutions to first-time problems. Organization tends to regulate the creative effort and can become overbearing or even stifling and counterproductive. Improvisation complements organization by dealing with the unforeseen and managing the extraordinary.

Communication.   By necessity, R&D involves communication—an exchange of ideas and findings or transfer of information from one individual to another. Communication plays a vital role in research as it links development personnel to the marketplace instead of letting them operate in isolation. In the mid-1950s, Bell Labs developed the picturephone, a strictly technology-driven product for which no market has developed in the more than thirty-five years since its inception. "Today Bell Labs would let the market determine whether it would develop a Picturephone."[6] In fact, to a growing extent, R&D people work closely with marketing and manufacturing personnel in a team effort. At Allen-Bradley Company such teamwork cut the development time for a new electrical contactor from six to two years.[7] Many development engineers even work directly with selected customers.[8]

While marketplace and manufacturing input are essential, internal communication among researchers is equally important. This can be difficult if they work in different locations, particularly if the labs are located in different countries. Many multinationals maintain research laboratories in a number of countries to take advantage of local talent, be responsive to host government demands for locally developed technology, and overcome the "not-invented-here" syndrome. To benefit from each other's insights and avoid inefficient duplication of effort under such a decentralized arrangement, regular dialog is necessary. General Foods holds semiannual meetings of its European product development managers, and IBM rents transatlantic phone lines to facilitate daily contacts between researchers on both sides of the Atlantic Ocean. In addition, each of IBM's European laboratories has "a full-time communications officer to maintain close contacts with other labs in Europe and in the United States."[9]

Wherever and whenever personal interaction is possible, the formal or informal discussion of roadblocks and results, of delays and discoveries, of side effects and by-products, of needs and outlooks, advances scientific progress. But the interchange of experience and insights should reach beyond the confines of a corporate family and cover the scientific community at large, even on an international level. Conventions of professional associations, scientific journals, industry-sponsored seminars, and workshops are among the many platforms on which this mutually beneficial exchange can take place. Of course, caution—including patent protection—must be taken not to reveal trade secrets gratuitously.

Money and Time.   Research and development often involves the expenditure of large sums of money, possibly over extended periods of time before a payoff is forthcoming. While economic advisability and technical feasibility have to be carefully checked and rechecked as development proceeds, it is self-evident that technological progress is unlikely to come about without sufficient investment. Lack of funds seriously hampers the completion of a project or may even render it impossible. Adequate funding is thus an essential prerequisite for success at the development stage.

The final element of research success is time. Performance pressure conflicts with the creative development and thorough testing of unique and technically mature products and is likely to affect the quality of the outcome. Tight scheduling may lead to shortcuts in design, testing, or refinement of new products. A product with superior performance, quality, and reliability can be obtained only from time-consuming cyclical series of design, test, and redesign until the optimum combination is found. Procter & Gamble is one company that firmly believes in this approach.

Make, Buy, or Sell Technology?

A company may decide either to develop the technology for a new product internally or to acquire it from external sources. Figure 8–1 lists the reasons that favor one approach over the other.

Internal Development

Cost: Internal R&D may be less expensive.
Familiarity: New technology builds on current R&D skills.
Growth: The firm wants to develop strength in a new area.
Protection: The firm wants to keep new technology confidential.
Pride: The firm believes in its own capabilities.

External Acquisition

Shortcut: Existing technology saves time and money.
Skills gap: The firm lacks skills to develop new technology.
Risk reduction: Proven technology cuts development risk.
Competition: There is a need to keep up with competitive technology.
Leverage: Market products that use existing equipment or channels.

FIGURE 8-1
Reasons for Internal Development or External Acquisition of New Technology
(*Source:*   Adapted with permission from Noel Capon and Rashi Glazer, "Marketing and Technology: A Strategic Coalignment," *Journal of Marketing* [July 1987]: 6)

A company with insufficient internal R&D resources or that wishes to short-cut the development step may be able to obtain a license to existing technology. Such a license may be available from a domestic or overseas competitor. Quaker Oats obtained a license from General Foods for manufacturing KenL-Burger, a soft-moist dog food. Ideal Toy and Union Carbide license and collect substantial royalties from a variety of firms abroad.

A license may also be available from a U.S. patent holder not currently active in the field. The U.S. Patent Office is the repository of hundreds of thousands of patents, most of which are not being actively exploited in the United States and could thus become the subject of a license agreement.

A third licensing possibility is to contact a corporation that is actively selling excess technology, such as General Electric Company. GE's domestic Business Opportunities Program, originated in 1961, aims to make available to outsiders technology that General Electric has decided not to exploit itself. A bimonthly journal informs subscribers about available opportunities and support. "Normally, GE sells more than a patent. Many transactions include, in addition to consultation, drawings, prototypes, manufacturing equipment, and whatever else is available at the time for the particular transaction."[10]

Another option for obtaining the necessary technology from outside the firm is to enter into a development contract with a commercial or university laboratory. In this event, the outside party undertakes to develop a marketable (and probably patentable) product on behalf of the corporate client for a fee and/or ongoing royalty (based on the product's eventual sales). Under this kind of arrangement, the sponsoring firm does not take advantage of existing technology but causes new technology to be developed at its request, on its behalf, and at its expense. In the process, it will typically become the owner of this technology, although the terms of the contract may vary.

A final—and certainly the most radical—way of obtaining technology from the outside is to acquire an entire company that currently possesses it. This would give the acquiring company full control over the requisite know-how, but it might also saddle the acquirer with considerable operating problems. Such a move, however, can represent a vital shortcut that could save valuable time—months or even years.

Needless to say, a company could reverse each of these relationships. Instead of buying technology from outsiders, it could sell its know-how to others in the form of licensing, contract development, or ultimately the sale of the entire business. And it can do so either domestically or internationally. In this way, the company can capitalize on internally developed technology and help amortize its investment.[11]

Types of Research and Development

Depending on the nature and purpose of the endeavor, R&D can be classified into four categories:

1. Basic research
2. Applied research
3. Product development
4. Product modification

The first two types are research or scientifically oriented and the last two are development or commercially oriented. In 1985, their shares of total R&D expenditures were as follows: basic research—12 percent, applied research—22 percent, and product development and product modification combined—66 percent or approximately two-thirds. These shares were virtually unchanged from those in 1965.[12]

Basic research aims to discover new technologies or materials. It involves a long-range program of scientific inquiry that is laboratory oriented and aims to advance the frontiers of human knowledge without seeking ready commercial applicability. Its key figure is an essentially self-guided scientist-inventor who can derive little guidance from marketplace input and instead is likely to be motivated by scientific zeal. Nylon and laser technology were invented within the framework of such a laboratory orientation. The transistor came out of Bell Laboratories, as did the laser, the solar cell, and the first communications satellite, while fiber optics came out of a joint effort with Corning Glass.[13]

The personnel, time, and money requirements of basic research are quite high, and substantial costs are incurred long before the marketability of any eventual end product is ensured. Because neither the timing nor the nature of the outcome can be predicted with any reasonable degree of accuracy and the risks are high, few business firms undertake basic research, leaving it instead primarily to nonprofit institutes and universities. Where it succeeds, however, basic research is crowned by a rare technological breakthrough that represents true progress and reaps impressive rewards.

Applied research evaluates the usefulness of the results of basic research and examines potential applications. It takes a material like nylon and expands its range of applicability from parachutes to circular knits (such as women's hosiery), broadwovens, warp knits, tire cord, textured yarns, and carpet yarns. Or it looks for applications for technologies such as laser (essentially nondiffuse, parallel-bundled, high-intensity light pulses) in such diverse areas as eye surgery, metal and fabric cutting, and communications. "The laser beam—a scalpel of light—can cut, weld, vaporize, seal, and even stimulate human tissue to heal itself."[14] Laser can cut through steel as if it were butter and transmit coded pulses over optic fiber at phenomenal speeds and far less expensively than the traditional copper cable. It is revolutionizing telecommunications and putting in question the future of satellite transmission.

The thrust of applied research is still scientific in nature. It strives to uncover potential uses, not marketable products. This additional step is taken in *product development*. This type of endeavor converts tested applications into commercially promising products. Clearly, the effort is market directed and profit oriented, governed not so much by technical considerations as by feature specifications generated through marketing research. Product development is only undertaken where sufficient demand has already been ascertained, so its financial risk is much lower than in the two preceding phases. Prospect-dictated performance standards must be met, making reliability and stability, durability, and ease of handling some of the key concerns of development engineers. Cosmetic aspects of product design—such as styling and color—should not be neglected, however. They can make a major difference in the initial market response.

The final category of *product modification* involves changes in existing products. It may mean the redesign or reformulation of an old standby to revitalize sales. This may simply represent a face-lift—that is, an alteration in appearance to give the product an updated, possibly sleeker look. Or it can incorporate functional improvements to support the powerful advertising claim "improved" in addition to "new," which could refer to a new package size or flavor. Because an ongoing product is involved, changes can be based on actual buyer experiences and feedback. Design and styling and aesthetic and psychological considerations play a major role in product modification.

In sum, basic research may show great promise, but its outlook is seldom clearly defined. Because of the radical newness of the discovery, the possibilities of realization are typically quite uncertain. The scientific potential of a new material or technology is proven in applied research where useful applications are determined and experimentally tested. Product development translates applications into products based on market measurements and economic feasibility studies. Once a product is established in the marketplace, it is refined and enhanced through product modification—by far the most frequent kind of development effort. It is usually crowned by success because it builds on an established track record and represents a response to marketplace demands and trends.

Stages of Product Development

Product development is a complex effort, involving several rounds of design, execution, testing, and redesign until a producible, marketable product emerges. For a better understanding of what happens during this process, here is a step-by-step description:

General Approach: Based on the preliminary technical feasibility study conducted in the business analysis stage and the product specifications submitted by product management as a result of marketing research, the project team should already possess a basic idea about how it plans to deal with the developmental challenge. This general approach is often driven by the desired application of a given material or technology. It would likely have been specified in the budget request for the development project. A general approach may, for instance, be photovaporization of an eye tumor via laser beam.

Detailed Approach: The general approach is broken down into components that can be assigned and developed separately. This division of labor permits the assignment of specialists and experts, perhaps even aided by outside consultants, thus expediting completion and ensuring the most efficient and effective use of the department's resources. It also enables special attention to problem components. A master development plan and timetable are formulated, possibly with the use of PERT.

Design Experiments: The component engineers work separately on design ideas for their assignments. They experiment with different ways of approaching their tasks, experience and overcome problems in execution, and start refining and improving their early ideas.

Rough Draft: After the various members of the project team have had a chance to pursue their assignments for a while, their early results are integrated into a rough draft of the entire product. This preliminary design incorporates all component parts. It provides an early checkpoint to see whether all the parts fit together and enhance each other's functions so that the whole is more than the sum of its parts. It also facilitates the identification of weaknesses and conflicts and, accordingly, their prompt resolution.

Stress Analysis: Where appropriate, materials and components undergo stress analysis to determine their physical limits, such as breaking point, melting point, and the like. This kind of laboratory testing under extreme conditions helps the project team conclude whether the tested materials and components are suited for their intended application or need to be redesigned or replaced. It also enables the computation of safety margins under normal use conditions, necessary limitations on product warranties, and advisable user warnings.

Model Design: After the component engineers have had an opportunity to improve on the early designs that they contributed to the rough draft, their refined designs are combined into the model design. This is a blueprint to instruct the model shop crew on how to construct the first working model. Although product appearance is included, the emphasis is on operational aspects.

Model Construction: A crude working model is built, by either the firm's own model shop or an outside specialized vendor. The model shop features the latest and best high-precision, multipurpose equipment and the most highly skilled workers. In other words, if the model shop cannot build the model, then it simply cannot be built. The model is accurate with respect to all operating characteristics but is likely to lack the styling elements.

Model Testing: The model is subjected to rigorous performance testing to see how well it holds up under operating conditions. Elaborate measurements uncover design strengths and weaknesses, including overengineering that builds redundant quality into the product. The model's endurance under continuous use may also be examined.

Prototype Design: The first cycle of design, execution, and testing has been gone through, and the flaws identified in model testing are now corrected in the improved prototype design. The changes are usually made on the model first in order to check whether they accomplish their purpose. Also, alterations are made to adapt the design to production line manufacturing conditions. Personnel less skilled than the model shop workers, using older single-purpose equipment with wider tolerances, will ultimately be making the product in quantity. The model design must be altered to reflect the real conditions on the factory floor, not the ideal conditions in the model shop.

Prototype Construction: Next, a prototype is built that reflects all these changes and comes as close to the finished product as possible. Ideally, it would be made with production line equipment. This might require expensive tooling, however, so the model shop may chip in once more and simulate production line conditions without requiring tooling. Unless the prototype comes very close to the final product, it could not generate a meaningful picture.

Prototype Testing: Completing the second cycle of design, execution, and testing, the prototype again undergoes extensive testing to examine its operating characteristics. Because this is the last laboratory test, the testing has to be particularly thorough to catch any deficiencies that could become liabiities.

Production Design: Any final adjustments indicated by the nature of the production process and equipment or triggered by weaknesses identified during prototype testing are reflected in the production design. Having been duly finalized, the design is then frozen and sealed with the project team's O.K. Its product development duty discharged, the team forwards the production design to the production department and stands ready to assist in smoothing out any transition problems.

Interaction between Marketing and Technical Research

Whereas in small companies often only one scientist is working on converting a product idea into tangible form, large firms typically capitalize on the advantages of teamwork. Project groups composed of engineers and product managers are held responsible for moving individual projects through their development phase on schedule and within budget. Because many project groups may be working simultaneously on their separate projects, coordination through a new product department becomes necessary. Whether or not formal project groups exist, however, the activities of marketing research on the one hand and technical research on the other should be closely coordinated for maximum benefit.

Table 8–1 illustrates the relationship between marketing and technical research. In the initiative stage of the evolutionary process, marketing research is at first concerned with the interpretation of secondary data. This inquiry is followed by an analysis of the company's market position and the market trend. This is further supplemented by a distributor survey and a detailed study of consumer habits, lifestyles, and wants as described earlier in the comprehensive consumer research program. This kind of broad-based investigation is helpful in setting the stage for new product evolution with solid facts.

For lack of guidance from marketing research, the technical researchers may engage in basic research during this initial phase. Although the payoff is quite uncertain, such research is a long-term investment in the future of the enterprise that, it is hoped, will bear fruit within a reasonable time. Scientific experiments can lead to important new discoveries. Other technical departments, such as production and purchasing, contribute their own inputs, further stimulating the thought process. The technical solution of existing performance or production problems often also indicates new ways, possibilities, and methods. Finally, external sources may serve as thought-provokers. Research institutes, professional journals and seminars, conventions and workshops, consultants and inventors, competitive activities, and foreign products are among the range of possibilities.

TABLE 8–1
Coordination of Marketing and Technical Research in the Evolutionary Process

Step	Marketing Research	Technical Research
Initiative	Analysis of sales data Market analysis Basic consumer study	Basic research experiments Examination of outside sources
Idea generation	Analysis of competitive offerings Customer/consumer suggestions	Applied research Reverse engineering Capability analysis
Business analysis	Concept testing Identification of desired features Demand and competitive analyses Break-even analysis	Teamwork Customer contacts Cost estimates Schedule projections
Development and market testing	Product testing Strategy testing Test marketing	Product development Laboratory testing Product changes Ingredients specifications Instructions for use
Introduction	Study of consumer, customer, and competitor reaction Revision of sales forecasts and strategy decisions	Review of warranty cases and customer complaints Materials testing Process control

The search phase is again characterized by a scarcity of product-related interaction between the two types of research units. Marketing research activity is directed toward obtaining suggestions from persons involved in the sale, use, and/ or consumption of the relevant product category. Surveys of wholesalers, retailers, and consumers or users solicit new product ideas and elicit comments about the comparative merits of competitive products.

With input from the marketplace still being generated and examined, technology feeds on itself. Applied research looks for innovative applications for materials and technologies originating from inside or outside sources. These new applications are analyzed for their practicality and efficiency to determine their usefulness and attractiveness. A survey of current capabilities in terms of personnel and equipment will prove helpful in assessing the outlook for new avenues. Simultaneously, the compatibility of new ventures with current production programs and facilities has to be investigated to identify the need for new equipment and/or personnel.

Analysis and Development

In the business analysis stage, marketing research begins to feed specifications into the R&D department. Consumers are called on to evaluate concepts that have meanwhile evolved from the ideas generated during the search phase. At the same time, they are asked to spell out desirable product features. To determine the economic prospects of the different proposals, market capacities and price levels now have to be estimated. Competitive structure and strategies are also in need of detailed assessment. Competitive selling techniques must be studied and their compatibility with the firm's current sales organization has to be checked. The cost and profit aspects of the proposed new products have to be calculated. Ultimately, the risk associated with each alternative has to be appraised.

In the meantime, technical research concentrates on the analysis and improvement of process characteristics. This effort is especially geared toward achieving process stability in terms of homogeneous output under conditions of mass production. Another task calls for the technical personnel to project the cost and schedule of product development and production, thus supporting the analytical effort of product management.

During the evolutionary phase of development and market testing, technical research carries out the specific assignment of product development. Durability, maximum output, and steady long-term performance characteristics are all thoroughly evaluated through the use of laboratory and stress tests under extreme conditions. Marketing research then receives the product for product testing. It presents a sample of the product to a carefully selected group of consumers, usually together with a comparable competitive model that remains unidentified, for free normal use or consumption during a specified period of time. The reported experiences of this panel typically prompt last refinements that are incorporated into the product before its design is frozen.

Other functions of technical research at this stage include a description of the product and its ingredients or components for the purchasing, production, and marketing departments, possibly even a patent application. The development engineers are also involved in the planning of the production process. They painstakingly examine the results of pilot production with regard to tolerances, quality of workmanship, and performance characteristics. They play a major role in the design of control mechanisms and methods for the production process. Because of their intimate familiarity with every aspect of the product they developed, the developmental engineers are in an excellent position to draw up instructions for use to be supplied to the consumer with the product. These instructions, however, tend to be written in engineering terms and often have to be edited and rewritten by a promotional writer to be understandable to the average buyer. Given their insight into product characteristics, they also have to outline the functional and time limitations of a meaningful and acceptable warranty for the product.

At the same time, marketing research is concerned not only with product testing but also with strategy testing. Product testing studies whether the product performs satisfactorily in the hands of prospects and whether they prefer it to available alternatives. It feeds back to the engineers suggestions for changes that would make the product more desirable and salable. Strategy testing investigates and attempts to optimize separately the various elements of the innovation's introductory marketing mix—brand name, packaging, price, advertising, and distribution channels. Due to possible shifts, and perhaps even increases, in cost, this kind of testing may require a revision of the original break-even analysis. Ultimately, the new product, after having been improved and finalized according to the results of product testing, has to undergo a final market test. The optimum marketing mix combination that emerged from strategy testing is applied in the introduction of the innovation in a few select test cities on an experimental basis. This serves as a last check of the product's salability and permits fine-tuning of the marketing mix for the national rollout.

The role of marketing research, however, does not end here. During the product's full-scale introduction, marketing research has the important task of ascertaining and appraising the reactions of consumers, the trade, and competitors to the innovation. It is possible, though unlikely, that the insights gained from this research will suggest adjustments in the product, its advertising, or some other element of the marketing mix. As the knowledge of the market increases, sales forecasts and strategies can be made more realistic and effective by modifying them in accordance with the actual results achieved and the underlying reasons as elicited in interviews.

The continued responsibilities of R&D personnel include possible market-prompted product adjustments and the investigation of reasons for warranty cases and customer complaints. This will enable swift corrective action in the event of product deficiencies, even to the point of voluntary recalls due to physical hazards. Beating the Federal Consumer Product Safety Commission or the National Highway Traffic Safety Administration to the punch in such a case can score important public relations points. Procter & Gamble promptly recalled its Rely tampon when the product became linked with toxic shock syndrome deaths, even to the point of offering to buy back free samples. This action helped maintain the company's reputation under tragic circumstances. Firestone, on the other hand, refused to acknowledge the blowout problems associated with its 500 tire, even while the National

Highway Traffic Safety Administration was actively investigating a growing number of accident reports. It finally recalled the tire only after being ordered to do so by this federal agency. The cost to the company: some $250 million and a damaged reputation. Procter & Gamble spent approximately $75 million on the Rely recall and suffered no measurable damage to its image, fully intending to reenter the feminine hygiene products market after the furor died down.

Development engineers are thus the beacons in an early warning system that is set to defuse emerging product problems and nip them in the bud. They may even participate in checking the quality of incoming material, particularly when variations from the specifications are suspected. And they are often involved in an advisory capacity in the control of the continuity and stability of the manufacturing process.

In summary, the interaction between marketing and technical research throughout the evolutionary process shows parallel rather than intertwining activities in its early stages. Marketing research has to do some groundwork first before it can give any meaningful guidance to R&D. So the scientists and engineers may use the time productively to do some basic and applied research, opening up new vistas of technological opportunity. Reversing the relationship, these possibilities can be checked for market appeal through concept testing. As their cooperation and mutual stimulation evolve, marketing research will draw up market-inspired specifications for the laboratory. The engineers come back with early product versions that are adjusted in accordance with market feedback. This fruitful dialog should not end with a product's introduction but should continue on a steady basis to feed naturally into subsequent product modifications and updates.

SUMMARY

As the evolutionary process moves along, authorized and funded new product development projects have to be converted into marketable products. This technical task falls upon the research and developmental department. But product management also plays a pivotal role in this process by engaging in an ongoing dialog with the engineers and providing crucial input from the marketplace at various checkpoints along the way. Technological capabilities are thus aligned with market opportunities.

Although most firms develop new products internally, there are a number of ways in which outside sources can be tapped. While outright acquisitions of innovative upstarts have often backfired in a loss of entrepreneurial zeal, joint ventures or similar forms of cooperation between large and small companies have on occasion born fruit. In such a relationship, the small partner contributes cutting edge technology and the large partner provides financing and marketing muscle. Conversely, a small firm may be able to obtain a license for excess technology that a large firm does not care to pursue. Wherever it takes place, R&D is more likely to succeed if these ingredients are mixed and managed properly: objectives, intelligence, knowledge, creativity, organization, improvisation, communication, money, and time.

Depending on its objectives, research and development can be classified into four types. Basic research is scientific in nature and aimed at the rare breakthrough that opens up an entirely new range of technological possibilities. These possibilities are then explored in applied research. Product development transforms applications into commercial products, and product modification alters these products in a functional or visual way to enhance their salability in a mature, competitive market.

Product development starts out with a conceptual clarification of the general design approach. After the work has been divided up among members of the project team, the component engineers engage in some early experimentation. From the subsequent rough draft until the final production design, several cycles of design, execution, testing, and redesign ensue, culminating in a product ready for large-scale production.

All along the way, the development process benefits greatly from close and continuous interaction between marketing and technical research. To be truly market-driven in their work, engineers need relevant market information. But what works well in the laboratory may not satisfy consumers. So hands-on testing is required to permit final product changes that are likely to improve salability. And R&D must be on hand to read early warning signals filtering back from the marketplace after introduction in the form of warranty cases and complaints.

NOTES

1. See Robert D. Buzzell and Bradley T. Gale, *The PIMS Principles* (New York: Free Press, 1987).
2. See "How Xerox Speeds Up the Birth of New Products," *Business Week,* 19 March 1984, 58, and John Bussey and Douglas R. Sease, "Speeding Up: Manufacturers Strive to Slice Time Needed to Develop Products," *Wall Street Journal,* 23 Feb. 1988.
3. See Geoff Lewis, "Big Changes at Big Blue," *Business Week,* 15 Feb. 1988, 95–96.
4. See Katherine M. Hafner, "Bright Smiles, Sweaty Palms," *Business Week,* 1 Feb. 1988, 22, 23.
5. See Gene Bylinsky, "The New Look at America's Top Lab," *Fortune,* 1 Feb. 1988, 60–62.
6. Ibid., 64.
7. See Bussey and Sease, "Speeding Up," 1. See also Paul A. Carroad and Connie A. Carroad, "Strategic Interfacing of R&D and Marketing," *Research Management* (Jan. 1982): 28–33.
8. See Michael G. Duerr, *The Commercial Development of New Products* (New York: The Conference Board, 1986), 23–25.
9. Vern Terpstra, *International Marketing,* (Hinsdale, IL: Dryden Press, 1987), 311.
10. E. Patrick McGuire, *Generating New-Product Ideas* (New York: The Conference Board, 1972), 45.
11. Concerning the reasons for selling technology or simultaneously exploiting and selling it, see Noel Capon and Rashi Glazer, "Marketing and Technology: A Strategic Coalignment," *Journal of Marketing* (July 1987): 7.
12. See "Research and Development," *Economic Roadmaps* (Oct. 1986): 2.
13. See Bylinsky, "New Look," 61.
14. Alan D. Haas, "The Kindest Cut of All," *American Way* (Aug. 1984): 99. See also Allen A. Boraiko, "A Splendid Light: Lasers," *National Geographic,* March 1984, 335ff.

CASE STUDY

A-ONE PRINTING CORPORATION

Background

A-One is one of the leading commercial printing concerns in the United States. Besides books and magazines, A-One is a leader in printing catalogs and advertising materials for retail outlets. In recent years, changes in technology, particularly the use of computers and digital imaging in the reproduction of pictures, has given the corporation new expertise in the use of electronics in providing information and graphics commonly available in a printed form. This experience, coupled with a recognition that many printed information forms are converting to electronic media, caused A-One to look for new business opportunities that could take advantage of its technological experience and the advent of electronic media.

Business Proposition

After considering a variety of alternatives and possible approaches, A-One decided to trade on its strong connection with the retail industry and offer an electronic shopping system to retailers.

Under a new business plan, A-One would provide potential clients with a total package for interactive electronic shopping, including all the necessary hardware and software and the design and plant capabilities to build freestanding shopping units, as well as a system for servicing units that are in place. The retailers would be responsible for all retail functions, including merchandising the system and providing a delivery system for orders and subsequent returns and payments.

Once the decision to pursue this new business was made, A-One gave its engineering division the task of assembling the necessary hardware and software, and commissioned a design firm to construct the prototype unit to house the various components.

This case was contributed by Douglas Mills, Vice President, Lieberman Research East, Great Neck, New York.

Product Configuration and Development Questions

After several months of trial and error, an electronic shopping product was completed. The initial design consisted of the following components.

- A two-screen system, including a video screen (for product shots) and a touch screen (providing a mode to show product information and a way for shoppers to interact with the shopping system)
- A personal computer and videodisk player
- A software package that provided a pathing system to allow shoppers to select the merchandise they wished to view and ultimately order (interactive shopping)
- An instruction sequence to explain to consumers how to use the shopping system
- A kiosk unit (looking much like an automatic picture booth) to house the unit

With this initial prototype came many questions about the product that had been designed. Because of these concerns, A-One decided that market research was necessary.

Objectives of Consumer Research

The consumer research commissioned by A-One was conducted to address one overriding concern of management: How do we know that this design for electronic shopping is acceptable to potential consumers? Specifically, consumer research was designed to answer the following questions about this electronic shopping prototype.

1. Do consumers understand how to use the system that has been designed? How effective is the instructional sequence in helping consumers to understand how to shop?
2. What are the areas of difficulty encountered by consumers that need to be clarified, improved, or changed? Do the various shopping functions

and pathing system allow shoppers to select the items they want? Are the words used to describe the shopping functions the right ones?
3. Are the various hardware components easy to use? Is the touch screen easy to use? Does the video screen adequately show the merchandise?
4. What advantages do consumers perceive this system to offer?

Research Design and Approach

Given the fact that electronic shopping is a relatively new concept to consumers and that specific reactions to the A-One system are needed, it was decided to utilize the following approach for the research.

- Personal one-on-one interviews would be conducted
- Both males and females would be interviewed (to determine if any differences exist in their reactions)
- An oversampling of younger people would be included in the research (because younger people tend to be the "leading edge" of new product acceptance)

Key to the research was the need to expose people to the A-One product. Therefore, the research called for a one-hour interview period, including twenty minutes for respondents to use and experience the electronic shopping system prototype, to be followed by forty minutes of questions regarding their experience with the system.

Findings of the Research

The Shopping Experience and Instructions
1. The instructional sequence that introduced people to this electronic shopping product told them how to use the various functions and how to shop the system was regarded as easy to follow.

Ease of Following Introduction and Shopping Instructions

Very easy to follow	32% ⎤
Fairly easy to follow	44 ⎦ 76%
Difficult to follow	11
Neither easy nor difficult	13

2. The majority of people also felt that the instructions provided by the introduction sequence adequately described their experience in using the system.

Instructional Match with Actual Experience
Match is:

Very good	31% ⎤
Fairly good	50 ⎦ 81%
Did not match	19

3. Although the instructions were well received by respondents, people felt that more complete explanations of various aspects of shopping the system were needed.

Areas of Needed Improvement

	% Rating "Needs Improvement"
How to move from one merchandise category to another	55%
Include a practice shopping sequence	50
More about how to go from one merchandise area to another (what types of items are for sale)	45

The Shopping Functions
1. Most respondents understood the various functions provided by the pathing program to actually shop the system.

Shopping Functions Correctly Identified

Functions	% Correctly Identified
How to *order* items	95%
How to get *product details*	90
How to *save* possible purchases for review	80
How to move *forward*	75
How to *back up*	70

2. Paramount among the least understood shopping functions as identified by respondents was the "help" shopping function. Designed to provide assistance to people who have specific problems while shopping the system, the help function did not perform this task adequately.

Use and Success of Help Function

	All Shoppers
Used "help" function	62%
It solved my problem	10
Didn't solve my problem	52
Didn't use function	38

Rating of System Components

1. The basic hardware of the electronic shopping system, the video screen and the touch screen, were generally rated favorably by respondents exposed to the system.

Clarity of Video Screen Picture

	All Shoppers	
Excellent	26%	71%
Very good	45	
Good	20	
Fair/poor	9	

Ease of Using Touch Screen Shopping Function Buttons

	All Shoppers	
Very easy to use	34%	78%
Fairly easy to use	44	
Not easy to use	21	

2. Although the touch screen and the shopping function buttons were regarded as easy to use, people did cite the following problem: an uncertainty as to whether a shopping function had registered after touching a particular button.

3. The design of the kiosk (the self-contained unit for the various electronic shopping components) was favorably received on the key design aspects.

Rating of Kiosk Design Aspects

	% Rating Item Excellent/Very Good
Offers privacy while shopping	80%
Is comfortable to sit in	60
Is eye-catching/attention-getting	59
Is well lit	55
Can easily see pictures	54
Can reach touch screen shopping buttons	49

Some respondents did complain about the distance of the seat in the kiosk as being too far to reach the shopping function buttons comfortably.

Advantages Associated with the System Tested

1. After experiencing this electronic shopping system, respondents were asked to cite specific advantages that the system might provide. The following were the most frequently volunteered advantages associated with electronic shopping:

"Is a more convenient way to shop"
"Provides more product information than salespeople in stores"
"More convenient than catalogs . . . no forms to fill out"
"Provides a way to compare product information all at once . . . in one place"
"Saves time . . . everything in one place"

2. In the course of obtaining the various advantages people associated with this mode of electronic shopping, a major problem also surfaced: Many respondents expressed a general fear of the impersonal nature of electronic shopping.

Results of the Research

At the conclusion of the research, A-One Corporation made specific improvements in the proposed electronic shopping product. Directing the engineering and design teams to enact these improvements, management required the following changes to be made in the prototype:

1. The introductory shopping instructions were modified to include a step-by-step practice of all the available shopping functions.
2. The help shopping function was totally redesigned by the engineering team to be more operational (told people *how* to solve their problems).
3. Each shopping function button was designed to change color when touched so that people would know the function had registered.
4. The design of the kiosk was changed to include an adjustable seat.
5. To alleviate the impersonal feeling, a telephone was installed for asking questions, placing orders, and so on.

Discussion Questions

1. Besides refining the electronic shopping system, to what other uses might A-One put the research?
2. What other types of consumer research should be conducted by A-One?
3. Discuss additional modifications that might be made to this shopping system when approaching different kinds of retailers (e.g., apparel, audio/video, sporting goods).
4. What benefits does this electronic shopping system offer to retailers?

CHAPTER 9

Market Testing

Engineers can, and do, ensure that the products developed by them perform to specifications. Perfectionists by training, they put their creations through rigorous laboratory testing to check every relevant performance characteristic. The outcome of the product development stage is thus a fully laboratory-tested product that has the engineers' stamp of approval. But in all due respect for technological perfection, the most critical hurdle for a new product to conquer is market resistance. For an innovation to become a commercial success, market reaction to its introduction has to be carefully and thoroughly investigated.

Consumers are complex and, at times, paradoxical creatures. Bored with endless repetition in their product purchases and looking for the excitement of change, they nevertheless frequently shy away from the uncertainty and risk associated with new products. A product should offer something new, but it should also be reasonably familiar. This is why improvements of existing products usually fare quite well. But when an innovation represents a significant departure from past offerings, market response becomes more difficult to predict. No amount of concept testing, however extensive it may be, nor the use of employee panels, will ever be a true substitute for actual field experience with the real product in the hands of consumers.

This essential live market feedback is generated through various types of market testing. One type is product testing, which involves a sample of relevant consumers actually trying the new product, preferably at their leisure in their own homes and under normal use conditions. Approaches vary. For example, test subjects may be given one or more products and the identities of these products may be hidden or evident. Whichever approach is chosen, the purpose of product testing is to determine whether the product performs to the satisfaction of the consumer and whether it is preferred to competitive alternatives.

Even if a new item does well in a product test, however, its commercial success is by no means guaranteed, as its salability has not as yet been tested. In moving to examine this vital issue, a few companies engage in some form of pre-market testing. This means that selected consumers are invited to carry out a simulated shopping experience. Its purpose is to obtain a sense of consumer choices in a competitive setting. This would allow final touch-ups in the marketing mix before "going public," thus enabling the company to fine-tune its approach at a very limited cost.

The final, and probably most hotly debated, round of marketing research before full-scale introduction is test marketing. Here the new product is actually offered for sale in an authentic competitive environment by making it available and promoting it in a select number of test cities. Whereas all earlier marketing research could be conducted without the competition learning about it, now the innovation is out in the open and competitors can buy and read test market data as well as the firm itself. So the company is not only incurring a sizable expense but also running a substantial risk, namely, the risk of competitive scooping.

If test marketing proves out, the signal is green for national introduction. Product design is finalized and frozen after product testing and is rarely altered after test marketing. But other elements of the marketing mix may still undergo final adjustments at this point, based on the feedback generated. Because the company now has every reason to believe that its national introduction will be successful, it should lose no time in gearing up for full-scale production. If it is to reap the full benefit of the initial response, it has to have an adequate supply on hand to "fill the pipeline" and satisfy the first burst of demand.

Product Testing

Although the new product has been thoroughly laboratory tested by its development engineers and there is ample evidence that it works well under the conditions for which it was designed, it would be a great mistake to assume without any further proof that all has been done and all the necessary pieces are in place to make it a commercial success. Consumers are fickle, and even if all their specified requirements have been met, it pays to check if they are satisfied and still interested. *Product testing* addresses this task.

Product testing involves having a representative sample of target consumers actually use or consume the product under normal use conditions. Ideally, this would take place during the everyday lives of the participants. For example, a wear test for a new type of pantyhose or shirt, for instance, would include several cycles of wearing and washing in a person's work environment and regular laundry, respectively. The purpose of such a wash and wear test (instead of just letting the consumer look at and feel the product) is to give a group of prospects firsthand experience with the innovation in their usual work and home environments. Their reactions provide live feedback to the company as to how the product actually performs in their hands and what they think of it in comparison to available alternatives.

Sophisticated firms use product testing as part of a continuous marketing research program that precedes, accompanies, and follows up on product development and subsequent improvements in the product's appearance, function, or composition. This procedure clearly points to the fact that, in an increasingly competitive world, companies try to explore every avenue of relevant communication with the consumer before disclosing the new product and its marketing approach to their competitors and committing their reputation to a potential failure.

Functions of Product Testing

In the context of a comprehensive step-by-step marketing research program, product testing is used to answer a number of interrelated questions. The following list shows its major functions and benefits:

- Report on the innovation's performance characteristics in the hands of the consumer.
- Identify areas of consumer dissatisfaction, thus suggesting opportunities for technical improvements.
- Point out spheres of product superiority to be exploited via advertising.
- Find out new uses to which inventive users put the product to broaden its range of applicability.
- Determine the intensity of consumers' feelings to evaluate their degree of interest and obtain a first indication of potential demand.
- Ascertain consumer reactions to the product to guide selection of advertising appeals.
- Compare the product with competitive offerings to obtain a first idea about the acceptable price range.
- Assess the product's overall desirability and marketability in order to direct management's decision making concerning additional investments and introductory marketing strategy.

As this lengthy outline indicates, the marketing research tasks performed during the product testing stage are quite varied, comprehensive, and crucial for the further progress of the evolutionary process. It is at this point that the new product is first subjected to real-life use or consumption conditions. Product management is understandably interested in utilizing this valuable opportunity to investigate a variety of concerns before finalizing the marketing program. As consumers are exposed to the actual product for the first time—rather than responding to a hypothetical description of a potential product, as in the preceding concept test—their reactions may differ significantly and prompt product reformulations.

Product Testing Methods

Resourceful product managers have a variety of options to choose from when determining the specific product testing approach. The various methods can be used either alternatively or in concert to yield the maximum amount of useful information prior to test marketing. Some companies will, for instance, routinely precede consumer product testing with employee testing. For reasons of secrecy and expediency, a few firms will even substitute employee panels for consumer panels and forgo consumer testing altogether.

Employees constitute a captive audience when it comes to product testing. They are readily accessible and can easily be persuaded to volunteer their services for this task. In cigarette companies, this is even true for nonsmokers. At R. J. Reynolds Tobacco Company, some 350 employee volunteers taste-test cigarettes for about 15 minutes two or three times a week under carefully controlled conditions. Having been screened for their sensory discrimination ability, panel members "help research-and-development staffs delicately adjust prototypes before expensive consumer testing. And they help the chemists, flavorists, and blenders keep a Winston tasting like a Winston, year in and year out, despite changes in tobacco crops, manufacturing processes and such things as the paper and glue used for the cigarette wrappers."[1] Besides smoking, they are asked to sniff, feel, and draw on unlit cigarettes. Their input assists those in charge of formulating new brands in determining the right blend of tobaccos and added flavorings, such as sugar and apple, prune, and raisin concentrates.[2]

Many businesses use employees as original test subjects. Garment manufacturers involve their workers in wear tests, and food producers invite employees into their test kitchens. When Kodak developed the Instamatic camera and cartridge system over a period of some ten years in the late 1950s and early 1960s, employees were used instead of consumers in order to maintain secrecy. Both cameras and cartridges were subjected to "customer-type" testing by a select group of company employees. This approach apparently worked well—20 million Instamatic cameras were sold in the first four years worldwide.

Two questions that arise in connection with the use of employee panels are the level of candor and representativeness. To avoid offending fellow employees championing the product, some participants may be inclined to be more laudatory in their statements than warranted by their actual experience and to hold back criticism. Thus a climate has to be created that encourages the frank expression of opinions in an effort to foster product improvement. The second issue is more difficult to resolve. Employees may well differ significantly from members of the target market. Their demographic characteristics, shopping habits, usage conditions, and consumption patterns may be different. Common sense would usually give a fair indication of such differences and marketing research could be used to confirm their nature and extent. But companies that want to play it safe will normally sidestep this issue by using both employee and consumer panels in product testing.

That is precisely what the Quaker Oats Company did in the evolution of its Chewy Granola Bars, which were taste-tested repeatedly during the development process by employee taste panels consisting of thirty-six employees each. These panels were administered by the Sensory Evaluation and Analytical Services Group, a part of Quaker Oats's research laboratories. "A variety of tests are administered. Panelists judge in Acceptance Tests, how much a sample product is liked or disliked; in Preference Tests, which of several samples is preferred; and in Difference Tests, if two samples are perceptibly different from each other."[3] They are supplemented by descriptive tests that yield detailed product descriptions, often containing comparisons with competitive products. Finally, the employee test panels assist in storage tests that "determine how long the product keeps its flavor and texture, using several temperature and humidity conditions."[4]

Although a great deal of useful information was derived from these employee tests that helped to refine the product's formulation, product management at Quaker Oats did not feel comfortable proceeding further until it confirmed the outcome with consumers. Variously called "prototype testing" or "in-home product concept test," this phase involved about 150 consumers. To qualify, prospective participants had to have eaten granola bars recently and be the food purchase decision makers in their families. "The consumers were shown a multicolor display board which described the product benefits. Since no packaging had been developed at this point, the consumers were simply given eight plain-wrapped bars to take home and try."[5] After one week, they were interviewed as to their experiences and feelings. Preferring Quaker's moist and chewy bar by 2 to 1 over the leading hard granola bar, the panelists described the results of their trials as "unexpected" and "amazing," two words that would become key themes in the subsequent advertising campaign.[6]

Consumer product testing is the most frequent type of such testing. It involves the actual use of the product by consumers in their own homes at their convenience, that is, in the absence of an interviewer, during a specified period of time. The selected sample of consumers, called a panel, is recruited by phone or personal contact and is supplied with the test product either by mail or in person. With regard to the procedure employed, the following can be said:

> The product is usually "blind"—i.e., the brand name is not shown and the product is identified by letter or by another code. This removes the brand name as a biasing influence and also assists in the maintenance of secrecy.
>
> If two variants of a product are being considered, both may be placed in the hands of each panelist, permitting direct comparison; or else product A may be given to one half of the sample and product B to the other half. The latter is called the "monadic design;" in theory it provides as valid a weighing of two alternatives as a direct comparison would. Generally, however, a comparison is more meaningful. It is often desirable to let the panelist compare the test product (or the two variations, as the case may be) with the company's present product, or with a competitive product against which it would be selling.[7]

As this quote suggests, blind pair comparison testing is the most common method at this stage. Its proponents suggest that branded testing would lead to distortions caused by preexisting (leading brand) or lacking (new brand) brand images rather than letting the innovation stand on its own merits through removal of brand identification. They argue that the new brand name, if any, should be tested separately in strategy testing and will automatically become a factor during test marketing.

This point of view has not gone entirely undisputed. Its opponents consider blind testing unrealistic, pointing out that under normal circumstances the consumer is fully aware of a product's brand name. They accordingly propose non-blind testing where the products to be compared are fully labeled. This perspective has, however, remained a minority viewpoint. Blind testing clearly carries the advantages of confidentiality and examination of the product's merits in regard to performance and preference without undue bias.

Pair comparison—that is, asking panel members to rate the relative merits of two choices—is methodologically preferable because it does not place unnecessary strain on a consumer's ability to distinguish and choose among several alternatives simultaneously. This latter method of rank ordering in order of preference may produce a false sense of accuracy by generating numbers that are ultimately fairly meaningless. Instead, a company attempting to choose among more than two product alternatives should use separate but matched samples of consumers to test the different versions against each other. This procedure can become quite cumbersome but yields more conclusive results.

To cite a case in point, a new liquid all-purpose household cleaner was being tested with regard to color and packaging material. In separate pair comparisons, consumer panels were asked whether they preferred a clear, bluish, or amber liquid and a plastic versus a glass container. This resulted in a six-cell research design, as shown in Figure 9–1. Accordingly, six consumer groups had to be formed and interviewed. Group A, for instance, tested the new cleaner as a clear liquid in one glass bottle and as a blue liquid in another. The winner was an amber liquid in a plastic bottle. This result supports the importance of consumer perception for the adoption and success of new products.

In-home testing with individually selected and screened consumers is the most frequent form of product testing, but other approaches also have their adherents. Civic groups are one such alternative. A guild of a local church, a high school association, or similar volunteer group may be recruited in an effort to reduce the time and expenses of test administration. As an example, the Mothers' Club of Sacred Heart Catholic Church in Moline, Illinois, was asked by Procter & Gamble to test eight formulations of a new powdered soap product. Each of the 200 participating women had to show up three times, receiving a different powder each time, and having her hands inspected by a dermatologist. In total, the club received about $1,000 for the test, which went to support the parochial school.[8]

Popular with some researchers, such groups have, over the years, tested hundreds of consumer products ranging from liquor to oatmeal and from paper towels to toothpaste. A frequently used location are the Quad Cities of Rock Island

Color / Package	Clear vs. Blue	Clear vs. Amber	Blue vs. Amber
Glass	A	B	C
Plastic	D	E	F

FIGURE 9–1
Six-Cell Research Design Example

and Moline, Illinois, and Davenport and Bettendorf, Iowa, because the results achieved in that area are viewed as representative of the full-scale response. But the degree of interaction among the group members causes concern among professional marketing researchers because it could affect the independence of the individual testers. Nonetheless, candor is not uncommon and careful screening of participating group members and combining several groups can ensure a reasonable representation.[9]

Mall testing offers another alternative. Many marketing research agencies operate storefronts in shopping malls across the country. They can recruit mall shoppers for an impromptu product test on their premises. Having been intercepted as they stroll down the mall, shoppers are invited to come in and try the new product, usually in blind pair comparison form. The on-premises trial is preceded by a product explanation and followed by a brief interview. Methodological questions concern the selection process, which, of course, excludes nonshoppers and favors easy-to-recruit shoppers. Also, a one-time trial of a very limited quantity produces results of less prognostic value than more extended and extensive in-home tests.

Unique problems are caused by the testing requirements imposed by the Food and Drug Administration for new drug approvals. Such tests have to be conducted under close medical supervision in carefully monitored circumstances. Prisons and hospitals, due to their controlled conditions, provide appropriate settings. According to FDA rules, human testing can only be undertaken after extensive prior testing with animals.

Less demanding and critical testing takes place when newly formulated pet foods are tried out on their prospective targets. Carnation Company runs a cattery with 500 feline residents that in 1983 taste-tested about 250,000 cans of wet cat food and 70,000 pounds of dry varieties. Their food preferences were recorded and computerized, guiding the marketing decisions of product management for cat foods, which, for the nation's number two pet food marketer, represented about $300 million in sales in 1983. Tests of food acceptance and food fatigue of this sizable cat population are strictly based on quantity consumed. The test cats are also involved if an existing product has to be reformulated because of the unavailability of a given ingredient.[10]

If a company produces a steady flow of new products and thus has a continuing need for product testing, it may want to avail itself of an ongoing panel. Such panels can be operated by a marketing research agency or the company itself on a continuous basis and obviate the need to recruit on a case-by-case basis. Corning Glass Works maintains an ongoing panel with rotating membership, as described in the following quote:

> In a large city near Corning, New York, we have over 1,500 housewives who cooperate with us in using new products and experimenting with product ideas. This operation is managed by our market research department. All the homes are card-catalogued by number in the family, number and ages of children, type of stove (gas or electric), ownership of special kitchen appliances, use of hard or soft water, age of housewife, and other characteristics. In any one test, a group of 200 families is used. They enjoy

participating in this work and are not paid for their cooperation. A constant turnover of participants is achieved by adding and dropping homes, so that panel members do not become "experts" in our problems and inquiries.

This panel is used to rate such functional characteristics of a product as size, shape, durability, usefulness, and other details which can be evaluated only in actual home use. After a participant has used a product in the home for a period of time, she is queried by personal interview, mail questionnaire, or telephone. This may be done several times during a test. On the basis of the panel member's experiences and preferences, subsequent design and engineering can "maximize" good features and "design out" weaknesses.[11]

This points up the fact that in some instances only the critical attributes of an innovation are fixed and panelists are presented with a choice of noncritical product elements. Product testing accordingly not only serves as a vehicle for evaluating product acceptance from the "take it or leave it" point of view of investigating a given product but also will often help to finalize the new product's formula or styling, size, or packaging.

The selection of panel participants is, of course, a crucial issue. As a general rule, panel members' characteristics should satisfy the test objectives. Because heavy users account for the majority of the sales volume in many product categories, a sampling plan favoring heavy users, such as disproportionate stratified random sampling or even exclusive simple random sampling of heavy users, may be quite in order. The latter approach was utilized by Standard Brands when it considered introducing a new large size of instant coffee:

> We knew that heavy users consumed about thirty per cent of all instant coffee sold. We were anxious to know what these heavy users thought of the new size. Therefore, the samples were restricted to heavy users, and they showed strong interest in the new size. If this research had been conducted among a random sample of the population, it would have included many people who did not use instant coffee, as well as others who were only light users. The answers obtained from a sample of this kind would have been quite different from those obtained from the heavy users who constituted the prime market.[12]

A similar approach concentrates on sampling only users of a company's own brand, thus eliminating from consideration the buyers of competitive brands. Some companies like to separate performance and preference testing. They use both employee and consumer in-home use panels to obtain feedback of performance characteristics of the innovation and conduct separate surveys, often in the form of mall intercepts, to determine buyer preferences with regard to color, styling, and packaging. Such an assessment of visual attributes can be accomplished independently from functionally oriented use tests by brief personal interviews based on limited exposure, for example, in a storefront location. Evidence indicates that although a respondent should definitely be allowed to choose among several alternatives, their number should be restricted to four or at the most six because a consumer's ability to discriminate, rate, and rank alternative choices diminishes rapidly as their number increases.

Limitations of Product Testing

Product testing, whether with employees, consumers, or both, is a most useful and important exercise. Any company that would proceed without this essential research loop risks introducing a product that represents a severe misreading of or mismatch with the market. But the reverse is not true. Product testing is not a life insurance for a new product, a surefire ticket to success. Rather, it is simply a necessary—but not sufficient—prerequisite.

Pillsbury learned this bitter lesson with Oven Crock. This preflavored baked beans product developed by Green Giant looked like a sure winner. In blind taste tests, it won out by substantial preference margins over bland pork and beans. "But Oven Crock was a disaster in a test market. Surveys later showed that people who ate heavily flavored baked beans added their own fixings to the bland variety and didn't want somebody to do it for them. 'Our beans were terrific, but they were a solution to no known problem,' " said a Pillsbury executive.[13] Similarly, the company decided to scrap a high-quality frozen croissant when consumers seemed confused about when to use it, even though the product had scored well in taste tests.[14]

And, of course, it can prove deadly to reformulate the product after the product test, sacrificing quality in an effort to make the product more convenient to use and less expensive. Appleasy, an easy-to-prepare dessert was reformulated to contain more starch and sugar and less apples when the price of apples more than doubled during its evolution. Needless to say, it failed upon market introduction for lack of repeat purchases.[15]

A product test does not in any way examine the marketing mix intended for the innovation. As a matter of fact, the marketing mix has likely not been finalized yet. While most immediately concerned with product characteristics, product testing can give some guidance in price level determination and the selection of promotional appeals. Even media habits and shopping patterns could be included in the interviews involved.

Although desirable and favored product characteristics, as well as the degree of product acceptance, should emerge clearly from a product test, and intention-to-buy scales can readily be administered in the process, product management will find it difficult at best to forecast sales on this basis. The lacking vigor of competitive aggression that is present in the marketplace makes a product test an unrealistic setting for sales forecasting. And the fact that consumers do not have to part with their money and actually purchase the items in question makes it dangerous to engage in premature euphoria. This danger can be lessened somewhat by offering to sell participants the product of their choice at a deep discount.

Perhaps the greatest shortcoming of product testing is the fact that it isolates and investigates only part of the total picture. Product features can be improved but no reliable indication of actual market reaction under authentic conditions can be obtained at this stage. "A concept test can show that the concept motivates; a use test can verify that the product works or tastes good; a package test can indicate that the package appeals. But you have not yet seen how these factors—concept, product, package, and so on—work in combination."[16]

Premarket Testing

Having completed product testing and having made product adjustments suggested by its results, it would appear that product management would now be ready to engage in that final round of preintroduction marketing research called test marketing. The test marketing stage, though, is a fairly expensive and unforgiving undertaking, hardly an appropriate setting for gambling with corporate resources. Accordingly, some companies like to take one or two more intermediate steps to answer a few more questions before taking the plunge.

The first such possibility is in-home "shopping" in a competitive setting, which could be described as a simulation of the purchase decision-making process. This kind of testing differs from product testing in several important ways:

- The product bears its brand name.
- It is fully labeled and identified.
- It is packaged the same way as that planned for national introduction.
- The innovation is priced as in a store environment.

A sample advertisement or some direct-mail promotional piece is likely to accompany the product, incorporating appeals identified in the earlier marketing research stages.

In order to duplicate the actual store purchase situation as closely as possible in the home environment, several fully identified competitive products are included in the test. Consumers are given a fixed amount to spend in the pseudo-store on the products of their choice within the product category being investigated. Each participant is repeatedly asked to make a selection from varying combinations of major brands and alternative new products being tested. Thus many of the ingredients of the true store environment are there, except that the decision is made at consumers' homes.

Because this kind of simulation is conducted over an extended period of time, repeat purchase patterns will emerge. Participants will repeatedly purchase from the interviewer the brands of their choice at discount prices that they are actually paying. This type of simulation could therefore be called an in-home market test. It has the great advantage that no public disclosure occurs because the new product is not yet advertised in mass media or available in stores.[17]

Another scheme uses simulated stores run either by companies themselves or by marketing research organizations. Procter & Gamble operates such a store at its Cincinnati headquarters. It is not an employee store, selling company wares to workers at a discount. Rather, it is a test arrangement that displays the company's products in competitive surroundings, differing from a regular grocery store only by a more limited assortment. Consumers are invited to shop under these controlled conditions that set the stage for displaying new products in their competitive context. Whether or not they buy an innovation, consumers can be subjected to exit interviews to determine whether they even noticed the innovation, and if so, why they did not buy it.

This kind of realistic setting is also offered by some marketing research agencies in the form of storefronts in shopping malls. While the cost is higher, the sponsoring firm remains unidentified, resulting in less bias on the part of the shoppers. Although this approach preserves anonymity, however, it should only serve as a forerunner to, and not as a substitute for, test marketing. There is simply no way to replace live sales experience in an authentic sales environment.

Test Marketing

Ultimately, a new product comes to the point where it has to own up to its destiny and fish or cut bait. Most elements of the marketing mix have been tested separately—from the product itself to its brand name, package, and advertising—but they have never been tried in combination. So the final round of marketing research involves the acid test of submitting them to the competitive conditions of the real marketplace, on a limited basis. This stage is called *test marketing* and consists of offering the innovation for sale in a select group of cities, using the intended introductory marketing mix.

Major differences between product testing and test marketing spring from the fact that product testing

- Utilizes a representative sample of the target market.
- Hands the test product and, if appropriate, the comparison model to the selected consumers in their homes at the company's initiative.
- Makes the new product or its use available for free to participating consumers and offers them an incentive to cooperate.
- Takes place in a sheltered setting, away from the onslaught of competition.

Test marketing, on the other hand, is distinguished from product testing by the following characteristics:

- Users are not selected by random sample; thus, at best, the test cities are representative of the national market but the actual distribution of test market buyers may be quite distorted in comparison with the later national patterns because of uncontrollable influences.
- The purchasers of the innovation have to take the buying initiative themselves.
- The buyers have to pay the regular (introductory) price and receive no special benefits.
- The innovation competes head-on with existing products and brands in the authentic sales environment of the chosen store and is thus typically just one among many products serving the same purpose.

Product tests may well yield favorably biased responses because the participants enjoy privileges for which they do not have to pay. Any expression of buying intentions on their part is usually noncommittal. In contrast, a test market should ideally constitute an accurate representation of the national market for this product. Socioeconomic structure, competitive conditions, and the distributive mechanism, to name but a few factors, should form a micropicture or model of the full-scale situation. It is the authenticity of the sales environment and the direct confrontation of the new product with the full range of competitive forces that make for the uniqueness and importance of test marketing.

Market tests are a method of risk reduction because they enable an empirical evaluation of an innovation's probability of success and allow for final adjustments in the marketing mix before the product is introduced full scale to the national market. Accordingly, companies conduct test marketing for one or more of the following reasons:

- To generate a more accurate indication of the product's sales potential
- To provide a final check of customer satisfaction with the product
- To identify the best combination of marketing mix elements

A sales forecast was, of course, made during the business analysis stage of the new product's evolution. But it was based on the information available at the time about the prospects of a product not yet in existence. Now this forecast should be updated with the help of real sales data for an existing product.

Similarly, consumer satisfaction with the emerging product was tested at various checkpoints along the way, principally in the form of concept testing and product testing. But at this point, satisfaction expresses itself in the most critical measure: the repurchase rate. It is relatively easy to sell somebody a new product for the first time. Curiosity and the excitement of change, of trying something different, propel such action. The proof of the pudding, however, lies in repeat purchases that indicate how many converts have been made. People will only buy a new product again and again if they are satisfied with its performance and consider it worth the price.

It is this latter element, purchasing and repurchasing the product, that is really new at this point. The consumer is exposed to advertising and sales promotion, has to find and select the product over a broad array of competitive choices, and has to pay for it. As it enters this final stage of preintroductory marketing research, product management may not be sure about one of the elements of the marketing mix and may still be considering several alternatives, such as different price levels, different packages, or different promotional approaches. These alternatives can now be tried out simultaneously in separate test cities to determine the most successful one. Thus test marketing can assist in finding the best marketing mix for the new product.

Test marketing, however, is too dangerous and expensive a tool to be undertaken frivolously. Ideally, product management should be able to predict the outcome of a test marketing program with a high degree of accuracy, based on previously generated information. It should never be used just to "see what happens." Rather, it should be employed to confirm management's predictions and create the confidence for a national launch. Statistics bear out the importance of using test marketing for this purpose, indicating that product management's prognoses are correct in less than half of all cases: "While the biggest and best marketers, such as Procter & Gamble, General Foods and General Mills, weed out approximately half of their new products in test market, as many as 30 percent of those that survive to be introduced nationwide fail to meet expectations."[18]

Mini-Market Tests

Test marketing is time-consuming and very expensive: "A single, classic test marketing exercise, including research, media costs, production and packaging, can cost upwards of $1 million. And in its last two major tests, Quaker Oats, for one, spent that sum on research alone."[19] According to International Multifoods, test marketing expenditures for a typical new product are composed as follows:[20]

Package design	6 percent
Production	15
Distribution	4
Advertising and sales promotion	30
Marketing research (telephone surveys, consumer diary panels, store sales audits, distribution studies)	45
Total test marketing expenditures	100 percent

Because of test marketing's sizable price tag, many product managers precede and focus it with a miniature market test:

> Rather than gearing up for a full test market—for which you must have a large volume of product, distribution channels organized and filled, and a fully-developed advertising campaign—you can undertake what might be called a "micro-market" or "mini-market" test. In this research, you put your product in just one, two or three stores in a town. If the town is small enough, the test stores might be all the suitable stores in it; if the town is larger, a selection of stores can be made.[21]

Mini-market tests typically involve communities with less than 50,000 inhabitants, whereas test marketing usually takes place in cities of more than 200,000. Mini-market tests are accordingly less expensive, quicker, and easier to carry out, offering more flexibility. But they should not be used as a substitute for test marketing. Instead, they should serve as forerunners, helping to fine-tune the marketing mix before full-scale trial. This permits product management to wring more productivity from test marketing, simultaneously making it more conclusive.

The two major methods of data collection employed in the subsequent market test are also applicable here: store audits to measure sales volume, and consumer interviews to reveal consumer reaction to the product and, in the case of nondurables, the extent of repeat purchase.[22]

Consumer interviewing should not be restricted to the test product but should also include competitive brands with which the respondent is familiar. Such a comparison provides the researcher with an indication of the magnitude of the product's potential market share. The main drawback of a mini-market test is its lack of projectability to the national level. It is thus the principal purpose of this phase to pretest the test marketing design rather than replace it, generating qualitative more than quantitative research.[23]

Another possibility is to conduct a simulated in-store market test, a low-budget procedure that may cost as little as $30,000.

> In a simulated test, a company may put its new product into a handful of stores for a period as brief as a weekend, and woo shoppers with gaudy displays, coupons and aggressive salespeople. Two weeks later, consumers are telephoned for their reaction to the product.[24]

Such simulations are not only inexpensive, they are also too short to be noticed by competitors. But there are serious methodological concerns. The hyped-up presentation is not characteristic of the national introduction or even a test market offer, the few participating stores can hardly serve as a reflection of the national scene, and repeat purchases are at best hypothetical.

Test Market Planning

Test marketing is an imperfect tool for guiding and predicting the marketing success of a new product. Pringles, the reconstituted potato chip from Procter & Gamble, test-marketed successfully but never lived up to its maker's expectations after nation-wide rollout. Rely tampons were test-marketed for three years prior to national marketing, never giving any cause for concern. Within one year after the full-scale launch, they were tragically connected with toxic shock syndrome and had to be recalled.[25] Nonetheless, test marketing is a crucial last screen, catching innovations that could otherwise prove to become a disappointment, an embarrassment, or a disaster. With few exceptions, the results of test marketing translate into a red or green light for national marketing.

One such exception was Pampers, the disposable diaper from Procter & Gamble. It failed in test marketing, which would normally spell a new product's demise. But the company had faith in and great hopes for the product. Several rounds of test marketing later, it had found the right price. The product took off and had to be rationed during national rollout, eventually going on to become the company's second-best-selling product, after Tide detergent.

But what decisions must be made in the preparation of a market test? Here are the main points of an outline suggested by a panel of experts:

- Market test objectives
- Criteria for evaluating results
- Pricing the test product
- Data-gathering techniques to be used
- Length of the test
- Coping with the results of disclosure
- Advertising and promotion in the test

- Budget requirements for the test
- Where to test
- Stores to be used[26]

It is obvious that without clearly enunciated objectives a meaningful test approach cannot be developed. To measure the achievement of the objectives, action standards have to be predetermined. If within a given time span a certain sales and/ or market share level is attained, what action should follow? Should, in other words, the plans for national introduction be implemented, cancelled, or altered?

While the price of the new product is important in the intermediary stages of in-home "shopping," simulated store tests, and mini-market tests, it now assumes a critical role. The prime dilemma of pricing new products (discussed at length later) derives from the fact that the price is supposed to be high enough to cover cost and generate a satisfactory profit but at the same time low enough to attract a substantial volume of purchases. The pricing task is additionally complicated by the fact that the direct price elasticity of demand is likely to be unknown at this point. Cost allocation, dependent on volume estimates, can thus only be very tentative during test marketing.

Techniques of Test Market Data Collection.   The two principal techniques of data collection employed in test marketing are store audits and consumer interviews. Whereas store audits report results, consumer interviews can delve into reasons. Store sales figures are absolutely essential, as they determine market shares and holding power. Where they rely on physical store audits, like those of A. C. Nielsen, intervals of two months between updates are inevitable. The advent of electronic scanners reading Universal Product Codes at supermarket checkout counters and other retail locations has expedited this data collection process to the point where minute-by-minute readings are possible.

However sophisticated their collection, sales data alone can be quite deceptive, potentially understating or overstating the true market response. Competitors buy market data from the same commercial sources and thus learn about test market results at the same time as does the company originating the new product. They may buy a supply of the product to analyze in *reverse engineering*. This procedure involves dissembling a competitive product to see how it was made in order to consider imitation or improvement. Worse yet, they may sabotage the results by lowering prices, increasing couponing or sampling, or using more aggressive sales tactics. In its eagerness to see the innovation succeed, product management itself may distort the results by spending disproportionately on advertising and engaging in an over-zealous sales effort.[27]

To shed light on the underlying behavior, consumer feedback is necessary. This can be obtained in the form of grocery diary panel data from such firms as MRCA or NPD, which enable longitudinal tracking of brand choices on a household-by-household basis. These data permit identification of first-time and repeat purchasers. Even the rhythm and extent of repurchasing can be determined this way, thus giving an indication of future national sales patterns.

The reasons for this observed behavior, however, are all but impossible to explore in this fashion. Participating households will state if they were stimulated by a coupon or cents-off deal but will otherwise not offer any insight into their motives, attitudes, perceptions, and level of satisfaction. These psychological factors have to be investigated via interviews. Consumer surveys can measure levels of awareness, brand trial, and satisfaction. And they can give insight into future behavior.

Duration of Testing.   To provide an accurate reading of market response, market tests have to be carefully planned and controlled. For this reason, they are usually carried out by independent marketing research agencies with professional staffs of project directors, statisticians, psychologists, and field supervisors. The duration of a market test can lie anywhere between six weeks and five years, depending on how long it takes to determine a stable repurchase rate, the company's ability to supply the market, and the comfort level of product management. On the point of supply capability: General Foods had to build a $5 million plant just to be able to supply its market test of Cycle canned dog food.

It is relatively easy for a firm to induce first trial or curiosity purchases of new products. The market success of most innovations, however, is determined by the percentage of initial purchasers who decide to adopt and thus continue to buy them. A spectacular initial burst of enthusiasm should not distract from the fact that only repeat purchases in the normal buying rhythm are profitable for the pioneering company. Three to six months of testing may well be sufficient for a frequently purchased and rapidly consumed convenience item. Durable consumer goods, on the other hand, which are bought or replaced infrequently and whose purchases are strongly influenced by economic conditions and other uncontrollable factors, will require longer market testing periods even though usually a repeat purchase rate is impossible to determine.

According to a group of experts

A test should be run long enough to accomplish three main objectives:
- Reveal the product's sales level after initial abnormal influences have run their course;
- Establish the fact, in the case of a nondurable product, that a satisfactory portion of this sales volume is accounted for by repeat purchases;
- Bring to light any product or merchandising deficiencies that should be corrected before national introduction.[28]

Test marketing is of little use if its results are distorted by temporary influences. Allowing sales patterns to stabilize is a condition for successful test marketing. Initial enthusiasm can lead to strong first-time sales. This pace can, however, be sustained only if a significant share of the triers become loyal buyers. This rate can only be determined with satisfactory accuracy after several buying periods have elapsed. Finally, test marketing provides a last chance to identify and overcome weaknesses in the marketing mix. It takes time for such weaknesses to filter back from the market-place, both from consumers and intermediaries.

The three objectives listed above would therefore advocate the motto: the longer, the better. This is counteracted, though, by the threat of competitive imitation during test marketing. While the pioneering company is test-marketing a new product, a competitor may be attracted by its sales results, which are readily available from such commercial sources as A. C. Nielsen. The competitor may proceed to obtain samples of the product through its sales force or a specialized product procurement service such as Marketing Intelligence Service, Ltd.[29] Using reverse engineering, the competitor could then create a similar product. This imitation may skip test marketing altogether and go immediately into national distribution while the original product is still being test-marketed. This danger of competitive scooping and preemption on the national scene grows in direct proportion to the amount of time spent in test marketing.

Besides premature imitation, cost is another factor that would tend to favor the approach: as long as necessary, as short as possible. The length of a market test is thus mainly dependent on three factors: the repurchase rate or the percentage of initial purchasers who carry out repeat purchases more than once, the danger of competitive imitation, and the cost of test marketing. The resultant dilemma facing product management is difficult to solve. The test should run long enough to yield reliable information on repurchase patterns and allow for meaningful forecasts of national sales. Yet it should be kept as brief as possible in order to prevent competitors from taking over the market even before the original innovation is introduced nationally.

Another major consideration in planning a market test is the kind of advertising and promotion support it will receive. It is obvious that the advertising plan has to be a scaled-down version of the intended national campaign. This is easier said than done, however. Local media do not necessarily offer the same programs, audiences, or opportunities as the elements of the national media plan do. Ideally, the test cities would be self-contained in terms of media influence. With regard to broadcasting, stations would neither serve areas beyond the city limits nor reach in from outside.[30] In the case of a conflict between coverage and cost, it is more important that the impressions or impact be comparable than that the cost of test market advertising be in line with the applicable portion of the national budget. Both broadcast and print media—even those of national scope—tend to be cooperative in facilitating local advertising for test purposes, for example, by inserting an advertisement only in those copies of a particular issue going to a particular test city.

Test Market Selection

The selection of test markets may be guided by the following criteria:

- Average income near the national average
- Not dependent on a single industry
- Not dominated by one ethnic or racial group
- Not subject to seasonal fluctuations in employment
- Suitable size (central city with at least 200,000 inhabitants)

- Self-contained with no dependence on neighboring area
- Adequate media coverage
- Not excessively used for testing by other companies

A recent survey produced the following list of cities most frequently used for test marketing:[31]

1. Albany–Schenectady, New York
2. Charlotte, North Carolina
3. Chicago, Illinois
4. Dallas–Fort Worth, Texas
5. Denver, Colorado
6. Fort Wayne, Indiana
7. Houston, Texas
8. Kansas City, Missouri
9. Minneapolis–St. Paul, Minnesota
10. Peoria, Illinois
11. Phoenix, Arizona
12. Portland, Oregon
13. The Quad Cities—Rock Island and Moline, Illinois, and Davenport and Bettendorf, Iowa
14. Sacramento–Stockton, California
15. Syracuse, New York

Number of Test Cities. The number of test markets to use depends on three factors: number of variations considered, representativeness, and cost. If different prices, packages, or promotional approaches are to be tested, only one variable should be altered at a time. Although using one test city per variation constitutes the bare minimum, it is advisable to use at least two and preferably four test markets per variation because of regional differences in consumer reaction. When Lipton was unsure which of three alternative prices to use in introducing its dehydrated Chicken Supreme Dinner, it employed two test cities per variation, finding that the medium price produced the best sales results.

The two criteria of representativeness and cost argue in opposite directions. To be truly representative, test cities should be chosen from different parts of the country, ranging from Sacramento to Houston and from Albany to Minneapolis. But representativeness increases the cost of a test marketing design. So a reasonable compromise has to be struck that endangers neither the integrity of the data nor that of the budget.

A last problem area to resolve before the market test can begin is securing dealer cooperation. This is not quite as easy as it may seem, for competition for shelf space is tight. It may well be that shelf space has to be rented and dealer cooperation paid for in order to make room for the innovation. This may be done in conjunction with forced distribution where the product is delivered directly to participating stores instead of winding its way through established distribution channels. This method is considerably faster and cheaper than conventional test marketing, particularly in mini-markets with populations in the 100,000 range, but it also reduces the realism of the experiment.[32]

Sometimes, however, store management is too cooperative—it makes a special effort to accommodate or promote the test product. Because this special support will hardly be duplicated during national introduction, it will bias the results and is therefore undesirable. Some of the questions that must be considered within the context of selecting retail outlets in test cities are

- What kind of stores should handle the test product—drugstores, department stores, supermarkets?
- Which chains or other retail companies should be selected?
- How many stores should be used?
- What sizes of stores should be included in the sample?
- Should the test product also be made available in stores that it is not planned to audit?[33]

As a general rule, test markets should be used only if their total costs are reasonably lower than the potential loss from failure at the national level if the product were introduced without test marketing. Marketing research should enable product management to predict the outcome of market testing with a high degree of accuracy based on knowledge gained in prior stages. If alternative marketing mixes are tested, their number has to be very small, two or three. The most frequently tested issues are level of advertising spending, price level, and promotional approaches.

In the test marketing of Vaseline Intensive Care, for instance, Chesebrough-Pond's used advertising only in two test markets and a combination of advertising and free samples in a third city. The results in this third location encouraged the company to choose the combination approach for the national introduction. While using just one city per variation is methodologically questionable, the opposite effect of excessive complexity can quickly occur if too many variations are tested at one time.

The difficulty and cost of administering a complex test marketing program involving a substantial number of sites have led some companies to experiment with a single large city and treat neighborhoods like separate markets. This greatly facilitates supply logistics as well as media purchases, thus lowering costs. Simultaneously, the danger of competitive intrusion is reduced. In any event, a test marketing program is definitely not the stage to try out a multiplicity of alternative approaches. This can be achieved more economically and less dangerously through simulation in the form of computer models.[34]

Interpreting Test Market Results

Whichever design is chosen, test market data have to be collected and interpreted. To produce meaningful insights and actionable information, the method chosen is often that of the *controlled experiment*. In this approach, two (or more) categories of test cities are created. The innovation is introduced to the experimental markets by employing a variant of the marketing mix and the introduction to the control markets is carried out using the basic version of the intended marketing mix. If two price levels are being considered, the new product will be presented in one group of cities at the price preferred by product management and in another group of cities at an experimental higher or lower price.

The term *controlled experiment,* however, not only means that comparable figures are being generated but also that all other influences on consumer purchasing behavior are being kept constant in both groups of markets. This condition is very hard to fulfill within the framework of everyday reality, even of geographically limited markets. It means that consumers should neither possess an extraordinary supply of the product nor stock up on the product category in question to an unusual degree.

A "before–after design with control group" uses comparative data—both in time and space—to control for this condition. "Before" data measure sales and market shares in the product category in both groups of cities during a reasonable period, four months, for instance, before the test. The "after" data collected during and after the test market experiment can then be compared to the "before" measurements to detect any unusual fluctuations in total category volume or brand shares. Similarly, cross-market comparisons before and after can identify exceptional deviations.

Also, competitive activity should not vary during the test period. Ideally, competitors' marketing mixes should remain unchanged—no price cuts, no special promotions, coupons, or rebates, and no product modifications. Where previously planned competitive campaigns or deliberate acts of sabotage interfere, the resultant data may become useless for predicting national reaction. Sufficient store availability and display of the new product would also have to be ensured—a question of both sales force sell-in and follow-through. Basically, any element of an innovation's marketing mix can be subjected to a last comparative check in the form of a market test. It is important, then, that only one variable be varied at a time or else its impact cannot be isolated.

Audits Alone Can Be Misleading.   An important part of the execution of a test marketing plan is frequently the collection of store audit data. In order to permit meaningful comparisons, pretest category sales and brand shares are utilized as points of reference. Store audits during the test should always include the chief rival brands. But even then, as experience indicates, sales figures taken by themselves can easily be misleading.

The four charts in Figures 9–2 and 9–3 bring out this fact. Here is how Bristol-Myers describes the situation:

> They deal with two specialty products, *A* and *B*, which we test marketed and then introduced. So we can compare sales estimates which might have been made on the basis of sales audits alone, with sales volume actually achieved after introduction. The first chart shows the sales volume developed by brand *A* in its six months of test marketing. This volume is represented by a solid line. The dotted line is our extrapolation of the indicated growth trend, a projection which could be considered reasonable or conservative.

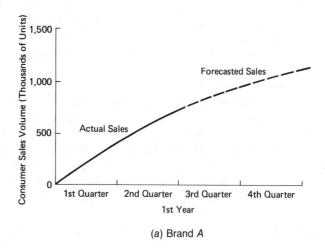

(a) Brand A

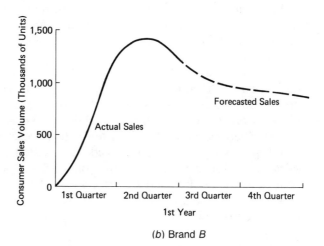

(b) Brand B

FIGURE 9–2
Actual Sales for First Six Months and Forecast from that Point
(*Source:* (Reprinted with permission from *Market Testing Consumer Products*
[New York: National Industrial Conference Board, 1967], 148))

The second chart shows that brand B apparently "trended off" after strong consumer trial. (Incidentally, this is the most familiar shape of curve for most new products which I have had experience with.) In our projection we forecast a continued, although gentler, decline.

But now see what actually happened. The third chart indicates that our forecast for brand A was too optimistic, and the fourth shows that our projection for brand B was too pessimistic. For both brands the intervals between repurchases were long. In the case of brand A, repurchase rates did not develop satisfactorily, so sales turned down. In the case of B, repeats were good, and this reversed the apparent downward trend which was initially reflected.

It is clear, ... that only by supplementing store audit figures with data obtained in consumer interviews can the probable shape of the test product's sales

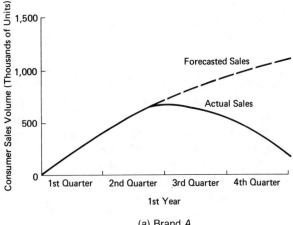

(a) Brand *A*

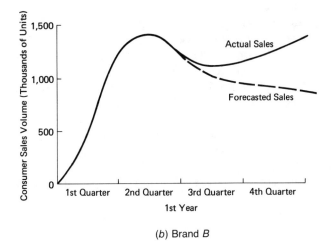

(b) Brand *B*

FIGURE 9–3
Comparison of Actual Sales for the First Year and Forecast Made at Six Months
(*Source:* Reprinted with permission from *Market Testing Consumer Products*
[New York: National Industrial Conference Board, 1967], 149)

curve be established. The repeat purchase rate information we obtained from consumer interviewing during the market tests of brands *A* and *B* enabled us to forecast
sales curves which more closely conformed to the volume later achieved.[35]

Thus the prime functions of consumer interviews during test marketing
are to

- Complement and/or modify sales audit data
- Enable more meaningful and reliable forecasts
- Identify the relevant characteristics of purchasers
- Elicit consumer reactions to the product

- Determine the repurchase rate
- Measure consumer awareness and trial rates
- Pinpoint consumer reasons for not trying and/or repurchasing the innovation

Obtaining direct consumer feedback is the essential difference that sets test marketing apart from mere sales tests. A sales test may look deceivingly like a market test. A new product is offered for sale in a few select areas, usually supported by a promotional campaign. The markets, however, are often chosen arbitrarily, based on the judgment of sales managers. And sales results are used as the sole measure of success. This can lead to unfounded optimism if competitive out-of-stock conditions or an influx of visitors inflate sales temporarily. Conversely, it can produce unnecessary pessimism if impending layoffs, competitive sabotage, lack of product availability on store shelves, or other temporary inhibiting factors distort sales. Only direct consumer feedback can help avoid such mistakes in the interpretation of sales results.

Such direct consumer feedback can be obtained in the form of consumer interviews or grocery diary panel data where participating households report all grocery purchases on a regular basis. But modern technology now offers another alternative: scanner-generated supermarket checkout counter sales and purchase data. Electronic scanners used to read Universal Product Code (UPC) imprints on grocery packages can provide instant and accurate sales or product movement data for a store as a whole. This information can be supplemented by a panel arrangement where shoppers identify themselves at the checkout counter and thus have their purchase diary produced and tracked electronically. This can be further amplified by using cable television to present experimentally alternative advertising executions to matched samples of households within a community and measuring differences in purchase impact, if any. Electronic data generation significantly expedites data gathering and processing in test marketing, thus facilitating an earlier national launch decision.[36]

By carefully evaluating both store sales data and the results of consumer diaries and/or interviews, product management is able to develop a more comprehensive picture of the product's chance of becoming a success in the marketplace. If the new product's test market performance lives up to the predetermined standards, the company is well advised to move ahead swiftly with its plans for national introduction. Loss of time at this stage generally means loss of market share because a successful product will attract competitive imitations in short order—which is precisely what happened to General Foods when it test-marketed Maxim freeze-dried coffee for an extended period. Having invented this new product category with its superior flavor-retaining ability, the company was preempted nationally by Nestlé, which quickly entered the market with its own brand, Taster's Choice. The latter consistently outsold the pioneering brand.

Once the decision to go national has been made, the company has to gear up for full-scale production to "fill the pipeline" to the consumer and keep it filled on an ongoing basis. Pilot production during the test marketing phase enabled production management to work out the bugs and produce the necessary tooling so that the production line can now function smoothly. Ideally, the capacity on-stream will be sufficient to satisfy at least the initial demand, with further expansions planned as they become necessary.

SUMMARY

Before a company puts its reputation and resources on the line by offering a new product to the national market, product management is well advised to engage in market testing. Without a sense of market reaction to the actual product and its marketing mix, it would be quite risky to proceed with a full-scale introduction. Far from merely testing market acceptance, market testing provides a feedback loop from the marketplace that can help product managers refine both the product offering and its supporting marketing mix.

Toward this end of developing the optimum introductory marketing program, a two-step procedure is usually employed, consisting of product testing and test marketing. Product testing means placing the new product in the hands of consumers and asking them to try it. Mostly this is done in the form of blind pair comparison testing where the innovation is compared against a major competing brand without label identification. The purpose of this approach is to permit performance evaluation without brand bias. Participating consumers are then queried as to which of the two products they prefer and why, simultaneously exploring suggested product improvements.

Before moving on to test marketing with a possibly modified product, some companies may utilize one or more forms of intermediary market exploration that are both less costly and less visible. Such premarket testing can take the form of in-home "shopping" in a competitive setting where consumers are asked to choose from an array of brands. Alternatively, product management may prefer to conduct simulated store tests in shopping mall storefront locations.

As an ultimate preintroductory check, many new products undergo test marketing. It is time-consuming, costly, and risky, but test marketing can offer invaluable insights into market reaction in an authentic sales setting. In a select number of cities that mirror the national scene, the introductory marketing mix is used on a trial basis to determine whether it produces the desired results. These results are measured in two ways: in the form of store sales (obtained through audits or scanners) and of direct consumer feedback (diary panel data and/or consumer interviews). As long as only one variable is altered at a time, even alternative marketing mixes can be tested in this fashion. The outcome of test marketing then governs the decision on whether to go national with the new product.

NOTES

1. Margaret Loeb, "Tasters of Cigarettes Find On-Job Puffing Isn't a Drag," *Wall Street Journal,* 22 August 1984.
2. See ibid.
3. "The Serpentine Path to New Product Success," *Quaker Quarterly* (31 March 1984): 13.
4. Ibid.
5. Ibid., 9.
6. Ibid.
7. *Market Testing Consumer Products* (New York: National Industrial Conference Board, 1967), 63ff.

8. See Craig Endicott, "Rating the Soaps in the Quad Cities," *Advertising Age,* 22 Feb. 1982.
9. See ibid.
10. See Ken Wells, "How 500 Cats Play Guinea Pig in Pursuit of the Purrfect Food," *Wall Street Journal,* 20 April 1984.
11. *Market Testing Consumer Products,* 64.
12. Ibid., 66.
13. Lawrence Ingrassia, "A Matter of Taste: There's No Way to Tell if a New Food Product Will Please the Public," *Wall Street Journal,* 26 Feb. 1980.
14. See ibid.
15. See ibid.
16. *Market Testing Consumer Products,* 72.
17. See ibid., 73ff.
18. Sandra Salmans, "New Trials in Test Marketing," *New York Times,* 11 April 1982.
19. Ibid.
20. Ibid.
21. *Market Testing Consumer Products,* 83.
22. Ibid., 85.
23. See ibid., 85ff.
24. Salmans, "New Trials."
25. See ibid.
26. See *Market Testing Consumer Products,* 94.
27. See Salmans, "New Trials."
28. *Market Testing Consumer Products,* 100ff.
29. See "New Products Museum Favors Good Ideas Gone Wrong," *Sunday Freeman,* 23 Sept. 1984, 49.
30. See Salmans, "New Trials."
31. See Salmans, "New Trials."
32. See Salmans, "New Trials."
33. *Market Testing Consumer Products,* 134.
34. See, for instance, Robert Blattberg and John Golanty, "Tracker: An Early Test Market Forecasting and Diagnostic Model for New Product Planning," *Journal of Marketing Research* (May 1978), and Henry P. Khost, "Pretesting to Avoid Product Postmortems: Simulated Test Marketing Delivers on Its Promises," *Advertising Age,* 22 Feb. 1982, M-10–M-11.
35. *Market Testing Consumer Products,* 147 (statements made by Mr. Pearson from Bristol-Myers).
36. See "Advances in Scanner-Based Research System Yield Fast, Accurate New Product Test Results," *Marketing News,* 18 Sept. 1981, 20.

CASE STUDY

A POT OF GOLD?

The Crystal Company is a manufacturer of liquid detergent for the hand dishwashing market that is sold under the brand name Crystal. Crystal is a subsidiary of Target Corporation, which was established in 1949 and had a domestic sales volume of more than $5 billion in 1987. Crystal's plant is located in suburban Chicago.

More than three-quarters of the households in the United States use liquid detergent for hand dishwashing. Total industry sales in this market amount to about $1 billion a year. Participating in this very competitive market, Crystal has been able to capture and hold a 5 percent market share for its brand. The market is dominated, however, by three firms:

Procter & Gamble	
Dawn, Ivory, Joy	45 percent
Colgate-Palmolive	
Palmolive, Ajax	30 percent
Lever Brothers	
Sunlight	15 percent

The remaining share of market is held by a number of minor brands and private labels. Retail prices for the popular 22-ounce bottle range from $1.39 to $1.59.

Testing Rainbow

Crystal's New Product Development Group has studied the market carefully and has come to the conclusion that, notwithstanding the lack of growth in the market, there is room for another entry, provided that it offers a clear advantage over competing brands. Marketing research has indicated that the majority of buyers display a surprisingly low incidence of brand loyalty. Considering most major brands to be interchangeable due to comparable performance characteristics, they readily switch from one brand to another during promotional campaigns. Concept testing has identified two key factors that consumers take for granted in any leading hand dishwashing detergent: cleaning power and gentleness on the skin.

The group has decided to position Crystal's new entry as its "fighting brand," a quality product at a bargain price. Its differential advantage will be its low cost of 99¢ for a 22-ounce bottle, considerably below competing name brands. The new product will be marketed under the brand name Rainbow. Product tests have confirmed that consumers like the product's fragrance and its grease-cutting performance that leaves their dishes shining. Blind pair comparison tests have not found any significant difference in performance when compared to current market leaders.

At a critical point in Rainbow's evolution, Don Willcox had been brought in to head its development effort as the new brand's product manager. Don is an enthusiastic, dynamic young man with an MBA from a prestigious business school and has more than five years' experience in marketing packaged goods.

Although there is consensus in the group that further market testing is needed before the introductory marketing program can be finalized, lively discussion centers on the choice of methodology. The company's marketing research manager, Carolyn Jones, favors test marketing because of the quality of the data generated in this fashion. In response, Don voices his concerns: "Our objective is to provide Rainbow with real-world, in-market exposure to help us evaluate its sales potential, consumer reaction, and our marketing program. But I am afraid of going into full-fledged test marketing. I am worried that the competition would try to scoop, preempt, or sabotage our program in any way it could. Also, test marketing is terribly expensive and time-consuming."

The choice of methodology was complicated by the fact that the group had formulated four

This case was prepared for instructional purposes by Sreedhar Kavil, Assistant Professor of Marketing, St. John's University, New York, New York. Although based on an actual business situation, names, places, and other data have been disguised..

alternative introductory promotions to speed market entry for Rainbow:

1. Free scrub sponge with full-price (99¢) purchase
2. Introductory price of 69¢ for 22-ounce bottle
3. Six-ounce trial size bottles for 29¢
4. Free 6-ounce samples mailed to homes

Given the range of alternatives to be investigated, several group members advocated mini-market tests because of their speed, versatility, and lower cost. The group also discussed the type of data to be collected and used in evaluating market test results and emphasized the importance of determining the extent, if any, of cannibalization of the company's established brand Crystal by the new brand Rainbow.

Discussion Questions

1. Do you recommend mini-market tests and/or test marketing? Explain the reasoning for your choice.
2. Describe the objectives of the research approach that you recommend, as well as the methodology that you would employ.
3. How long would you run the market test? What kind of budget would you allow? How would you prevent competitors from interfering with your market test?
4. In your research design, how important are consumer interviews? What can the company benefit from this component that it cannot learn in other ways?

PART THREE

The Introductory Marketing Program

The decisions concerning the marketing mix for a new product—although discussed here separately for easier identification and comprehension—are in reality closely interwoven with the other stages of new product evolution. At the time of the final decision on whether or not to go ahead with the introduction of the innovation, the entire marketing program has necessarily been drawn up in the desired detail. Packaging thus cannot be separated from the development and design of the product itself nor from its promotional campaign. Other influences on product design come from the choice of distribution channels, as well as from pricing and advertising decisions. The decisions concerning the various elements of the introductory marketing mix are highly interdependent and cannot meaningfully be made in isolation from each other. Rather, they have to be carefully coordinated and integrated with each other. Their joint application is designed to achieve optimum profits through the satisfaction of customer needs and the solution of customer problems.

The marketing mix is a highly versatile instrument, composed of all the means that a firm employs in order to stimulate and promote the sale of its products. The traditional keyboard of product and pricing policies, channels of distribution, and advertising has been enlarged by additional manuals. Product management's degree of freedom in choosing a marketing program for an innovation depends in part on the product's degree of newness or stage in the life cycle. The more revolutionary the product is, the more revolutionary the methods can be that are utilized in its marketing. The marketing mix for substitute and complementary products in mature markets, however, is typically largely predetermined by industry practice, leaving product managers with little flexibility.

The elements of the marketing mix, together with some key decision complexes related to the individual marketing tools, are listed below:

- Product policy
    Determination of target markets—who, what, when, where, how, how much
    Product mix—product lines, quality levels, degree of differentiation, diversification
    New products—design, features and benefits, additional research and development projects
    Production method—make or buy
- Packaging policy
    Function—protection, promotion, profit; primary versus secondary package
    Type—disposable, returnable, refillable, recyclable, biodegradable, ecologically safe; secondary use, multiple packaging
    Material—choice of packaging material, texture, dimensions and specifications, color
    Design—styling, size, appearance, perception of package
- Branding policy
    Brand ownership—manufacturer's brands, distributor's brands, mixed brands, unbranded merchandise
    Branding options—individual versus family brand names
    Selection of a brand name—meaningful, easy to remember, registerable
    Brand strategy—extension, repositioning, multiple brands
- Customer service policy
    Warranty—extent of coverage
    Spare parts—availability, cost
    Training—competence and professionalism of service personnel
- Pricing policy
    Pricing philosophy—skimming versus penetration
    Margins—manufacturer's margin, wholesaler's margin, retailer's margin
    Pricing flexibility—rigid versus negotiated prices
- Credit policy
    Conditions—delivery, payment
    Terms—installments, returns, accommodations
    Allowances—rebates, discounts, trade-ins, bartering
- Channels of distribution
    Route from producer to customer—direct and/or indirect
    Intensity of market coverage—intensive, selective, and exclusive distribution
    Channel control—manufacturer versus intermediary, multiple channels
    Intensity of cooperation—distributor training, motivation
- Physical distribution
    Warehousing—plant, field, or distributor warehousing
    Transportation—air, road, rail, water, pipeline
    Inventory—when and how much to order, inventory cost versus cost of lost sales

Handling—convenience, safety, efficiency

Plant location—raw materials, energy, labor, consumption oriented

- Advertising policy

Advertising focus—trade versus consumer advertising

Platform—image or benefit advertising

Agency—current or new agency

Budget—amount, allocation, frequency, reach

Media mix—print and broadcast media

- Sales promotion policy

Program focus—sales force, dealers, customers

Methods—samples, trial sizes, coupons, deals, displays, premiums, demonstrations

Approach—techniques for securing display and use of sales promotional materials

- Personal selling

Selling task—sell-in and restocking versus continuous selling

Sales force options—existing organization, new sales force, temporary sales force, manufacturer's representatives

Sales effort execution—training, motivating, compensating, evaluating

This list gives only a flavor of the variety and complexity of marketing mix decisions that product management has to make with regard to the launching of a new product. To be successful, these decisions have to be made in concert with each other and in tune with marketplace conditions. Only then can the innovation be transferred smoothly in its most critical phase from internal technological perfecting to external market offering. This challenge calls on the full range of experience and talent of the product manager and renders product management a true proving ground for advanced marketing management positions.

CHAPTER 10

Product-Related Marketing Mix Decisions

The elements of the introductory marketing mix can be broadly classified as product-related policies and other marketing tools. The product-related factors encompass product, packaging, and branding policy. Although these three are very closely connected, forming what has been called the "tangible product"—the bundle of benefits immediately surrounding and virtually inseparable from the core benefit sought by buyers—they can and should be decided on separately, though not independently. A change in any one of them may readily mean a new product to the ultimate user. And a mistake in any one of them can prove fatal—even if the other two components have been honed to perfection. Only their proper combination as guided by marketing research will provide the right basis for amplification by the other elements of the introductory marketing mix.

Product Policy

With regard to product policy, the major decisions have already been made throughout the evolutionary process. In sequential stages, the new product has been conceptualized, formulated, designed, tested, and reformulated and redesigned to ensure its success in a market fraught with unknowns. In the process, its materials, components, and features have been decided on, thus determining the benefits that it will be able to offer to one or more market segments. Some further decisions still have to be made though.

One of these decisions is whether the innovation, which has been developed in the firm's own research facilities, should also be manufactured in the company's own production facilities. In other words, should the firm make all the parts on its own production equipment, or should certain components, or even the whole product, be bought from another firm? If the company cannot build up and bring on-stream adequate production capacity in a reasonable amount of time, it may have to rely on outside sources for some time to come in order to supply the market with sufficient quantities of the new product.

Also, if management wants to minimize the potential loss from failure at the national level, it might at first have the innovation manufactured by an outside vendor. Such temporary or permanent "outsourcing" is not without its risks, however. Temporary outsourcing of an entire product carries the danger of creating a competitor upon termination of the contractual relationship, unless the originating firm is adequately protected by a wall of patents. Permanent outsourcing results in a dependency relationship, as the pioneer becomes dependent on the supplying vendor for punctual delivery, adherence to quality specifications, and restraint in price increases.

Besides making such complex make or buy decisions, management further has to decide on the dimensions of the product mix. As a general rule, radical innovations are introduced with little variety to choose from. At this stage of the product life cycle, it is the acceptance or rejection of the new product concept, not the extent of the available choice, that makes or breaks the sale. When adding new products in an already established market, however, it may be desirable to offer a greater selection in a new subcategory. A new car size may thus come in several body types with several engines and options to choose from, not to forget color and upholstery.

Another key decision area within the product policy complex is the innovation's relationship to current products and product lines of the company. Will it displace or complement current products? Should any existing products be deleted now or at some more or less specific future date? Many companies are willing to compete with themselves by introducing new products in product categories where they already have established a presence. In the mid-1960s, for instance, Colgate-Palmolive, which had long marketed its flagship Colgate brand in the toothpaste market by emphasizing cavity prevention, introduced Ultra-Brite as a dentifrice with a tooth brightener effect and advertised it using a sex appeal theme. In such cases, "cannibalization"—the migration of buyers from the established to the new product—may occur.

Corporate philosophies as to the acceptability of the cannibalization effect differ. At one end of the spectrum, it is abhorred and such products are simply not introduced. Other managements subscribe to the "survival of the fittest" philosophy and do not hesitate to launch innovations that may send some of their established brands into a tailspin. A frequent and prudent attitude of product management is to scrap present breadwinners only after a new product has proven its worth and appeal in the marketplace and an old product has fallen off in sales and profit contribution significantly.

A final product policy consideration involves initiating the development of a successor product even before the latest one has been rolled out nationally. This approach is based on the conviction that new product evolution should not be a sporadic, intermittent activity that is triggered by the business equivalent of a fire alarm to combat acute threats. Rather, it should be an ongoing program that continuously prepares a firm for future challenges and opportunities. Product life cycles are constantly shortening, requiring companies steadily to update and strengthen their offerings. Long evolutionary lead times call for a carefully planned and executed program of product addition and deletion.

Packaging Policy

The importance of packaging ranges from mere in-transit protection to major selling tool. The term *packaging* refers to both the design and execution of a container and/or wrapper for a product. More specifically, the *primary package* is the immediate container of the product that usually stays with the product throughout its entire period of use, such as a tube or a bottle. Often the product becomes inseparable from, and closely identified with, its primary package—for instance, Campbell's familiar red and white soup can. All so-called "package goods" are presented and sold in at least a primary package. It is this primary package that constitutes the essential focus of this section.

Two other types of packages should be mentioned for the sake of completeness. The *secondary package* represents the wrapper around the product container. It is usually discarded when the product is first used, since its principal function is in-transit protection of its contents. The box that a tube of toothpaste comes in provides a good example. This example also points out that the secondary package may further serve a display purpose and shares a promotional responsibility with the primary package.

The *shipping package* is typically made of corrugated cardboard and serves mainly to protect the product during transportation and handling. In the case of a durable good, it contains just one unit of the product, for example, an electric dryer. In the case of a nondurable good, a master shipping carton contains several units of the product, a dozen bottles of ketchup, for instance.

In this latter case of self-service convenience items, the significance of careful (primary) package design is particularly evident. Today's supermarkets display on average some 20,000 items. With a typical shopping trip lasting about twenty minutes, a shopper may pass 1,000 items per minute. Accordingly, many products are never considered, or even noticed, unless special efforts are made to attract the shopper's attention through displays, shelf-talkers, and eye-catching packages. For lack of sales personnel, the package has to assume the selling function as the "silent salesperson on the shelf." Having been presold through presentation in advertising, the recognition of a familiar brand name and package greatly increases a shopper's likelihood to stop and purchase.

Functions of Packaging

Grocery manufacturers have long realized that a package is not merely a container. Properly designed, it can be a strong motivating force behind the purchase and consumption of a product. It is the package that makes the promise that the new product will perform in a manner superior to any of its competitors. A poorly designed package is likely to doom a new product, regardless of its merits.

The functions of packaging can be described by *three Ps:* protection, promotion, and profit. The *protection* heading should be expanded to include identification and convenience, and the promotion heading should also cover communication. It is only natural that a seller would want to protect a product against evaporation, spilling, spoilage, and physical damage en route to the consumer. Damaged goods cannot be sold at full price, if they can be sold at all.

Of greater and steadily increasing importance, however, is the protection of the consumer in dealing with both the package and its contents. Following several deaths from cyanide-laced headache remedy capsules in the early 1980s, tamperproof packaging of many products became a key concern. Baby food had long been vacuum-sealed, resulting in a popping sound when a container is opened for the first time. Factory-sealing of many other products soon became routine, in some cases employing three separate seals: glued flaps on the secondary package and outer and inner seals on the primary package. One product using this approach is Tylenol.

Other concerns relate to injuries sustained from containers. When a well-known consumer goods firm introduced pudding in cans with pull-off tops, parents complained that their children cut their tongues and lips when licking out the cans. Because of the dangers inherent in the consumption of drugs and caustic household liquids by children, child-resistant tops for their containers were mandated by law, causing unintended difficulties for arthritic persons.

Besides protecting both the product and its users, packages are increasingly called on to protect the environment from litter and pollution. Ecological concerns have risen sharply in recent years and have led to calls for biodegradable packaging. McDonald's has been urged by New York State officials to discontinue use of styrofoam containers because they are not biodegradable and clog landfills. The trend has also been away from one-way disposable containers for beverages because their method of disposal contributed significantly to the litter problem marring the nation's roadsides. So-called "bottle bills" in several states require returnable beverage containers and impose deposits. Although recycling of beverage containers has not exactly become a national pastime, it has assumed such proportions that a significant share of beverage containers are now made from reclaimed materials. When pull-off can tops littered the landscape, the beverage industry adopted tops that remained attached after opening.

In conjunction with branding and the closely related tool of labeling, packaging also helps to identify a product. It enables repeat purchasing and facilitates the development of brand loyalty, effectively reducing the likelihood of competitive substitution. Also, the buyer can use the package to identify the manufacturer and/or distributor to present inquiries or claims. The convenience aspect of packaging refers to purchasing, carrying, storing, using, opening, closing, and refilling or reusing. Packages that are more convenient than those of the competition carry valuable extra appeal.

The *promotion* function of packaging has already been alluded to. As the "silent salesperson on the shelf," the package has to attract the shopper's eye and sell the product, and in the home, it should entice consumption and encourage repurchase. But the package also serves as a crucial means of communication. The package has to communicate its contents and their ingredients, instructions for use, indications, recipes, warnings, price, Universal Product Code (UPC), weight or volume, nutritional information, product appeal, size, color, flavor, expiration date, number of servings, brand name, and manufacturer. These multiple communications requirements place great demands on the creativity of package designers, who, on a more subtle level, must also establish credibility and distinctiveness.

Direct *profit* impact of packaging can be achieved in a number of ways. Holiday or gift packaging of a product such as men's aftershave lotion can be so attractive in itself that the markup for the special container can exceed its cost, thus generating an extra profit. Multiple unit packaging, for example, a six-pack of beer or a carton of cigarettes, simultaneously cuts down on handling costs and increases consumption due to in-home availability of the product.

Designing the Package

A well-designed package is one that gets the product to consumers intact and motivates them to purchase it while simultaneously enhancing the product's value and attractiveness. Most package design tasks can be classified into one of three categories: package for a new product, package for an extension of an established product line, and redesign of an existing package.

A designer enjoys the greatest amount of freedom and flexibility in designing a package for a dramatically different new product that is unrelated to the company's existing product mix. The design goal in this instance is to develop a unique, distinctive style in terms of shape, materials, and graphics. It should provide the product with identity and visibility, communicating the character and benefits of the product. Identifying and differentiating the innovation, the new package has to incorporate due consideration for potential additions to the new line.

In contrast, developing a package for an extension of an established product line is relatively simple. Under a *family packaging* policy, the packages of related products resemble each other closely. An individual entry, such as a certain flavor, may be distinguished only by its generic description (e.g., Campbell's cream of mushroom soup) or by a different color (e.g., d-CON insect sprays) in combination with a generic description. Even where such an explicit philosophy is absent, similar uses generally suggest similar packaging.

Easy as it seems, the redesign of an existing package is possibly the most challenging of the three types of new package design tasks. It appears reasonable and appropriate to adjust a product's package to changes in competitive conditions and buyers' life-styles, updating it periodically to conform to current expectations and usage patterns. But creating this contemporary new look and thus, in essence, a new product is a difficult assignment at best, often requiring the services of specialized design firms. Unless the utmost care is exercised and thorough marketing research undertaken, serious damage to a firm's reputation and sales, profits, and market share could result. And occasionally it may turn out that the existing package, in spite of its relative age, may have the most staying power and sales appeal of all alternatives considered. When Warner-Lambert reviewed the packaging for its Listerine mouthwash, a marketing research study indicated that it already had the best possible bottle. The container's comparatively unattractive looks and medicinal appearance suggested high germ-killing power. Any change would have detracted from the product, the leader in its field.

Researching a new package design can be frustrating. When hard-core users of a popular pound cake mix were asked to pick the current package from an array of ten choices, they identified a design that had never been on the market. Successful redesigns, however, can significantly enhance the appeal and salability of a product, giving it a new lease on life. Ovaltine, an old-line energy-oriented beverage, benefited greatly from the impetus of a new package. Moving away completely from the traditional metal can packaging for automotive motor oil—which required pouring spouts and left users' hands greasy—Quaker State introduced a new convenience in oil changes, most of which are done by automobile owners themselves: Translucent plastic bottles (whose use does not increase the price of the oil) allow grease-free application and ready content level identification.[1]

It can be dangerous, however, to alter a package design just for the sake of change. Rather, a change should be instituted only if it is likely to increase the product's sales and profit potential. This can, for instance, be done by eliminating some of the current package's negative features and incorporating additional benefits in the new design. Three basic questions to be considered before any change in packaging are

- Is a package change really necessary?
- Will a package change do the job? In other words, will changing the package be enough to accomplish the marketing objective?
- Is the company's management willing to make the necessary investment in the package and in introducing it properly?

These preliminary questions should be augmented by a number of other considerations:

- How will consumers respond to the change?
- What potential damage could a packaging change produce?
- Given a certain consumer response, how will the trade react to the new package?
- Will the packaging change influence the price of the product?
- Can the new package be filled with existing packaging equipment?
- How will the physical distribution of the product be affected?
- How will the new package compare with and stand out from competitive packages?
- How high are the expected additional sales and profits?

All these questions, and many more, are being contemplated with great care and concern by Campbell Soup Company as it prepares to undertake the unthinkable: abandoning the familiar tin soup can. The Campbell can has been synonymous with soup in the United States since 1897, when a company executive chose the red and white colors of the Cornell University football team for its label.[2] Although Campbell is the third-largest manufacturer of cans in the United States, selling more than 2 billion cans of soup a year, Gordon McGovern, its president and chairman, is worried that cans have outlived their usefulness.

"The major rap against the soup can is inconvenience. Consumers don't like having to use a can opener, mix the can's soup with water if the soup is condensed (which it usually is), heat the mixture and then clean several utensils."[3] So Campbell is experimenting with a variety of alternative packaging approaches. Leading contenders are plastic microwavable bowls with plastic lids. But a seventeen-member task force, led by the company's packaging director, is also investigating, through laboratory tests and consumer surveys, a plastic container that resembles a can.[4]

A packaging innovation was just what McKesson was looking for when California inventor Richard Hagan came along. He had developed a heavy-duty but lightweight plastic bottle for old-fashioned seltzer with its high-pressure carbonation, accompanied by a separate, reusable siphon nozzle. McKesson's Alhambra National Water Company expects to do well with the product in national distribution.[5]

Package design tasks are usually executed by one or more of the following sources: the package design function of the company itself, the design department of a packaging supplier, product management, the company's advertising agency, or a specialized packaging design firm. The result of their efforts, a new packaging design, has to add new value to the product, be easily recognizable, and be capable of economic reproduction and filling. To provide for continuity of product presentation, packaging changes for an ongoing product should be gradual and evolutionary rather than abrupt and revolutionary. An example is provided by Ivory soap, which has undergone many packaging changes in its history of more than 100 years.[6] Similarly, fictitious characters incorporated into the package design may need to have their appearance updated periodically to reflect changing tastes. The White Rock soft drink and Morton salt girls have been redesigned several times, and Betty Crocker has been altered repeatedly to the point where she appears younger today than when this character was first used.

Color is an extremely important element in packaging design. The investigation of optimum colors and color combinations on packages has gained such emphasis that specialized agencies have been founded that dedicate themselves exclusively to color. Extensive color research was conducted for the packaging of a new cigarette that is directed toward women and named Satin. Even taboos have been broken. In spite of the unwritten rule that no consumer products in the United States should be packaged in black, Players cigarettes were reintroduced in this packaging color. Because silver and gold connote elegance and prestige, such premium products as Benson & Hedges 100s and Michelob beer liberally use these colors in their packaging.

Consumers have emotional and symbolic reactions to colors. They associate specific colors with certain things, such as the "refreshing" colors green and blue with men's aftershave lotions.[7] In soft drinks, the color red symbolizes cola. When Canada Dry changed its sugar-free ginger ale can from red to green and white, sales increased by more than 25 percent.[8] The preference rating of a color depends on the rarity of its appearance, the retention power in a person's mind, and its symbolic meaning. When a new cosmetic product was displayed side by side in yellow and pink containers, the pink package outsold the yellow one 96 to 4. When another cosmetic firm changed its package color from blue to yellow, sales immediately tripled.

These examples indicate that colors produce definite emotional responses. They can be stimulating or calming, soothing or irritating, harsh or soft, cold or hot. Colors also create symbolic meanings in the mind of the viewer. They can symbolize delicacy, elegance, femininity or masculinity, strength, dignity, quality, and even danger or safety.[9]

These emotional and symbolic reactions are common to every purchase, although consumers typically are not aware of them. Such reactions were confirmed by a color study concerned with the package design for a new powdered detergent. Besides identifying the most appealing package color, the study was designed to determine if the consumer was influenced by the color of the package in judging the performance of the product. The detergent was put into three different boxes: one all yellow, one predominantly blue without any yellow, and a third one blue with splashes of yellow. Participants were asked to try all three. Their reports stated that the detergent in the yellow box was too strong, allegedly ruining clothes in some cases. The detergent in the blue box reportedly left clothes dirty-looking. The third box, however, received favorable responses, indicating the right combination of gentleness and cleaning power. As the detergent in each box was identical, the respondents' judgments were based solely on their psychological reaction to the package colors.

As mentioned earlier, the rarity of appearance is another factor in color preference. Common colors become monotonous, tiresome, and boring, prompting consumers to look for the excitement and surprise of new color sensations. For this reason, green does not sell well to farmers because it is so much a part of their daily environment. City dwellers, on the other hand, are attracted to green because they see less of it. Salem cigarettes use green extensively both in packaging and advertising to suggest the refreshing excitement of the great outdoors.

The appropriate color will attract and hold the attention of the shopper in a self-service shopping environment characterized by competitive clutter. The brighter the package, the easier and farther it will be seen. Red, for one, is a powerful signaling color with great stopping power. Consideration must, however, be given to the fact that colors undergo modifications when viewed at a distance. Yellow appears white, blue appears black, and crimson appears orange. Perceptual studies can help determine the strong and weak points of a new package design by asking participants to rate not only colors and color combinations but also shapes, illustrations, and graphics. Package designers are thus greatly helped in their task by working closely with marketing researchers.

The Role of Packaging in the Marketing Mix

Because more than half of all supermarket purchases are based on in-store decisions, grocery product packages assume the promotional function of serving as the "silent salesperson on the shelf." In fact, packaging—although depicted here as part of the tangible product—acts in both a product-related and a promotional capacity. Creative packaging, often prominently incorporating the word "new," attempts to stimulate initial and repeat purchases.

Often the launch of a new product is facilitated by scaled-down versions of the full-size product package in the form of free samples or trial sizes. Sunlight dishwashing liquid was introduced with a free sampling program. Trial sizes are increasingly preferred by many marketers because they not only substantially reduce the cost of a nationwide free sampling program but also attract only consumers who are genuinely interested because they have to pay a modest amount for them.

Modern packaging has evolved from a mere attribute of a product to a major marketing force in its own right. No longer is a package a more or less irrelevant container for a new product. Rather, a package can create a "new" product even if its contents remain unchanged, as in the case of Quaker State motor oil. Packaging, therefore, impinges more or less directly on every other element of the introductory marketing mix: product policy, pricing policy, branding, channels of distribution, advertising and sales promotion, and personal selling. A company's product policy as well as the characteristics of an individual item in the product mix are major determinants of packaging.

Through its dual impact on both cost and profit, packaging becomes intimately involved in the determination of an innovation's price. Packaging can create a difference and establish a preference in the marketplace, but it has to be in line with the pricing, positioning, and distribution of the product. Expensive, high-quality, stylish packaging is in order for high-priced luxury goods like perfume or twelve-year-old whiskey, whereas an inexpensive, utilitarian container is appropriate for discount merchandise like Suave shampoo.

Packaging also works hand in hand with branding to build and reinforce the product's positioning. Because the owner of a brand decides on its packaging, this powerful combination enhances the owner's control of the market. Campbell's firm grip on the soup market, for instance, derives in no small part from the consistent combination of its family brand with the well-known family packaging. Del Monte employs a comparable strategy in canned fruits and vegetables.

Closely related promotional tasks make for a strong interdependence of packaging and advertising as well as sales promotion, requiring careful coordination for maximum effectiveness and mutual reinforcement. In self-service categories, packages are typically presold through presentation in advertising so that the shopper easily recognizes the familiar package on the shelf. Conversely, the package often becomes the main focus of a sales promotion campaign, conveying the cents-off message, carrying the coupon, or containing the premium.

New product packaging has thus become an ever more important ingredient of the total new product offering, closely interwoven in function and impact with the other components of the company's marketing mix. Its role has changed from that of a mere wrapper to that of a complex marketing tool using a wide range of materials, shapes, and methods. Its significance at the point of sale will continue to increase as competition for shelf space and consumer spending becomes even more intense.

Branding Policy

Another key decision that product management has to make concerns the branding of a new entry. A *brand* can be defined as a name, symbol, or design that is intended to identify the products of the seller and to differentiate them from those of competitors. Any distinctive means of identification and differentiation can thus serve as a brand. Best known, and subsequently discussed in this section, is the brand name. But a corporate logo, unique color combination, or distinctive package shape—the Mercedes star, the yellow, black, and red color combination on Kodak's packages, and the unique shape of the Coca-Cola bottle—are also brands.[10]

A brand becomes a *trademark* when it is registered with the U.S. Patent Office for exclusive use by one seller. Within the American legal system, this protection requires prior and continued use. A highly recognized and respected trademark can become an extremely valuable asset—so much so that the Coca-Cola Company has put a vice president in charge of trademark protection.

Branding is thus the activity of a seller designed to establish a means of identification and differentiation for its products. To the seller, this presents an opportunity to imbue these products with distinctive personalities and aggressively stimulate demand for them. Unless a new product is branded, a prospect has no meaningful way of singling out the item that this particular seller is offering. Only branded merchandise can successfully be advertised and distinguished from competitive entries. Accordingly, branding enables a buyer to develop loyalty and carry out repeat purchases. A brand further identifies the firm behind the product and offers a guarantee of consistent quality.[11]

The use of a brand name assures its owner that it can make all crucial marketing decisions, such as packaging, advertising, pricing, channel selection, and even product design, and thereby keep close control over the market. Because branding can create a difference in buyers' minds, even between chemically and physically identical products, price differentials can be maintained. This is evident in the controversy surrounding the use of generic versus brand name drugs. While the Food and Drug Administration favors generic substitution because of the price advantage to consumers, leading drug manufacturers suggest that a difference does exist.

Options in New Product Branding

In choosing a brand name for a new product, product managers are likely to be governed by two basic options: family branding and individual branding. In *family branding,* a company places the same brand name (usually the corporate name) on all products in a product line or even its entire product mix, distinguishing individual entries simply by their generic description. Campbell, for instance, uses its name on its entire "family" of condensed soups, supplemented by generic identification, such as Campbell's tomato soup. "Campbell's" is a registered trademark, but the generic description "tomato soup" cannot be protected for any specific company.

Family branding enjoys the distinct advantage of instant recognition, benefiting from the "halo effect" of the brand's established reputation.[12] A new entry using the family brand name thus gains instant credibility and visibility. A new soup variety offered by Campbell would automatically be assumed to be of good quality.

This quality image of well-known trademarks has led some companies to leverage them by entering new fields under the same name, a practice known as "brand franchise extension."[13] Consider, for example, the following report: "In Britain, Cadbury's have, over the years, increasingly extended the Cadbury name to embrace not only chocolate and candy products but such mainstream food products as mashed potatoes, dried milk, soups and beverages."[14] But such a move may prove to be counterproductive if buyers see no meaningful relationship between the old and new businesses.[15] When Campbell introduced a tomato sauce under its name, consumer response was very poor. After the product was renamed Prego, it became a runaway success story, quickly carving out a major share in this attractive market. Consumers would likely have even stronger reservations about the competence of a soup maker in baking bread. The company is thus well advised not to offer Campbell's bread. It is, however, a successful competitor in this market under the Pepperidge Farm brand name.

Similarly, Ralston-Purina was understandably reluctant to apply its well-known name to a new line of frozen gourmet dinners. Consumers would not have taken well to the association with pet foods. Loath to give up its corporate identity altogether, the company named the new line Checkerboard Restaurant, in an allusion to its corporate symbol. The line failed because of the company's lack of experience in this field.

While the reputation of the established brand name can facilitate the introduction of a new product, any problems with the new product can, conversely, affect the salability of all items bearing the same name. In other words, family branding places high demands on quality control because every single item is considered representative of the entire line. An innovation that is rushed to market without adequate testing and debugging can do significant damage to the image of all members of the brand family. This is a real concern to Bic, a company known for its inexpensive, disposable products, as indicated by the following statement from Bruno Bich, its president: "If you're going to leave your name on all your products, you should never produce a bad product. If you make a mistake, you'll hurt your whole company."[16]

This danger, though, rarely exists for the other major branding option, *individual branding*. Separate, individual brand names for several products in the same category help to contain any potential damage. The association of Rely tampons with toxic shock syndrome that prompted Procter & Gamble to recall this product has not prevented the company from reentering the feminine hygiene field with a new product under a different name. And Johnson & Johnson not only avoided any spillover ill effects from the Tylenol disaster to its other product lines but skillfully managed to reestablish this brand as the category leader after convincing the public of its innocence and triple-sealing the product.

Individual branding requires product management to create a brand franchise from scratch. When first presented to the public, the new name has no meaning to the consumer and bears no association with the product or category. Heavy advertising spending is necessary to imprint this information in the buyer's mind and generate demand for the product. Considering the magnitude of registered trademarks, it has become increasingly difficult to come up with registered brand names. For this reason, computers are frequently used to develop short, distinctive, and easy-to-remember letter combinations as brand names for new products that can then be registered as trademarks.[17] Given the growing importance of international marketing, it is imperative that names be selected that are inoffensive in any of the countries where they may be used.[18]

Companies employing individual brands can have multiple entries in the same product category, thus essentially competing with themselves. The rationale behind this approach is to segment the market, as no single brand can hope to capture an entire market. This fact is exemplified by such market leaders as Marlboro cigarettes, Colgate toothpaste, Coca-Cola, and Tide detergent. None of these well-known brands is left to fight a lonely battle for preeminence. Rather, all of them are surrounded by *flanker brands,*[19] such as Ultra-Brite, Tab, and Bold, respectively. Different brand names enable product management to imbue multiple entries with different brand personalities in order to appeal to separate market segments. This differentiation may involve different product characteristics, price levels, and/or quality levels. For instance, a company wishing to compete in both the prestige and economy segments of a market can simply use individual brand names to set the two product lines apart—a practice common in the liquor industry where Heublein markets both Smirnoff and Popov vodkas.

Individual brands possess another significant advantage: They permit easy market introduction and withdrawal on an experimental basis without damaging a firm's reputation and established business. They also foster internal competition among the brand managers of the competing lines, thus sharpening their market impact.

Although family and individual branding are the two major options in new product branding, two other choices are employed on occasion. One approach combines family and individual branding by pairing the company's name with an individual product name, such as Kellogg's Rice Krispies. This combination attempts to capitalize on the recognition of the corporate name and amplify it with a distinct product identity that cannot be copied readily by the competition, as in the case of a generic description. Although this procedure combines the benefits of the two major options, it also suffers from their disadvantages, such as the snowballing effects of product problems and the heavy introductory spending necessary to establish the individual brand portion.

The second alternative unites separate product line names with generic product descriptions. Utilized mainly by leading retailers, this approach attempts to develop separate departmental identities. Sears, Roebuck and Company uses the Craftsman brand for tools and Kenmore for appliances. This approach differs in two important ways from the preceding method: It is more specific in that product line names are used instead of the corporate name, and it is more general because it applies generic identifiers instead of protectable names. But even Sears has proven itself more flexible in its branding policy by offering such brands as DieHard batteries, Cheryl Tiegs fashions, and Levi's jeans.

Alternative Branding Strategies

Alternative branding strategies bring up the subject of brand ownership. As the name suggests, a *manufacturer's brand* is owned by a manufacturer, whereas a *distributor's brand* belongs to a wholesaler or retailer. Brand ownership is a crucial consideration because the brand owner can control the marketing effort for its brand. Alternatively labeled "national" and "private" brands, respectively, these two ownership patterns enable the owners to build loyalty for their brands. A manufacturer's brand facilitates comparison shopping because it is available in a variety of outlets. It also tends to be heavily advertised and command a premium price. A distributor's brand, on the other hand, translates into store loyalty because it can be bought only in a retailer's own stores. Relying primarily on in-store promotion and appeal, private brands are usually priced below national brands. They create a following of their own, particularly among better educated, higher-income consumers.

A company subscribing to a manufacturer's branding strategy emphasizes its own brands and is committed to an active national marketing effort. Smaller firms, however, are often inadequately capitalized to mount such extensive and expensive campaigns. They serve as contract manufacturers for other companies that buy and resell merchandise under their own names—be they producers who have farmed out this production or retailers. Manufacturing concerns that follow this kind of private branding strategy become more or less captive suppliers to their major customers without a market identity and control of their own.

To reduce this dependence and vulnerability, it is advisable to employ a mixed branding strategy in which manufacturer's and distributor's brands coexist. Skillfully played and carefully balanced, this philosophy can bring together the virtues of both extremes by permitting market presence and control through national brands as well as steady employment and market share via private brands. Most major manufacturers have adopted this approach to maintain both their position and volume in the marketplace.

To create visibility and leverage, many producers offer a new product initially only as a manufacturer's brand, giving it time to build up momentum in the market. As volume expands, the pressure for private branding and even licensing to competitors increases. Eventually, it may prove wise to cooperate with these requests and produce the innovation under both manufacturer's and distributor's brands. Even exclusive designs for certain large customers may be possible.

One last alternative that has gained some limited popularity is the use of *generics*. Forgoing branding altogether in favor of generic identification and employing no-frills packaging, such unbranded items compete strictly on price. Introduced in the 1970s, first by Carrefour in France and then by Jewel Cos. in the United States, generics seemed to offer an attractive solution to inflation-weary consumers. Their success, however, has been quite limited, showing more resilience in nonfood items. Given the high prices of name-brand prescription drugs and tight supervision by the Food and Drug Administration, however, generic drugs are gaining more favor with consumers and hospitals alike. Introducing innovations in generic form would be self-defeating because it would afford no identity or control, and profits would be very low. Responding to generic competition with price cuts is equally futile and hurts both a firm's reputation and operating results. Instead, it is beneficial to emphasize quality.[20]

SUMMARY

Simultaneously with the development and testing of a new product, product management has to determine the marketing mix for the product's introduction to the market. Many of the preparations involved require considerable lead time, such as selecting and protecting a brand name, hiring and training sales personnel, designing an advertising campaign, buying media time and space, designing the package, and developing promotional aids. To coordinate all these, and many more, activities in the marketing mix, an integrated marketing program becomes a necessity.

Product features and styling, as well as the composition of the product mix, have been decided on before and during the development stage. The company must also decide whether to make the product itself or buy it from an outside source for resale under its own name.

Packaging has been assuming growing importance, particularly under the influence of self-service. Both on the store shelf and in the home of the consumer, the product's package acts as a "silent salesperson." A change in packaging for an existing product alters its appearance, potentially creating a "new" product. Packaging's prime functions are protection, promotion, and profit. They may be executed by a combination of primary and secondary packaging. Package design considerations are governed by the question of whether the new item should be packaged in a way similar to or different from the company's other products. Packaging colors and color combinations have to be chosen and researched very carefully. A highly visible component, packaging should be fine-tuned with the other elements of the marketing mix.

In branding a new product, product management has a range of options and a number of aspects to consider. Decisions in this area have far-reaching implications: They influence distribution and market coverage, pricing policy, the size of the funds necessary for promotional support, the extent of market control, the ease of introducing subsequent innovations, the degree of production capacity utilization, product and company image in the consumer's mind, and many other factors. It is the brand that, often in combination with the package, identifies the product to the consumer and communicates some real or imaginary qualities about it. Branding thus assumes an important role in the introductory marketing mix, especially since the brand—in contrast to the other elements—cannot be changed during the market life of the product. Ranging from family to individual brands and from manufacturer's to distributor's brands, branding decisions make a significant contribution to the success potential of a new product.

NOTES

1. See "Quaker State Expects Sales Gains with New Packaging System for Oil," *Marketing News,* 3 Feb. 1984, 7.
2. See Ronald Alsop, "Color Grows More Important in Catching Consumers' Eyes," *Wall Street Journal,* 29 Nov. 1984.
3. Paul A. Engelmayer, "Campbell Plans to Drop Its Tin Soup Can, Reflecting New Emphasis on Convenience," *Wall Street Journal,* 28 March 1984, 35. See Also Bill Abrams, "Packaging Often Irks Buyers, but Firms Are Slow to Change," *Wall Street Journal,* 28 Jan. 1982.
4. See Engelmayer, "Campbell Plans," 35.
5. See Joan O'C. Hamilton, "Old-Time Seltzer in New-Fangled Bottles," *Business Week,* 14 Sept. 1987, 164.
6. For an illustration of these changes see Leon G. Schiffman and Leslie Lazar Kanuk, *Consumer Behavior,* 3rd ed. (Englewood Cliffs, NJ: Prentice-Hall, 1987), 180.
7. See "Color Needs To Be Integrated in Marketing Plans," *Marketing News,* 11 Nov. 1983, 3.
8. See Alsop, "Color Grows More Important," 37.
9. See E. P. Danger, *Selecting Colour for Packaging* (Brookfield, VT: Gower Publishing Co., 1987).
10. Kodak has been able to prevent other firms from using its unique color combination. See Alsop, "Color Grows More Important," 37. Recently, Owens-Corning even obtained trademark protection for the exclusive use of the color pink in fiberglass.
11. See John M. Murphy, "Developing New Brand Names," in *Branding: A Key Marketing Tool,* edited by John M. Murphy (New York: McGraw-Hill, 1987), 86.
12. See Kenneth Dreyfack, "The Big Brands Are Back in Style," *Business Week,* 12 Jan. 1987, 74.
13. See Edward M. Tauber, "Brand Franchise Extension: New Product Benefits from Existing Brand Names," *Business Horizons* (March–April 1981): 36–41, and Bill Abrams, "Exploiting Proven Brand Names Can Cut Risk of New Products," *Wall Street Journal,* 22 Jan. 1981.
14. John M. Murphy, "What Is Branding?" in *Branding: A Key Marketing Tool,* edited by John M. Murphy (New York: McGraw-Hill, 1987), p. 5.
15. See Al Ries and Jack Trout, *Positioning: The Battle for Your Mind* (New York: McGraw-Hill, 1981), 119, and Abrams, "Exploiting Proven Brand Names," 27.
16. See Abrams, "Exploiting Proven Brand Names" 27.
17. See Murphy, "Developing New Brand Names," 91–92.
18. See ibid., 87. See also George Anders, "Ad Agencies and Big Concerns Debate World Brands' Value," *Wall Street Journal,* 14 June 1984, 33. For examples of mistakes in international branding see David A. Ricks, *Big Business Blunders: Mistakes in Multinational Marketing* (Homewood, IL: Dow Jones-Irwin, 1983), 36ff.
19. See Tauber, "Brand Franchise Extension," 36–37.
20. See Hasso G. Nauck, "Mit Markentechnik gegen 'No-Names,'" *Marketing Journal* (1984): 8–12.

CASE STUDY

THICK OR CRISPY?

Frito-Lay, Inc., is the leading player in the snack food market, generating more than $2 billion in annual sales and contributing substantially to parent PepsiCo's bottom line. The company was founded some fifty years ago by Elmer Doolin, who paid $100 for a corn chips recipe. Making the chips in his mother's kitchen, Doolin peddled them personally wherever he could. Meanwhile, in Nashville, Herman Lay was producing and marketing potato chips in a similar manner. The two companies merged in 1961 and were bought in 1965 by PepsiCo.

Thorough Testing

From its humble beginnings, Frito-Lay has grown to be one of the most sophisticated packaged goods marketers. Its management routinely reviews several hundred new product suggestions every year. The screening is so rigid, however, that only five or six ideas move beyond the early stages of the evolutionary process. To qualify for market introduction, innovative chip concepts have to progress systematically through test kitchen, consumer taste testing, naming, package design, advertising planning, manufacturing, and test marketing. Unsatisfactory results at any point along the way or an ill-chosen brand name or advertising approach can derail a concept. If it is successful in the marketplace, the company may enjoy up to $100 million in additional sales. In fact, Frito-Lay will not even consider introduction unless it can expect at least $50 million in additional revenues. And any new brand that cannibalizes a current Frito-Lay product too heavily stands little chance of going national.

Forever looking for new ideas, the company has tested hash-brown and batter-fried potato chips, as well as whole grain chips made of wheat, corn, and oats. Carrot chips and plantain chips failed quickly in market tests. Besides product formulation,

This case was adapted from Janet Guyon, "Fixing a Snack: The Public Doesn't Get a Better Potato Chip without a Bit of Pain," *Wall Street Journal*, 25 Mar. 1983.

a great deal of research goes into branding and packaging. Tiffles light corn chips produced poor test market results before being renamed Sunchips, the "corn chips for potato-chip lovers."

New thick, white tortilla chips tasted good, although they would cause some problems in production. Competing products used twist ties, but they are expensive and cumbersome to apply. And what should the new chips be called? Managers consulted Spanish dictionaries and Latin American maps. "Mamacita's" was already protected and "Captivas" referred to prisoners. The winner was "Sabritas," which means "little tasty ones" and is already owned by Frito-Lay.

Packaging decisions include sealing method and color. Questions of wording arise: "potato chips" or "potato crisps"? If the chips show through a window in the package, packaging costs go up by at least $1 million a year.

Attractive Alternatives

Frito-Lay's management faces the dilemma of making a choice between two attractive new product alternatives. The group assembled around the table consists of Willard Korn, senior vice president for sales and marketing; Brad Todd, the marketing director for new products; George Reynolds, the potato chip marketing director; and John Cranor, marketing vice president.

The two front-runners before them are Ta-Tos and O'Gradys. Both products are made from potatoes, but Ta-Tos is described as "super-crispy wavy," while O'Gradys is "extra-thick and crunchy." According to Willard Korn, "Small differences can build big brands. Ta-Tos and O'Gradys have different textures, different mouth feel, and potato impact."

To make them particularly crispy, Ta-Tos are soaked in a salt solution before being fried. The production process not only makes them wavy but also strengthens them. Although some consumers found them too hard in taste tests, most indicated a likelihood to buy some, so the product is being test-marketed. The extra-thick and crunchy chip has also recently begun test marketing. But O'Gradys first had to overcome a manufacturing problem: Thick potato chips fry well on the outside but remain white in the center. Ingenious ridge cutting solved this problem and helped the chips fry all the way through.

In branding the extra-thick chips, it was essential to give the right impression: "This product was of the earth, it was thicker, a natural-tasting product," explains Brad Todd. Looking for a hearty name that suggested a local origin, the company had come across O'Gradys. Consumers said that a person named O'Grady would be fun, jovial, male, happy-go-lucky, hearty, and big. This kind of image served Frito-Lay's intentions well.

As far as advertising is concerned, Frito-Lay wants consumers to realize that Ta-Tos is "a chip with the crispness of a regular chip, with the potato taste of a ridged chip," points out John Cranor. He recognizes the difficulty of achieving this objective in a 30-second commercial, though. After having a number of people describe the taste on camera, the agency suggested that viewers "listen" to the taste.

Discussion Questions

1. Which of the two new brands would you recommend for national introduction? Why?
2. What do you think of the brand names chosen? Would you care to offer alternate suggestions?
3. Issue package design specifications and explain their rationale.
4. Do you anticipate offering this product in additional flavors at a later point in time? If so, why? If not, why not?

CHAPTER 11

New Product Pricing and Distribution

Although product-related decisions have been presented separately, they are in reality closely interwoven with all other marketing mix decisions for the introduction of a new product. Because they affect each other and are interdependent, introductory marketing mix decisions have to be made in concert. Decisions about product features and design, for instance, determine cost aspects of its price. Conversely, the price at which a new item can be sold in the marketplace often influences the materials, styling, and sources used. The nature of the distribution channels chosen shapes such packaging decisions as quality and graphics. Branding decisions, too, are intimately related to channel arrangements and control.

Even though they interact closely and are mutually influential, the different elements of the introductory marketing mix have to be discussed separately to facilitate a better understanding of their specific options, conditions, and considerations. This approach was accordingly taken in the preceding chapter and will continue to characterize the remaining chapters in part three. This chapter is thus devoted to a discussion of issues related to new product pricing and distribution. These two complementary marketing mix components are as influential for an innovation's success as are its design and formulation.

Pricing Policy

Within the framework of new product evolution, price determination is a strategic factor of prime importance, strongly affecting the sales and profit performance of a new item. Price determination is important for a number of reasons: First, a company can employ pricing policy in such a way as to discourage competition from entering the market where this threat is present. Second, in accordance with different demand elasticities throughout a market, pricing determines the kind and number of market segments that can be penetrated. Third, a new product's price shapes its image in terms of quality perception and thus its acceptability to various market segments. Fourth, price directly influences the profit margin and profit contribution of a product.

A new product's *price* is the amount of money in exchange for which its seller is willing to do either of two things: transfer possession and title to a tangible good, or perform a service. *Pricing* is thus the activity on the part of product management by which it sets prices for its product offerings. *Pricing policy* involves choosing both objectives and approaches for pricing.

Because of its significance for the survival and growth of a firm, price determination is a key management responsibility. Before any meaningful pricing decision can be made, however, certain types of information must be assembled:

- The nature of the product being priced
- The projected production and marketing costs of the product
- Prices of competitive products (if any)
- Any competitive development of a comparable product and the stage of this development
- Consumer sensitivity to price (direct price elasticity of demand)
- Likely reactions of wholesalers, retailers, and consumers to alternative pricing structures

Of all these price determinants, the costs of development, production, promotion, and distribution are easily the most influential—if only to set a "floor" or minimum level. Where a cost-based price is likely to be unacceptable to the marketplace, modifications have to be made to render the product marketable.

Competitive products also have to be carefully analyzed. While adequate consideration has to be given to existing substitutes and their price and quality levels, potential competition could pose an equally significant or even more imposing threat. In fact, new product pricing decisions may be used to reduce this threat by selecting the minimum price possible at a given profit constraint. A low price trims per unit profit but results in a higher market share, discouraging competitive market entry due to lessened market opportunity.

Varying levels of consumer sensitivity to price are useful bases for market segmentation. Many markets contain at least two such segments: a prestige-oriented segment and a price-oriented segment. The prestige-oriented segment is typically price inelastic, in other words, it does not respond favorably to lower prices. As a matter of fact, it may well possess inverse elasticity, where demand increases as the price goes up. The price-oriented segment, on the other hand, is very price elastic and thus quite responsive to price stimulation.

This kind of dichotomy exists, for instance, in the liquor market, where the same company often markets simultaneously in the same category an expensive, heavily advertised name brand and an inexpensive unpromoted alternative. An example of this strategy is provided by Heublein, Inc., which leads the vodka market with its well-known, high-priced Smirnoff brand. At the other end of the spectrum,

Heublein offers Popov vodka at a considerably lower price without any promotional support. Ideally, the lower-priced brand will not cannibalize sales from the flagship brand but, rather, attract buyers from other brands at its level. In essence, the two entries are differentiated only in name and price without any inherent differences in chemical or physical characteristics.[1] Nonetheless, they are perceived as different products. Procter & Gamble pursues the same strategy with its Charmin and Banner brands in the toilet tissue market.

Likely reactions of wholesalers and retailers to alternative pricing structures are easier to obtain than those of consumers. Although a representative sample of consumers could readily be interviewed, asking them what a new product is worth or what they could be willing to pay for it is a dangerous undertaking. Because they do not have to pay the price they quote at the time of the interview, they can freely state an exaggerated amount—due more to their eagerness to please than to a realistic appraisal. In fact, of all the issues that new product research can investigate at the consumer level, pricing is easily the least valid. Wholesalers and retailers, on the other hand, being more rational in their judgments and looking primarily at the profit impact of alternative prices, will tend to give more meaningful answers, looking at the same time for such supportive information as planned promotional expenditures.

Pricing Objectives

Pricing decisions are governed by *pricing objectives,* which give direction to the pricing effort. They represent desired end states or perspectives and are often profit or volume oriented. Profit objectives come in many permutations. First of all, there is the question of time frame. Pricing directed toward short-term profits will tend to result in higher prices than will the pursuit of long-term profitability. The long-term orientation is aimed at building a steady long-term business by charging moderate prices. Second, there is the issue of the reference base for profitability percentages. Fixed or category-specific markup percentages on the cost of an individual item include a provision for profit. Conversely, a profitability objective may be expressed as a target return on sales revenue, or it may be stated as a target rate of return on investment (before or after taxes).

Volume-oriented pricing objectives may, at their very minimum, strive for mere survival, keeping the plant operating during difficult times with a view toward minimizing losses rather than maximizing profits. More meaningfully and more frequently, volume objectives take the form of market share objectives. This can simply mean defending the status quo, that is, maintaining the firm's current market share in a given category. Or it can imply striving for a given market share such as in the cigarette business, where a market share of .4 percent means profitability and staying power. A third, and the most aggressive, market share objective is to increase market share and/or achieve market share leadership. The PIMS (profit impact of market strategies) project has concluded that there is a strong positive correlation between market share and profitability. This means that the pursuit of market share growth is likely to be rewarded by increased profitability.[2]

Another frequent pricing objective is to meet the competition. In this case, a firm simply adapts to the price set by a market leader because products in this market are considered interchangeable. This precludes any price initiative or differentiation of its own and suggests a "me-too" perspective of price imitation. This kind of going-rate pricing shifts the burden of competition and differentiation to the other elements of the marketing mix.

A final pricing objective is image oriented. Because the quality and status perception of a product are closely linked to its price in the minds of most consumers, a high-priced offering will tend to earn an image of quality and luxury. The image-oriented objective will set a firm apart from the competition, but it may also limit the firm's customer base.

Approaches to Pricing

Actual price determination can be either cost based or market based. Figure 11–1 illustrates these alternative approaches and their subcategories.

Cost-Based Pricing.   Cost-based pricing is in some way related to the cost of an item. In its most frequent method, *cost-plus pricing,* a company computes its cost of making or acquiring an item and marks up this figure by a standard percentage. This markup ("plus") may be straight profit (before taxes) or it may contain an allowance for operating cost. Although often used because of its ease of administration, cost-plus ignores demand and competitive considerations altogether.

Marginal cost pricing is employed by some firms when their capacity remains underutilized. It is based on the marginal (incremental or additional) cost of producing and distributing an additional item that is largely identical with a product's variable or direct cost of labor and materials. The underlying philosophy is that fixed cost is incurred regardless of the level of production and is hopefully recovered by the output sold at regular prices. Incremental business that utilizes existing facilities

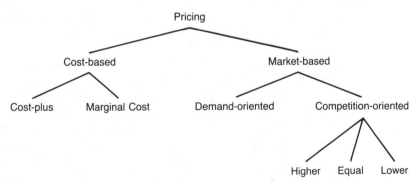

FIGURE 11–1
Pricing Options

then helps to sustain continuity of employment and generate a modest profit if it is obtained at prices exceeding out-of-pocket cost. As is evident, this procedure is more of a stopgap, temporary measure than a solid long-term approach. It is thus little suited for pricing new products.

Market-Based Pricing.   Market-based pricing uses market considerations and valuations in setting the price of a product. Instead of being guided by what it costs to make/buy and sell an item, this perspective is psychologically oriented toward consumer perception. In one of its incarnations, *demand-oriented pricing,* it selects a price in accordance with the value that prospective buyers place on a product, a practice that is colloquially known as "charging what the traffic will bear." Although this is a solid premise that may actually lead to higher sales from higher prices, because of a perceived greater value and higher quality, it is operationally difficult to apply. As pointed out earlier, surveys are ill suited for discovering consumer value perceptions, so demand-oriented pricing remains a matter of judgment or experimentation.

In an attempt to identify the right price for a new product, Thomas J. Lipton, Inc., charged three different prices in a number of test markets. The company found that the lowest price produced poor results because of suspected inadequate quality and the highest price appeared excessive to consumers. The medium price, however, generated satisfactory sales results and was consequently adopted for the national introduction.

Competition-oriented pricing, another type of market-based pricing, deliberately relates the price of a product to those of competitive entries. Depending on the underlying philosophy, the resulting price may be higher than, equal to, or lower than competitive price levels. According to the psychology of pricing, a higher price suggests that a company's offering is superior to the competition, incorporating either better quality or more sophisticated features. The expected greater value has to be obvious to consumers in terms of the appearance and/or performance of the product for this approach to succeed. Match-the-competition pricing implies a parity or "me-too" product that more or less homogeneously blends into the competitive field. Most cigarettes are sold at such a prevailing price. To succeed under such conditions, product management has to employ nonprice competition such as heavy brand advertising.

Pricing a new product lower than competitive alternatives is aimed at conveying a better value to consumers. The success of this strategy depends on a company's ability to establish a satisfactory quality perception. C & C Cola was not able to believably communicate its message to a substantial number of people that this beverage's quality was comparable to that of industry leaders even though it cost less. To the average consumer, a lower price simply means lower quality unless convincing evidence to the contrary is presented. The vulnerability of its lower price claim became particularly evident when Coke and Pepsi engaged in a price war and undersold C & C. For well-established brands, pricing below competitive levels can serve as a temporary measure to move merchandise, gain market share, or enter a new market.

Differentiated Pricing Structures

In many markets, charging a single price to all buyers of a product would produce less than optimum results. Such markets are capable of segmentation based on buyer sensitivity to price. The existence of differences in demand elasticity among buyers due to disparities in income, taste, location, function, or availability of competitive alternatives enables a seller to partition a market by setting differentiated prices for each market segment. Market segmentation in the manner described here, where applicable, can serve to increase sales as well as profits by enlarging production beyond the level that would be generated by a single price aimed at only one segment of demand.

Such a policy of charging different prices for the same product to different market segments is referred to as *price differentiation*. As described below, this practice is legal and not in violation of the Clayton or Robinson-Patman Acts because it does not discriminate among buyers possessing the same characteristics and satisfying identical conditions. To succeed, price differentiation requires that the individual submarkets be clearly separated from each other. If segment-to-segment arbitrage can take place where members of a higher-priced segment manage to supply themselves in a lower-priced segment, the scheme inevitably collapses. A German manufacturer of elastic watchbands sold these products at lower prices to French dealers than to German retailers. German jewelers promptly crossed the Rhine and bought the watchbands from their French colleagues.

One type of price differentiation is sequential in nature. A new product is introduced at a relatively high price and the price is subsequently lowered to reach other submarkets. "Launching a new product with a high price is an efficient device for breaking the market up into segments that differ in price elasticity of demand. The initial high price serves to skim the cream of the market that is relatively insensitive to price. Subsequent reductions in the price tap successively more elastic sectors of the market."[3] This approach has been called a "skimming policy" and is exemplified by the systematic succession of a book's editions, sometimes ranging from high-priced hardcover edition to low-priced paperback printings. Thomas J. Peters and Robert H. Waterman, Jr.'s, bestseller *In Search of Excellence,* for instance, appeared first as a hardcover edition by Harper & Row in 1982 at $19.95. After 1.3 million copies were sold, a softcover edition was published in 1984 by Warner Books. By fall of 1984, this paperback version had sold an additional 1.5 million copies at $8.95 and was still going strong.[4]

Another type of price differentiation works on a geographic basis by, for instance, charging different prices in domestic and foreign markets or in different domestic locations.[5] The divergence in prices may be due either to variances in actual cost (mainly for transportation) or to differences in regional demand elasticities, inflation rates, standards of living, or competitive price levels. Whatever the reason, if the price increases as a continual function of the distance from a plant or basing point, the respective local prices of the item—given a highly competitive product— will determine the size of the territory that can be successfully served by the company.

This situation is depicted in Figure 11–2, where ex-factory prices are identical for both companies A and B, located in two different cities. Local delivered prices, however, differ greatly: Through economies in physical distribution, such as shipping

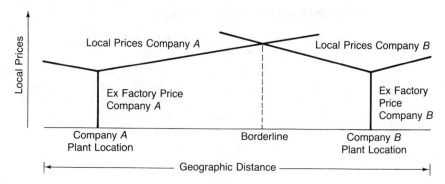

FIGURE 11–2
Geographic Price Differentiation and Market Area

full carloads or truckloads, containerization, piggybacking, or operating its own truck fleet, company A was able to penetrate a larger geographic area than company B. The borderline between the two competitive territories is defined by the intersection of the local price curves of the two competitors. On either side of this intersection, the local price of one of the competitors is higher than that of the other, thus effectively delimiting the trading area for products that are perceived as being homogeneous by consumers.

A third type of price differentiation uses a functional or customer-type orientation. Essentially the same product may be offered at different prices for different uses. In order to avoid arbitrage, the lower-priced version is often made unfit for application in the higher-priced segment. Low-priced rubbing alcohol and rock salt, for instance, contain additives to prevent internal consumption by humans and avoid conflicts with high-priced distilled spirits and table salt. Functional price differentiation is also found in wholesaler versus retailer price lists as employed by manufacturers that make allowances for the functions performed by these intermediaries. Customer-type segmentation occurs in the form of multiple branding or in the use of manufacturer's versus distributor's brands.

Whichever criterion the distinction of submarkets is based on, the example presented in Table 11–1 demonstrates how the system of price differentiation works. If management chose to employ a single-price policy, the maximum revenue that could be generated would be $250 at a price of $5. While this might satisfy volume-oriented objectives, it would not produce the highest possible profit. In this case, the maximum profit, given a single-price policy, would be realized at a price of $6.

On the other hand, a multiple-price policy employing five different prices significantly enlarges demand and profits: At a total volume of 90 units sold, sales revenues reach $410 and profits amount to $130. The example also illustrates that once the point of highest profits (called the point of negative returns) is reached, further price reductions are no longer beneficial to the company and will result in decreasing profits. According to this "law of diminishing returns," the company

TABLE 11–1
Effect of Price Differentiation on Sales Revenue and Profit

					Multiple-Price Policies					
	De-	Total	Single Price		5 Prices			9 Prices		
Price	mand	Cost								
P	Q	C	R	Z	R	Z	Z_m	R	Z	Z_m
10	0	100	0	−100	0	−100	−100	0	−100	−100
9	10	120	90	−30	90	−30	+70	90	−30	+70
8	20	140	160	+20				170	+30	+60
7	30	160	210	+50	230	+70	+100	240	+80	+50
6	40	180	240	+60				300	+120	+40
5	50	200	250	+50	330	+130	+60	350	+150	+30
4	60	220	240	+20				390	+170	+20
3	70	240	210	−30	390	+150	+20	420	+180	+10
2	80	260	160	−100				440	+180	± 0
1	90	280	90	−190	410	+130	−20	450	+170	−10

R = sales revenue = $P \cdot Q$; Z = profit = $R - C$; Z_m = marginal profit.

should restrict itself to charging four different prices of $9, $7, $5, and $3. This would result in revenues of $390 and profits of $150. The additional price of $1 increases revenues by $20 but cost by $40, thus leading to a net loss of $20.

As Figure 11–3 illustrates, a firm can expand its sales considerably by applying a multiple-price policy instead of a single-price policy. Under a single-price policy, consumers who are willing to pay a higher price actually save money. This phenomenon is referred to as consumer savings. For instance, ten buyers willing to pay $9 save $4 each at a uniform price of $5. On the other hand, sales to consumers who will respond only to lower prices are lost to the company. For instance, prospects willing to buy at $4 will not buy at $5. So the company loses at both ends with a single-price policy—in the form of consumer savings and lost sales.

These revenue and profit losses can be reduced by utilizing multiple prices. In this particular case, the highest total sales volume would be achieved by using nine different prices to tap all market segments. By so doing, the firm reduces consumer savings to their bare minimum and eliminates lost sales altogether. In accordance with the law of diminishing returns, however, a full-range price differentiation program, extending to the lowest conceivable price, ultimately results in decreasing profits. The optimum combination of volume and profit is achieved with a seven-price policy ranging from $9 to $3. In practice, though, it will likely be difficult to effectively separate seven market segments from each other and avoid intersegment arbitrage. Even if price differentiation is carried out in a sequential manner, some potential buyers who are basically willing to pay the current price might wait for a later date in order to save money. Thus it seems more realistic to use four rather than seven different prices.

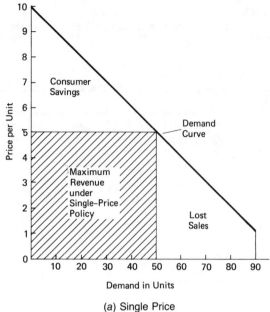

(a) Single Price

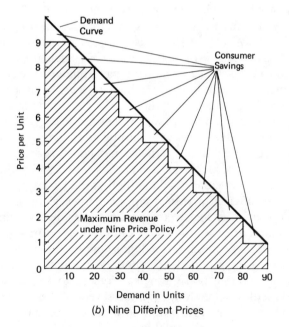

(b) Nine Different Prices

FIGURE 11–3
Effect of Price Differentiation on Sales Revenue

New Product Pricing

In setting prices for new products, a firm has a variety of factors to consider and a number of options to choose from. It will typically combine cost-based and market-based considerations by adopting a cost-plus price as the minimum level and examining whether market forces permit charging more. Conversely, if market conditions predetermine an innovation's price, a reverse computation process can help management determine how much it can afford to pay for the item's ingredients and manufacture. The objectives governing new product pricing may be identical to those applicable to established products. Alternatively, they may be unique to a particular new venture, such as early payback of research and development expenditures or discouraging competition.

The latter two objectives are among the characteristics distinguishing two approaches that have been suggested specifically for new product pricing: skimming and penetration. *Skimming* uses high introductory prices followed by subsequent price reductions, whereas *penetration* pricing employs modest prices from the outset and attempts to keep them stable for some time. These two approaches represent extremes whose selection has to be based on pricing objectives, cost figures, and market conditions.

Skimming versus Penetration Pricing

Market-based pricing for new products derives from a careful assessment of demand and competitive factors. These include the level and intensity of demand, as well as its initial price elasticity. The external review also covers the stage of the product life cycle, the degree of market penetration desired over a given time period, the extent and nature of current competition, and the threat of market entry from potential rivals.

A firm examining its new product pricing options can essentially choose between two basic alternatives:[6]

Skimming—A relatively high initial price, followed by subsequent price reductions to tap successively more elastic market segments.
Penetration—A relatively low introductory price to create and maintain mass market appeal.

A high-price policy is particularly well suited to the introduction of dramatically different products, such as electric cars and personal computers, that create entirely new markets. Under such circumstances, demand is usually fairly inelastic with respect to price, simply because consumers have no meaningful idea as to what such a product is worth. A substantial change in consumer behavior is required, so market resistance is high, and only a very limited number of people are willing to assume the risk inherent in an untried product. This affluent group can well afford the product and may actually be attracted by a high price because of its implied exclusivity. Because the innovation does not yet have real rivals, its vulnerability to competitive pricing decisions is low. As the product becomes better known and more widely accepted, however, and competitive entries appear on the market, consumer responsiveness to price incentives increases markedly.

Accordingly, skimming can result in significant, if not rapid, price reductions. Penicillin dropped to one-tenth of its introductory price within only two years. Aided by advances in semiconductor technology, digital timepieces moved from a $2,500 Pulsar to $5 disposables, and electronic calculators decreased in price from a bulky $400 Sharp calculator to $10 pocket items.

The idea behind setting introductory prices high is to recover the cost of development and introduction before competitors enter and involve the pioneer in a price-cutting contest. A large percentage of the cost of a new product is incurred before the first dollar of revenue is generated. In such a situation, high initial prices shorten the time span needed to reach the break-even point. This approach is particularly attractive if the available production capacity is too small to supply a large original demand and additional facilities require considerable lead time before they can begin full-scale production. Price can then be used to control demand until sufficient capacity comes on-stream. Even so, for quite some time Du Pont was unable to fill all the orders it received soon after the introduction of the synthetic elastic fiber Lycra and was forced to ration supplies.

A company can afford to use skimming if it is likely to be the sole supplier of a new product for some time into the future. This may be due to advanced technology, a patent or license, or simply a wait-and-see attitude on the part of potential competitors. In light of the uncertainties associated with the launching of a novel product in the marketplace, skimming is the safer approach. It also serves to establish a quality or even luxury image for an innovation that later price reductions can benefit from. It is always easier to reduce a price that is too high to generate sufficient volume than to increase a price that is too low to yield a satisfactory profit. Further, a high initial price reflects the high current cost of production and distribution at a limited output level. If market response is favorable, economies of scale and perhaps advanced technology can lower cost and prices.

Penetration pricing, on the other hand, enters the market with a deliberately modest price to obtain substantial volume from the beginning. It is an appropriate approach if demand is price elastic—a condition that is likely to be present in the more advanced stages of the product life cycle. This policy is also advantageous if the threat of potential competition exists. The low price reduces the profit potential of would-be competitors and thus may well prevent them from entering the market altogether. Manufacturers of products for which they cannot achieve patent protection or which are easy to imitate (such as food products) will typically set prices that enable them to penetrate a significant part of the market before competition could react effectively. If there is a large market potential for such a product, a penetration pricing policy serves long-term sales and profit objectives well.

A penetration policy is thus meaningful if a sufficiently large market volume can be expected. Such a procedure serves at the same time to discourage potential competitors and to build an established position in the marketplace. A policy of fairly low, stable prices is much more likely to create brand loyalty than are high initial prices. Relatively low prices make for a mass market from the outset and guarantee economic mass production of products with limited distinctiveness. Supported by a product design that appeals to a large number of people, penetration pricing makes the product affordable for a large portion of the market. Based on a philosophy of "profit through volume," penetration pricing keeps the profit per unit low and relies on quantity to propel total profit to a satisfactory level. This kind of price restraint erects entry barriers by requiring entrants to make large-scale investments to meet or undercut the price of the pioneer.

Selecting the Best Approach

Marketing situations exist where neither one of these pricing policies is clearly superior to the other. If the various segments of a market differ in price elasticity, it may very well pay to apply both policies simultaneously in different parts of the market, for example, by using multiple brands, as described earlier in the Heublein case.

In attempting to identify the right price for a new product, increasing numbers of companies use simulation to predict market response. Because only a very limited number of alternative prices can be tested under real market conditions, these firms utilize simulated test markets to find the winning price. One such service is ASSESSOR$_{FT}$, from Information Resources, Inc., which has been applied to predict the volume or market share potential of hundreds of new products worldwide. This tool examines the relationship between price level and purchase behavior. It can also help product management to simulate the impact of competitive response, for instance, price-cutting, on a new product's sales performance. This facilitates the selection of the most profitable price and enables the development of sales forecasts.[7]

A practice to be avoided when setting prices for new products is pricing low for easy market entry with the intent of pricing up after a projected share of the market has been achieved. Introducing a new product at a low price creates a certain price/value relationship in the consumer's mind that is very hard to change. Besides, it may result in charges of predatory pricing to put existing competitors out of business. Another, potentially even more dangerous, pitfall is to neglect the impact of inflation by introducing innovations at prices based on current direct cost. It is better to anticipate cost increases for the foreseeable future and build them into a price structure from the beginning than to risk price increases early in a new product's market life.

In attempting to select the best approach to pricing a specific new product, the criteria presented in Table 11–2 can serve as useful guidelines. The following comments will serve to shed some light on the suggestions made there.

- Where a low promotional budget exists, a low price often has to "do the talking." A high price, on the other hand, permits and/or necessitates more generous promotional spending. But there are exceptions to this rule: Some of the highest advertising-to-sales ratios are found in everyday staples while a relatively modest percentage is spent on promoting some luxury items.
- A commodity-type product that is available from many sources has to be price-competitive but a unique, patented item can command a premium price.

TABLE 11–2
Criteria for New Product Pricing Policy Selection

Criteria	Conditions Typically Suggesting	
	Skimming	*Penetration*
1. Advertising budget	High	Low
2. Product type	Proprietary	Commodity
3. Mode of manufacture	Custom-made	Mass produced
4. Degree of market coverage	Selective	Intensive
5. Product obsolescence	Short-lived	Long-lived
6. Technological changes	Rapid	Slow
7. Production emphasis	Labor-intensive	Capital-intensive
8. Market share goal	Small	Large
9. Channels of distribution	Long	Short
10. Stage of market	New/declining	Mature
11. Profit perspective	Short-term	Long-term
12. Product versatility	Multiple-use	Single-use
13. Effect on firm's other products	Low	High
14. Ancillary services	Many	Few or none
15. Product life in use	Long	Short
16. Turnover	Slow	Fast
17. Price differentiation	Applied	Not applied
18. Amortization of investment	Fast	Slow
19. Threat of competitive entry	Absent	Present
20. Sales objective	Gradual expansion	Early maximization

Source: Adapted with permission from William Crissy and Robert Boewadt, "Pricing in Perspective," *Sales Management,* 15 June 1971, 44.

- If an item is mass produced, economies of scale permit a lower price. On the other hand, the specialized talent required to produce to order results in a higher price.
- The degree of market coverage desired also affects the choice of price level. Intensive distribution, that is, offering the product for sale in virtually every outlet that is willing and able to carry it, is both the cause and the result of lower prices. Low prices are needed to achieve such widespread coverage, and the resulting volume permits lower prices due to economies of scale. Selective distribution is considerably more restrictive, producing higher prices in return.
- If an extended market life span is anticipated for a new item, its cost can be spread out over a longer period. Conversely, a limited market life is compensated for by higher prices.
- Prices and the speed of technological change in an industry are often correlated positively. Rapid turnover of technologies requires short recovery periods for the invested capital. Also, technological innovations can frequently command a premium because they typically offer more convenience or better performance. Where change is slow, its financing requirements are low.
- If production is highly automated, large-scale production permits lower unit prices. Labor-intensive production, however, means slower productivity gains and a built-in wage inflation factor.
- Market share and price normally move in opposite directions: The higher the market share desired, the lower a product's price has to be.

- The more levels there are in the channel of distribution, the higher the price has to be in order to allow for the cost and profit of each intermediary.
- High prices are likely to be applied during the introductory stage of the product life cycle due to inelastic demand and during the decline stage because of shrinking volume and rising cost. In mature markets, competitive alternatives limit pricing flexibility.
- A short-term profit orientation suggests high prices; a long-term perspective advocates low prices.
- A broad range of product applications supports a high price; a single-purpose item translates into a low price.
- If there is strong interaction between an innovation and the rest of the product mix, a low price would be advantageous. When the innovation stands more or less by itself, a high price is justifiable.
- The cost of ancillary services, such as installation or training, should be built into the product's price.
- The length of a product's life in the hands of the ultimate buyer is another factor: A throwaway item has to be priced attractively, whereas a product of lasting value justifies a higher ticket.
- Slow-moving items require a higher markup than do products that turn over frequently.
- Price differentiation as an active marketing tool is not used under a penetration policy but is practiced within the framework of skimming.
- Payback of the money invested in a new product is fast with a high price but slow with a low one.
- A low-price policy is generally preferred in order to deter an existing threat of competitive entry. Where no such danger is present, skimming is frequently chosen.
- A firm that aims for gradual increases in sales can afford to choose the skimming route. If early volume gains are important, penetration pricing is the appropriate route.

The criteria presented in Table 11–2 will assist product management in choosing the approach best suited to a particular set of circumstances. The choice will not always be clear-cut, and it is possible that a combination of the two extremes, using multiple brands and channels, may be the right way to go in order to accomplish the new product pricing objectives of a given firm. Product management should also keep in mind that the pricing of a new product begins long before its birth, with projected cost/price ratios governing the decisions to authorize its development and invest in its introduction. As the product life cycle takes its course after the introduction of the innovation, careful monitoring and periodic reviews permit price adjustments in line with evolving conditions.[8]

Distribution Policy

A *channel of distribution* is the route that the title to a product takes from producer to ultimate buyer—as distinct and possibly separate from physical distribution, which refers to the physical movement of tangible goods, such as transportation, storage, and handling. The chain of ownership transfers involved in a channel of distribution can be either direct or indirect. In *direct distribution,* title to the product is transferred directly from the producer to the ultimate user. In *indirect distribution,* the product's ownership changes hands several times, involving independent intermediaries.

Intermediaries actually come in two forms, as agent and merchant middlemen. *Agent middlemen* are matchmakers that bring the two parties (seller and buyer) together. In the strict sense of the definition of a channel distribution, they are not part of the channel because they do *not* take title and thus do not assume the risks inherent in ownership. In practice, they are typically treated as partners in the distribution process, although they earn a commission rather than a profit. This is particularly true in the service sector, where insurance or travel agents are major revenue producers for their principals.

Merchant middlemen, on the other hand, buy and resell the merchandise they handle and thus take title to it. Their involvement makes for indirect distribution, which reduces both the risk and the control of the manufacturer. Only tangible goods can be distributed in this fashion because intangible services cannot be owned and resold.

In this context, it is useful to distinguish between the institutions and functions of wholesaling and retailing. Both the functions of wholesaling and retailing can be performed by many different types of organizations because the distinction is based on the buying purpose rather than the identity of the seller. The function of wholesaling is to sell goods for business purposes, whereas the function of retailing is to sell for personal use. Manufacturers selling to retailers are assuming the wholesaling function themselves. If they also open or acquire their own retail outlets, they have moved further into the retailing function. In contrast, the institution of wholesaling is a wholesaler, that is, a business that specializes in wholesaling. Similarly, the institution of retailing is a retailer, an independent firm that concentrates on retailing. As will be discussed later, the institutions of wholesaling and retailing can be eliminated, bypassed, or replaced, but the corresponding functions always have to be performed by someone. Producers that cut out wholesalers from their channels have to take over the wholesalers' role and establish their own distribution networks.

It is the role of distribution channels to provide widespread exposure and availability for a manufacturer's products. The more extensive and efficient a distribution system is, the better it serves this purpose. The process of inventing and producing a new product is ultimately futile if the product cannot effectively reach its intended target group. As a matter of fact, distribution contributes significantly to a nation's standard of living by providing both many jobs and the goods necessary for material comfort.

New Product Channel Selection

Often a firm will find itself constrained by its own past patterns or prevailing industry practice in choosing the channel(s) for a new product. Current intermediaries handling the company's established brands will want to benefit from the appeal of a new product. Also, the company will want to leverage this immensely valuable asset of trade relations. So the most likely solution to the new product channel selection issue is to use existing channels. This is especially appropriate if the new product is closely related to the present product mix and is likely to be bought as an alternative to or in conjunction with other company products. The synergism involved in this relationship would make it imprudent to seek another approach.

Existing channels and an established distribution organization can be tremendously valuable assets. The goodwill and momentum inherent in such an arrangement would then simply have to be mobilized in favor of the new product. Dealer support is absolutely essential for the success of many products. It can be gained much more easily by an established sales force calling on current accounts. As a matter of fact, this kind of leverage can be so valuable that firms wishing to enter a new business may acquire companies already active in this business because of their distribution organization and trade reputation rather than starting from scratch in building a new distribution network. This procedure gives the new product instant credibility by association with the established organization and thus greatly facilitates its introduction.

Where such considerations are less important, prevailing industry practice can still act to constrain the range of meaningful choices. The way in which an industry typically distributes its products creates customer expectations and behavior patterns that make it advisable to follow a similar path. If consumers, for instance, routinely shop for residential fluorescent lighting fixtures in hardware and department stores, it makes only a limited amount of sense to pick supermarkets as a major distribution channel. It is not likely that buyers will significantly alter their shopping patterns in response to one firm's deviating marketing approach, although some impulse sales could result. Consumers tend to favor shopping situations where they have a choice of competitive offerings available and can make on-the-spot comparisons of features and price. Also, they have simply come to expect to find a given type of product in a certain kind of store and will habitually shop for it there.

It may, however, make sense to consider multiple channels in order to reach different target markets. A new product could provide the impetus for such a rethinking of traditional practices. In the food industry, for example, separate channels serve the needs of consumers through grocery outlets and the needs of institutional feeders through specialized distributors and direct sales. Multiple channels may require repacking—soup in larger cans for restaurants, peanuts in portion packets for airlines—or even rebranding, but they enable a seller to reach out to new audiences, thus enhancing a new product's appeal and sales potential. Appliances for singles, for instance, could simply be sold through established appliance dealer channels or additionally be marketed and distributed directly to developers and builders. Accordingly, a firm may take a promising new product as an occasion to add to its existing distribution capability by creating a separate sales and distribution organization directed at a different market. Such a move, although costly and time-consuming, is all the more likely if other products are being developed that are likely to benefit from this arrangement.

Occasionally, though, a company will venture into unfamiliar territory without the option of using or buying an established distribution network. Then product management faces the challenge of building a new channel structure from the ground up. Typically, this will mean hiring a sales force and going the indirect route by calling on wholesalers, which, in turn, can promote the innovation to their associated retailers.

That is what Pfizer did when it invented the broad spectrum antibiotic Terramycin and decided to market the drug itself rather than license it to another pharmaceutical manufacturer with established trade channels. At the time, Pfizer was a major supplier of ingredients to the pharmaceutical industry but did not have a sales organization to market finished products to pharmacies. Instead of joining or buying a pharmaceutical firm with existing channels, Pfizer hired an initial sales force of twenty people to call on 800 pharmaceutical wholesalers across the nation. On approval by the Food and Drug Administration, the product quickly caught on, the sales organization expanded rapidly, and Pfizer became a household word in pharmaceuticals around the globe.

During the introduction of a new product, indirect distribution can generate widespread exposure and availability faster and cheaper than shorter, more direct channels can provide. It is physically impossible and prohibitively expensive for a fledging sales force to call on all relevant retailers or other potential buyers of the innovation. Wholesale intermediaries can speed up the implementation of this contact and promotion function significantly and lower its cost by spreading it over many products. But the selection of these trading partners should be executed with great care because it locks the firm into long-term relationships with distributors and dealers that are difficult if not impossible to break. And it may require some wooing, as establishing distribution channels is a matter of choosing *and* being chosen. A firm gets judged by the company it keeps and is dependent for its success on the integrity, capability, and dedication of its channel members.

In selecting new product channels, product management should also be acutely aware that the type of channel arrangement chosen will affect all other marketing decisions. This interdependence between channel choice and the determination of other elements of the marketing mix is apparent in the area of pricing. If product management chooses exclusive distribution, placing the product in only a few carefully selected stores and thus combining a high level of support with tight channel control, the product becomes a luxury item that entails high margins and prices. On the other hand, producers aiming for intensive market coverage classify their products as mass merchandise with low markups and prices, exercising very little control over merchandise distribution and presentation. Also, different advertising methods, themes, and media are needed, depending on the way in which a product is distributed and offered for sale. Even product and packaging design may depend on the nature of the distribution channels: Merchandise suited for self-service is designed and packaged in a different manner than expensive items requiring expert advice and explanation.

The selection of a specific channel of distribution further determines the type and size of the target markets by delimiting the numbers and kinds of buyers that can be reached through these trade partners. When General Foods developed and launched a line of fancy foods, distributing them through the fancy foods departments of major department stores rather than through its established supermarket channels, the venture failed. Department store customers viewed the line as being inferior to other high-priced items while grocery shoppers might well have perceived it as offering higher quality. Ideally, channel structures should be designed to reach precisely the intended target groups.

At times, innovative channel arrangements can offer exciting growth potential. When Avon found traditional cosmetic counters in leading department stores too crowded for effective competition, it set up its own door-to-door selling operation. Tupperware has also successfully deviated from competitive marketing practices, using its direct distribution party selling approach internationally. Electrolux has acquired a fine reputation in many countries, selling vacuum cleaners through in-home demonstrations. As these examples illustrate, it can well pay to be different and choose a distribution setup that makes a company stand out in its industry. Going direct is costly, however, and requires relatively high markups to cover the higher cost of distribution.

Implementing Channel Decisions

The first order of business within the framework of channel design is the formulation of channel objectives. The objectives may include growth through new products within existing markets or through invasion of new markets. Market expansion can usually be achieved by having present distributors carry additional products, although it may require giving up some established products to make room for the innovations. Market extension, on the other hand, often requires new, separate distribution channels and thus new trade contacts that may have to be opened and serviced by a new sales force.

Creating an efficient distribution system may be another objective of channel policy: to reach the right customers at the right time at the right place at the right price with the right merchandise. This requires considerable cooperation from channel members, particularly in the form of information feedback. Another consideration is whether a given channel will be able to utilize fully existing plant capacity and secure continuous sales and employment. It might well be necessary to adopt a policy of multiple channels to achieve this objective, which may involve supplying complementary or even competing channels.

The cost of alternative channels and their support requirements as compared to the benefits they provide for the sponsoring firm are another factor to consider in channel choice. Because the marketing cost of a product can constitute a substantial share of its price, economies in channel design render it more price-competitive.

Once the strategic decision has been made concerning the type of channel structure to use, the actual selection and recruitment of individual partners in the distribution process is a tactical task that should not be delegated to the sales force. Product management should work closely with sales management in executing this crucial assignment. The actual sell-in of the chosen wholesalers and retailers is then largely the responsibility of the sales force.

Key employees of intermediaries, such as inside counterpeople, field sales-people, floor salesclerks, or repair and maintenance personnel, will often require specialized training. This may involve knowledge of the product and its applications, comparative competitive information, familiarization with the production process, and/or instruction on how to install or service a piece of equipment. Typically, such training programs serve both informational and motivational purposes, creating both the necessary understanding and the desire to sell and service. Usually, the cost of such new product training programs is borne by the manufacturer, which may conduct them at the factory or in the form of a traveling road show. If the need for training is fairly limited, videotapes may be substituted for live instruction.

SUMMARY

Introductory marketing mix decisions have to be made in concert, requiring careful coordination to achieve synergistic relationships among all the elements. In addition to product-related decisions, this involves integrating pricing and distribution decisions into a cohesive framework.

New product pricing is governed by pricing objectives that may be either profit or volume oriented. These objectives may be pursued by using cost-based or market-based pricing. Cost-based pricing is mostly of the cost-plus variety, which suggests a minimum level for the alternative of market-based pricing. Marginal cost pricing is, and should be, used rarely as a stopgap measure to generate higher capacity utilization. Market-based pricing, on the other hand, can be either demand or competition oriented. A particularly useful tool for increasing revenues and profits is price differentiation, which can be practiced in a sequential, geographic, or functional manner.

The two major choices in new product pricing are skimming versus penetration pricing. A variety of considerations govern their selection. Essentially, skimming creates a high-quality, luxury image but restricts the initial volume and attracts competitors. Penetration establishes a mass market from the outset and erects barriers to competitive entry, relying on volume to generate profits. Accordingly, it depends on the firm's objectives and capacity, as well as on the product's stage in the life cycle and the nature of competition, which approach is most likely to succeed in a particular case.

As discussed, the selection of one or more channels of distribution has to be carried out in concert with other introductory marketing mix decisions. Channels of distribution refer to chains of title transfers. They determine the distribution structure for an innovation for many years to come and outline the nature and number of buyers that can effectively be reached. In choosing a channel for a new product, a firm may find itself constrained by its own past patterns or by prevailing industry practice. At times, however, innovative channel arrangements that deviate from industry norms can offer attractive growth potential, and multiple channels enable product management to reach several target markets. Prudent channel decisions can greatly enhance the market impact of an introductory program.

NOTES

1. See Philip Kotler, *Principles of Marketing,* 2nd ed. (Englewood Cliffs, NJ: Prentice-Hall, 1983) 335.
2. See Robert D. Buzzell and Frederik D. Wiersema, "Successful Share-Building Strategies," *Harvard Business Review* (Jan.–Feb. 1981): 135–144.
3. Joel Dean, "Pricing Policies for New Products," *Harvard Business Review* (Nov.–Dec. 1976): 147.
4. See " 'Excellence, Inc.': Lectures, Spinoffs, and a TV Special," *Business Week,* 5 Nov. 1984, 88.
5. Concerning the reasons for setting different prices in domestic and overseas markets, see Vern Terpstra, *International Marketing,* 4th ed. (Hinsdale, IL: Dryden Press, 1987) 524–528.
6. This section is based on Dean, "Pricing Policies," 147–148, and Eberhard E. Scheuing, "Pricing New Products," in *Marketing Update* (New York: Alexander Norton Publishers, 1977).
7. See Robert L. Klein, "Right Price on New Product Boosts Profit Potential," *Marketing Review* (Sep.–Oct. 1985): 24–25.
8. See John B. Frey, "Pricing and Product Life Cycle," *Chemtech* (Jan. 1985): 40.

CASE STUDY

COOKING WITH WINE

Founded as an importer of gourmet food products, the Dutchman Company has a current sales volume of $54 million, earning a profit before taxes of $8.1 million. The company distributes its product mix through specialty food distributors to grocery stores. In its nationwide distribution system, it also employs food brokers (at a 5 percent commission) to "ride herd" on the distributors to motivate them to buy and, in turn, push Dutchman items. Over the years, its product mix has grown, and the firm is well respected by its distributors, which operate on a 25 percent margin on their selling prices.

Supermarket operators like specialty food items primarily for three reasons:

1. The gross profit is high—on average, 33 percent of the retail selling price.
2. The products are delivered on a store-door basis (like bottled soda, bread, and snacks).
3. They are price-marked and placed on the shelves by the distributors' salespeople.

Because the only cost to the stores is providing shelf space, the stores get to keep most of the gross profit from these items.

Expanding the Product Mix

Forever intent on increasing the business, founder and chief executive officer Jacob Irwin has come up with a new product idea. He is aware of the fact that in many states wine cannot be legally sold in food stores because food stores cannot obtain alcoholic beverage licenses. He has, however, been able to secure the federal government's permission to sell cooking wine in food stores because technically it is considered nonpotable. Irwin satisfies this require-

This case was contributed by B. Felix McGuigan, Instructor in Marketing, St. John's University, New York, New York.

ment mainly by adding a small amount of salt to the wine. This fact is not identified on the label and it does not affect the performance of the wine in cooking.

Ellen Blair is the company's one-person marketing department. In this capacity, she is responsible for pricing recommendations and reports directly to Irwin. Blair earned an M.B.A. in marketing from a well-known private university, joining the company one year ago. She has convened a meeting with John Blum, the sales manager, and Nick Fusco, the controller, to develop a recommendation on the pricing of the new line of cooking wines. Their deliberations are governed by the fact that the three most popular varieties of wine used in cooking are red wine, white wine, and sherry. Accordingly, it has been decided to offer initially only these three varieties. Also, the company is not planning to advertise the cooking wines.

Ellen opens the meeting by stating that "we are really fortunate in that potential competitors have not caught on to our idea yet. By the time they do, we should be well enough established to fight off any challengers. What chain would want to carry two lines of cooking wines anyhow? Our only competition at this point is table wine. Most consumers are confused there and can get little help from liquor store clerks. Our proposition, in contrast, is simple. We offer three varieties of wine to be used in cooking, and shoppers can buy them in the same stores where they buy groceries."

Nick Fusco presents his cost estimates to the group: "I estimate that we can obtain and distribute a case of twelve 16-ounce bottles at a cost of $4.20. To enter this new business would require an additional investment of $540,000. In addition, we would expect each case to carry a $1.05 share of general overhead. Assuming that we recommend a retail selling price of $1.49 per bottle, we could profitably sell a case at $8.98 without infringing on the traditional distributor and retailer margins."

Considering a New Distribution Arrangement

Fusco continues: "The wine market has grown substantially in recent years and a high percentage of households use wine. Consequently, I wonder whether we should not consider going directly to supermarket chains with this line. If we bypass our distributors, we will make substantially more profit per case, even after counting delivery costs. I think the volume we will generate will be up to the levels demanded by the chains for a direct item. Why should we let the distributors get this profit?"

John Blum cannot believe his ears. "Nick," he says, "if we go directly with this line, we will lose the support of our distributors on our other items and they will simply drop us. They will not appreciate being cut out of this business and will simply hit the roof. You know how they talk to each other—we will be dead as soon as they hear of this. Forget it."

Ellen is also taken by surprise by Nick's recommendation. She feels, however, that his proposal should at least be studied. She knows that sales managers often resist changes in distribution channels. Perhaps John overstated the distributors' probable reaction.

Discussion Questions

1. What price level should Ellen Blair recommend? Why?
2. At this price, how many cases would the company have to sell to break even?
3. What will Dutchman's profit be if it sells (a) 300,000 and (b) 540,000 cases of cooking wine?
4. Should the company sell the cooking wine directly to supermarkets and thereby bypass the distributors? Why?

CHAPTER 12

New Product Promotion

The promotion element of the introductory marketing mix consists of three major ingredients: advertising, sales promotion, and personal selling. Advertising and sales promotion are treated in this chapter and new product selling is the subject of Chapter 13.

Advertising is the paid presentation of promotional messages through mass media. It takes a long-term perspective, building an image and following for a brand. *Sales promotion,* in contrast, involves the short-term stimulation of demand by various means. Otherwise put, the term "sales promotion" refers to all those promotional activities that are neither advertising nor personal selling. This kind of definition highlights the fact that sales promotion encompasses a broad variety of tactical tools. Advertising aims to build position and recognition; sales promotion attempts to generate sales. Both are important, and neither should be favored to the exclusion of the other. Advertising without sales promotion increases awareness and familiarity without much current sales impact. Sales promotion without advertising support moves merchandise for the short term but without much lasting impact. In concert, they can be great revenue generators: Advertising creates interest and a favorable attitude, and sales promotion provides the added incentive to stimulate immediate action. Jointly, they can break down substantial barriers of resistance on the part of prospective buyers of an innovation and greatly facilitate its adoption throughout a target market.

In new product introduction, advertising is used as the major instrument of demand creation and sales support. It plays a key role in communicating the product's existence and benefits to potential buyers. The creative challenge is formidable: communicating uniqueness, creating a product identity, and preselling the innovation. Most product managers prefer to address this challenge by seeking professional help from an advertising agency. This agency may be one that the company currently works with, or it may be specifically recruited and selected for this particular purpose.

It is the agency's responsibility to develop an advertising campaign for the new product in close cooperation with product management. Toward this end, campaign objectives have to be formulated and the advertising budget determined. The agency then develops a copy platform and translates it into finished advertisements. Choosing the right media mix and schedule for carrying the new product message to the intended audience requires considerable skill and experience.

Most new products, however, cannot live on advertising alone. They also need a substantial dose of sales promotion to succeed during the critical introductory period. Although advertising can familiarize them with the features and benefits of an innovation, most prospects need an extra incentive to overcome their natural reluctance to assume the risk inherent in its adoption. Product management can direct sales promotion efforts toward these ultimate buyers, the company's own sales force, or the intermediaries involved in the product's distribution. A broad range of tools is available to resourceful product managers, spanning from contests to trading stamps.

Advertising in New Product Introduction

Most new product launches are inconceivable without advertising. Whether industrial or consumer, good or service, a product is only new once in its lifetime. The excitement inherent in this newness can be leveraged by headlining it: "Announcing/ Introducing New (brand name) (product category), (benefit claim)." After all, "new" is one of the most powerful words in the English language, one that is well worth leveraging while appropriate. "Improved" is another action word that suggests progress in a progress-minded society. Clearly, new product advertising has an announcement function that no other marketing mix element can adequately fulfill.

The principal functions of new product advertising are to create awareness of and interest in the innovation. From these overall goals derives a gamut of individual objectives:

- Attracting attention and alerting prospects to the existence and availability of the product
- Informing them about the new product's features and benefits
- Generating and maintaining a favorable attitude toward the firm and its product, possibly helping to defuse negative feelings
- Creating a desire for the new product by activating and focusing needs
- Orienting the generated willingness to buy toward the firm's new product and thus establishing, expanding, and securing market position and market share
- Bringing about buyer preference for, or even insistence on, the firm's new brand, granting the company a level of pricing freedom
- Speeding up purchase and consumption rhythms through psychological obsolescence of former models

Essentially, introductory advertising has to address the dual tasks of demand creation and sales support. Depending on the nature of the product and its stage in the life cycle, the demand to be created at the end user level may be primary or selective. If a new market is being created by a dynamically continuous or discontinuous innovation, demand for the new category has to be generated from ground zero. Its occurrence will automatically benefit the sole supplier of the innovation. If a new product is introduced at a more advanced stage of the product life cycle, selective demand generation is the required approach. This means that advertising has to produce a following for the specific brand because primary demand already exists. The latter procedure is particularly evident in a *pulling strategy,* which is aimed at producing brand insistence at the end user level, thus serving to pull the brand through the channel of distribution.

In terms of sales support, advertising has to smooth the way for salespeople. It has to create buyer awareness of the innovation's existence and principal features, thus enabling sales representatives to build on this prior knowledge rather than having to acquaint uninitiated prospects with its availability. This kind of concerted effort allows for better utilization of salespersons' time by shifting the emphasis in sales presentations from education to persuasion.

New product advertising can further help to focus the sales effort on promising candidates by generating leads. A *lead* can be defined as an expression of interest in a firm's offering by a potential buyer. Such sales leads can be triggered by advertising in a number of ways. An advertisement can carry a coupon for a free catalog or brochure, or it can list a toll-free telephone number to call for such informational materials. A postage-paid information request card addressed to the company may be bound or inserted into a magazine together with an advertisement, or a magazine-sponsored reader inquiry card at the end of an issue may invite readers to circle reference numbers relating to specific advertisements in order to obtain further information.

Whichever method is used, advertising can play a vital role in new product introduction by soliciting expressions of interest that can be followed up by salespeople, thus eliminating the need for cold calling. Of course, not every sales lead produced in this manner indicates a potential sale. Because some inquiries might be brought about by mere curiosity without the appropriate authority or intention to buy, it is preferable to qualify inquiries by phone before embarking on a personal visit.

In some businesses, such as groceries, new product advertising contributes in yet a different way to personal selling. One of the major factors affecting the decision of a supermarket buyer to carry or not to carry a particular innovation is its level of advertising support. In other words, the buyer is concerned with how much the manufacturer will spend on advertising to generate consumer demand in its trading area. Regardless of the merits of the product, a salesperson will have difficulty convincing the buyer to carry the innovation if the level of advertising support appears insufficient. On the other hand, a mere me-too product enjoying a generous level of advertising support is likely to succeed in making it onto the shelf.

The Role of the Advertising Agency

In designing and executing the advertising program for a new product, product management will usually avail itself of the services of an *advertising agency*. An advertising agency is an independent organization composed of creative and business people who develop, prepare, test, and place advertisements in media for clients trying to sell their goods and services.[1] Historically, advertising agencies came into being as sales agencies for print and broadcast media, selling space and time to prospective advertisers. For these services, they were compensated with a 15 percent commission on sales revenues generated (or billings) by the media. In order to attract a sufficient volume of business, these agencies had to assist advertisers in designing advertisements. As the need for this assistance became more extensive, advertising agencies started working for the client firms rather than the media, contracting for media space and time as needed for specific client campaigns.

These historical roots explain why advertising agencies to this day derive the majority of their compensation from commissions received from the media in return for placing advertisements with them. Because this discount is granted only to advertising agencies and not to advertisers that place advertisements directly, product management should retain the professional services of an advertising agency.

A modern full-service advertising agency consists of

- A creative department that designs advertising campaigns and individual advertisements
- A media department that formulates and executes a media plan, buying media space and time on the client's behalf
- An account management department that acts as the interface with product management
- A production department that produces the actual advertisements to be sent to the media
- A traffic department that handles the physical flow of advertising copy to and from the media
- An accounting department that handles client billing and media payments
- A marketing research department that carries out market and sales, product, and advertising research tasks
- Various other administrative and support services

Thus, a full-service agency is ideally equipped to serve as a comprehensive marketing adviser. It could and should enter the picture in the product conceptualization stage to apply its varied talents for maximum client benefit.

In fact, an agency's contributions can even begin with the product idea itself. The concept underlying Cycle dog food was developed by the creative personnel of an advertising agency who reasoned that the nutritional needs of canines differ throughout their life cycles. This suggestion resulted in four formulations marketed by General Foods, namely, for puppies, adult dogs, overweight dogs, and older dogs.

Account executives become intimately involved with their clients' businesses and offer recommendations with respect to product mix, packaging, branding, pricing, distribution, merchandising, and sales promotion, in addition to their core responsibility of advertising.[2]

Advertising can generate and sustain sales success only if the product itself is in tune with the market. In fact, it can be said that good advertising can help bury a poor product faster because it induces more people to try the product earlier and find out for themselves how disappointingly it performs. Many advertising agencies, therefore, demand to be brought in early in the game and have their say in new product design.

Before a new agency took on the account of Ballantine's Scotch, for instance, it conducted a study to determine the existing image of this brand of whisky. It found that at the time Ballantine's Scotch was mainly consumed by blue-collar workers and was considered a heavy drink because of the dark color of the liquid and the bottle. Because a prime objective for the advertising of this brand was to broaden its base by repositioning it as a high-class social drink, the agency requested some changes before it would take on the account. The bottle was stretched to make it look more elegant, and clear glass was used to suggest lightness, which was enhanced by lightening the color of the liquor itself through charcoal filtering. The agency's suggestions were quite valuable and helpful in modifying this product to fit its new target market.

Selecting the Agency

The advertising agency chosen to handle the new product may well be one that has an existing account relationship with the firm. If the innovation represents a line extension or modification of a current item, it will typically be appropriate for the present agency to be assigned the new product also. Under such circumstances, splitting the responsibility for established and new products within the same line between two agencies would likely be counterproductive. Having one agency serve the entire line will usually result in efficient effort and integrity and continuity of presentation. This arrangement also facilitates the communication and learning process because most factors required for an effective agency relationship are already in place and working.

A number of reasons, however, could prompt a search for a new agency:[3]

- Management is dissatisfied with the performance of the current agency and takes the new product as a catalyst to change agencies.
- With the new product, the company's advertising and marketing support needs have outgrown the resources and capabilities of its current agency.
- The new product conflicts with a competitive account that the present agency is handling, thus preventing it from accepting the new assignment.
- The new product represents an additional brand in a product category where the company already has other entries so that the same agency could not do justice to competing brands from the same source.

- The new product is an entry in a new product category where the current agency does not offer appropriate expertise.

Under any of these circumstances, the following four-step procedure provides a useful framework for the systematic selection of a new advertising agency:

Step 1: Product management acquaints itself with the services offered by advertising agencies.

Step 2: In conjunction with the advertising department, product management identifies the new product's advertising needs and establishes criteria for agency selection.

Step 3: Product management conducts a comprehensive search, appraisal, and selection program aimed at matching an agency's capabilities with the new product's advertising needs.

Step 4: Management makes a final choice and commitment after competing agency presentations, negotiating a mutually satisfactory working and financial agreement.

In step 1, a listing of advertising agency departments offers a glimpse at the range of services rendered. This range will greatly depend on the size of an agency, which can extend from a small creative boutique to a multinational agency with a global network. A large advertiser will typically retain a full-service agency but utilize smaller agencies for special creative assignments on a project basis, particularly if a new product's budget is too small initially to be profitable for the main agency.

With regard to step 2, it is essential to realize that advertising must be managed by the advertiser, not the agency. The fundamental responsibility for originating new product marketing strategy and thus its advertising strategy rests with product management. The new product's advertising needs and service requirements should thus be defined on the basis of its strategic marketing approach. These needs will determine the degree of involvement that product management expects from an agency. For example, product management may

- Require only advertising assistance because the company is reasonably self-sufficient in other marketing areas, such as marketing research and packaging development.
- Need a number of additional services beyond the preparation and placement of advertisements, such as marketing research and design of sales promotion materials.
- Look for more comprehensive marketing advice, reaching beyond advertising into broader marketing strategy decisions, such as channel strategy formulation.
- Desire all-inclusive marketing guidance, looking to the agency to initiate research projects on its own and suggest new product development programs.

The capabilities and characteristics that an agency would ideally possess should be reflected in the selection criteria. A list of criteria and information needs for agency selection is presented in Table 12–1. This comprehensive checklist covers

TABLE 12–1
Criteria for Agency Selection

A. *The Agency*
  1. Location of headquarters and branch offices
  2. Agency management—names, titles, and backgrounds of principal officers; extent of top management participation in client service
  3. Agency philosophy—agency's own business goals and strategies; basic philosophy of doing business; types of accounts and services agency specializes in; reputation for integrity
  4. Financial stability—credit rating; cost accounting practices; bill paying procedure; ownership; passing on of discounts to clients

B. *Account Management*
  1. List of current accounts by name and type
  2. Turnover of accounts—accounts added and lost in last three years, and reasons for loss
  3. Billings—analysis by size range of billings (smallest and largest account); media billing mix; growth rate through new billings and new accounts in last three years
  4. Evidence of success with present accounts—sales results, share of market, ratings, other measurements
  5. Potential conflicts with existing accounts—policy on account conflicts
  6. Account team—backgrounds, talents, personalities of people scheduled to work on the account; need for hiring additional personnel to handle the account; type of expertise sought
  7. Rate of employee turnover in last three years
  8. Marketing capabilities—ability to provide assistance in development of a marketing plan; ability to convert a marketing strategy into a workable advertising plan; evidence of sound marketing thinking; experience with new product introductions

C. *Creative and Media*
  1. Agency's creative and media philosophy, especially with respect to specific account
  2. View of agency's and client's responsibilities in creative and media fields
  3. Flow chart showing how creative work is planned, developed, executed, and approved
  4. Importance placed on background material in developing copy
  5. Forecast of trends in media costs and circulation
  6. Media rating services used by agency and benefits derived from their use
  7. Examples of outstanding work produced by the agency's creative people

D. *Marketing Research*
  1. Agency's ability to gather and analyze marketing data—internal capabilities; use of outside suppliers; examples of recent marketing research studies conducted for clients
  2. Measuring advertising effectiveness—methods used for copy pre- and post-testing; nature of media research; use of outside services; importance placed on effectiveness research; examples of adjustments made based on results of such research

E. *Compensation and Facilities*
  1. Commission—nature and extent of services to be provided under agency commission
  2. Charges and fees—policy on charges for creative work, production costs, expenses, studies, promotional help, public relations work, training assistance, etc.; at cost or with profit margin
  3. Sample of agency-client contract, reflecting any suggested changes
  4. Facilities for production or purchase of typography, finished art

Source: Reprinted with permission from Jerome W. Stein, "How to Select the Right Advertising Agency," in *Marketing Update* (New York: Alexander-Norton Publishers, 1977), pp. 3–4.

agency characteristics, details about its account management track record, its creative, media, and marketing research capabilities, and its usual compensation arrangements.

With the evaluation framework established, step 3 is devoted to the search and screening process, often conducted as a joint effort of product management and the advertising department. An initial list of agency candidates drawn from personal recommendations and published sources will be reduced by applying the screening criteria. The list can then be further refined by considering each agency's reputation, creative excellence, and capabilities in other areas, such as media, marketing research, and sales promotion.

Geographic access may be important, ruling out some otherwise qualified agencies. Account conflicts are also a common deterrent, rendering an agency ineligible if it handles a competing account. Still other agencies may not have the experience or desire to take on the account. Many are too large or too small, or possess an inadequate degree of marketing sophistication, or have conflicting business philosophies. Product management may also be constrained by the size of the new product's budget, the amount and type of work required from the agency, and the degree of specialized knowledge required to service the account.

The remaining agencies are then approached and invited to bid on the account. This contact function involves mutual wooing, as agency selection is a process of choosing and being chosen. Thus, product management has to be sure to present its business in an attractive light, pointing out growth opportunities from a possibly modest start. Contacted agencies may be asked to submit information about themselves in the form of a questionnaire, forward names of current and former clients, and present samples of their creative work. This information should be supplemented with an analysis of an agency's credit rating and other indicators of its financial stability. The most appealing agencies should be visited in order to obtain personal impressions of their capabilities, operations, and people.

Indeed, its people are the key asset of an advertising agency. Their talents, experience, philosophy, and dedication make the agency unique. Knowledge of a market's needs and characteristics and creativity in problem solving are among the most important abilities that an agency's personnel can offer to a client. The depth and substance of an agency are also dependent on the quality of its support and service personnel. What all this adds up to is the intangible property of "chemistry," which is essential to the success of an agency relationship.

In step 4, management invites the semifinalists to give oral presentations and bid for the new account. No more than a handful of agencies should have survived the prior selection procedure and be serious candidates at this point. A selection committee, typically composed of product management, advertising management, and senior management, will use these presentations to assess each agency's approaches and capabilities.

Two types of presentations might be considered. A standard new business presentation is totally unrelated to any specific new product but is, instead, intended to acquaint an advertiser with the agency's history, organization, talents, capabilities, and past successes. Such a presentation demonstrates the agency's basic philosophy and experience, the way in which it approaches marketing problems and creative challenges, what services it offers, and what kind of work it has done in the past.

In addition to or instead of this standard type of presentation, the competing agencies might be asked to make speculative presentations. Such presentations are designed to outline how an agency would handle the new account, including creative and media strategy, copy platform, and media schedule. In other words, the winning agency is expected to be ready to implement its proposal through the account team as identified at the time of presentation. A speculative presentation addresses itself to the specific new product advertising challenge at hand and sketches out proposed approaches or solutions. To make it meaningful, product management has to spell out what it is looking for in the presentation, offering adequate guidance and support in terms of factual input and access to product and facilities. It is also common to reimburse the participating agencies for the, at times, substantial expenses incurred in preparing the presentation.

Each agency presentation should also propose an appropriate compensation system that will be attractive for both advertiser and agency. In addition to the standard media commission, fees may be necessary to cover extraordinary services that can be involved in developing an advertising campaign for a new product, particularly if the initial budget is somewhat modest. Such a compensation proposal is frequently subject to further discussion and negotiation before a final agreement is reached.

Working with the Agency

Once an agency has been retained to service the new account, the product manager has to work closely with the account executive assigned to it. This account executive represents the liaison or interface of the client with the agency and can bring all of the agency's resources to bear in servicing the account—including research, copy-writing, art, production, media planning and buying, and a variety of other services.

In working with the agency to develop the advertising strategy and subsequently the campaign for the new product, product management has to give both direction and support. The product manager in charge typically serves as the company's contact person with the agency and thus as the account executive's counterpart. Jointly, they have to establish the new product's advertising objectives and review them with senior management. They analyze internal data and research findings and discuss evolving creative approaches and media options on an ongoing basis. The product manager acts as the conduit of internal information to the agency and communicates inputs from other units of the organization. The product manager also directs and evaluates the agency's efforts on the product's behalf, carefully coordinating it with the other elements of the introductory marketing mix.

In its day-to-day relationship with the agency working on the new product account, product management should attempt to achieve a number of goals:

- Proper use of the agency's resources and talents
- Proper direction of the agency's work on the account
- Constructive criticism of the agency's output and performance

- Proper relationship with agency personnel
- Balanced involvement in the agency's operations

To make balanced use of the agency's capabilities, its role in the new product effort has to be clearly defined and understood by both parties. To what extent should the agency participate in product and/or packaging design or the choice of a brand name? To what extent should it become involved in marketing research? And what should be its role in formulating marketing strategy? This understanding should, of course, be reflected in the compensation agreement. At one extreme, the agency's capabilities go severely underutilized by an overprotective product management that wants to do everything itself. At the other end of the spectrum, the agency is called on for every conceivable marketing decision by an indecisive product management.

In directing the agency's work, product management should share its insights into emerging shifts in the marketplace. Overly directive product management simply tells an agency what to do in terms of creative executions and media choices, thus forgoing the benefit of expert recommendations from the agency. An underdirected agency is completely left to its own devices without any meaningful input from the client. Balanced direction results from mutual respect and synergistic interplay of product and account management.

Uncritical acceptance of the agency's suggestions shows little judgment, lulling account management into a false sense of security and producing mediocre advertising. Frequent criticism and excessive changes, on the other hand, are very demoralizing and costly, possibly culminating in the agency resigning the account. Constructive criticism measures individual advertisements against agreed-upon criteria and strengthens them with suggestions for improvement.

Frequent interaction with agency personnel, particularly account management, can breed friendship and cloud judgment. This kind of closeness compromises objectivity and does not serve the best interests of the firm. The other extreme is an aloof, even condescending and antagonistic product manager who discourages personal commitment and exceptional dedication on the part of agency personnel. A balanced relationship is friendly but firm and businesslike.

To work optimally with the agency, the product manager should have a solid understanding of agency operations. An overparticipative product manager interferes in the agency's operations and tells it what to do. An underparticipative product manager does not understand the agency's operations and is accordingly dominated by it. Balanced involvement results in a healthy interchange of ideas and a mutually supportive relationship.

Designing a New Product Advertising Campaign

The purpose of hiring an advertising agency for the new product is to have it design an advertising campaign for the innovation's introduction. A *campaign* is a series of advertisements designed around a unifying theme and presented in concert in one continuous schedule. Table 12–2 details the steps involved in developing an advertis-

TABLE 12–2

Steps in Developing a New Product Advertising Campaign

Campaign Step	Advertising Activities	Research Activities
A. *Pre-Campaign Phase*		
1. Market Analysis		Study of competitive products, positioning, media, distribution, and usage patterns
2. Product Research		Identification of perceived product characteristics and benefits
3. Consumer Research		Demographic and psychographic studies of prospective consumers, investigation of media, purchasing, and consumption patterns
B. *Strategic Decisions*		
4. Set Advertising Objectives	Determine target markets and market targets (user profile, exposure goals)	
5. Decide on Level of Appropriation	Determine total advertising spending necessary to support objectives	Investigation of competitive spending levels and media cost necessary to reach objectives
6. Formulate Advertising Strategy	Develop creative approach and prepare "shopping list" of appropriate media	Examine audience profiles, reach, frequency, and costs of alternative media
7. Integrate Advertising Strategy with Overall Marketing Strategy	Make sure that advertising supports and is supported by other elements of marketing mix	

ing campaign. It indicates clearly that a sound campaign is based on continuous marketing research that stimulates the creative talents of advertising professionals.

Consisting of five stages subdivided into sixteen steps, the campaign development process begins with the pre-campaign phase, which is exclusively devoted to marketing research. This includes market analysis, that is, the study of competitive products, their characteristics, positioning, distribution, and usage patterns. The purpose of this step is to understand the nature and intensity of competition and thus to establish a frame of reference for product positioning and potential comparative advertising.

The second step of product research focuses on the identification of perceived product characteristics and benefits. This is useful input in formulating a copy platform and selecting specific advertising appeals that should reflect relevant target

TABLE 12–2
continued

Campaign Step	Advertising Activities	Research Activities
C. *Tactical Execution*		
8. Develop Detailed Advertising Budget	Break down overall allocation to spending on media categories and individual media	
9. Choose Message Content and Mode of Presentation	Develop alternative creative concepts, copy, and layout	Conduct concept and copy tests
10. Analyze Legal Ramifications	Have chosen copy reviewed by legal staff or counsel	
11. Establish Media Plan	Determine media mix and schedule	Conduct media research, primarily from secondary sources
12. Review Agency Presentation	See entire planned campaign in perspective for approval	
D. *Campaign Implementation*		
13. Production and Traffic	Finalize and reproduce advertisement(s), buy media time and space, and deliver ads	
14. Insertion of Advertisements	Actually run ads in chosen media	Check whether ads appeared as agreed and directed
E. *Campaign Follow-Through*		
15. Impact Control		Feedback on consumer and competitive reaction
16. Review and Revision	Adjust advertising execution or spending levels to conditions	Check whether changes made yielded desired results

Source: Reprinted with permission, from Jerome W. Stein, "How to Develop a Successful Advertising Campaign," in *Marketing Update* (New York: Alexander-Norton Publishers, 1979).

market concerns. Additional potential uses for the new product could also be researched at this point, as well as the viability of the product's packaging in the context of advertising. The package may well have to be redesigned to tie in more closely with advertising in its effort to presell the product.

The third step, consumer research, focuses on the demographic and/or psychographic profiles of prospective buyers and investigates their media, purchasing, and consumption patterns. In other words, it seeks answers to the questions: What do they read, watch, or listen to? Who buys, when, where, what, how, how much, and why? Who consumes, when, where, how, how much, and how often? What is the product used for?

With this kind of background information available as an input, the campaign development process proper can begin with a series of strategic decisions. Like other strategic choices, advertising strategy for the new product can only be determined meaningfully if its marketing, and consequently advertising, objectives have been spelled out clearly. As indicated earlier, they might be awareness, lead generation, or creation of primary or selective demand. Target customers have to be outlined demographically and/or psychographically, and market targets such as distribution or sales levels and exposure goals specified. This typically involves some trade-off between *reach* and *frequency*, that is, the number of people to be potentially exposed to the new product message and the number of times that the message will be presented to them. Other potential new product campaign objectives could be the achievement of an attitude change that facilitates product acceptance, inducement of product trial, or realization of a target market share necessary for long-term viability.

As the initial advertising budget is decided, traditional methods for determining the level of appropriation fail. The *affordable method* has one person, usually the controller, arbitrarily decide what the firm can afford to spend on advertising. For a new product, this approach would inevitably produce insufficient appropriations, thus probably dooming it. The *competitive parity method,* which matches competitors' outlays, is hardly applicable because the innovation may not have direct competition.

A third traditional method, the *percentage of sales method,* relates the level of advertising spending to past or projected sales. As there are no past sales for a new product, only projected first-year revenues would qualify. Whatever percentage is more or less arbitrarily picked for ongoing advertising would be inadequate to break through the initial barrier of resistance. In an extreme form, however, this method is occasionally used in new product advertising: A rule of thumb used by some firms says that advertising spending during the first year should equal anticipated sales revenues. These firms consider such heavy spending necessary to break through marketplace clutter and firmly establish the product. Needless to say, they sharply reduce advertising expenditures in the second year of the product's market life.

The ideal approach to new product advertising budget determination is the *objective-and-task method.* It follows a four-step procedure:

1. Formulate advertising objectives.
2. Identify tasks necessary to achieve these objectives.
3. Analyze cost of task implementation.
4. Appropriate funds sufficient for task implementation.

In this manner, the precise amount needed to achieve the new product advertising objectives is allocated—not more, not less.

Governed by the advertising objectives specified, creative and media strategies compatible with the budget constraints can now be formulated. They will attempt to create a unique position for the product, building on its perceived benefits. The advertising theme used to build this position must be powerful and possess relevance and appeal for the target market. In other words, it has to incorporate a unique selling proposition, or USP. A creative approach that contains nothing special is not likely to give a prospect a good reason to buy and try the new product. And simply describing it as "new" is not enough. A unique claim has to be made that makes the product stand out from the competition. New product advertisements should always contain at least one proposition that offers a relevant specific advantage or benefit to the buyer. Glorifying the product is a dangerous route to take because prospects are only interested in what the product will do for them. Effective advertising copy presents the benefits of the product to the consumer in concise form, using a single selling idea instead of overloading an advertisement with a variety of appeals. And this has to be done in a persuasive fashion so that the prospect is moved to action.

Step 7 in the development of a new product advertising campaign highlights the fact that advertising cannot and should not be created and executed in a vacuum. Rather, for maximum impact it has to be carefully coordinated and integrated with the other elements of the introductory marketing mix. The product manager is the pivotal point in this endeavor.

Once this strategic framework has been established and fine-tuned, the campaign development process enters its tactical execution stage. Among the tasks to be undertaken is the allocation of the total new product advertising budget to media categories and individual media as well as time periods. This may well involve "flighting," where heavy multimedia exposure during a limited time period is chosen as opposed to distributed expenditures that maintain a steady level of advertising presence. The concentrated exposure of a flight breaks through advertising clutter and creates high top-of-the-mind awareness, strongly supporting simultaneous sales promotion in stores aimed at inducing initial purchases and product trial.

The next step concerns the creative work of copywriters and art directors. Within the framework of the new product advertising objectives and strategy, these people are called on to determine what should be communicated and how. Based on factual input generated by marketing research in the precampaign phase, they develop alternative creative concepts, copy, and artwork. These are then subjected to concept and copy testing with target consumers to determine their relative merits and impact.

The winning advertisements have to be reviewed by legal experts to analyze the legal ramifications of the statements made and the features or benefits implied. Truth-in-advertising laws require that claims made in an advertisement be substantiated by evidence presented by independent outside organizations. Comparative advertising, however, that states factual deficiencies of competing products is permissible.

Meanwhile, the media department has been putting together an appropriate media mix and schedule. In formulating the new product media plan, it is assisted by media research outlining audience profiles of individual media that can be matched with the characteristics of the target market. Increasingly, the right media mix for a new product emphasizes "narrowcasting" as opposed to broadcasting. Whereas broadcasting addresses vast, fairly amorphous audiences, narrowcasting allows product management to zero in on smaller, more clearly defined groups—for example, by means of special interest magazines. This cuts a lot of waste circulation from the media plan, increasing advertising efficiency and effectiveness. Electronic media hold some promise in this regard but have yet to gain the necessary leverage.

The planned campaign is then presented in its entirety to the client for approval. This includes both creative execution and media plan and brings together not only the account team and product management but also senior management. Although minor changes may yet be undertaken, the approval of the basic formula is hardly in question at this point. The continuing dialog between account and product management prevents any serious misalignment.

In the campaign implementation phase, the carefully designed advertising plan is put into effect. The production and traffic departments of the agency have to finalize and reproduce the finished advertisements, buy the specified media time and space, and physically deliver the advertisements to the media. These advertisements are then run by the media at the specified times. Marketing research verifies that they actually appear as agreed and directed.

No strategic endeavor is complete, however, without a control element. In the campaign follow-through stage, impact control is exercised by examining feedback on consumer and competitive reaction to the advertising campaign. Where the differences between intended and actual advertising results are controllable, corrective action is indicated. This may mean increasing the spending level or redesigning the advertisements themselves. Where uncontrollable market conditions cause the discrepancy, the advertising plan should be revised to reflect the new reality. Marketing research then reports on whether the changes made produced the desired results.

Sales Promotion for New Products

New product promotion will work best if its various ingredients are used in concert, reinforcing and building on each other rather than being designed and implemented separately and independently. Advertising alone cannot meaningfully assume the entire burden of the communication and persuasion function related to the new product. Ideally, it creates an initial burst of awareness and excitement for the innovation, giving it visibility, identity, recognizability, and a first lease on market life. Because the initial spending level for advertising cannot and should not be sustained in the long run, its role thereafter is often confined to reminder or maintenance advertising.

In its long-term demand-building role, advertising works closely with the personal selling effort on behalf of the new product. It generates interest and communicates factual information about the innovation, thus reducing the amount of time that a salesperson has to spend educating a prospect about the merits of the new product. It can produce leads, provide credibility, and give postsale reassurance to buyers.

Advertising for the new product should also tie in closely with its sales promotion effort. As pointed out earlier, sales promotion consists of a variety of tactical tools used for short-term sales stimulation. In new product introduction, the extra inducement that a sales promotion tool often represents may be crucial to overcoming initial buyer resistance. Even firms that do not usually employ sales promotion programs in their marketing effort (such as industrial marketers) will often use them during the launch period of a new product.

New product sales promotion builds on its advertising, or may even use an advertisement to deliver a coupon. It can stir up excitement at the point of sale, possibly featuring the presenter who appeared in the advertising for the innovation. Advertising is also often used to announce a particular sales promotion program, such as a contest or sweepstakes. It can feature a premium available with the purchase of the new product or promote attendance at a trade show where it is exhibited.

Furthermore, sales promotion interacts with personal selling in various ways. For one, salespeople will often deliver sales promotion materials to dealers or stores, frequently even setting up and stocking special displays. For another, sales promotion programs provide sales personnel with a selling point in persuading intermediaries to take on and feature the new product. Last, not least, sales promotion can offer a direct incentive to the sales force to expend exceptional effort in selling the new product.

Alternative Sales Promotion Thrusts

In designing a sales promotion program, product management can choose from three alternative thrusts. Sales promotion can be directed at the company's own sales force, at intermediaries, or at ultimate buyers. Whereas any of these thrusts can be employed independently of the others, it is not uncommon to find them used in combination with each other.

A *sales force promotion* is aimed at giving the company's salespeople a special reason to exert themselves during the introductory period. Because the success of the innovation depends to a great extent on their enthusiasm and effort, giving the sales force an extra incentive to devote particular attention to the new product can pay substantial dividends. Selling-in an innovation is often difficult because intermediaries' shelves are crowded and many new products are clamoring for space. A sales force promotion in the form of a bonus or contest recognizes the fact that it is difficult to succeed under these circumstances and offers appropriate rewards for the special effort necessary.

A *trade promotion* is directed at wholesalers and/or retailers (distributors, dealers, or agents), attempting to enlist their cooperation in carrying and promoting the new item. The support of these intermediaries is critical in making it available to ultimate buyers. Accordingly, they may be offered display materials, deals, or cooperative advertising funds in return for agreeing to give the new product a chance. Like all other sales promotion programs, these inducements are available for a limited time only to add a sense of urgency and impress the fact that it is important to act now.

A *consumer promotion* is a tool used in a pulling strategy to create demand, traffic, and purchasing action at the retail level. If consumers do not buy and keep the merchandise moving, filling the pipeline has been futile. Even if a sales force and trade promotion yield the desired results, a lack of consumer enthusiasm will cause the flow to back up. These ultimate buyers can be given a variety of incentives to try the innovation, ranging from coupons to premiums and samples to contests. Whereas the trade may or may not pass on savings obtained during a promotion period to its customers, consumer promotions go directly to the consumer.

As is evident from this discussion, new product sales promotion objectives differ with the nature of the target audience. Sales force promotions encourage and reward special effort to obtain orders for and display the new product. Trade promotions attempt to get intermediaries to carry the new item, give it shelf space, promote it, and keep an adequate supply on hand. Consumer promotions aim to induce purchase and trial, followed by an effort to expand usage and build brand loyalty.

Tools of New Product Sales Promotion

"Sampling is the most effective and most expensive way to introduce a new product. S. C. Johnson & Sons spent $12 million on sampling its new shampoo Agree."[4] The effort produced the desired results: Agree is now well established as a top-selling shampoo. Free *samples* eliminate a consumer's financial risk associated with a new product altogether. Whichever method of distribution is chosen, they produce trial in three out of four cases, with 25 percent of the triers subsequently purchasing the product.[5] This purchase is even more likely to occur if the sample is accompanied by a coupon.

Coupons are savings certificates that reduce the price of an item on a one-time basis. They differ from samples in that they require interest, initiative, effort, and expenditure on the part of the consumer. Only some 4 percent of the approximately 200 billion coupons distributed annually are accordingly ever redeemed. Although a 15 percent discount is the minimum, the highest rate of redemption results from a coupon that provides a saving of about one-third off the regular price of the new product.

In contrast to samples, *trial sizes* are sold through retail stores at special prices. They are enjoying increasing popularity with product managers because they eliminate the waste and substantially reduce the expense involved in free sampling. Consumers have to take the initiative in selecting and paying for the trial size container of the new product. This requires a sufficient level of interest and acts as a prospect-qualifying device.

Price packs or *cents-off deals* are often used in new product introduction. They induce trial but do not distinguish (as coupons more readily would) between buyers who would have bought the innovation at its full price and those who required the special price incentive to make the purchase. Everybody receives the savings (on the deal packages only), regardless of buying readiness stage.

Premiums are items sold at an attractive price or given for free with the purchase of the new product. A carefully selected premium that is meaningfully related to the innovation itself can greatly enhance its salability because it offers added value. The premium can also attract attention to the new product and serve as a reminder for its repurchase if it bears the new brand's name, such as a T-shirt or mug.

Contests are a powerful tool that can be used at any or all of the three levels. Sales force and dealer contests aim to spur the sales effort on behalf of the new product. Consumer contests and sweepstakes attempt to expose prospects to the benefits of the innovation. "When Allied Chemical introduced a new line of Anso nylon carpeting, a $25,000 'It's on the House' sweepstakes was used. Sweepstakes participants received entry forms at department stores, furniture stores, and carpet stores and were invited to inspect the new carpet line at the same time."[6]

Point-of-purchase promotions involve such in-stores devices as displays, shelf-talkers, and demonstrations. Special displays can attract a great deal of attention and move a lot of merchandise, provided retailers make space available for their use. L'eggs pantyhose used a combination of imaginative packaging and freestanding displays in supermarkets to create a new distribution channel for this product category. Point-of-purchase demonstrations of the new product can greatly enhance its salability as they illustrate its versatility and ease of use. Letting shoppers taste a new food product and handing them a coupon is yet another way to generate interest.

Trade promotions often use *buying allowances*—temporary price reductions (e.g., one dollar off per case) during the introductory time period. Or they may offer free goods with the purchase of a specified quantity (e.g., one free case with every four cases bought). These incentives are used to encourage a dealer to stock up on the new product and may be accompanied by an advertising allowance that reimburses the dealer in part for advertising expenses related to the innovation. A display allowance is a payment to the intermediary for permitting a special display of the new product, thus adding to its visibility. Clairol routinely uses all of these tools in its new product introductions.

A final means of promotion are *trade shows*. A manufacturer can participate by renting a booth and presenting the new product to the visiting public, which may consist of industrial, retail, or consumer buyers. Trade associations often sponsor trade shows in conjunction with annual conventions, inviting sellers to display and demonstrate their wares. "Over fifty-six hundred trade shows take place every year, drawing approximately 80 million people. The participating vendors expect several benefits, including generating new sales leads, maintaining customer contacts, introducing new products, meeting new customers, and selling more to present customers."[7] Home and recreation and automobile shows, for instance, enable producers or intermediaries to present new products directly to the ultimate consumer who might not otherwise become acquainted with them.[8]

SUMMARY

The market success of a new product depends substantially on the firm's ability to communicate its features and benefits to the intended target market. Promotion is the element of the marketing mix that informs the target audience about the innovation and persuades it to buy. It consists of three major ingredients: advertising, sales promotion, and personal selling.

New product advertising has to attract attention to the innovation and alert prospects to its existence and characteristics. It also has to create demand and support the selling function, by generating leads, smoothing the way for salespeople, and/or producing traffic at the ultimate buyer level.

Most companies employ the services of an advertising agency in planning and executing their new product advertising, with the firm's product manager in the role of interfacing with the agency's account executive. For a number of reasons, a search for a new agency is ideally carried out in four steps: (1) familiarization with agency services, (2) identification of advertising needs and selection criteria, (3) review of agency candidates, and (4) selection and agreement.

In working with the agency on a daily basis, product management should be supportive and directive. It should make proper use of the agency's resources and talents but also offer constructive criticism of its output. The product manager should not become so friendly with agency personnel as to cloud objective judgment but should engage in a healthy, ongoing dialog with the account team.

A series of steps are involved with designing the advertising campaign for the introduction of the new product. They include the precampaign phase of market, product, and consumer research to provide factual input into the advertising process. Strategic decisions cover new product advertising objectives, spending level, and creative and media strategies. The tactical execution stage translates these strategic decisions into actual advertisements and media schedules. During implementation, the advertisements are reproduced and inserted in the chosen media. Follow-up research may suggest adjustments in advertising execution or spending levels.

But advertising cannot accomplish the new product promotion task on its own. It needs to be employed in concert with the other ingredients of the promotion mix. In particular, it has to tie in with sales promotion, which encompasses a variety of tactical tools for short-term sales stimulation. Sales promotion can be directed at the company's own sales force, at intermediaries, or at ultimate buyers. The resourceful product manager can choose from a gamut of sales promotion tools: samples, coupons, trial sizes, cents-off deals, premiums, contests, point-of-purchase promotions, trade promotions, and trade shows. All of these aim to add urgency to the purchasing decision during a limited time period and thus expedite new product trial and acceptance.

NOTES

1. See *What Advertising Agencies Are: What They Do and How They Do It* (New York: American Association of Advertising Agencies, 1976), 8–9.
2. See ibid., 14.
3. This section is based on Jerome W. Stein, "How to Select the Right Advertising Agency," in *Marketing Update* (New York: Alexander-Norton Publishers, 1977). See also *Selecting an Advertising Agency* (New York: Association of National Advertisers, 1977).
4. Philip Kotler, *Principles of Marketing,* 2nd ed. (Englewood Cliffs, NJ: Prentice-Hall, 1983), 467.
5. See *How to Create Advertising That Sells* (New York: Ogilvy & Mather, n.d.), 16.
6. David L. Kurtz and Louis E. Boone, *Marketing,* 2nd ed. (Hinsdale, IL: Dryden Press, 1984), 618.
7. Kotler, *Principles of Marketing,* 469.
8. See Thomas V. Bonoma, "Get More Out of Your Trade Shows," *Harvard Business Review,* (Jan.–Feb. 1983): 75–83.

CASE STUDY

PREDICTABLE RELIEF

Laxative products are used by consumers to obtain relief from constipation. The products essentially fall into two categories:

- Chemical stimulants that induce bowel action. Competing brands include

  Ex-Lax Pills (Sandoz)
  Correctol Pills (Schering-Plough)
  Phillips Milk of Magnesia (Sterling Drug)

- Natural fiber products that are bulk-forming. Competing brands include

  Correctol Natural Fiber (Schering-Plough)
  Metamucil (P&G)
  Citrucel (Dow Chemical)
  Fiberall (S. C. Johnson & Sons)

In 1986, total category sales amounted to approximately $500 million. This represented a 5 percent increase in dollar sales but a 1 percent decline in unit sales—a pattern that had held steady for three years, indicating a stagnant industry. Total industry spending on advertising amounted to $43.6 million, an increase of 33 percent compared to the previous year. Industrywide, three-quarters of this amount were spent on network television, with an additional 12 percent going to spot, syndicated, and cable television. This left a mere 3 percent for radio and only 10 percent for print advertising. Industry advertising was dominated by ten brands, which collectively accounted for 90 percent of all laxative advertising spending.

This case was contributed by Lorinda Ash, Account Supervisor, Grey Advertising. Invaluable support from E. Lawrence Deckinger is gratefully acknowledged.

The Dulcolax Difference

One of the top five brands in this category is Dulcolax, made by Boehringer Ingelheim of West Germany. Before 1981, Dulcolax was a successful prescription laxative promoted exclusively to professionals, hospitals, and drugstores. In 1981, Boehringer Ingelheim Pharmaceuticals, Inc., of Danbury, Connecticut, converted the product to proprietary status. Distribution was ultimately expanded to include nondrug outlets.

Today, Dulcolax is available over the counter in tablet and suppository forms. It is carried by 98 percent of all drugstores and 47 percent of food stores. Nonetheless, 83 percent of its sales volume comes from drugstores and only 17 percent from food outlets. The latter share stands in marked contrast to the industry average of 31 percent of total volume.

The active ingredient in Dulcolax is bisacodyl. Upon contact with the nerve endings of the colon, bisacodyl causes the nervous system to initiate evacuation. Its action is distinctive from that of any other laxative type. Dulcolax is nonirritating and its use produces the desired results within a predictable period of time: overnight (or about 8 hours) for the enteric-coated tablets, and (uniquely) 15 minutes to 1 hour for suppositories.

In 1981, Boehringer Ingelheim retained Grey Advertising as its agency on the Dulcolax account. Since then, Dulcolax annual sales have grown by 171 percent, outpacing the category, which increased by 43 percent in the same period. In a highly competitive market, the brand's market share in 1986 was 4.5 percent, supported by advertising that represented approximately 10 percent of total industry expenditures.

Discussion Questions

1. Given the situation in the laxative market as described in the case study, which target groups would you select to help broaden the brand's consumer franchise in this nongrowing market? Why?
2. How would you differentiate Dulcolax from competitive brands in the minds of buyers?
3. How would you support your claim?
4. What kind of media mix would you use in your campaign?

CHAPTER 13

New Product Selling

In the introduction of new products, the single potentially most effective promotional tool is *personal selling*. Personal selling can be defined as the person-to-person effort of a salesperson to obtain an order from and build a continuing business relationship with a customer. This effort of well-trained salespeople in face-to-face confrontations or phone contacts with prospective and current buyers is vital to the success of most innovations.

Wherever direct selling is used, the door-to-door sales representative becomes the only means of distribution. It is not unusual in this type of business to pay sales personnel commissions of 30 to 50 percent of the consumer price. Even the other extreme, the "missionary salesperson," who does no selling whatsoever but, rather, sets up store displays or explains an innovative drug to a physician or a new industrial product to a purchasing manager who might then place an order with a distributor, plays an important role by supporting the introduction of an innovation. In the selling of complex new systems, almost inevitably a team effort of a salesperson and a sales engineer or systems consultant will be required. The engineer or consultant analyzes a prospect's situation and needs and recommends an appropriate solution, leaving it to the salesperson to obtain a commitment and negotiate terms.

Like advertising and sales promotion, personal selling is part of the promotion mix and has to be carefully coordinated and integrated with these other ingredients. All too often, a company's salespeople are uninformed or ill-informed about the content and/or timing of its new product advertising. For a consumer product, trade advertising aimed at obtaining support from wholesalers and retailers would ideally precede and accompany the initial sales effort. This sell-in period is intended to "fill the pipeline," that is, stock the shelves before consumer advertising breaks. The sales force should have tear sheets of consumer advertisements to show to retailers and should be well acquainted with media mix and schedule to use as a powerful sales tool in presentations to the trade. Consumer advertising translates into store traffic and is absolutely essential to win the cooperation of the trade. It is part of a pulling strategy that assists sales representatives in selling to the members of the new product's chosen channel of distribution.

Advertising and personal selling alone, however, are seldom enough to launch an innovation on its way to market success. Channel members often exhibit a great deal of resistance to the change required by the new product. Shelves are typically full with merchandise, and a current product would have to be displaced in favor of the new one. Intermediaries need strong incentives to do so. Consequently, getting a product on the shelf is no less challenging than moving it off the shelf.

The sales force needs a well-designed sales promotion program to gain distribution for the new product. Ideally, this program would have a triple thrust: It would fire up the sales force in the form of a contest, extra bonus, or special commission. It would solicit dealer enthusiasm through buying allowances or free goods, an advertising allowance, and a display allowance. And it would induce consumer purchases via sampling or trial sizes and coupons. This kind of combination may prove irresistible, stimulating all three target audiences into timely action and enabling the new product to gain a foothold in the marketplace.

Personal selling thus plays a key role in launching a new product in the marketplace. The nature of this task can range from a one-time sell-in followed by restocking to a continuous creative sales effort. Although the existing sales force is utilized most often, it may be appropriate to consider other options, depending on the circumstances of a particular introduction. For maximum impact, the new product sales effort should be carefully planned and orchestrated.

In implementing the new product sales plan, training is used to communicate new product knowledge to the sales force and instill proper sales approaches. Sales manuals are often used to support and enhance this indoctrination program. What remains, then, as a joint effort between product and sales management is to motivate, compensate, supervise, and evaluate the sales organization's new product effort.

The Personal Selling Task

Personal selling is always a challenging responsibility and opportunity. It requires people who possess at least three basic traits: empathy (sensitivity to the customer's situation, needs, and feelings), drive (aggressiveness or a powerful desire to succeed), and knowledge (familiarity with business conditions, company operations and policies, and the characteristics of the new product). Assuming that knowledge is present or can be taught, the relationship between the other two character traits will strongly influence the outcome of a salesperson's activities. An ideal combination would be high levels of both qualities. If they are out of balance, the salesperson will either make a good impression but no sale or force customers into one-time purchases with no likelihood of repeat orders.

In most instances, a salesperson's first and foremost responsibility is to generate sales revenues. This cannot successfully be accomplished over the long run without creating customer satisfaction as the basis for continued patronage. Accordingly, salespersons have to serve two masters: their employers, who want sales volume, profits, and market information, and their customers, who want information, delivery, favorable conditions, service, and support. Serving as the company's outpost and interface with the target market, salespeople have to reconcile these, at times, conflicting interests for mutual benefit and long-term growth.

For a new product, this personal selling task is even more challenging than usual because it cannot rely on an established track record and typically has to try to make room for the innovation by displacing a competitive product on the shelf. Because of the change that it requires on the part of the buyer, new product selling often encounters a great deal of resistance due to sheer inertia. Overcoming this resistance to obtain first orders needs solid preparation and dogged persistence.

The nature of the product and its distribution system determine whether salespeople are mere order-takers or aggressive order-getters.[1] Order-takers characterize intensively distributed, frequently purchased low-value convenience items, such as cigarettes or bread. The driver-salespeople visit outlets frequently, even daily, carry fresh merchandise on their vehicles, and simply replenish racks to predetermined stock levels. Order-getters characterize selectively distributed, higher-value semidurable or durable products, such as clothes or appliances. These kinds of goods require a continuous creative effort of selling and servicing for sustained patronage and growth.

In an order-taking situation, new product selling involves a one-time sell-in, followed by periodic restocking to agreed-upon levels. No ongoing creative selling effort combined with servicing and support is necessary. This greatly facilitates the selling task. In contrast, order-getting is a relentless effort, forever threatened by competitive overtures and necessitating constant vigilance and frequent follow-up. Whereas an order-taking sell-in may succeed with a simple flip-chart presentation, introductory advertising, and some point-of-purchase materials, more support for the personal selling function is usually called for in an order-getting situation. Because the products can be technically complex (personal computer, textbook, suit, microwave oven), intimate knowledge of the new product and its competition is a must. Demonstrations of the product and its advertising may be necessary. Substantial advertising, as well as trade and consumer promotion, may be required to enable the sales force to achieve its goals.

Organizing the New Product Sales Force

New product sales forces are organized according to the same principles as those for established products. In fact, the two are often identical in that an existing sales force structure takes on the new product as an additional item in its product mix. The most frequent principle of sales force organization is an assignment of territories (i.e., accounts) on the basis of geographic parameters (e.g., counties). This arrangement is appropriate for a firm with a limited product mix and a fairly undifferentiated customer base. All accounts are then simply identified by their geographic location and divided up among the members of the sales force, resulting in smaller territories in densely settled metropolitan areas and larger territories in rural areas with low customer density. In this kind of organization, a new product is usually given to the existing sales force as an additional item to sell along with the established product mix, supported, of course, during its launch period by a special introductory push.

Rarely is an entirely new sales force created for a single new product, as Pfizer did when it first marketed Terramycin. The firm anticipated introducing other drugs and was entering the field of pharmaceutical sales for the first time. So it assigned rather large territories to its original sales force of twenty ethical pharmaceutical salespeople, leading to fairly thin coverage but nonetheless a very successful launch and transforming the nature of the entire company.

A second principle of sales force organization structures assignments according to product classifications. Large multidivisional corporations offer a variety of products that require different talents and approaches. IBM, for instance, uses separate sales forces to sell its office products (e.g., typewriters) and its mainframe computers. A product-oriented sales force structure is particularly appropriate for technically complex products that require specialized, in-depth understanding of the technology involved in order to advise a knowledgeable clientele properly. Similarly, conglomerates that are active in several industries will employ several sales forces to ply the diverse products to their different target markets.

When a new product merely represents an extension of an existing line, the appropriate product specialists will normally be assigned to handle it. They are usually very pleased to have something new to talk to their customers about, all the more so since the product often evolved from their own suggestions. If the innovation represents a diversification move, however, additional product specialists with the proper expertise may have to be hired to do justice to its characteristics and potential. For a highly specialized, high-priced, high-tech product, they may roam the country to visit the few prospects in the market for this kind of device. Should the nature of the new product warrant it, a completely new product–oriented sales force may be initiated by its existence and outlook.

The third principle of sales force organization revolves around customer categories. This approach becomes necessary and appropriate if various customer groups have different needs and operating characteristics. It is, for instance, common for food processors to have separate sales forces dealing with grocery stores, on the one hand, and institutional feeders like hospitals, restaurants, and airlines, on the other. Institutional feeders need larger (e.g., soup, pickles) or smaller (e.g., crackers, peanuts) containers than do consumers who shop in supermarkets. Support needs and prices are different, too. Manufacturers of information-processing devices also organize their sales forces by industries because requirements and conditions vary substantially from industry to industry.

When a new product is introduced into a customer-structured sales organization, it is typically absorbed into the existing structure and presented to the different customer groups in appropriate ways. Only if it represents a significant departure from established products and channels, addressing itself to a totally new audience, will a new solution have to be found. An additional sales force will then have to be built that possesses expertise in and concentrates on serving the needs and characteristics of the new target market.

Occasionally, combinations of the three forms of sales organization are used. One group of customers—national accounts, say—may receive special treatment while the rest are served by a territorially or product-structured sales organization. Or product specialists may call on designated customer groups. Procter & Gamble, for instance, has seven separate product-oriented sales forces (powdered detergents, bar soaps, paper products, etc.) calling on grocery stores in an effort to maximize product sales.

The New Product Selling Process

The personal selling process follows the general pattern outlined in Figure 13–1.[2] If the effort focuses on a particular new product, this time-tested pattern takes on some unusual aspects. It is in this context of new product selling that the selling process will now be discussed.

The *personal selling process* consists of a series of steps involved in obtaining an order from a particular buyer. The new product selling process is simply a variant of this basic procedure that focuses on selling a new product.

The first step, *prospecting,* involves identifying prospects, that is, potential buyers. This requires the salesperson to generate and qualify leads. A lead is a person or organization that might have an interest in or need for the innovation. As pointed out, advertising can be geared to lead generation for the new product by inviting requests for informational brochures, particularly in the case of industrial products. Of course, an established sales force has its own customer base to draw from or may ask current accounts for referrals. Trade show participation is a fertile source of leads, as are data sources, such as membership or subscriber lists, trade or alumni directories, and business periodicals.

Leads, however, are merely names and addresses. To become prospects for the new product, leads have to be qualified or screened to determine whether they

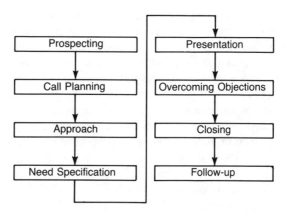

FIGURE 13–1
Steps in the Personal Selling Process

are worth pursuing. The most important lead qualifier is need or applicability. Any lead that has no use for the innovation has to be eliminated. Ability, authority, and eligibility to buy are other considerations that may qualify a lead.

The *call planning,* or preapproach, step encompasses the homework that salespersons have to do to decide what they want to accomplish in a sales call and how they propose to go about it. This means research into the nature of the industry, the history and operations of the prospect company, and the background and personal characteristics of the contact person. Where possible, external and internal buying influences should be identified and studied. Sales representatives should specify their call objectives and selling strategies and then contact the prospect in writing or by telephone to set up an appointment. In these initial contacts, they provide just enough information about the innovation to whet the appetite of the prospective buyer.

The *approach* step is aimed at establishing rapport with the prospect and generating interest in the new product. A positive relationship already exists if salesperson and prospect have done business before. Otherwise the sales representative may first have to create credibility. The very newness of the product, however, may be sufficient to arouse interest, especially if it offers unusual benefits that can be easily demonstrated and are supported by a special introductory deal.

A salesperson, though, who then simply proceeds to engage in a standard spiel is often ill-advised. Although preliminary need identification is part of prospecting, a more detailed *need specification* is necessary at this point to tailor the problem solution and presentation to the unique situation of the prospect. Two of the most important skills of a salesperson—questioning and listening—are exercised at this step. Learning about the prospect company's mode and size of operation facilitates the formulation of an appropriate proposal. Experienced salespersons who are familiar with the prospect's business may be able to dispense with this step.

In the *presentation* phase, the salesperson presents a proposition that centers around the purchase and use of the new product. This may well involve a full-scale demonstration of its operation and benefits. The purpose of this step is to convince the prospect company that the innovation satisfies its need or solves its problem. As an increasing number of corporate buying decisions are made by committees, the presentation step may require a group or team selling effort that involves technical specialists and occasionally even a senior executive.

As the proposition is made and the new product is heralded as an ideal problem solver, *objections* will occur that can range from its size to its cost, appearance, advertising support, technology, and many other aspects. A well-prepared salesperson anticipates these objections in the call planning step and thus has appropriate answers readily available to overcome these objections. If well handled, objections can be turned around and become powerful selling tools.

Closing means asking for the order. This is a bit harder for a new product without an established track record than for a proven seller. Although a variety of closing techniques is available to the resourceful salesperson, it may well take a special incentive to land the first order for the new product from a particular prospect. This is where the sales promotion program becomes essential in providing a sense of urgency and value.

But obtaining the order does not complete the personal selling process. Intelligent salespeople *follow up* with buyers to find out whether the order was delivered and the product performs satisfactorily. This contact provides an opportunity to thank the buyer for the order, ask for referrals, and sell accessories or other complementary items. And it identifies the need for after-sale service. It is axiomatic that satisfied customers are a salesperson's most valuable asset.

It should be mentioned in this context that it is common, and advisable, for product managers to become involved in the personal selling effort for their new products. Many product managers spend up to 50 percent of their time in the field, traveling and visiting prospects with salespeople. There is no substitute for this firsthand, frontline experience in streamlining the innovation's marketing program. Product managers can give individual salespeople substantial moral and factual support. Also, their personal presence in the field ensures that their new products receive the proper attention and effort—a result that can hardly be achieved by sitting at a desk. The field intelligence gathered in this fashion can provide valuable inspiration for redesigning the product, offering additional versions, or developing future offerings. Product managers cannot and should not replace sales representatives. In concert, however, they can have a powerful impact in the marketplace.

Planning the Sales Effort for New Products

To succeed in the long run and achieve an innovation's marketing objectives, the new product sales effort has to be thoroughly planned. Without a sales plan, product and sales management become mired in short-term tactical decisions without the necessary long-term direction. Sales planning, therefore, has to be an integral part of the new product planning process, particularly the introductory marketing plan. The procedure for new product sales planning is the same as for established products: specifying objectives, formulating strategies, outlining tactics.

Before the sales effort for a new product can meaningfully be planned, the nature of the sales force used to promote it has to be determined. Essentially, four options are available: using the existing sales force, hiring a new sales force, employing a temporary sales force, or utilizing manufacturer's representatives. The particular option chosen determines the content of the new product sales plan.

Sales Force Options

A company introducing a new product will usually favor using its *existing sales organization* to promote the innovation. Because the product can, so to speak, take a "free ride" with current salespeople, considerable operating efficiencies can be anticipated. Travel cost can be shared with other products, the fixed compensation portion remains unchanged, and training expenses are reduced because present members of the sales force are already familiar with company history, operations, and procedures. For line extensions, this approach is appropriate as they offer more choice to current buyers and involve the same technology.

This reasoning, however, does not apply when a firm with an established sales organization enters a new field that is somewhat but not too closely related to its current business. Retraining the existing sales force to add the new line and distribution structure to its repertoire and calling patterns can readily prove counterproductive. Current salespeople have often developed a routine in servicing their accounts and maintaining a steady stream of orders from their present product mix. They are likely to feel insecure about, if not hostile toward, the new line and customer type.

Furthermore, current salespeople may resent the expectation of splitting their time and loyalty between two customer bases and technologies that are only marginally related to each other. They cannot and will not do justice to both, so the overall effect will be a decline in sales force productivity. Because they would be required to split their selling time between the established mix and the new line, they would tend to give the new product only a halfhearted effort. This might well doom the innovation while the established business would suffer simultaneously from neglect. Thus, finding some other solution is necessary in order to give the new product a true chance to succeed without interfering with ongoing business relationships and patterns.

Hiring a *new sales force* in addition to the existing one will increase both cost and internal competition. Because the livelihood of the new salespeople depends entirely on their success with the new product line, they have every reason to work hard at realizing the new product sales objectives. They are much easier to train, having a positive attitude toward the innovation and no preconceived notions about how to sell the new line and to whom. Selected for this particular purpose and new to the company, they do not possess established patterns or habits that they may have to unlearn to do justice to the new product. Their presence can introduce a healthy rivalry into the sales function, putting current salespeople on notice that they are no longer the firm's only "game in town" and will have to try harder to maintain their own momentum in the face of the new internal competition. Obvious detriments are the expense and effort of recruiting and selecting the new sales force, its extensive need for training, and the increase in fixed cost associated with its presence.

A third, and often overlooked, possibility is a *temporary sales force*. Such an outside sales force can be contracted for on a project basis with specialized agencies. The agency supplies experienced salespersons who will call on a given list of outlets or all stores of a specific type in a certain area. The temporary sales personnel are quite adept at learning a specific sales presentation, answering objections, and then setting up and stocking a display or putting initial stock on the shelves. Although the cost of this approach is considerable, it is quite acceptable on a per call basis when prospects are located close to each other. Using a temporary sales force to blitz a market has proven effective for a variety of manufacturers. A brief description of an actual case history illustrates how this approach works.

A producer of consumer products had been successful in establishing a good working relationship with and steady growth of sales volume through a nationwide network of distributors handling its products. The distributors, in turn, employed sizable numbers of driver-salespersons who worked their assigned routes regularly, taking inventory in drugstores and supermarkets of the products they carried and automatically replenishing shelves and stockrooms. When the manufacturer decided to take on a dramatically new line of products to be distributed through the same channel and challenging an industry giant that had virtually monopolized the market, it could not rely on its distributors to do the selling job for the innovation and open up this additional market. On the other hand, hiring and training a new company sales force in order to enlist retailer support would have been unwise and extremely costly. It was expected that after initial market resistance was overcome, the new product line would virtually sell itself, provided it received sufficient advertising support and would be kept well stocked in freestanding displays by the driver-salespersons employed by the distributors.

Under these circumstances where the driver-salespersons did not possess the requisite creative selling skills, a temporary sales force was the answer. Consisting of experienced sales professionals, the temporary sales force would only require one day's sales training and would simply be dismissed after the contracted length of time. Each distributor was advised that the manufacturer's temporary sales force would not only be calling on every one of the distributor's accounts but in addition would visit any store that the distributor wanted to sign on as a new customer. The salespeople were provided with a brochure that outlined the new program in a flip-chart presentation format for across-the-desk selling. Incentive programs were set up to cover everyone involved in the distribution of the new line—the distributors, their sales personnel, the retail store managers, and even counter clerks. Complementary channels of distribution were tapped subsequently. The company's decision paid off: It met its objectives and is now firmly established in its new market.

A fourth product sales force option gives a company the least amount of control and is therefore used only to the extent that the other approaches are not applicable. A *manufacturer's representative* is an independent businessperson who represents several manufacturers in noncompeting lines. Because the manufacturer's representative is not an employee and is compensated strictly on a commission basis, the company has very little control over this independent contractor.

There are a number of potential reasons why producers might want to utilize manufacturer's representatives in the introduction of new products.[3] Among the market-related factors are instances where the market potential for the new product is too small and simply does not warrant a company sales force. Or the location of a market area may be too far from the producer's headquarters to justify the overhead of a company-sponsored sales organization. This is particularly true in the initial stages of international marketing. Company-related aspects include insufficient financial resources to support a company sales force. Or the range of products offered may be too restricted to have a company sales force earn its keep. The new item may require a distribution channel that differs from the company's established business. Or product management wants to gain distribution for the innovation quickly.

New Product Sales Planning

Once the suitable sales force option has been chosen and appropriate organizational arrangements have been made, new product sales planning can begin. New product sales planning involves specifying sales objectives to inspire and guide the new product sales effort. It requires formulation of sales strategies to achieve these new product sales objectives. And it means mapping out the tactics needed to implement these strategies. Finally, the process culminates in a feedback feature that closes the planning loop. As is evident, new product sales planning represents a special application of the new product management cycle and new product planning process discussed in Chapter 2.

Accordingly, the new product sales management cycle can be said to consist of the four components analysis, planning, implementation, and control. For lack of a historical sales record, new product sales analysis involves a review of market and sales trends of related products and a sales forecast for the innovation. Sales planning proper means developing the blueprint or road map of new product sales action. Implementation involves executing the new product sales program. New product sales control then compares actual and planned new product sales data, investigating reasons for any divergence between the two. If the reason is controllable, the sales effort has to be improved. If the cause of poor sales results is competitive interference or other uncontrollable circumstances, however, the new product sales plan may have to be revised.

New product sales objectives typically consist of generating and maintaining predetermined levels of sales revenues, market share, and profits. These objectives are guidelines for action and are derived from the overall new product objectives. Sales volume objectives are often expressed in terms of the number of units to be sold during a given time period, for example, x cases in three, six, or twelve months. Such dealer loading reflects a push strategy that aims to fill the pipeline and is usually supported by end user advertising and a sales promotion campaign. Alternatively, the volume objective can be stated in terms of sales revenue dollars. The difference between the two ways of volume formulation is only significant if the price varies by customer type or with the quantity purchased.

Sales volume in dollars can easily be translated into market share by dividing it into total category volume. A certain minimum market share is usually needed to make the new product a viable entity over the long run. Market share is an attractive new product sales objective because it reduces a brand's vulnerability to competitive attacks, it increases pricing independence and flexibility, it facilitates future new product introductions, and it is directly related to a brand's profitability.[4] In some industries, groceries, for instance, a market share sales objective for a new product is typically formulated in terms of percent distribution obtained in a specified time period. In this context, distribution means shelf presence in appropriate outlets, for example, 90 percent distribution in six weeks.

The overall new product sales objectives are divided up among the members of the sales force and assigned to them as individual quotas. These personal sales objectives or quotas become the basis for individual new product sales performance measurement and evaluation. Personal compensation is linked directly to the level of quota attainment, which can be turned into a powerful motivating tool through a special incentive program.

Carefully chosen new product sales objectives are a reflection of marketing and corporate objectives and thus an integral part of the company's planning system. They have to be precise and attainable and specify responsibility and accountability for their attainment. Once set, the new product sales objectives govern the entire new product sales planning process. Sales strategies are then developed as broad guidelines for sales action, marshaling the sales function's resources in pursuit of the objectives.

The choice of new product sales strategy depends on the thrust of the new product. If it is a line extension, the existing customer base will be worked heavily. If it represents an entry into a new market, new accounts have to be acquired. If it is intended to leverage the company's market presence by broadening its base, a healthy mixture of current and prospective accounts has to be called on. A decision also has to be made as to the intensity of market coverage. Should the innovation be made broadly available by deeply penetrating the market? Or should it be marketed selectively in return for more substantial dealer support and commitment? This choice closely relates to the issue of control: The more widely a product is distributed, the less control a company has over its marketing.

After the new product sales strategy has been determined, detailed tactics for its implementation have to be decided. This involves classifying accounts according to sales potential and selecting methods of prospecting. Usually, a salesperson's customers are classified as A, B, or C accounts, depending on the size of their past purchases. A accounts are the best customers that deserve and receive the most attention, whereas C accounts make infrequent, smaller purchases. This classification, if applicable to the new product, will affect calling patterns, with A accounts receiving the greatest emphasis because of their significant sales potentials. To the extent that new accounts are desired, salespersons should also be given guidance as to how to develop leads and qualify them as prospects.

Other tactical sales planning decisions concern the nature and size of special sales incentives for the new product. Should a contest be conducted or a special bonus be offered during the introductory period? Methods of sales force indoctrination and types of sales support materials have to be chosen. Furthermore, an appropriate and sufficient sales budget has to be developed and approved.[5]

Executing the New Product Sales Effort

Once the sales effort for the new product has been duly planned, integrated, and approved, product and sales management continue to cooperate closely in implementing the sales plan. Specifically, this involves training the sales force in new product–related knowledge, skills, and attitudes. It means deciding on the role and designing the contents of a sales manual for the innovation. It encompasses the development of such selling aids as flip charts and other audiovisual aids. It covers preparing and conducting sales meetings and dealer briefings. And it may even extend into the day-to-day management of the introductory sales effort, such as guiding and supporting individual salespeople.

Sales Training

Because product managers do not have any direct authority over the sales force and are competing with each other for salespeople's attention, time, and effort, the product manager in charge of the new product has to "sell" the company's salespeople on the concept and merits of the innovation and gain their support. This is usually done at sales meetings where the new product and its marketing mix are announced with some flair, excitement and hoopla, capturing the imagination of sales force members and generating enthusiasm. Such new product kickoff meetings are as much motivational as they are informational: The innovation is not likely to succeed without an all-out effort by the sales organization.

Some firms with large sales forces numbering in the thousands spend a great deal of time and money preparing for such inspirational extravaganzas. They fly their entire sales force to a city with a modern convention center, ask their advertising agency to produce a multimedia new product campaign presentation, and may even hire a Broadway or Hollywood producer to direct a specially designed show. If the product is important enough for the company, similar care may be lavished on dealer briefings aimed to inform and win the support of the trade.

New product sales meetings and dealer briefings, however, are not substitutes for, but rather complements to, a sound new product sales training program. *Sales training* could be described as a systematic activity intended to improve the sales performance of company sales personnel. A well-designed new product sales training program should instill appropriate knowledge, skills, and attitudes. Omitting this vital activity and leaving the sales force to its own devices could well prove to be a fatal mistake.

With regard to product-related *knowledge,* the product manager may want to become personally involved in the sales training program. The product manager knows the product best and can convey its rationale and history, as well as its nature and features, most accurately. Performance characteristics and ingredients may have to be explained, the production process outlined or even shown, and the product's operation demonstrated. Still, knowing the product well is not sufficient. The sales representative also has to become acquainted with the features and performance data of competitive products, learning their relative advantages and disadvantages for use in sales presentations. If the trainees are newcomers to the firm, they will also have to be introduced to the firm's history, operations, product mix, and procedures.

New product salespeople require the normal arsenal of selling *skills,* ranging from how to size up and approach a prospect to handling objections and asking for the order. Beyond this basic range, however, they may have to be trained in how to assess and analyze relevant customer needs in order to design and propose an appropriate solution. They may also have to learn how to operate and demonstrate, even debug, the new product.

The third ingredient in a new product sales training program refers to *attitudes*. Probably the most important attitude to inculcate in the new product sales force is pride. To succeed in the competitive marketplace, company salespeople have to believe that their new product is excellent, if not superior. They have to be proud of the company they work for and take pride in their personal appearance. And they should be happy with their job, aiming to please the customer and establish a lasting, mutually fruitful relationship.

Support Materials

A valuable tool in preparing sales representatives for their new product responsibility and assisting them in its execution is a specially designed sales manual. Such a manual is intended to acquaint salespersons with all relevant product-related information so as to enable them to make powerful presentations and competently answer all pertinent questions. Ideally, it will supplement and enhance an in-person new product sales training program, continuing to serve as a handy portable resource and reference during the introductory sales activity. Figure 13–2 outlines the contents of a typical new product sales manual.

The introduction section of the manual describes the introductory campaign, its objectives, importance, and rewards. The background and rationale section goes into the reasons why the new product was developed and what its purpose is in the company's overall product lineup. From the historic evolution section, the salesperson can learn how the innovation evolved from the initial idea to finished product, including product design and redesign, package design, and the choice of brand name. The target market and distribution section defines the intended ultimate buyer in socioeconomic and possibly life-style terms. It also sketches the planned distribution pattern with regard to type of store and percent distribution targeted by certain dates. The marketing research section analyzes the results of studies made at various points in the new product's evolution, particularly test market data about its initial market acceptance and sales and market share performance in representative cities. This provides powerful ammunition vis-à-vis new product-weary retail store buyers.

The technical data section describes the new product's formulation, composition, ingredients, construction, design, structure, and components to enable the salesperson to answer basic engineering questions. The test results section reports performance characteristics as obtained in internal laboratory testing or analysis by outside independent test institutes. The competitive products section reviews the relative merits and demerits and strengths and weaknesses of competing offerings, explaining the innovation's advantages and benefits in the form of a comparative analysis of design, performance, and price.

The section on pricing discusses the economics of the situation for the retailer by looking at both sides of the pricing issue, that is, the purchase price and sale price. It outlines the new product's list price to the trade, including appropriate quantity discounts. By relating the purchase price to the suggested resale price, an average markup and profit can be computed, supplemented by the projected number of stock turns.

Introduction
Background and Rationale
Historic Evolution
Target Market and Distribution
Marketing Research
Technical Data
Test Results
Competitive Products
Pricing
    List price, Quantity discounts
    Suggested resale price, Markup, Profit, Turnover
Introductory Advertising
    Media mix, Schedule, Spending level
    Tear sheets, Storyboards
Promotional Incentives and Support
    Trade promotion
        Introductory deal
        Point-of-purchase materials
    Consumer promotion
        Nature and size
        Schedule
Launch Information
    Sell-in
        Call objectives
        Prospecting and calling pattern
    Ordering Information
        Order forms and minimum orders
        Order placement and delivery dates
Compensation Information

FIGURE 13–2
Contents of a New Product Sales Manual

In its introductory advertising section, the manual highlights the media mix, insertion schedule, and spending level. It should also supply tear sheets (reproductions) of finished print advertisements and storyboards depicting television commercials in the form of frame-by-frame still shots and text. This is supplemented in the promotional incentives and support section with information about the simultaneous sales promotion program insofar as it refers to trade and consumer promotion (details on the sales force promotion component can be found in the compensation information section). With regard to trade promotion, the sales manual sets forth the nature and duration of the introductory deal intended to entice the cooperation of the trade. It also spells out what point-of-purchase materials, such as freestanding displays, will be made available. As to consumer promotion, it details the nature of the incentive and the quantity used, as well as the distribution method and dates, such as free samples and/or coupons.

The launch information section presents details on sell-in activities and ordering information. It specifies the objectives to be achieved in individual sales calls and establishes a schedule and procedure for prospecting and calling on accounts. It also includes order forms (if different from regular forms) and other relevant ordering information, such as minimum order size and dates for order placement and delivery. The final section, compensation, contains information on the sales force incentive package and reward system applicable to the new product, such as a sales contest or bonus.

A new product sales manual is an extremely valuable tool in instructing and guiding the sales force for the selling of the new item. Many companies further support their salespeople with flip-chart presentation materials. Depending on the nature of the product and the selling situation, these may range from a few pages of typewritten materials with some photographs of display materials to elaborate, glossy, printed ring binder sets, which are used in canned presentations where the salesperson simply recites a standard text. Properly designed and employed, flip charts can greatly enhance the effectiveness and efficiency of sales presentations without reducing the salesperson's flexibility in tailoring them to each particular selling situation and account.

Other audiovisual aids that could prove useful as support materials for the new product sales force are brief slide/cassette or filmstrip/cassette presentations that can be built into a sales call. Prospective retail buyers may also appreciate receiving a preview of television commercials. For presentations to buying groups or committees, it will be helpful to convert important information to transparencies and use an overhead projector, possibly amplified by developing a specific proposition on an easel pad.

Managing the New Product Sales Force

Salespeople report to sales managers, not to product managers. To leave them to their own devices is to leave introductory sales results to chance. Planned sales results are more likely to materialize if the day-to-day implementation of the new product sales plan is actively managed. As stated earlier, product management can and should give sales management as well as individual sales representatives active support and guidance in the pursuit of new product sales objectives. It is a delicate but vital cooperation that takes place at this critical point in the new product's life cycle.

The joint product/sales management effort may begin with recruiting and selecting individual salespeople or an entire new sales force. In this case, a job description would have to be developed that specifies the purpose of the new sales positions, specific duties and responsibilities expected of the new salespeople, working conditions, and desired applicant qualifications and characteristics (including abilities, knowledge, skills, educational background, prior work experience, and personal qualities). The cooperative effort may even extend to joint interviewing of sales candidates.

Once hired or identified as members of the existing sales force, the new product salespersons have to be trained specifically for the selling of the new product.

Both in formal classroom instruction and informal on-the-job training, the product manager in charge is likely to be involved to the extent possible due to intimate familiarity with the product, its target market, and its introductory marketing program. The product manager also has to "sell" continually the new product sales force on aggressively promoting the innovation in line with the objectives and approaches specified. Traveling with individual sales representatives and calling with them on prospects will alert the product manager firsthand to emerging problems or previously undiscovered opportunities related to the new product launch. This frontline experience, when thoroughly investigated and put in proper perspective, can help refine the product and its marketing mix at an appropriate point.

Motivating the sales force to emphasize its product is a continuous task for product management, even more so than for sales management, which has less interest in any specific product than in the overall sales volume being achieved. Directing and supervising the new product sales force in action is, however, clearly the exclusive prerogative of sales management. Product management would be out of order and ill-advised to give direct orders to salespeople. Because sales management is being held accountable for delivering the planned sales results, it must possess sole authority for making them happen.

The special new product compensation scheme was, of course, devised jointly by product and sales management with the aim of achieving maximum impact for the amount spent. To add urgency to its implementation, its duration has to be limited to the introductory period and then phased back to normal compensation levels, making the meanwhile established product one among many carried by the sales force. Performance evaluation takes place in various ways and may be reflected in special rewards. Clearly, managing the new product sales force on a day-to-day basis represents a significant challenge that provides the firm with a substantial growth opportunity.

SUMMARY

The personal selling effort for a new product is one of the most critical factors affecting its success in the marketplace. It begins with organizing the new product sales force according to some relevant principle—geography, product classification, or customer category. Putting this sales organization to work in selling the new product follows the generalized pattern of the personal selling process as applied to a new product situation. This may, for instance, involve additional prospecting among new buyer groups and encountering objections related to the product's newness.

New product sales planning is an important responsibility that begins by determining which of several sales force options will be chosen. Resourceful managers can select from four alternatives: using the existing sales force, hiring a new sales force, employing a temporary sales force, or utilizing manufacturer's representatives. Which option is preferred depends on the circumstances and objectives. These new product sales objectives also govern the sales planning process. They typically consist of obtaining and maintaining predetermined levels of sales volume or market share. The new product sales objectives guide the selection of appropriate sales strategies, which, in turn, relate to the desired intensity of market coverage. These are then translated into detailed tactical implementation decisions.

　　In order to carry out the new product sales plan successfully, the sales force has to be adequately trained to possess sufficient product-related knowledge, skills, and attitudes. In executing their challenging task, new product salespeople are greatly assisted by a specially designed sales manual and other audiovisual aids. Both in the conceptualization of the new product sales effort and in the day-to-day management of the new product sales force, close cooperation between product and sales management is essential.

NOTES

1. See Dan H. Robertson and Danny N. Bellenger, *Sales Management* (New York: Macmillan, 1980), 43.
2. See Eugene M. Johnson, David L. Kurtz, and Eberhard E. Scheuing, *Sales Management: Concepts, Practices, and Cases* (New York: McGraw-Hill, 1986), 60–82. See also Rolph E. Anderson and Joseph F. Hair, Jr., *Sales Management: Text with Cases* (New York: Random House, 1983), 579–609.
3. See Robert D. Hisrich and Michael P. Peters, *Marketing Decisions for New and Mature Products* (Columbus, OH: Charles E. Merrill, 1984), 352.
4. See Robert D. Buzzell and Bradley T. Gale, *The PIMS Principles* (New York: Free Press, 1987).
5. See Johnson, Kurtz, and Scheuing, *Sales Management,* 150–163.

CASE STUDY

PLAYCLOTHES

Over a period of fifty-five years, Fisher-Price had made and marketed a steadily growing assortment of safe educational toys. It claimed to have penetrated 99 percent of the homes where a child under the age of six lives. Now the company was ready to branch out into related fields that would allow it to capitalize on its reputation for quality and well-known brand name.

To gain a perspective on the industry they were about to enter, several executives of Fisher-Price Toys were observing and listening in on a live focus group session. For four hours, they peered through a one-way mirror and eavesdropped as a dozen women in Cleveland complained about their battles with the zippers, buckles, buttons, and snaps on kids' clothing. The participants were "veteran" mothers, having been prescreened to possess at least five years' experience with two children. The complaints from these and other disenchanted mothers convinced Fisher-Price's management that a combination of customer-driven design and a respected name could spell success in the lucrative but highly competitive children's wear market.

A Point of Difference

In 1984, the Quaker Oats Company subsidiary introduced its first line of preschool playwear. None of the clothes had buttons, zippers, or buckles. Most closures were made of Velcro, supplemented by a few snaps. Although competitive products looked attractive, it was difficult and time-consuming to get kids in and out of them.

Fisher-Price playwear showed other signs of listening to battle-fatigued mothers. It featured padded knees and elbows, extra-long shirttails, cuffs that grow with children, and bigger neck openings. These features are all very practical, useful aspects, but style often matters more than durability in this

industry, given the growth patterns of children. And the field is becoming more crowded as other experienced firms enter the fray. In 1983 and 1984 alone, the Gerber Products Company acquired no less than three children's clothing companies, including the Buster Brown brand.

Troubled by sagging sales of jeans to adults, Levi Strauss & Company launched baby Levis in 1985. The company offered blue denim pants and diaper covers for infants as well as T-shirts with the inscription "My First Levis," For parents who considered it inappropriate to clothe newborns in Levis, the company offered more conventional infantware under the Petite Bijou and Little Levis brand names.

Attractive Outlook

Levi Strauss foresees more than 8 million babies by 1990. Already the population of under five year olds has increased to 17.8 million. Marketers are excited about the fact that a growing proportion of babies represents first births. This spells greater selling opportunities due to the lower likelihood of hand-me-downs. In fact, the preschool clothing market has been estimated at $6 billion a year.

"The outlook is tremendous," enthuses Gerber's president. "There are more working mothers who have the money to spend and who are going for better quality merchandise." They also have prompted children's wear companies to simplify their designs.

Fisher-Price is advertising its playwear line as "children's clothing that mothers helped design." It is clearly counting on its high brand name recognition. Fliers promoting the apparel line are inserted into toy packages, and all children featured in toy ads are dressed in the company's playwear.

Recognizing that it had no experience in making children's clothes and would face a steep learning curve, Fisher-Price farmed out manufacturing and distribution to a girls' dressmaker. The company insists on tight control over design and

This case was adapted from Ronald Alsop, "Fisher-Price Banks on Name, Design in Foray into Playwear," *Wall Street Journal,* 2 Aug. 1984.

marketing, though. It also adamantly refuses to license its trademark, as Tonka and the Playskool division of Milton Bradley Company have done.

Research indicates that parents do not appreciate paying a premium for logos imprinted on T-shirts of quite ordinary quality.

Discussion Questions

1. What do you think of Fisher-Price entering the children's playwear market? Was the company well advised to use practicability appeals in its advertising?
2. What kinds of stores should the company target?
3. Should Fisher-Price use its current toy sales force or hire a completely new group of salespeople? If so, what kind of salesperson should the company be looking for?
4. How could the sales force overcome store buyer resistance to a newcomer to the field?

PART FOUR

The Product in the Marketplace

*I*nnovations are of vital importance to the health and growth of both individual companies and the economy as a whole. In the buyers' markets that characterize an affluent society, however, market success depends largely on the selective perceptions and reactions of prospective buyers to the new products' concepts and communications efforts. This dependence on complex psychological factors, on perceived rather than actual product benefits, explains why it has become crucial for product managers to study buyer behavior. In particular, it is essential to understand the processes by which information and opinions about new products are spread and accepted or rejected. Product management has to acquaint itself with the stages through which individual buyers go in making up their minds about an innovation. Such knowledge will enable a determination as to when and how this decision-making process can be influenced in the company's favor.

One of the most important tasks of product managers is the successful handling of product-related communication. In order to optimize the communications programs for their new products, they need to become familiar with the processes and factors involved in the communication and acceptance of innovations. These can be subsumed under the two sequential processes of diffusion and adoption. Diffusion means communicating the new concept to its target audience; adoption is the process by which members of the target audience determine how to respond to this information.

Diffusion occurs when an innovation is spread throughout the target market. It involves personal influence in the form of opinion leadership, which takes place when an adopter offers comments and recommendations about the innovation to others who follow this advice. The communication sources active in the diffusion process can be grouped into four categories: advocate impersonal sources are advertisements in mass media, independent impersonal sources are impartial published reports, advocate personal sources are salespeople, and independent personal sources are friends. The rate of diffusion is dependent on five factors: the innovation's relative advantage over competing products, its compatibility with the prospect's life-style and/or operation, its complexity in comprehension and use, its ability to be tried on a limited scale, and the observability of its benefits.

The adoption process consists of five stages: awareness, interest, evaluation, trial, and adoption. It is a continuum that leads from first exposure to information about the innovation to the ultimate decision to continue its use. A group of predispositional factors can serve as indicators to product management for a person's likelihood to adopt early in the game, thus helping to sharpen the focus of the marketing effort. These factors are venturesomeness, social integration, cosmopoliteness, social mobility, and privilegedness. They enable product management to understand better the five adopter categories—innovators, early adopters, early majority, late majority, and laggards—which are classified according to their respective degrees of innovativeness.

Once they have been introduced in the marketplace, new products will ideally move through a series of stages that differ significantly in their sales patterns. Collectively, they tend to form a bell-shaped curve called the classic product life cycle. This cycle can be subdivided into five stages labeled introduction, growth, maturity, saturation, and decline. Because the competitive situation and demand elasticity vary substantially from one stage to the next, it is essential for effective strategy development to determine a product's precise position on the life cycle curve. This can be accomplished by simultaneously examining a product's sales volume, its rate of growth of sales volume, and its profit/loss curve. These three variables show a different combination for every stage of the cycle.

Because of varying conditions, marketing mixes have to be different for the various stages of the product life cycle. During the introductory stage, the pioneer uses heavy advertising to create primary demand, accompanied by high prices to help recoup developmental expenses. During the growth stage, the emphasis is on broadening distribution and market acceptance while keeping the product mix small. In the maturity phase, intensifying competition puts pressure on prices and encourages selective demand advertising. When saturation arrives, prices bottom out and products proliferate. When decline hits, all signs point toward retreat. Advertising is slashed, the product mix undergoes radical surgery, and prices are increased.

Fortunately, decline is not inevitable. Rather, three alternate patterns have been observed. Stability has occurred if sales plateau without showing any indication of permanent decline. A pattern of increase can result from the inherent dynamics of the marketplace as a product continues to enjoy popularity after reaching a first sales peak. And extension is produced by a strategic effort to build one product life cycle on top of another by continuing to market a mature product while introducing a popular but more expensive improvement.

Knowledge of the product life cycle enables product management to strategically manage its shape. If it chooses substitution, product management continuously replaces one life cycle with another. With extension, on the other hand, existing products or applications are continued while further variants or uses are added to extend the concept's market life.

CHAPTER 14

Diffusion and Adoption of Innovations

After a new product has been conceptualized, analyzed, designed, tested, refined, and finalized, and its introductory marketing program has been put in place, the new product's virtues and merits need to be presented and advocated to its target market. It is axiomatic that a prospect who is not aware of the existence of a given innovation cannot consider buying it. It is, therefore, of utmost importance to create expeditiously widespread awareness of the new product in the target group.

This communication task is referred to as diffusion. It represents the communications flow concerning an innovation that leads from the producer to ultimate buyers. The process of diffusion encompasses several elements and describes the ways in which information and influence related to a new product are spread to and throughout its target market. This influence has been said to take place in two steps: from the company via mass media to opinion leaders and from opinion leaders to their followers. This theory requires some updating and modification. Reference groups also affect their members' adoption decisions in varying degrees, depending on the nature of the innovation.

Diffusion, in and of itself, however, would serve little meaningful purpose unless it was followed by adoption. The two processes are necessarily sequential and closely dependent on each other. With regard to diffusion, the various types of communication sources that may be utilized are of great interest, particularly because each of them assumes prominence at a different stage of the adoption process. As would be expected, they bear varying degrees of credibility and thus influence.

The speed with which diffusion occurs is determined by a number of factors. They include the extent of the innovation's advantage over available alternatives. Compatibility with a user's life-style and/or operation is another. The rate of diffusion will also be affected by the new product's complexity. Word will spread faster if the innovation can be tried on a limited scale. And ready observability of its benefits facilitates communication, too.

As word about an innovation reaches individual consumers via the diffusion process, they may become intrigued by the concept and consider purchasing the product. This sequence of search and deliberation is known as the adoption process. It is both triggered and guided by the information received through diffusion. The complementary processes of diffusion and adoption thus ideally go hand in hand in producing new product knowledge and acceptance.

Of course, the individual process that culminates in commitment to the new product can be elaborate and time-consuming. This is a function of the innovation's degree of newness, its price tag, its personal relevance to the prospect, and the decision-making style of the individual. In any event, the adoption process can be broken down into five stages that range from first exposure to ultimate commitment. During these stages, the different communication sources mentioned earlier assume varying importance and influence. Also, the consumer's social system can exert different degrees of impact, depending on the nature of the innovation.

In their adoption decisions, members of the target market are affected by a number of factors that are either related to their personalities or to the innovation. One group of factors represents basic character traits of the decision makers. They are called predispositional factors. The other group is entitled exposure and response to the communications flow concerning the innovation.

With the help of these factors, adopters can be placed in one of several categories. Their members differ with regard to their degrees of innovativeness and can be called innovators, early adopters, early majority, late majority, and laggards. This classification is of considerable consequence because the members of these subgroups exhibit different communication and behavior patterns and accordingly should be approached differently.

The Diffusion/Adoption Dyad

The *diffusion process* is a communication process that takes place between people and thus occurs in the social sphere. In contrast, the *adoption process* is a decision-making process that evolves within one person and thus belongs in the individual sphere. It can be defined as "the mental process through which an individual passes from first hearing about an innovation to final adoption."[1] Figure 14–1 illustrates this relationship between the diffusion and adoption processes.

As Figure 14–1 indicates, diffusion comprises the transfer of new product information and opinions from the company via various communication channels to individual consumers. Diffusion of a new idea is a necessary but not a sufficient prerequisite for its adoption. Only after consumers have learned about the existence, availability, applicability, and desirability of a particular innovation can they decide about its adoption in a multistage decision-making process. Information about the new product is passed on from the producer by means of mass media and opinion leaders to individual consumers.

The diagram highlights the original *two-step communication flow theory,* which states that a company uses mass media to influence opinion leaders (stage 1), who, in turn, take the initiative in influencing their followers (stage 2). As discussed

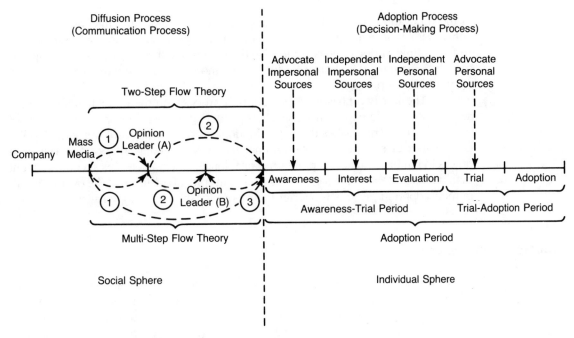

FIGURE 14–1
Diffusion and Adoption of Innovations

earlier, this requires some modification to a more complex, up-to-date multistep flow theory. For one, opinion leadership is often a sequential process where opinion leader A begets opinion leader B, who, in turn, affects a number of followers. For another, mass media simultaneously inform both opinion leaders and other target market members. What sets opinion leaders apart from others, then, is the fact that they respond faster and more positively to the product information and subsequently pass the word on to nonleaders.

The right-hand portion of Figure 14–1 depicts the adoption process as a multistage decision-making process occurring within an individual. It proceeds from awareness over interest to evaluation and trial and finally adoption. As consumers move through the sequential stages of the adoption process, they are influenced at various points by the different communication sources outlined earlier. At the final stage of adoption, the consumer's own experience with the product will become the most powerful influence on the ultimate decision.

The length of time that elapses from first hearing about an innovation until its final adoption is called the *adoption period*. Its duration varies considerably from one person to the next. Used as a measure of a person's degree of innovativeness, it provides the basis for classifying adopter categories. The adoption period can be broken down into two segments, namely, the awareness-trial period and the trial-adoption period. This subdivision is meaningful because the first three stages that compose the first segment can be viewed as mental stages, as they do not involve actual product use experience. Rather, they constitute exposure to and examination of the innovation. The awareness-trial period encompasses the interval between a consumer's first hearing about an innovation and the decision to try it. Although it requires time, it does not as yet involve the commitment of funds. Significantly, this first decision period is shorter for the earlier, more decisive adopter categories than for the later adopter groups.

The last two phases of the adoption process, on the other hand, comprise actual product use experience as well as product purchase and/or continued use of the innovation. This makes the trial-adoption period crucial from the seller's point of view. Because earlier adopters do not have a substantial body of experience of others to fall back on at this point, they take longer to complete this second segment than do later adopter categories. This occurs in spite of the fact that the overall length of their adoption periods is shorter than those for the later adopter groups.

Diffusion of Innovations

The diffusion process can be defined as "the spread of a new idea from its source of invention or creation to its ultimate users or adopters."[2] It can thus be described as "spreading the news" about the innovation to the intended audience, informing potential buyers about its characteristics and availability. An analysis of diffusion reveals four constituent parts that will now be examined more closely.

Elements of Diffusion

The diffusion process consists of four major components:

- An innovation
- Its communication from one individual to another
- In a social system
- Over time[3]

Innovations are ideas that an individual perceives as new.[4] Even if a product has been on the market for years, it is new to consumers who hear about it for the first time. Moxie is a popular soft drink in some parts of New England but virtually unknown outside that area. To visitors encountering it for the first time, Moxie is an innovation, even though it has been consumed for generations. Whether something is an innovation, therefore, depends more on subjective perception than on objective reality. This fact has far-reaching implications for product management. It means that the objective length of time that a product has been on the market is less important than an individual consumer's reactions to it. And it has two important consequences: (1) An idea does not have to be objectively new in the sense that it has never been around before; it qualifies as an innovation if consumers perceive it as being different. (2) Even if an idea is objectively new and has never been presented before, if prospects do not perceive a significant difference, it is not an innovation to them. Several examples will illustrate these points.

In 1927, commercially prepared baby food was introduced to the American market. In 1956, it was made available in Germany. Although objectively almost thirty years old, the idea was perceived as new by German mothers at that time. On the other hand, Jergens did not succeed in conveying to potential buyers that it had a new product to offer when it launched Jergens Extra Dry. Instead of a liquid lotion, it was a creamy product. But the similarity in name and package appearance misled the consumer. Only when Chesebrough-Pond's introduced Vaseline Intensive Care did the idea assume an identity of its own.[5]

Accordingly, the greatest technological breakthrough will not necessarily make a product an innovation. Only if consumers view it as being different is it an innovation to them. And only then do they have a reason to buy it, try it, and talk about it. Because most new products compete more or less directly with existing products, communication about them will occur only if consumers perceive distinct differences.

Another crucial point to realize is the fact that ideas, not products, are being diffused. Unless the underlying idea is accepted by the target market, the characteristics of the actual product are irrelevant. When a fashion concept called the "midi" was widely rejected by American women as unattractive, material, workmanship, label, price, and other factors no longer mattered. Similarly, family planning as a concept is fairly unpopular in India, so features of actual products become insignificant.

Thus, diffusion could be said to be a process of educating a target group to the merits of a new concept, a new way of doing something. Clearly, this requires change. But unless the basic concept is accepted, a product that is simply a tangible manifestation of the concept will not sell. Even if consumers see differences, they do not necessarily develop preferences. This is where skillful communication comes into the picture. *Communication* can be defined as the transfer of information, ideas, opinions, or emotions by verbal or nonverbal means. Product management aims to communicate messages to the target market that are both informative and persuasive, that is, present the necessary facts about the new product and convince the prospect to try it.

Although these promotional contacts between manufacturer and consumer can be termed controllable communication, because management controls advertising and the sales force, most of the information exchange concerning its products is beyond the control of the producer. Advertising and sales personnel of competitors and intermediaries, independent professional evaluation by testing laboratories, and the exchange of personal opinions among consumers cannot be influenced directly by the manufacturer.

When mass media are used to transmit messages about a new product, there is no direct contact between the creator of the message and its recipient. This is the reason why feedback is needed in the form of advertising research to measure the impact of the appeals used on consumer decision making.

The third element of diffusion is a *social system,* which can be defined as a group of people who interact more or less frequently due to a common interest, employer, or neighborhood. For purposes of this discussion, it suffices to say that the social system in question here is the target market, that is, the group of consumers the company is trying to serve. Its individual members have earlier been described as prospects or potential buyers. Needless to say, they have certain common characteristics, such as demographics, life-style, income, and media habits. Thus, they can be reached in similar ways and can be expected to exchange information if they find the product's newness worth talking about.

The final element of diffusion is *time,* the time that it takes to get word to every potential buyer. This time, speed, or rate of diffusion varies from one innovation to the next, depending on a number of determinant factors that will be explored later in this chapter.

Personal Influence

Research has indicated that the communication element of the diffusion process is not a simple one-step or one-way phenomenon. Rather, information and opinion flow in several steps from sources to influentials to influencees. Personal influence thus plays an important role in diffusion. It can be said to have occurred if a consumer's attitude, opinion, or behavior changes as a result of interpersonal communication. Although there should be no doubt about the necessity of advertising, the influence coming from personal conversations is much more powerful.[6] The change in predisposition and/or behavior takes place because the human mind has the unique ability to learn from communication of other people's experiences, knowledge, or opinions.

One theory advanced about the role of personal influence in diffusion suggests that "innovations spread from sources of new ideas via relevant channels to opinion leaders and from them by way of personal communication channels to their followers."[7] *Opinion leaders* are those persons within a social system to whom others turn for information and advice and whose behavior others emulate. These individuals influence the decisions of fellow members of the group with regard to the adoption of innovations. Because "opinion leaders and the people whom they influence are very much alike and typically belong to the same primary groups of family, friends and co-workers . . . it appears that influence is related (1) to the personification of certain values (who one is); (2) to competence (what one knows); and (3) to strategic social location (whom one knows)."[8]

Evidence suggests that often several types or levels of opinion leaders are involved in the communication process about a particular new product. This phenomenon has been particularly well researched and documented with regard to the diffusion and adoption of new drugs among physicians in a community.

Figure 14–2 illustrates a frequent pattern in the form of a *sociogram,* a diagram showing communications and influence flows. In this instance, physician A is a respected local authority whose advice is highly valued by peers. While this individual is exerting considerable direct influence on colleagues B to G, doctor F, in turn, takes the initiative as a satellite opinion leader to spread the word about the efficacy of the new drug to fellow practitioners H and I. It is not uncommon, in other words, that opinion followers, after having tried the innovation themselves, in turn become opinion leaders among their friends, thus multiplying the impact of the original influencer and producing a chain reaction or "snowballing" effect.

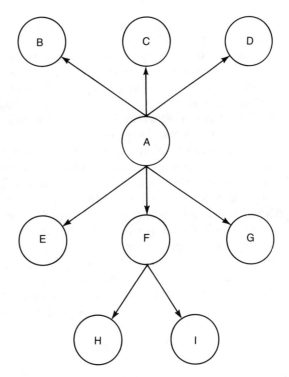

FIGURE 14–2
Sociogram of New Drug Diffusion

Clearly, the two-step flow theory as originally formulated requires modification. For one, it is more likely to be a multistep than a two-step process. For another, the initiative for personal influence may just as well originate with the opinion receivers as with the opinion leaders, making them active opinion seekers instead of passive opinion followers. Also, opinion leaders tend to be influenced as easily as they influence, making the situation one of mutual instead of one-way influence. Further, opinion leaders are not the only members in their social systems who are exposed to mass media messages. They are only more susceptible and responsive to impersonal information sources than are their influencees.[9]

Another theory concerning the spread of new ideas, called the *trickle effect*, suggests that members of lower social classes imitate the purchasing behavior of high-status consumers, especially in fashion adoption. This hypothesis has not gone undisputed. More recent evidence indicates that the horizontal flow of ideas between members of the same social system has considerably greater impact on consumer behavior than any imitation of higher-status people: "Though some vertical flow undoubtedly exists, it does not represent the dominant movement in adoption. Given simultaneous adoption across socioeconomic strata and freedom of choice among consumers, the innovators and the influentials tend to direct fashion adoption within social strata."[10]

Whatever the direction of the communication flow and the number of steps between the original information source and the individual consumer, there can be no doubt about the significance of personal interchange of ideas within a social system for the success of an innovation. There is also a wealth of evidence demonstrating that certain persons, the opinion leaders, exert considerable influence over the opinions and decisions of other members of their social systems. The success of a new product in the marketplace thus hinges to a great degree on its acceptance by these trendsetters and tastemakers.

Although opinion leaders are very important and influential in new product diffusion, it represents a major problem and challenge for product managers to identify these centers of influence and win their backing. Opinion leaders are not easily and readily distinguished from their followers because they do not act in a deviant manner but rather "are, in a certain sense, the most conformist members of their groups—upholding whatever norms and values are central to the group."[11] The task is further complicated by the fact that "influentials and influencees may exchange roles in different spheres of influence."[12] Opinion leadership is, therefore, not a general and permanent personal feature, associated with certain outstanding individuals throughout their lives. Rather, it is a social phenomenon subject to continuous changes and shifts, depending on the adoption behavior of individuals with regard to specific innovations.

Product management can utilize opinion leadership in three ways in the diffusion and adoption of innovations.[13] First, it can *stimulate opinion leadership* by encouraging satisfied customers to tell others about the new product or name friends for sales contacts. Conversely, an advertising slogan like "ask somebody who has one" aims to motivate opinion seeking, thus initiating personal influence. The first buyer of a swimming pool or central air-conditioning system on the block may well receive a particularly favorable price from the installing firm with the hope that other households on the block will want to "keep up with the Joneses" and follow suit. When the author had central air conditioning installed in a house on an eight-house suburban block, the entire neighborhood flocked to the scene. In a similar vein, sellers of major industrial equipment, such as printing presses, may give an early purchaser a break in price with the understanding that prospects may be brought to the facility for inspection and questioning. The implication is that satisfied customers make powerful advocates.

Second, product management can *simulate opinion leadership* by using a "chain of communication" approach in its new product advertising. When Procter & Gamble introduced Bounce dryer sheets, its advertising featured an interview with a user. Upon questioning, the person revealed that a friend had recommended the product. Flashback to this friend revealed the same pattern, and so on.

Third, product management can attempt to *create opinion leaders* by enabling carefully selected individuals who are likely to have relevant influence on a significant number of others to experience the new product firsthand at no cost. Local car dealers have been known to loan a new car model to prominent citizens for a few days or weeks with no strings attached to benefit from the implied endorsement when these citizens are seen driving the car. Travel agents are routinely treated to free trips and weekend accommodations by airlines and hotel operators because of their influence on the traveling public.

Communication Sources

In the diffusion process, communication flows from a source to a recipient. The original source of communication is always the producer of the innovation. It is, however, essential to determine how and when relevant factual and persuasive information is transferred to individual members of the target market. Four major types of communication sources play a role and bear influence in this process:

1. Advocate impersonal sources
2. Advocate personal sources
3. Independent impersonal sources
4. Independent personal sources[14]

They are classified according to whether they have a commercial interest in promoting the innovation (advocate sources) or not (independent sources). A second distinction is based on the nature of the source: Either a person is communicating directly with the consumer (personal sources) or an object is the immediate source of information (impersonal sources).

The principal characteristic of *advocate impersonal sources* is that they represent attempts by the innovating firm to persuade prospective buyers via paid standardized messages. Mass media advertising is the main component of this group of sources. It includes the broadcast media television and radio and the print media magazines and newspapers. These media have in common large, anonymous audiences who are exposed to their advertising messages in noncommercial settings. Due to the diverse nature of most audiences, the messages have to be fairly vague and general and have to be repeated in order to register and produce an impact. This impact of mass media advertising is reinforced by direct-mail campaigns, free samples, coupons, brochures, point-of-purchase displays, and other sales promotion materials. And, of course, the new product itself can be considered an advocate impersonal source. This fact, that a product may be its own best advocate, was utilized in the introductory campaign "Test drive a Mac" (free overnight loan of a Macintosh personal computer from Apple by a dealer). The expectation was that a trier would become a buyer.

An *advocate personal source* is an individual who attempts to influence the opinions and actions of target market members in favor of trying and buying the innovation.[15] In most cases, this change agent will be a new product salesperson, trying to get a prospect to consider the new product in the face of a bewildering array of competitive alternatives. It is due to the high degree of competitiveness in mature markets that the role of the sales force in new product introduction has steadily been gaining in relative importance in the promotion mix. In some areas, such as in the adoption of new farming products or ethical drugs, salespeople are the most important source of original information for farm operators and physicians, respectively.

Consumer Reports and editorial coverage by mass media, such as test-drive reports in *Road & Track, Motor Trend,* and *Car and Driver* magazines, as well as government publications (such as the Surgeon General's report on the health hazards of cigarette smoking), are *sources of independent impersonal information.* In many cases, these reports are based on careful testing according to a multiplicity of criteria in order to inform and protect the consumer. The behavioral impact of this kind of information, however, depends on the consumer's personal involvement with the brand or product category in question.

The importance of *independent personal sources* of communication in the diffusion process cannot be overestimated. Neighbors, friends, colleagues, and relatives belong in this category. Their advice and opinions are sought because they might have had prior experience with the product or because their acceptance and support of the new idea is essential to the consumer. The significant difference to advocate personal sources lies in the fact that consumers let their guard down and converse casually with people they know and trust and of whom they do not suspect any ulterior, selfish motives. Not only do these communicators enjoy great trustworthiness, but as reference persons they can exert considerable influence in the form of their expectations and opinions. A product recommendation by a trusted friend, also known as word of mouth, can very well be the immediate cause of a purchase decision. This is particularly so if the amount of financial and/or social risk that a consumer perceives in a potential new product purchase is high.[16]

As has become evident, the four major types of communication sources—advocate impersonal, advocate personal, independent impersonal, and independent personal—are organized in ascending order of credibility and thus influence. Unfortunately, only the advocate sources related to the new product are largely under the direct control of product management. Independent sources are, by their very nature, more elusive and, although more powerful and effective, cannot be controlled by the firm. But they are not entirely beyond reach and can be accessed via the three means of tapping into opinion leadership that were discussed earlier.

Factors Affecting the Rate of Diffusion

The *rate of diffusion* is the amount of time that it takes to diffuse an innovation throughout its target market. The speed can be said to depend on a combination of five factors: the innovation's relative advantage over competing products, its compatibility with the prospect's life-style and/or operation, its complexity in comprehension and use, its ability to be tried on a limited scale, and the observability/communicability of its benefits.[17]

A new product's edge over the competition is a critical factor. The more significant the differential, the more reason there is to talk about it and pay attention and the faster it will diffuse. A new personal computer with a memory capacity 10 percent larger than the competition would hardly be perceived as an innovation. But a new design with double or triple the standard capacity would become known virtually overnight. A minor modification will barely be noticed, whereas a technological breakthrough will attract a great deal of attention. But the seemingly obvious conclusion "the more, the merrier" is not necessarily correct. A large performance differential claim may produce a credibility gap in that it may be ahead of its time and simply not appear believable. Consumer risk perception may grow simultaneously, particularly if the advanced design carries a markedly higher price tag. And, of course, the advantage can appear excessive, wasteful, unnecessary, counterproductive, irrelevant, and frivolous.

Thus, relative advantage has to be managed carefully and may actually benefit from gradual introduction that is geared to actual, current market needs and leaves room for further improvement in the future. This approach is also safer from a delivery and liability point of view because significant advances in the laboratory are difficult to translate into stable production output so that "less (differential) may be more (stable)."

An innovation will be accepted more readily if it blends in easily with prospects' established behavior patterns. Compatibility with existing user life-styles and/or operations greatly facilitates diffusion and adoption of a new product. This aspect clearly favors continuous and dynamically continuous innovations. But it works against discontinuous innovations because they are incompatible with current patterns and require substantial changes in behavior. A personal computer, for instance, requires major adjustment and learning of new skills on the part of a computer-illiterate person. A new flavor or size of a presently consumed product, on the other hand, is quite compatible and accepted without difficulty.

The simpler an innovation is to understand and operate, the more popular it will prove to be. Complexity in design and use is inimical to smooth diffusion and adoption. The more explanation, study, and training a new product needs, the more slowly its acceptance will spread. Complexity necessitates education, and education of prospects takes time, money, and effort. The value analysis technique can serve as a valuable aid in eliminating unnecessary complexity and streamlining a product's design so as to deliver the desired functions most effectively and efficiently.[18] Again, simplicity should not be overdone and become a detriment by making the new product look like a poor value for the money.

If a new product can be sampled on a small scale, its communication and acceptance are enhanced considerably. Consumers perceive financial, functional, psychological, social, and even physical risk in the adoption of innovations. This risk can be reduced to a more acceptable level by scaling down the extent of the risk exposure. Trial sizes or free samples are a meaningful way for product management to respond to this desire of the consumer and speed up the diffusion process. Groceries are among the product categories that can be tried in limited quantities. Durable goods, however, pose a problem in this respect. Because they have to be tried full scale, purchase may have to precede trial. This kind of high-risk situation can be partially defused by a performance warranty or a money-back guarantee. Services, too—a haircut, a surgical procedure, or an insurance policy—can usually not be tried on a limited scale. Lack of trialability slows down the diffusion of these types of offerings.

The final factor of observability refers to the ease with which the benefits of the new product can be observed or communicated. This is where durable goods often excel and services suffer. Features and performance characteristics of durables are frequently quite evident and highly visible. When the author bought a new car a few years ago, a neighbor inquired whether he could test-drive it and then promptly acquired the same model. Because of new services' lack of tangibility, their benefits are difficult to comprehend and communicate, which hampers their diffusion. Nondurables, such as groceries, on the other hand may use package design or product color to create a visible difference. A mere color change in a product's package can have deep psychological impact:

> When designers at Berni Corp. changed the background hue on Barrelhead Sugar-Free Root Beer cans to beige from blue, people swore it tasted more like old-fashioned root beer served in frosty mugs. No matter that the beverage itself remained exactly the same. Similarly, consumers ascribe a sweeter taste to orange drinks the darker the orange shade of the can or bottle.[19]

Adoption of Innovations

Diffusion means spreading the word; adoption involves use of the new product. Essentially, adoption represents a decision-making process that takes place in a number of stages ranging from mere awareness of the innovation's existence to full-scale commitment to its continued use. The responsiveness of individual prospects to the innovation's lure is moderated by a number of personality characteristics. They are called predispositional factors and include venturesomeness, social integration, cosmopoliteness, social mobility, and privilegedness. The group of people who ultimately adopt can be subdivided according to their speed of response to the diffused information into innovators, early adopters, early majority, late majority, and laggards.

Stages of the Adoption Process

As shown in Figure 14–1, the adoption process consists of five distinct phases:

- Awareness
- Interest
- Evaluation
- Trial
- Adoption

During the *awareness* stage, consumers cognitively learn about the existence of the new product, but this information remains incomplete as to availability, features, and price. Awareness is more than mere exposure because it requires some degree of attention to the material presented and retention of some of its content. It nonetheless represents passive learning because it takes place at the initiative of the seller, not the buyer.

To reach the majority of the target market's members quickly and at a relatively low cost (per thousand readers, viewers, or listeners), mass media advertising is typically used at this point. Print and broadcast media—possibly amplified by the impact of opinion leaders—are especially well suited for the purpose of creating widespread product awareness because they can establish this first contact at a lower cost than any alternative channel of communication, given the size of the audience. Mass media can, however, only transmit fairly generalized, vague messages with limited informational content due to the short attention span usually devoted to passing advertising impressions.

From the product manager's point of view, the purpose of the awareness stage is to communicate the introduction of the innovation and stimulate interest in it. If consumers gain the impression that it might be applicable to their situations and could offer them relevant, significant benefits, they have moved into the *interest* stage. This phase differs substantially from the awareness stage in that prospects will engage in an active search effort.

To expend time and energy on information gathering, consumers must really feel it worth their while to find out more about the innovation. In other words, some affective learning must have taken place that drives this effort, which tends to be constrained by the amount of information available or wanted, whichever comes first. Major sources of information at this stage are promotional materials, such as folders and descriptive brochures, and independent impersonal sources, such as *Consumer Reports* or government studies. The consumer's goal in this phase is to obtain a comprehensive picture of the new product by collecting a satisfactory amount of objective facts and data.

This data collection leads into the next stage of *evaluation,* which involves a careful and thorough examination of the factual material gathered. Potential buyers weigh the pros and cons of the product and determine in their own minds whether or not they should try the innovation. This requires go/no go decisions on the part of these consumers, who have to judge not only the applicability and suitability of the item for their particular situations but also the probable reactions of significant reference persons.

Every innovation involves *perceived risk* for potential adopters because they cannot be sure of the consequences of a purchase. This risk can have five dimensions:

Financial risk	Potential loss of money if the product does not perform satisfactorily
Functional risk	Possibility that the innovation will malfunction or fail to live up to performance expectations
Physical risk	Possibility that the new product will inflict physical harm on the user
Psychological risk	Potential psychological discomfort resulting from a poor choice
Social risk	Potential loss of face or respect in the eyes of relevant others caused by their rejection of the innovation.[20]

Experiencing perceived risk can produce substantial tension in potential buyers, who may, therefore, attempt to reduce this risk before making a commitment or even just trying an innovation. This can be done in the evaluation stage of the adoption process by consulting with two types of reference groups or persons: "experts" and affected persons.

"Experts" are friends, neighbors, colleagues, or relatives who possess relevant product experience, even though they are unlikely to qualify as trained experts in the strict sense of the word. Rather, they have tried or own either the innovation itself or a comparable product so that they have some meaningful, experience-based input to offer. This kind of advice is solicited and encouraged by potential adopters because it comes from trusted, independent sources.

The second category of advisers used at this point are persons who will be affected by the consequences of a possible adoption. In other words, they will have to live with the innovation if the individual goes through with it. Prime candidates for this category are family members who may have no relevant product experience to offer but whose reaction is crucial to the comfort level of the consumer. Ascertaining it beforehand prevents unpleasant surprises.

Essentially, what the consumer is looking for at this stage is reinforcement from trusted associates. Mass media messages are far too general and commercial to have much impact at this point.

The evaluation stage completes the mental, inquisitive portion of the adoption process. Consumers who have come to the conclusion that it would be appropriate to try the innovation will now enter the *trial* stage. After all, few buyers will adopt an innovation without first trying it. Trial means testing the new product on a limited scale, if possible. This can be done with products that are divisible, that is, capable of being consumed in small quantities. Such is true for grocery products and consumer nondurables in general, but it is definitely not applicable for durable goods and services, which can only be tried full scale. Here, trial usually occurs not before but rather after purchase of the product.

Some exceptions are possible, however. Consumers who have narrowed down their choice to a particular new automobile can rent this particular model for a few days to find out how it operates. Rental qualifies as a trial, whereas a test drive around the block does not—it does not adequately simulate normal usage conditions. Similarly, if the owner of a house rents it with the option to buy, the rental period can be construed as a trial. Finally, mail-order houses often grant a free ten-day trial of their merchandise with full return privileges. And speed-reading institutes may offer free initial lessons to enable prospective students to try their service without obligation.

In the process of obtaining and sampling the new product, the consumer typically interacts with a representative of the seller. This makes the salesperson (advocate personal source) the potentially most influential source of information at the trial stage. Because the salesperson is assumed to be more knowledgeable in this field than the uninitiated buyer, the advice given can be a powerful purchase influence. In the case of a service, the person doing the selling may also be the performer, thus encouraging the formation of a personal bond.

Upon conclusion of an innovation's trial, consumers determine in their own minds whether or not it has proven itself to be useful and desirable in their particular situations. At the *adoption* stage, a decision is thus made to continue the use or consumption of the new product. Adoption is, therefore, not the first purchase of an innovation but the conscious and deliberate decision after its trial to continue using or consuming it. The consumer's own trial experience is the most powerful influence at this point. Curiously, though, while satisfaction facilitates adoption, it is not a necessary prerequisite. In other words, consumers will at times adopt innovations that they do not like. This may happen if a particular innovation is the only choice available or affordable to them. Or social pressure may prompt them to do so. This brings up the relationship between individual adoption decisions and consumers' social systems.

As pointed out earlier, a social system is a group of people who interact more or less frequently due to common interests. A consumer's social systems are, therefore, reference groups made up of family members, co-workers, or neighbors. With respect to these social systems, four types of adoption decisions can be distinguished that can be depicted in the form of a continuum ranging from total freedom of the individual to total system control (see Figure 14–3).

At one extreme, the consumer decides to adopt in accordance with personal preferences and without regard for other members of a given social system. This kind of independent decision making is characteristic for socially irrelevant, inconspicuous items that are of no interest to any reference group and do not reflect substantially on the individual. Groceries and such ubiquitous products as radios are examples.

A second category covers new products that are bought by a consumer because it is fashionable to do so. Such "keeping up with the Joneses" ensures the individual's continued acceptance and thus reduces the perceived social risk of being out of tune with a given reference group. Such innovations are socially desirable because they keep the purchaser's consumption patterns up to date. Fashion items, appliances, cars, vacation trips, vacation homes, fitness clubs, and personal computers may be among the innovations adopted under social pressure.

The third type of adoption decision requires prior group adoption before a consumer can individually decide whether or not to join in. The facilitating decision by the social system serves as an enabling, not necessarily compelling, factor. The individual member is free to decide for or against personal adoption. Without the prior group adoption, however, this possibility would be precluded because going it alone without the group's support and commitment would be beyond the means of the individual. Any project that requires a cooperative effort falls into this category, such as a charter flight or a cruise for members of a particular social organization.

The final type of adoption decision leaves the individual no choice. The social system adopts an innovation by majority vote and all members are forced to comply. This extreme is, of course, an exception rather than the rule and involves community projects such as the adoption of local zoning laws. In a such case, real

Consumer decides according to personal preference without regard for social system (1)	Consumer adopts because others have adopted ("keep up with the Joneses") (2)	Group makes facilitating decision, enabling consumer to join in (3)	Group adopts by majority vote, consumer is not given a choice (4)

Individual Freedom   System Control

FIGURE 14–3
Types of Adoption Decisions

estate in the community is zoned in certain uniform ways, regardless of the desires and preferences of individual property owners.

As these examples clearly indicate, the diffusion and adoption of innovations do not occur in a social vacuum but are shaped and often even initiated by the interaction of people belonging to a particular social system. The norms, values, attitudes, and behavior patterns prevalent in a given social system may make or break an innovation. This is why product managers have to look beyond the characteristics of the product to the characteristics of the target market. A number of large, sophisticated companies have failed in overseas markets with domestically quite successful products because they did not adjust their marketing mixes sufficiently to different cultural settings.

In reviewing the adoption process, it becomes evident that its five stages evolve over varying time spans for different products. They may take years to come about or, as in the case of impulse trial purchases, occur within short periods of time. This indicates that knowledge of the adoption process can be employed in a strategic manner. Manufacturers will, for instance, be able to realize desired profits at an earlier point in time if they succeed in shortening the average time span that elapses between consumers' first hearing about a new product and their trial of the innovation.

This can be achieved by means of free samples, distributed door to door, through the mail, or in a more selective fashion. Consumers who receive a sample of a new product free of charge and without any obligation are apt to try it, if only out of natural curiosity and because any perceived financial risk has been eliminated. This promotional approach is used extensively by leading grocery manufacturers. They mail unsolicited samples of new products to households across the United States, achieve high instant trial rates, and retain a substantial number of triers as long-term adopters. With free sampling, they penetrate their target markets much faster than with any alternative approach—a factor that is essential in today's tough competitive climate where consumer preferences and product market shares can shift rapidly.

On the other hand, consumer *rejection* of an innovation can occur at any stage of the adoption process. Nonsmokers eliminate a new cigarette from further consideration already at the awareness stage as being of no interest to them. Consumers may dismiss an innovation as being inappropriate in the course of data collection, having discovered that its features are not suitable for their conditions. Or their weighing of the innovation's benefits and drawbacks in the evaluation stage may lead to the conclusion that trial is not desirable or appropriate. They may discard the innovation after trial if its performance was unsatisfactory. A rejection at the adoption stage, however, represents a discontinuance or termination of brand loyalty because it follows an earlier, often carefully deliberated adopted decision.

An understanding of the interplay between the adoption and discontinuance of an innovation is of considerable importance for the design of a successful marketing strategy. Many companies restrict their analysis to a study of the adoption rate, which is defined as the quotient of actual and potential adoptions. An increasing adoption rate can, however, be misleading because it suggests growing popularity while in reality purchasers may be fluctuating heavily. If one investigates, instead, the interplay of adoption, discontinuance, and readoption, one might well find that while more and more of the original nonadopters convert into adopters, a lesser or larger percentage of former adopters discontinue the use of the innovation over time. It is an important step toward market success through stabilization of brand loyalty to research the reasons for such discontinuance by previously loyal buyers.

Factors Influencing Adoption

It would be of great strategic value for product managers to be able to predict who among the members of a target market (social system) is likely to adopt at what point in the game. In that case, they could simply concentrate their early promotional efforts on the relatively few consumers who will probably be innovators and early adopters and then let the diffusion and adoption processes take their courses. This would greatly improve both the efficiency and effectiveness of promotional activities and expenditures in the introduction of new products.

Unfortunately, the situation is not quite that easy. Nobody can predict before-hand which individuals *will* adopt at what point in time and accordingly fall into a given adopter category. But there are certain indicators that suggest which prospects *are likely* to adopt earlier or later. These are called *predispositional factors* because they represent basic characteristics of an individual that exist independent of any particular innovation. The higher a person scores on one or more of the predispo-sitional factors, the greater is the probability that this individual will adopt earlier than other consumers with lower scores. Predispositional factor scores can thus be used as points of reference when estimating probable magnitude and speed of new product acceptance.

The group of predispositional factors is composed of five separate variables: venturesomeness, social integration, cosmopoliteness, social mobility, and privi-legedness. All of these factors are indicators of a person's open-mindedness or *innovativeness,* which can be described as an individual's readiness to adopt inno-vations. A consumer's innovativeness can be measured retrospectively by determin-ing the length of the personal adoption period. Although this determination can take place only after the fact, that is, after adoption has occurred, predispositional factors can be investigated beforehand and give a reasonable indication of probable adoptive behavior.

Venturesomeness is a buyer's willingness to accept one or more types of perceived risk in the adoption of innovations. A venturesome person has a higher tolerance for risk than other consumers, perhaps even a bit of a gambling spirit that seeks the thrill of newness and uncertainty. The extent of perceived risk will, of course, vary with an innovation's degree of newness, price tag, and conspicuousness and may even encourage venturesome people to engage in risk reduction behavior.

Social integration can be defined as the degree of involvement in community affairs. A highly socially integrated person is very active in public life, well known in the community, and popular with fellow citizens. Typical for such community leaders are activities in political parties, religious organizations, charitable organizations, and prominent local clubs and committees. In short, socially integrated consumers are characterized by intensive participation in community life.

Cosmopoliteness is the extent to which individuals' information and values come from outside their social systems. Cosmopolite persons receive such inputs from scientific sources, trained professionals, traveling, overseas sources, and social contacts. Due to this diversity of inputs and sources, they tend to be more open-minded and receptive to new experiences. Localite consumers, in contrast, restrict themselves to inputs from inside their social systems and are thus necessarily more narrow-minded in their mental horizons, interests, and activities.

Social mobility refers to people's willingness to make significant changes and commitments in their lives. It encompasses three subcategories—geographic mobility, educational mobility, and career mobility.

Geographic mobility concerns the willingness to move and relocate to a new place of residence. Although geographic mobility has dropped somewhat in recent years, in any given year 16 percent of the U.S. population change their place of residence. This type of mobility has assumed a new dimension in the era of dual-career couples where every second married woman is gainfully employed. Hardships can be wrought if only one of the spouses receives an out-of-town job offer. This is why enlightened employers assist the other spouse in finding a job in the local economy. Moving on to a new assignment elsewhere had long been considered the price of career success and progress in the United States. Fortunately, employers have become more aware of and sensitive to the substantial human toll that such an approach can exact on a family and its roots in a community. So turning down a new assignment that entails a move does not quite carry the same stigma that it once did.

Some geographic mobility, too, is simply the result of changes in the family life cycle. As family size and housing needs change, consumers may move from a city apartment to a suburban house, then back to a center city condominium and ultimately to a nursing home or retirement community. This may also explain why most geographic moves are intrastate in nature.

Educational mobility implies the pursuit of advanced degrees. This requires a considerable commitment of time and financial resources, often carried in addition to a full-time job and family obligations. The purpose is usually career advancement which is presumed to be linked to the attainment of the coveted degree. *Career mobility,* on the other hand, is the willingness to change careers, that is, to terminate a past occupation or path and seek a new career in another field. Although this is not uncommon for today's active retirees, it has spread to many other groups, for example, teachers, civil servants, and entrepreneurs. Whatever the type, socially mobile people show open-mindedness and tend to adopt earlier than others.

Privilegedness relates to an individual's financial situation as compared to other community members. Privileged persons have an above average income and are thus more readily able to afford the financial risk inherent in buying an innovation. In contrast, community members of more limited financial means are forced to wait until a relatively late point in the game because they can ill afford to take the functional risk of an innovation and have to wait for the price to come down to a more affordable level.

Adopter Categories

On the basis of the factors previously described, a comprehensive picture of the various adopter groups can now be drawn. Obviously, only persons who have gone through all the stages of the adoption process, that is, adopted the product after trial, can be considered adopters. The classification of adopters is based on their innovativeness, which is measured by the length of the adoption period. In accordance with this criterion, five categories can be distinguished:

- Innovators
- Early adopters
- Early majority
- Late majority
- Laggards

These groups tend to be distributed normally: In any given population of adopters of a specific innovation, there will be, on average, 2.5 percent innovators, 13.5 percent early adopters, 34 percent early majority, 34 percent late majority, and 16 percent laggards.[21] Table 14–1 contains summary profiles of the five adopter categories, which will now be described in more detail.

Innovators are clearly distinct from all other adopter types. They have been said to be "in step with a different drummer" because they do things that nobody else does—yet. Because they are the first consumers to try a particular new product,

TABLE 14–1
Summary Profiles of Adopter Categories

Adopter Categories	Key Characteristic	Personal Aspects	Communication Sources	Opinion Leadership
Innovators	Venturesome	Young; high social status and income	Scientific and impersonal sources	Some
Early Adopters	Striving for respectability	Community leaders	Local sources	Greatest
Early majority	Deliberate	Above average social status and income	Early adopters	Some
Late majority	Slow	Below average social status and income	Early majority	Little
Laggards	Tradition-oriented	Lowest social status; small income	Peers	Very little

Source: Reprinted with permission from Eberhard E. Scheuing, "How Do Consumers Adopt a New Product," in *Marketing Update* (New York: Alexander-Norton Publishers, 1977), p. 7.

they must possess a considerable amount of curiosity and courage. They tend to be young and are usually quite comfortable financially so that they can afford to take a chance on an untried product. Innovators are likely to be well educated, well read, and well traveled, take an interest in the affairs of the world at large, and may even speak several languages. This makes them cosmopolites who receive their decision-making input from scientific and impersonal information sources. Innovators are mobile and decisive, though open-minded and venturesome as well as affluent. But they are only marginally integrated into their local communities and interact mainly with early adopters, thus exerting only a limited amount of opinion leadership.

The *early adopters* are the true trendsetters. They are the local leaders, deeply rooted in the life of the community and actively involved in shaping it. Early adopters interact readily and frequently with others in the community. They are well known and popular, enjoy high prestige, and command sizable incomes. The other members of their social system respect them and ask them for advice, imitating their behavior. Their adoption decisions have far-reaching impact because they set examples for others. By their support, they remove the social risk inherent in the adoption of a new product. In contrast to innovators, early adopters have a strong local orientation. They have close contacts with local businesspeople and are thus well informed about the latest innovations. Where they can be persuaded to try a new product extensively and conspicuously, ostensibly or even overtly endorsing it, the impact could be considerable.

As the news about an innovation spreads, the *early majority* enters the scene. They are deliberate people whose goal it is to "keep up with the Joneses," the latter being represented by the early adopters. The income and social status of the members of the early majority are above average. Although somewhat older, they are strongly influenced by the early adopters, while their own opinion leadership is limited to members of their group and of the late majority. They are less flexible and more set in their ways than the members of the preceding categories.

From the early majority word is spread to the *late majority*. Members of this group are slow to adopt because they have to be cautious in their spending and wait until the price drops to a level that they can afford. As time passes and the price decreases, pressure builds for them to join the previous adopters. By now, the new product is already well represented in the households of the target market and is no longer news but a fact of daily life. Late majority members respond less to mass media advertising and instead rely more on personal contacts with individuals in the early majority and their own group as important sources of information. Their opinion leadership is restricted to fellow members of their own category.

The final category of *laggards* is made up of people who are tradition-bound and oriented toward the past. They buy less on impulse and more due to long-established habits. Laggards are often somewhat isolated from processes in their environment, interacting less frequently with other groups and living in a world of their own. This world includes active interchange with other people like themselves. They are mostly older people with fixed retirement incomes, which gives them little social status. Their resistance against anything new is hard to overcome. They are virtually immobile and are frequently among the first to discontinue an innovation because they quickly find out that they cannot handle it or cannot afford it.

Thus, the picture of consumer reaction to the introduction of a new product becomes complete. It was shown that potential buyers react differently, though predictably, in accordance with their psychological makeup, financial situation, and interaction patterns. The spread of new ideas via various communication channels is closely intertwined with individual adoption decisions. The discussion indicated how product managers can manipulate the information input at each stage of the adoption process, how they can differentiate between adopter categories with varying characteristics, and how the acceptance of an innovation by a target market can be speeded up strategically. Thorough familiarity with the sociological and psychological processes in the adoption of new products is, therefore, an important prerequisite of marketing success in a society and business environment where a steady stream of new products is vital for the survival of individual companies and the growth of the economy as a whole.

SUMMARY

The spread and acceptance of new ideas are governed by two interrelated processes: diffusion and adoption. Diffusion is concerned with getting the word to ultimate buyers, whereas adoption refers to the subsequent decision-making process.

Diffusion is the spread of a new idea from an innovating company to the members of a target market. This process consists of four elements: an innovation, its communications flow, in a social system, over time. An innovation is an idea perceived as new by an individual, regardless of whether or not it is objectively new. On the other hand, only innovations whose newness is successfully communicated will produce the desired response.

New product communication can flow from source to receiver in several steps, often involving one or more opinion leaders—persons to whom others turn for advice and whose recommendations they value. Accordingly, opinion leaders can exert a powerful positive or negative influence during the diffusion process. Their potential support can be tapped by stimulating, simulating, or creating opinion leadership.

The communication sources utilized in the diffusion process can be classified into four major categories. Advocate impersonal sources are mainly represented by mass media advertising and sales promotion materials. A prime example of an advocate personal source is a salesperson. Independent impersonal sources include *Consumer Reports* and government reports. Independent personal sources, in contrast, are composed of friends, neighbors, colleagues, and relatives. The impact of these sources varies throughout the adoption process.

The rate of diffusion is the speed with which information about the innovation is diffused throughout the target market. It is affected by five factors: the extent of the new product's relative advantage over competing products, its compatibility with a prospect's mode of living or operating, its user-friendliness, its trialability on a limited scale, and the ease of observation or communication of its benefits. The presence or absence of these factors affects nondurables, durables, and services differently.

After members of a target market have been exposed to information about an innovation, they may go through a decision-making process that eventually leads to adoption. Conversely, prospects may reject the new idea for a variety of reasons at any stage of the adoption process. These stages are awareness, interest, evaluation, trial, and adoption.

At the awareness level, consumers merely know that a particular new product exists. If their interest is aroused, they will collect more information about it. This information will subsequently be evaluated to determine whether or not the product should be tried. At the trial stage, consumers sample the innovation on a limited scale, if possible. If they like it, they will probably adopt it and thus continue its use.

It is of considerable interest for product managers to be able to identify different categories of adopters. This permits a fine-tuning of the marketing mix to the specific conditions of the various subgroups, which greatly improves its effectiveness. The means by which the different adopter categories can be identified are provided by a group of predispositional factors: venturesomeness, social integration, cosmopoliteness, social mobility, and privilegedness.

Among the resulting adopter categories, innovators tend to be the youngest as well as the most aggressive and dynamic. They possess the highest social status and income, are very cosmopolite in their outlook, have close contact with scientific sources, and exert only a limited amount of opinion leadership. The real movers and shakers are the early adopters, who are respected, well-known community leaders. Their orientation is very localite in nature. Members of the early majority are deliberate in their adoption decisions, even though they still enjoy an above average income. The late majority drops below the average income level. Laggards are tradition-oriented and somewhat isolated from the rest.

NOTES

1. Everett M. Rogers, *Diffusion of Innovations* (New York: Free Press, 1962), 76.
2. Ibid., 76.
3. See Everett M. Rogers, *Diffusion of Innovations,* 3rd ed. (New York: Free Press, 1983), 10.
4. See ibid., 11.
5. See Al Ries and Jack Trout, *Positioning: The Battle for Your Mind* (New York, McGraw-Hill, 1981), 141.
6. See Elihu Katz and Paul S. Lazarsfeld, *Personal Influence* (New York: Free Press, 1955), 169ff. See also Rogers, *Diffusion of Innovations* (1962), 217ff.
7. Rogers, *Diffusion of Innovations* (1962), 213.
8. Elihu Katz, "The Two-Step Flow of Communication," in *Perspectives in Consumer Behavior,* edited by Harold H. Kassarjian and Thomas S. Robertson (Glenview, IL: Scott, Foresman, 1968), 349, 347.
9. Compare Rogers, *Diffusion of Innovations* (1983), 273–274, and Katz, "The Two-Step Flow" 349. Concerning the modified, multistep communication flow theory, see also Leon G. Schiffman and Leslie Lazar Kanuk, *Consumer Behavior,* 3rd ed. (Englewood Cliffs, NJ: Prentice-Hall, 1987), 572–573.

10. Charles W. King, "Fashion Adoption: A Rebuttal to the 'Trickle Down' Theory," in *Dimensions of Consumer Behavior,* 2nd ed., edited by James U. McNeal (New York: Appleton-Century-Crofts, 1969), 182. See also Henry Assael, *Consumer Behavior and Marketing Action,* 3rd ed. (Boston,Kent Publishing Co., 1987), 455–456.
11. Katz, "The Two-Step Flow," 347.
12. Ibid., 349.
13. See Schiffman and Kanuk, *Consumer Behavior,* 577–581, and Assael, *Consumer Behavior,* 436–437.
14. See Alan R. Andreasen, "Attitudes and Customer Behavior: A Decision Model," in *Perspectives in Consumer Behavior,* edited by Harold H. Kassarjian and Thomas S. Robertson (Glenview, IL: Scott, Foresman, 1968), 503.
15. See, for instance, Rogers, *Diffusion of Innovations* (1983), 28.
16. See Johan Arndt, "Word-of-Mouth Advertising and Perceived Risk," in *Perspectives in Consumer Behavior,* edited by Harold H. Kassarjian and Thomas S. Robertson (Glenview, IL: Scott, Foresman, 1968), 330ff., and Raymond A. Bauer, "Consumer Behavior as Risk Taking," in *Perspectives in Consumer Behavior,* edited by Harold H. Kassarjian and Thomas S. Robertson (Glenview, IL: Scott, Foresman, 1968), 187ff.
17. See Rogers, *Diffusion of Innovations* (1983), 15–16.
18. See Eberhard E. Scheuing, *Purchasing Management* (Englewood Cliffs, NJ: Prentice-Hall, 1989), chap. 10.
19. Ronald Alsop, "Color Grows More Important in Catching Consumers' Eyes," *Wall Street Journal,* 29 Nov. 1984.
20. For a discussion of perceived risk and consumer risk-reduction strategies, see Schiffman and Kanuk, *Consumer Behavior,* 214–221.
21. See Rogers, *Diffusion of Innovations* (1983), 246–247. Concerning the following description of adopter categories, see Schiffman and Kanuk, *Consumer Behavior,* 247–259.

CASE STUDY

CHANGING FABRIC

Founded in 1922 by the Malkon family, Malkon Mills, Inc., is a leading manufacturer of fabrics. At its headquarters, in Greenville, South Carolina, the company manufactures both greige goods (unfinished woven fabrics sold to converters for further processing) and finished woven fabrics (sold to garment manufacturers and used in the production of clothing).

Malkon Mills employs 2,500 people, operates 1,140 looms, and generates sales of $105 million. The last two years, however, have seen mounting losses of $2.5 million and $3.2 million, respectively. Because of its importance in the fashion business, the company's marketing department is located in New York City. Its sales force covers the entire country, though, from sales offices located in key cities from Miami to Seattle.

Examining the Business Portfolio

Malkon Mills is composed of three divisions that make the following contributions to its total sales:

Greige Goods Division	18.2%
Apparel Fabrics Division	79.5
Chemicals Division	2.3
	100.0%

The Greige Goods Division, Malkon's original business, manufactures staple, commodity-type fabrics that are sold by specification rather than by sample. All such mills basically produce identical products, which are only semifinished and are bought and sold as commodity items.

In 1932, the company's management decided to modify the operation and built a finishing plant. Its motivation for this vertical integration was improved customer service, better quality control, and greater profit. Today, the Apparel Fabrics Division

not only commands the largest volume but is also the most profitable. Exhibit 14–A shows the composition of its 1987 sales by department and product category.

Notwithstanding the success of the Apparel Fabrics Division, the company has witnessed difficult times since 1980 as more and more of its customers started buying imported fabrics. Malkon Mills began to experience market resistance as price considerations assumed increasing importance. Imported fabrics often enjoyed a price advantage of 10 to 35 cents per yard, representing a savings of 10 to 20 percent for the garment manufacturer. Retailers added to the challenge by importing entire garments from East Asia. This practice started in the 1970s but has spiraled since 1980.

In 1952, Malkon Mills created a Chemicals Division as a means of obtaining dyestuff at a lower cost by eliminating the outside manufacturer's profit. Eventually, this division started selling dyestuff and textile-related chemicals to outside companies. Today, the Chemicals Division supplies a limited number of customers with specialty chemicals under long-term contracts.

New Blood

In an effort to revive the company's flagging fortune (its sales had hit a peak of $125 million in 1980, with profits of $11 million), its president, David Malkon, Jr., hires a new vice president of marketing to head the company's entire marketing effort.

Harry Kay is a graduate of North Carolina State University with a B.S. degree in textile technology. In recent years, he has also completed the University of Virginia's Executive Management Program. He previously worked as vice president, marketing, for a smaller manufacturer of knitted fabrics where he had started as a trainee seventeen years ago. Although he has no prior experience in woven fabrics, he is an excellent administrator and merchandiser.

This case was contributed by George Papalian, Instructor in Marketing, St. John's University, New York, New York.

**EXHIBIT 14–A
Composition of Apparel
Fabrics Division Sales,
1987**

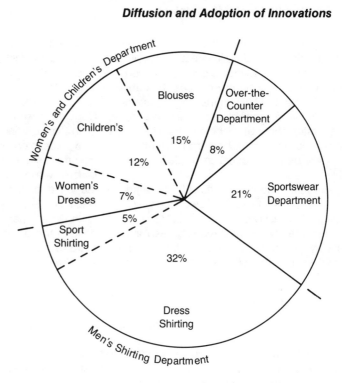

Harry quickly sets out to acquaint himself with the operation. He learns that Malkon produces yarn-dyed plaids and stripes, Oxford cloth, and piece-dyed solids. The company offers an "open" line for general distribution to all customers. It also sells "confined" styles to customers desiring exclusive, customized designs. Malkon Mills has a styling staff that creates a design or pattern, an art studio that paints it, and a pilot plant that weaves a sample for the customer's approval before manufacturing the full warp or order.

Open line items are carried in inventory. Delivery can be made within one week. The time frame for confined styles includes two weeks for creativity, two to three weeks for samples from the pilot plant, and twelve to fourteen weeks for the production of an order. This adds up to an order lead time of sixteen to nineteen weeks as compared to eighteen to thirty weeks for imported fabrics, which also require letters of credit to be established.

Analyzing the Men's Shirting Market

Harry knows that David looks to him to help return the company to profitable operation. He feels that the

Men's Shirting Department holds the greatest promise for a quick turnaround and studies its situation carefully.

The department encompasses two product categories, namely, sport shirting and dress shirting. Sport shirting fabrics are made of either a 65/35 blend (35 percent cotton, 65 percent polyester) or a 50/50 blend, both with a permanent press finish. Dress shirting consists of 60/40 Oxford cloth. Last year, Malkon Mills added an all-cotton Oxford cloth. The Men's Shirting Department sells its fabrics to manufacturers of men's and boys' shirts. Their number has decreased over the years, leaving only a few large firms that produce for both segments. These manufacturers sell shirts under many different labels (national, company, and private brands, as well as unbranded) to various types of retailers.

After reviewing the department's product offering, Harry examines its merchandising and distribution policies, as well as its sales records. He also analyzes the import statistics for fabrics and garments. Imports of cotton fabrics had steadily climbed over the years, reaching 83 percent of domestic production in 1985. In the same year, imports of men's and boys' shirts exceeded domestic production by 66 percent.

In the course of his research, Harry further learns that in Europe, especially in Great Britain, all-cotton, wide-stripe men's shirts are being packaged differently and are selling at higher prices. This approach is beginning to diffuse in the United States. Better specialty and prestige shops are introducing 100 percent cotton shirts as fashion items. He becomes convinced that the fashion trend for men's dress shirts will be in the direction of 100 percent cotton.

Every year since 1983, sales of 60/40 blend Oxford button-down shirts have shown steady increases. During the past two years, Malkon Mills has sold this fabric at a very modest markup, resulting in short supply throughout this period. Imports of men's Oxford shirts and cloth declined sharply in 1984 and stayed low in the subsequent years. This is due to the fact that they do not enjoy the same kind of price advantage as sport shirts and their fabrics.

Harry concludes that the Men's Shirting Department should add 100 percent cotton Oxford cloth to its offering for regular distribution. It should also experiment in producing 100 percent Pima cotton, a superior quality cotton, in the pinpoint Oxford weave, which sells for approximately twice the price of the regular all-cotton Oxford cloth. Because the cost of manufacturing pinpoint Oxford cloth is less than twice that of regular 100 percent cotton Oxford cloth, this will result in better profit margins. He also instructs the department to develop a lightweight all-cotton Oxford cloth for summer wear.

Discussion Questions

1. Evaluate Malkon Mills's current product strategy.
2. Do you agree with Harry Kay's plans for the Men's Shirting Department? Why, or why not?
3. How should Malkon Mills combat the rising tide of imports?
4. Should the company pursue more custom work? If so, from whom? Or do you recommend a completely different approach?

CHAPTER 15

Managing the Product Life Cycle

As new products are launched in the marketplace, their sponsors have high hopes that they will be successful and make significant contributions to the company's bottom line. Considerable amounts of time and money are often invested in their internal evolution, as well as in the formulation and testing of their introductory marketing programs. Now they face their greatest test yet: their full-scale introduction in the competitive marketplace and thus the question of whether they will establish themselves and grow into profitable revenue producers or wither quickly.

Ideally, after their market introduction, innovations will, over time, move through a series of stages in their external or market evolution. This process of a new product's evolution in the marketplace is referred to as its product life cycle (PLC). The life cycle concept is borrowed from biology, where an organism is born and subsequently evolves through infancy, childhood, adolescence, adulthood, maturity, and decline to ultimate death.

Understanding the product life cycle and its implications is vital to the successful management of a product in the marketplace. This chapter is devoted to developing this knowledge and facilitating its strategic application. It outlines the stages of the product life cycle and their particular characteristics. And it suggests appropriate ways of dealing with or capitalizing on stage-specific conditions.

The product life cycle is a very useful concept because it helps product managers understand and describe changes in market growth rate, competitive intensity, and profitability during a product's market life. Many products follow a fairly predictable pattern that could be called the classic or traditional product life cycle. This common pattern represents a key subject in this chapter. The chapter also concerns itself with the question of how to determine a product's position on the cycle in order to choose the most effective marketing approach. The chapter further contains a review of the changes in a product's marketing mix that are necessitated by changes in environmental conditions that occur during the different stages.

After the discussion of the classic PLC, potential alternate patterns are presented, and product managers become acquainted with strategies for overcoming stagnation or decline. Because many product life cycles have reached the stage of maturity or even saturation, a final section deals with the issue of how to manage mature products.

Mapping the Market Life of a Product

The *product life cycle (PLC)* is a basic model of the sales trend for a product (line, category) during its market life. It is shown in a two-dimensional diagram in the form of a bell-shaped curve, where the vertical dimension represents sales and the horizontal dimension indicates time. Sales is preferably expressed in physical units. If this is impractical, dollar sales, which are used as a substitute figure, have to be adjusted for any price changes that would distort the statistics over time. For instance, if in a given year, sales revenues increased 10 percent but this was caused by a 10 percent price hike, the adjusted figure reflects no change in unit consumption. If the level of nondurable consumption expenditures varies during the observation period, it may become necessary to adjust the raw sales data to eliminate the impact of population growth, inflation, and the business cycle.[1]

The effect of such adjustments can be dramatic, significantly altering the magnitude and pattern of the data. The adjustments are necessary to purify the raw data from any extraneous influences not germane to the product's market acceptance. The adjusted figures more accurately portray changes in the level of market acceptance.

The product life cycle concept refers alternately to three different levels of aggregation: product categories, product lines, and products. Markedly different shapes and stages result, depending on which level of aggregation is chosen. For instance, in the same market a product may be in its decline stage, a product line in its growth stage, and the product category in the maturity stage.

A *product category* (also called product class) includes an entire classification or market that addresses itself to the satisfaction of a particular type of need. Product categories are, for example, represented by passenger cars and cigarettes. Individual products within a given category serve basically the same need configuration in slightly different ways, thus competing against all other entries in the category for the same consumer dollars.

For most companies, it is not practical to operate at this highest level of aggregation. Only giants in their industries would see merit in taking the movement of the entire market into account. Also, it has been argued that many product categories seem to enjoy almost indefinite maturity stages, so that the product life cycle at this level of aggregation can be of little strategic consequence.[2]

A *product line* (also called product form) is a group of related products that serve the same purpose and compete directly with one another. Frequently, the purchase of one item within a product line precludes the purchase of any other. In a product line of portable black and white television sets, for example, the purchase of a 19-inch set usually means that no other items in the line will be chosen. This level of aggregation is normally the most meaningful for analysis and strategy formulation because most firms have several entries in a product line and different product lines within the same category tend to show sharply varying patterns.

A *product* (also called brand) is an individual item within a product line, representing a specific version of the basic product idea. In the following discussion of the product life cycle, the term *product* is generally used to refer to the underlying concept rather than to specific executions or variations of the basic idea. Although an analysis is possible, and to some extent meaningful, at any of the three levels of aggregation, the following discussion will focus on life cycles for product lines for the reasons outlined above. This will permit the presentation of a complete picture of competitive strategy and interaction at the various stages of market evolution. Figure 15–1 illustrates differences in cycle behavior based on aggregation level.

Stages of the Classic Product Life Cycle

The classic model of the product life cycle with its bell-shaped sales curve can be divided into a number of stages with distinctly different characteristics that prompt differences in strategic approaches. Although the number of stages is somewhat arbitrary and has been known to vary from two to nine, depending on individual preference and perspective, the pattern described here distinguishes five stages. This five-stage model differs slightly from the frequently used pattern of four stages in that it divides the peak period (commonly referred to as maturity) into two stages, namely, maturity and saturation. Because sales behavior (slow growth versus no growth) and appropriate strategic responses differ, this refinement aids product managers in formulating successful strategies.

In analyzing the nature of the product life cycle stages, the distinction between market capacity and market volume (discussed earlier) can serve as a valuable tool. Market capacity tends to remain stable over time. Accordingly, the relationship between market capacity and market volume offers a good indication of the stage that the life cycle has attained at a given point in time, as well as its future growth prospects.

The analysis benefits further from a consideration of the degree of *market resistance*. Initial market resistance to an unknown innovation is often very high, leaving it to a limited number of daring innovators to break the ice and give the new product a chance to succeed in the marketplace. As the innovation's popularity and thus sales gain momentum, market resistance drops markedly. It resurges, however, as market growth slows because buyers have developed loyalties and perceive few significant differences among competing brands.

An alternate useful indicator is the *market growth rate*. It can be measured at any point by dividing the industrywide sales increment in a given year into the market volume at the end of the preceding year. This rate accelerates in the early portion of the cycle, peaks in the middle of the growth stage, and becomes zero at the saturation point. The Boston Consulting Group matrix uses market growth rate to classify strategic business units and to select appropriate strategies.

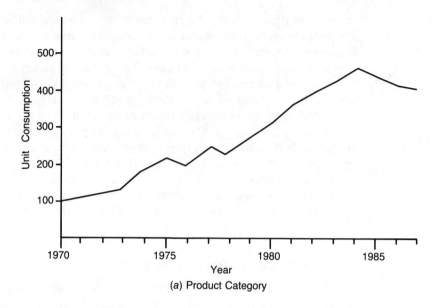

(a) Product Category

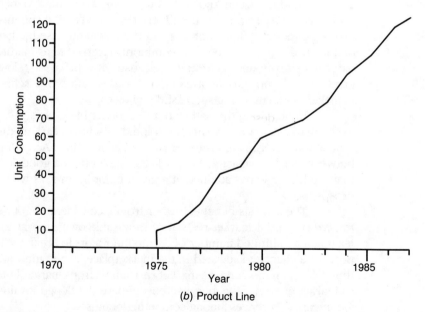

(b) Product Line

FIGURE 15–1
Comparison of Life Cycle Patterns at Different Levels of Aggregation

FIGURE 15–1
continued

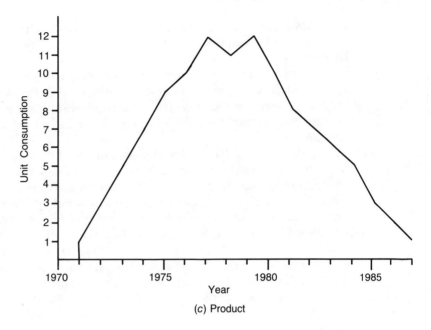

(c) Product

Introduction.   The introduction stage of the product life cycle represents the full-scale launch of an innovation in the marketplace. Notwithstanding painstaking marketing research and financial analysis during the preceding stages of new product evolution, this remains not only a challenging but also a risky undertaking. In fact, introduction could well turn out to be the make-or-break stage for an innovation.

One description of the first phase of the product life cycle attributes its pattern of slow sales growth to four possible causes:

1. Delays in the expansion of production capacity
2. Technical problems, that is, "working out the bugs"
3. Delays in making the product available to customers, especially in obtaining adequate distribution through retail outlets
4. Customer inertia, arising primarily from reluctance to change established behavior patterns[3]

Assuming that a new product line is being launched and thus essentially a new market is being created, the introduction stage requires the generation of primary demand. This task of converting part of the market capacity into market volume falls on the *pioneer.* This term refers to the first company to offer a new product concept in the marketplace. In spite of the risks involved, if the innovation responds to a real need in the marketplace and its marketing is well conceived and managed, it helps to be first. Clearly, the opportunity exists to become the leading brand in the emerging market. And if this opportunity is seized and defended with relentless vigor, it can become a franchise for years to come. A survey showed that of twenty-five leading brands in 1923, 80 percent were still in first place sixty years later.[4]

Implementing an innovative idea can give a firm a jump on the competition and provide it with some lead time to fortify its position. Although the pioneer's product is unique at the outset, its competitive distinctiveness will tend to decline over time as competitive imitations copy or surpass its appearance, performance, and value.

The pioneer has to shoulder the burden of creating a market for the new product from scratch, possibly against considerable odds. Apple single-handedly created the market for personal computers, only to see the field of competitors expand to more than 150, including IBM, the most formidable player in the computer industry. Because people generally resist change of any nature and prefer to continue established behavior patterns, market resistance is very high at the outset of a new market. Intensive promotion and extensive buyer education to the benefits of the new concept are needed if a radical innovation is to catch on. A great many unknowns and, therefore, substantial financial and social risk are involved for potential buyers. They discourage all but the most venturesome. Innovators belong to this category of purchasers who respond first to the pioneer's promotional efforts in introducing the new product.

Growth.   The initial success of the pioneer attracts competitors that enter the market with carbon copies of the original product. They, in effect, represent imitators whose entry in the marketplace facilitates and fuels a rapid expansion of market volume. This has been the case for disposable cameras, a product category pioneered by Fuji Photo Film Company, which was quickly followed by Eastman Kodak Company and Konica Corporation.[5] As the innovation gains greater acceptance, market resistance decreases sharply: "The transition to rapid growth is explained partly in terms of an imitation process among consumers, and partly in terms of intensified promotion as competitors of the innovating company introduce 'me-too' products."[6]

On the buyers' side, two additional types join the market—the early adopters and, later on, the early majority. After the innovation has been tried and accepted by the innovators, early adopters step into the picture as powerful opinion leaders whose endorsement provides the impetus for fast growth. After all, their behavior is quickly emulated by members of the early majority (who want to "keep up with the Joneses"). Although the limited demand presented by innovators during the introduction stage was rather insensitive to price changes, the appearance of lower socioeconomic strata explains an increase in price elasticity.

Competition is carried out by expanding market volume and entering new market segments. Product availability is a major factor, but price reductions also begin to play a role in attracting business to a firm. The pioneer's virtual monopoly has been replaced by an oligopoly, with several firms competing for the buyer's dollar. These imitators were attracted by the promising profit potential combined with the pioneer's inability to satisfy primary demand due to limited production capacity.

Maturity. As the volume of the new market grows further and sales of displaced products decline, conservative sellers experience pressure to switch to the new product for sheer survival. This pattern of displacement, where a new product with superior technology supersedes an established one with now obsolete design, is illustrated in Figure 15–2.

A modern-day version of this familiar pattern can be seen in Figure 15–3, which depicts unit sales of instant and 35-millimeter cameras over a nine-year span. The diagram shows that "since the 35-millimeter camera became the camera of choice for young professionals in the late 1970s, Polaroid's instant-camera sales worldwide have plunged to 3.6 million cameras last year from 9.4 million in 1978."[7]

To reverse the decline, the company introduced a third-generation instant camera in April 1986 with great fanfare. The report about the kickoff event continued: "Polaroid has spent millions of dollars developing Spectra and will spend tens of millions marketing it over the next year alone. . . . To revive its fortunes, Polaroid's ads will sell not just a camera, but what Polaroid executives almost religiously refer to as the 'instant experience'—the magic of seeing a photo develop before one's eyes."[8] Time will tell whether the decline is indeed reversible and the life cycle of instant cameras can be revitalized.

As the life cycle of a new product enters the growth stage, a market has been created. This means that initial market resistance has been overcome and the innovation has caught on with buyers, gaining steadily in popularity and momentum as it moves farther through the growth stage. As it enters the maturity stage, the market has been established. The product is no longer news. It is now widely accepted and has been integrated into the consumption or usage patterns of a variety of buyers. This fact significantly reduces the financial risk involved for both buyers and sellers that now join the market. However, the rate of growth of sales volume has slowed down significantly in this stage at the very time that sizable numbers of additional entrants change the competitive picture to a polypoly—competition among many firms.

This explosive combination translates into fierce fighting for market share. Price wars are common in mature industries. In addition, a whole gamut of nonprice

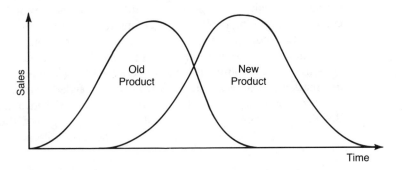

FIGURE 15–2
Product Life Cycle Displacement Pattern

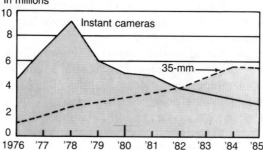

FIGURE 15–3
Displacement in the Camera Market (*Source:* Reprinted with permission from *Wall Street Journal,* 25 March 1986, 33)

competition takes place to help differentiate a company's products from those of its competitors. Typically, a firm's product offering also proliferates at this point in the life cycle.

Another large group of buyers, the late majority, has now decided to follow the lead of the earlier adopter categories. They are eventually joined by the laggards as the market volume approaches saturation. Price elasticity is now substantially higher than in the growth phase, reflecting increased responsiveness to price changes.

Saturation. Once the saturation point has been reached, sales stabilize because the market capacity has been exhausted. Few new buyers will be entering the market after this point, and most purchases are repeat or replacement rather than first-time purchases. Secondary market resistance is now in force because competing entries resemble each other closely in buyers' minds. Buyers either display inertia, continuing brand patronage for convenience's sake, or switch readily from brand to brand, depending on the price incentives given. The direct price elasticity of demand thus reaches its peak in this phase as many purchasers are looking for good buys and consider competing products largely interchangeable.

Consequently, the fight for market share heats up further and becomes increasingly more expensive. Although market volume has plateaued, some sellers are still belatedly joining the market, encountering a rather hostile climate. Because the market is flooded with products and crowded with competitors, sellers use differentiation and modification to create a differential advantage in the marketplace. But the handwriting is on the wall. Dynamic companies therefore intensify their diversification into other markets with higher growth potential.

Decline. The saturation stage "may last for many years. With few exceptions, however, all products are thought ultimately to reach a stage of decline, during which sales will decrease more or less steadily."⁹ "The sales decline may be slow, as in the case of oatmeal cereal; or rapid, as in the case of the Edsel automobile. Sales may plunge to zero, or they may petrify at a low level and continue for many years at that level."¹⁰

The sales decline may be due to any number of reasons. Buyers may simply have tired of and lost interest in the "old" product. Lost sales from "dropouts" are no longer compensated for by new buyers. Or the product may have been superseded by a superior, or at least different, alternative, causing the displacement depicted in Figure 15–2.

The onset of decline has accelerated over the years, due to increasing pressure both from domestic and foreign competitors. Attempting to examine this hypothesis of shortening life cycles in a given industry at different points in time, one study analyzed the electric appliance industry. The authors found evidence to support the hypothesis. Twelve household appliances introduced prior to World War II (1922–1942) took an average of 46.3 years to move through the introduction and growth stages. Sixteen appliances with commercial origins after World War II (1945–1964) took an average of only 26.5 years. For nine products introduced during the period from 1965 to 1979, the combined duration of the first two life cycle stages had shortened to 8.8 years.¹¹

This process of acceleration continues unabated. Due to more aggressive competition, better communication, and more affluent, free-spending consumers, new types of appliance products, from microwave ovens to videocassette recorders to compact disc players, have been moving more quickly through their life cycles. In the cosmetics industry, many products complete their entire life cycles within one year.

Ultimately, market shrinkage seems fairly inevitable in most cases. The laggards, although late to join, discover that they cannot handle the product financially and intellectually and leave the market. Innovators become bored with this "old hat" and seek new thrills. Whatever the reason, the continuous decrease in market volume is precipitated by the discontinuance decisions of an ever-increasing number of adopters. Accordingly, the pioneer and imitators are likely to leave this now more or less rapidly declining market completely, relying instead on the growth of new markets into which they had diversified earlier. As more and more sellers withdraw from the scene, the market structure gradually shifts back to that of an oligopoly.

The remaining firms will tend to engage in some streamlining. They "may reduce the number of product offerings. They may drop smaller market segments and weaker trade channels. They may cut the promotion budget and reduce their prices further."¹² Price reduction may be difficult to do from an economic point of view, however. Lot sizes will have shrunk, reducing economies of scale. Unless costs are trimmed rigorously, perhaps even through transfer of production overseas, there may be limited room to "give."

All is not necessarily bleak in a declining market, though. In fact, resourceful product managers may be able to choose from five alternative strategies:

• Building the firm's position by selective investment
• Holding the firm's investment level until the industry outlook becomes clearer

- Concentrating the firm's investment on the most lucrative niches of enduring demand
- Harvesting the firm's investment by minimizing expenditures
- Divesting the business unit promptly[13]

     The choice of marketing strategy depends on the industry's relative attractiveness and the company's competitive strength within the industry. It also depends on the cost and profit outlook and the contribution that the declining product makes to the salability of other products—otherwise known as synergism.

Measuring the Product Life Cycle

     In order for the product life cycle concept to be an operational guide in strategy selection, product managers must be able to determine their company's position on the life cycle. Sales volume alone is not a sufficient indication of the stage that a market has reached: "The implications of the difference between a temporary or even an extended pause in sales growth versus a true topping out of growth are profound."[14] The fact that the market is still growing might cause euphoria that is not justified in terms of the profit and sales outlook. To get a better handle on the situation, it is advisable to analyze simultaneously three curves: sales volume, the rate of change of sales volume, and the profit-loss curve. Taken together, these three related factors provide a fair indication of the stage of the product life cycle, particularly if trends are being examined instead of short-term fluctuations. Figure 15–4 presents a comparative analysis of these three curves, demonstrating that their combination differs for every stage.

     During the introduction stage, sales volume is growing very slowly because initial market resistance is high and hard to overcome. Also, the diffusion and acceptance of the new idea require time. The rate of growth is increasing faster than the sales volume itself because the latter is very low and every added dollar represents a higher growth percentage than at any later stage of the cycle. Because the initial outlay for product development and introductory advertising is typically quite large, this stage is normally characterized by a loss. By the end of the introduction phase, however, the company should break even, that is, the total revenue for the product should at least equal its cost. As competitors appear on the scene, the pioneer should have paid off its up-front investment.

     Booming sales are characteristic for the growth stage. The rate of growth continues to increase but reaches its peak approximately in the middle of the stage. From this point on, further increases in sales volume will produce decreasing growth rates. A sales increase from $5 million at the beginning of the growth phase to $15 million in the middle, for instance, translates into a growth rate of 200 percent. A further, even higher increase from $15 to $30 million at the end of the growth stage, however, then only means a 100 percent rate of growth. Composite industry profits reach their highest level in this stage. This is due to the fact that still only relatively few competitors are operating in this fast expanding market. They, too, begin to decline, however, as prices come under pressure while costs are still substantial.

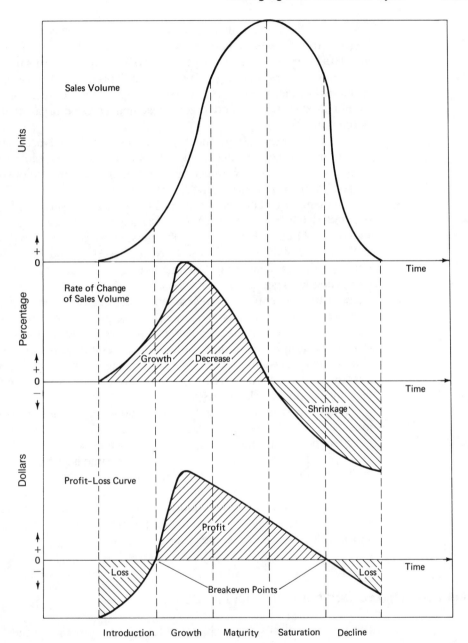

FIGURE 15–4
Determining a Product's Position on the Life Cycle

Although sales still grow considerably in the maturity stage, they are doing so at a markedly slower pace. The rate of change is decreasing rapidly. It reaches the stagnation level at the end of the stage when market volume approaches market capacity and the saturation point is attained. Even though profits are diminishing, additional competitors continue to enter the market.

As the product life cycle enters the saturation stage, all three curves show a negative trend. Sales volume begins to decrease at this point as some of the earlier adopters lose interest. The rate of change of sales volume turns negative as it mirrors the onset of sales shrinkage. There are still profits to be made, but they decline continually under the influence of rising costs and increasing competitive pressure. Eventually, they are reduced to zero, reaching a second break-even point at the end of the stage.

In the decline stage, the shrinking of sales volume is accelerated by exploding sales of more recent products. The rate of change of sales volume becomes increasingly negative. Costs may exceed revenues because of smaller lot sizes and the rising costs of labor and materials, thus creating a loss.

Temporary aberrations in a positive or negative sense will usually not change the underlying trends of these three variables, which might prove to be valuable indicators of future developments. The most important decision point clearly occurs in the middle of the growth stage. Here, the reversed tendency of the rate of change curve predicts a slowdown of the market's growth pace. Quite in contrast, rapidly expanding sales generally create considerable euphoria on the part of product managers at this moment. Nonetheless, an objective evaluation of the market outlook should lead to the decision to develop a new product to supersede eventually the most recently introduced one. The lead time required for the research and development of an innovative product and its successful launching in the marketplace makes early decisions necessary. After all, the prospective innovation has to be introduced early enough to build up sufficient volume by the time that the currently growing product market starts declining.

A synopsis of the stages of the product life cycle and its characteristics is presented in Table 15–1. In the table, the term *market structure* refers to the number of sellers present in the marketplace at any given point in time. The categories type of seller and type of buyer report the market entry or departure of the different types of players. *Elasticity of demand* denotes the responsiveness or sensitivity of demand to price changes. The listings under *technological changes* and *marketing changes* relate to the six types of new products identified in Chapter 1. The last three columns summarize the changes in the configuration of the three variables used to determine a product's position on the life cycle.

Marketing Mixes during the Product Life Cycle

The previous discussion highlighted key characteristics and measurements of the classic product life cycle stages. The marketing literature has traditionally assumed that the life cycle acts as a determinant of marketing strategy. This is not entirely correct: "A more realistic view is that life cycle analysis serves several different roles in the formulation of strategy, such as an enabling condition, a moderating variable, or a consequence of strategic decisions."[15] As an enabling condition, life cycle evolution is a driving force by creating varying threats and opportunities. As a moderating variable, it affects the outcome of marketing decisions in the form of market

TABLE 15-1
Characteristics of the Product Life Cycle

Stages	Market Structure	Type of Seller	Type of Buyer	Elasticity of Demand	Technological Changes	Marketing Changes	Sales Volume	Rate of Change of Sales Volume	Profit/Loss
Introduction	(Virtual) monopoly	Pioneer	Innovators	Inelastic	New product	Market creation	Slow growth	Increasing	Loss
Growth	Oligopoly	+ Imitators	+ Early adopters + Early majority	Elastic	Modification	Expansion	Rapid growth	Increasing/ decreasing	Very high profits
Maturity	Polypoly	+ Conservative competitors	+ Early majority + Late majority	Highly elastic	Modification Differentiation	Expansion Extension	Growth	Decreasing	Decreasing profits
Saturation	Polypoly	+ Ultraconservative competitors	+ Late majority + Laggards	Extremely elastic	Modification Differentiation Diversification	Extension	Stagnation	Negative	Decreasing profits
Decline	Oligopoly	– Pioneer – Imitators	– Laggards – Innovators	Elastic	Diversification	New market	Decrease	Negative	Loss

shares and profits. Consequently, the shape of the life cycle curve is influenced by the marketing actions of the participating firms.

Notwithstanding these complex relationships, it is of great interest and importance to product managers to identify typical, if not ideal, strategies for the different phases of the product life cycle. These strategies translate into marketing mixes that a company uses to achieve its marketing objectives during each stage. Although every company has to formulate its own unique configuration, depending on its objectives and market conditions, a typical approach can be pinpointed for each stage.

Within the framework of the marketing mix, the term *product policy* encompasses all decisions that deal with the composition of the product mix and with the features of individual products. Its responsibilities include the evolution of new products, as well as a systematic program for the phasing out of old, unprofitable, and obsolete models. It is this very balance between old and new products that constitutes one of the greatest challenges for product policy. There is a real danger of proliferation of the product mix if new products are constantly added without a corresponding reduction in the number of established products.

Product policy takes a vital interest in product design, which consists of both the interior construction and the exterior styling of a product. The key task of product design is to convert a raw idea, as modified by marketing research findings, into a technically mature, fully functioning product that delivers the desired benefits. Technical maturity is characterized by satisfactory stress performance, the freezing of the design, and the stabilization of the production process. Although this condition is an absolute prerequisite of successful introduction, it by no means precludes further development, refinement, or improvement of the product. Undoubtedly, however, a technically immature product, introduced too early because of internal or external pressures, may well seriously endanger the survival, or at least the growth potential, of a company.

Product design has two emphases, performance and styling. The product has to solve the technical problems of the purchaser. It also has to be easy to handle and service and fit the buyer's requirements with regard to capacity and price. The more advanced the stage of the life cycle, the more aesthetic considerations assume prominence. Available products are, meanwhile, so far advanced that further technological improvements can only be minor. With performance characteristics of competing products being fairly homogeneous, buyers might be influenced to select products based on attractive styling.

The second aspect of product policy besides the appropriate design and improvement of individual products consists of the formation of a powerful product mix. Even if the pioneer is initially successful with only one version of its basic product concept, buyers insist on differentiation as demand expands. Prospects want to choose among a wide range of products, differentiated according to quality, size, performance, styling, and price. In combining individual entries to form a cohesive product mix, sellers have to decide whether to make or buy part or all of the merchandise involved.

Conditions policy can be viewed as another element of the marketing mix. It, too, relates to two aspects: terms of payment and conditions of delivery, the latter including delivery periods. Another instrument is added by *service policy,* which encompasses availability and reliability of service, as well as decisions concerning the extent of warranties. *Channel policy* determines the product's market size and distribution structure. *Advertising policy* covers the entire gamut of decisions ranging from budgeting to message content, copy execution, media mix, and scheduling.

Last, but not least, in *pricing policy,* product managers have to decide whether they want to discourage potential competitors from entering the market or reap the highest possible revenues before their entry. The effectiveness of pricing decisions in the various stages of the life cycle depends on the product's distinctiveness and buyer preferences—in other words, the direct and cross-price elasticity of demand. The more sales dollars that can be won or lost through price changes, the more effective pricing policy will be. The greater the dependence on the prices of substitute products, the more restricted the pricing autonomy of the firm will be.

The Introduction Stage

It is absolutely vital that a new product be technically mature when it is launched in the marketplace. Stability of design and presentation is needed to gain the confidence of innovators, who take a considerable risk in buying the innovation. Working out the bugs during product introduction indicates premature launching and inadequate testing. Early changes irritate initial buyers and confuse potential customers about the innovation's degree of maturity, thus postponing the real takeoff.

In product policy, no changes in the product or product mix should occur during this initial period of educating the target market to the new concept. All product-related decisions have to be made before the creation of the new market starts. Product testing and test marketing enable a company to identify potential product or marketing problems and to make final changes prior to market introduction. The product mix is very small, consisting only of the innovation itself and perhaps one or two variations of its basic concept. After all, it is not the breadth of choice but the new way of need satisfaction or problem solution that attracts the innovators.

Conditions policy is relatively unimportant at this stage. Innovators are looking for the thrill of change, and the pioneer is at this point the only source of supply. Thus, the features and performance of the new product are more important for the innovators' purchase decisions than conditions of payment and delivery. Generally, innovators are affluent and thus readily able to pay cash. They may even tolerate a delay in delivery because they are eager to be among the first to try the innovation. The service network may still be in the process of being created. Most innovators will, however, accept a certain amount of service problems in return for the privilege to be among the first to use the new product.

With regard to channel policy, the introductory stage constitutes a vital phase. Will the company be successful in enlisting the cooperation and support of the chosen intermediaries? The ability of a manufacturer to secure maximum timely availability in chosen outlets and thus to establish optimum distribution can make or break the creation of a new market. Channel decisions lock a company into long-term commitments to selected intermediaries. They also determine the character and size of the market. If exclusive distribution is chosen, only a small group of high-income people can be reached. Intensive distribution, in contrast, establishes a mass market from the outset. Selective distribution represents a compromise between these extremes, combining control with broader market exposure.

Pioneers tend to choose indirect distribution involving wholesalers in creating a new market. Wholesalers have close working relationships with many retailers in their areas. They are thus able to ensure fast widespread distribution at a cost far below that of the manufacturers' own sales forces calling on individual retailers.

Diffusion and acceptance of the new product are enhanced by heavy advertising pressure, aimed at creating a new market against high initial market resistance. Its main tasks are to communicate the basic idea of the innovation and to induce prospective buyers to try it. Many promising new products fail because the pioneer does not have the financial means to back the innovation with a strong advertising program that is able to cut through the clutter and create primary demand for the new type of offering. Advertising expenditures at this stage have to be considered an investment in the future of the new product because they are usually far higher than the sales generated by them.

Because potential buyers are not in a position to develop their own ideas about price, the pioneer enjoys a great deal of freedom in setting the introductory price. Under a skimming policy, it would be set fairly high to allow for subsequent reductions. Under a penetration policy, it would be set deliberately low to discourage potential competition and appeal to larger numbers of buyers. For dramatic innovations, the approach of choice is skimming because it controls the size of the market and permits quick recovery of the up-front investment.

The Growth Stage

As sales gain momentum and the profit picture begins to look more and more attractive, imitators enter the market with carbon copies of the original product. Product policy is still relatively unimportant because there are no major differences among competitive offerings. Minor improvements have been made, though, to smooth out wrinkles in the product. The product mix continues to remain small. Only very few variations of the basic concept are being offered at this point because the original model is selling so well that there is no need for costly product differentiation. The market volume for these virtually homogeneous products grows fast. This makes a manufacturer's supply capability more important at this stage than differences in product design. Intermediaries want to ride the boom and buy wherever they can get the merchandise. The pioneer would not be able to supply this exploding volume of demand all by itself.

While conditions of payment still exert little influence on the market, delivery terms gain paramount importance. Delays in the delivery of promised goods cause customers to switch to more reliable suppliers. With competitive products being fairly homogeneous, superior service becomes a prime consideration in the sale of the innovation. If the product needs to be serviced periodically, it will not develop a substantial following unless convenient, fast, reliable expert service is available to the final buyer.

In advertising policy, the emphasis shifts from informing prospective buyers about the existence, uses, and advantages of the new product to an expansion of market volume. Even horizontal cooperation is sometimes undertaken toward this end. Because at this stage any advertising will tend to benefit the entire industry by expanding primary demand, a campaign jointly sponsored and financed by all players can provide an additional impetus. Cooperation does not prevent any company from launching its own campaign but is, instead, likely to enhance its impact. A cooperative effort is, however, only meaningful if all or at least most of the competitors contribute to the common budget.

A high-price policy in the introduction stage served to cover the initial outlay of the pioneer before prices would deteriorate due to competitive pressure. As lot sizes increase, the learning curve advances, and economies of scale come to bear, price reductions become possible. Early on in the growth stage, there is little incentive for price reductions because output sells briskly. But as technology advances and cuts costs and additional entrants begin to crowd the scene, the inevitable happens and prices start to soften.

The Maturity Stage

The competitive picture changes completely in the maturity stage. The field becomes crowded and the former peaceful coexistence of competitors now turns into aggressive marketing warfare: "To be successful today, a company must become competitor-oriented. It must look for weak points in the positions of its competitors and then launch marketing attacks against those weak points."[16] During the growth stage, the homogeneity of competing products facilitated the rapid expansion of market volume. Now competing firms utilize all means at their disposal to create differential advantages in buyers' minds by making their products appear as heterogeneous as possible. Cooperation turns to civil war. Although market volume is still growing, the expansion of an individual company's sales volume depends primarily on the attainment of a larger share of the market—at the expense of competitors. All players, therefore, try to establish brand preference and brand loyalty for their own products and to distinguish them from competing brands.

Product policy now begins to play a more significant role in a firm's marketing mix. The products are now technologically so highly developed and features of competing products are copied so quickly that competitive entries in effect differ only slightly. Design, consequently, can exert a powerful influence on market success if the designers are able to distinguish the product from its competition in the consumer's mind. Their unique styling was certainly a strong contributing factor in the success of the Taurus/Sable series of Ford. In contrast, the Chevrolet Beretta did not generate the hoped-for excitement.

Because further performance improvements are difficult to achieve at this point, product policy emphasizes product refinement. Differentiation is used to segment the market and zero in on the specific needs of particular groups in the market. With the size of their product mixes steadily expanding, companies are confronted with the decision of make or buy. It may actually be more profitable to buy part of the merchandise offered from other manufacturers, either domestic or foreign, and merely act as a reseller under private branding arrangements.

With regard to conditions policy, the market participants undertake every effort to employ it as a competitive tool to stimulate sales. Easy credit, liberalized terms of payment, and discounts are all used in an effort to win over customers with limited funds. Prompt delivery, too, becomes vital. Improvements in service, lower repair charges, and extended warranties make service policy an important weapon in winning and satisfying customers.

In channel policy, distribution structure and cost are revisited. There is a certain tendency in the maturity stage to eliminate the independent wholesaler. This move is driven primarily by two reasons: The seller wants to capture the wholesaler's profit margin and assert tighter control over the distribution system. At this point in the life cycle, the product is well enough diffused and sales volume high enough to substitute the manufacturer's own sales force, in combination with the establishment of regional warehouses and service centers.

As far as advertising is concerned, product management has to strive for *selective demand* creation. This involves generating brand preference by highlighting the comparative features and benefits of the company's brand and attempting to create a difference in buyers' minds. The purpose of brand appeal is to presell the product through advertising so that the prospect recognizes and prefers the brand even in a competitive environment.

The substantial effort notwithstanding, however, the effectiveness of advertising decreases sharply, making it increasingly more expensive to "buy" market share. This is due to the fact that demand has become less responsive to promotional stimulation because of growing brand loyalty and, as a consequence, growing secondary market resistance. As more and more brands and varieties hit the market, the consumer becomes confused and insecure, facing a bewildering array of choices. Feeling unable to judge product differences, consumers buy brands familiar through heavy advertising. They will continue to repurchase this brand, deliberately disregarding all other brands, unless they experience dissatisfaction.[17]

In order to stimulate earlier replacement purchases for durable products, advertising has to suggest psychological obsolescence. In the minds of buyers, it has to make established models obsolete by extolling the satisfaction of owning the latest version with its advanced technology.

Prices decline further to appeal to less affluent adopter categories. Because actual differences among competing products are minimal and the elasticity of demand is high, price differences among competitors gain in importance, opening up the remaining portions of market capacity. But eventually prices have to stabilize as cost pressures catch up with the sellers. Product proliferation has reduced production lot sizes and increased design, inventory, and advertising costs. If product management has been able to create brand loyalty for its products among its customers, it will enjoy a certain pricing discretion. This will enable it to adjust prices as needed—up to a point. Figure 15–5 illustrates the interdependence among sales, prices, and advertising expenditures during the early stages of the instant coffee life cycle. Prices and sales show a strong negative correlation: The higher the price, the lower the sales volume, and vice versa.

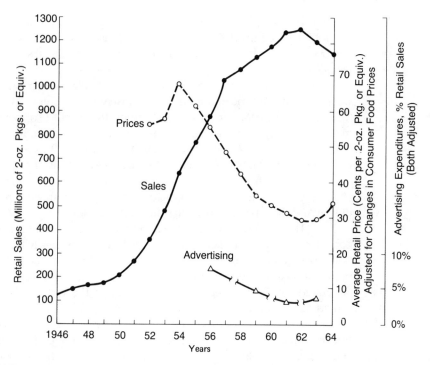

FIGURE 15–5

The Early Life Cycle of Instant Coffee (*Source:* Reprinted with permission from Robert D. Buzzell, "Competitive Behavior and Product Life Cycles," in *Proceedings of the 1966 World Congress* [Chicago: American Marketing Association, 1966], p. 55)

The Saturation Stage

During the saturation stage, the intensity of competitive warfare escalates to its highest level. Market volume is no longer growing and market capacity is virtually exhausted. Under such conditions, a company's sales volume can grow only at the expense of competitors. Efforts to win over competitors' customers accordingly become increasingly aggressive, involving every element of the marketing mix, from product design to promotional pricing.

In product policy, modification and differentiation are used in combination at least to maintain and protect a firm's position in the marketplace. The number of variations offered by each company seems to grow endlessly and in some cases dangerously approaches custom production. Although diversification activities should have been set in motion much earlier, they now have to move into high gear to ensure the firm's continued growth. It is usually not necessary or even advisable to withdraw completely from the current market. To the very contrary, at this point this business is likely to throw off a steady stream of cash that can be used to build other, more promising businesses.[18] For reasons of stability and growth, it is prudent to add other businesses at this point. Facing increasing public hostility to their original business, cigarette manufacturers have long pursued such a strategy: R. J. Reynolds has acquired Nabisco, and Philip Morris has bought General Foods. General Electric has similarly diversified aggressively into financial services by buying Kidder Peabody.

Easy credit terms and attractive payment plans become powerful competitive weapons. The American automobile industry has become a veritable battlefield of financing plans trying to outdo each other. In an effort to move cars in a stagnant market climate, American automobile manufacturers have at various times offered interest rates on car loans of 3.9, 2.9, 1.9, and even 0 percent! Prompt delivery is taken for granted under such circumstances. As to service policy, a large network and fast, reliable, competent service are absolutely essential. No major changes occur in channel policy. Efforts are undertaken, however, to gain even more intensive distribution and thus maximum availability and exposure.

The objective of advertising policy in the saturation stage is to defend the company's present market share. Its emphasis shifts slowly from product to institutional advertising. This is done to associate the firm's name in the consumer's mind with quality and need satisfaction. In this way, the transition to a new market will be facilitated by capitalizing on the goodwill of the old product in introducing or imitating a new one.

The direct price elasticity of demand reaches its highest point at this stage. Because many buyers consider competing products interchangeable, price differences offer valuable selling points. But the general trend is not toward lower prices because most opportunities for cost reduction have been exhausted. This fact notwithstanding, manufacturers' cash rebates to buyers may well become a frequent occurrence. They are a form of promotional pricing that helps move merchandise and trim inventories during specified time spans. Particularly visible in the automobile and small appliance industries, they can also be found in many consumer goods industries, including wines and liquors.

Sales have topped out, and profits are diminishing rapidly under the vise grip of competitive and cost pressures. Diversification leads many companies into new and more promising areas where demand has already been created and better growth opportunities exist.

The Decline Stage

As the market volume declines and eventually goes into a tailspin, a growing proportion of the total production capacity is being idled. This causes the participants either to close some of their plants and consolidate production or withdraw from this market altogether. Some firms weather the storm quite well, though, and remain profitable by trimming cost to the bone.

In product policy, product management categorically phases out weak products and concentrates on its best-sellers. In its channel policy, it moves from intensive to selective distribution, cutting out the smaller accounts. It also tries to economize by increasing minimum order sizes.

While easy credit plans and fast delivery remain in effect, loyal buyers continue to favor their established suppliers. Service costs have become exorbitant, however, which leads to cutbacks in warranties.

Advertising support is almost entirely withdrawn because the product line has gone into a harvesting mode. What little advertising remains is intended to serve as a reminder to retain the patronage of buyers still active in the marketplace. Continuing to do some advertising may help delay the decline and smooth the transition to a new market.

Prices have nowhere to go but up. They tend to increase because of rising costs and a decrease in price elasticity—the buyers still present in the market really want the product and are willing to pay what it takes to get it. With steadily shrinking volume, however, a seller's eventual withdrawal from this disappearing market becomes inevitable. Early diversification has taken the pain out of this abandonment decision.

Alternate Patterns

The concept of the product life cycle has been around for some time. Empirical evidence indicates that it conforms reasonably well to reality. This is particularly true for the first three stages during which most sales curves demonstrate an S-shape. There is also proof that some products ultimately reach a stage of decline. Nonetheless, many product markets are characterized by sales remaining at relatively high levels without showing any signs of impending decline.

This suggests that the classic product life cycle may have to be modified, at least in its more advanced stages, to conform more precisely to actual sales patterns. As pointed out earlier, the product life cycle is as much a consequence of a firm's strategic actions as it is their cause. The classic pattern is not inevitable, forcing a company to adjust reactively to its dictates. Rather, cycle participation can and should be managed proactively for maximum sales and profits. Astute observers of the product life cycle can see the handwriting on the wall at an early point in the game and act accordingly to manage strategically their firm's future.

As Figure 15–6 indicates, four alternative empirical patterns have been observed in the analysis of actual product markets:[19]

Decline—After reaching the *saturation point* or peak of the sales curve where market volume and market capacity are virtually identical, sales decrease first slowly then precipitously as consumers lose interest in the product and switch to more attractive substitutes.

Stability—Having attained a certain level or plateau, sales remain virtually unchanged over an extended period of time. In this setting, the market has entered a maintenance mode where sales revenues are almost exclusively derived from replacement demand and only minimally from first-time purchases. This may make market volume quite vulnerable to downswings in the economy. The reason for this phenomenon lies in the fact that most durable goods replacement purchases are

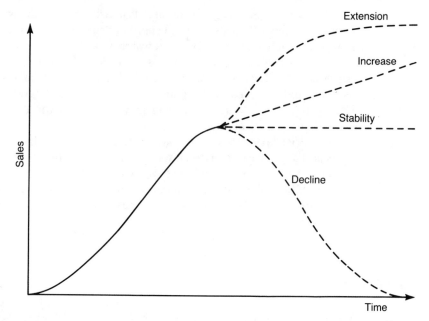

FIGURE 15–6
Alternative Cycle Patterns

postponable. If times are difficult, consumers will repair their possessions instead of replacing them with the latest models. Market volume drops as consumers postpone replacement purchases until economic conditions improve. Then pent-up demand hits the market and things return to "normal."

The U.S. passenger automobile market has long displayed signs of such an uneasy stability pattern. Over the long term, unit sales have remained fairly stable. When they are disrupted by temporary dips in demand, the industry typically tries to reinvigorate sales with incentive programs that can seriously affect the manufacturers' bottom lines.

Increase—After arriving at a first peak through relatively fast growth, sales continue to grow due to the inherent dynamics of the marketplace. In other words, the product continues to enjoy increasing popularity, it is simply a "winner." No extraordinary efforts on the part of the sellers are required. As a matter of fact, tampering with the winning formula could prove quite unhealthy. In contrast, complacency can pose a real danger. Product managers have to remain vigilant and leery of unexpected attacks when things are going so well and the product seems to sell itself. Quality has to remain superior, product design has to be kept up-to-date, and periodic promotional programs have to continue to move substantial quantities of merchandise and keep the brand name fresh in the buyer's mind.

Extension—As the life cycle of the original product flattens out, the concept receives a new lease on life from a number of strategic moves. While continuing the original product or application, product management breathes new life into sales by essentially building one product life cycle on top of the other. This can be achieved in a variety of ways, including promoting different usage patterns, introducing new product variants, or offering the product to new markets.

For each of these four alternative patterns, an empirical example is presented in Figure 15–7. Diagram (a) illustrates the situation of evaporated milk, which, during the period pictured, showed steadily, if not rapidly, declining sales. Originally developed to overcome the problem of fresh milk spoilage due to inadequate refrigeration, this product lost a great deal of its appeal when refrigerators became widespread. The resulting decline in sales could not even be stemmed by reduced prices. Although a residual market remains to this day, only a few players continue to participate.

Diagram (b) shows the postwar retail sales trend for flavored gelatins and pudding mixes. Such a pattern of stability is common across a broad spectrum of industries. It tends to produce fairly stable market shares because market share gains can only be achieved at the expense of competitors—a feat that has been becoming increasingly difficult and costly. Significantly, prices remain stable, too, in this example.

The case of a market whose volume continues to grow after a first peak is demonstrated by the sales pattern for peanut butter shown in diagram (c). Not coincidentally, the sales increase is accompanied and supported by price reductions while advertising expenditures remain stable. For the participants, this is certainly an enviable situation, but it will require effort to sustain it in the long run. Other markets following this pattern are salad dressings and cooking oils.

An example of an extension pattern is presented in diagram (d). Sales of the "regular" subcategory are virtually flat during the period depicted. The growth in total ready-to-eat cereal sales, however, was fueled exclusively by the contributions of the two more recent subcategories. These are presweetened cereals and nutritional cereals. According to the diagram, the presweetened subcategory can be said to be in its early growth stage, whereas the nutritional subcategory is still working its way through the introduction phase. And all this was achieved in spite of a steady upward adjustment in prices.

Strategic Cycle Alteration

As a mere description of empirical occurrences, the product life cycle concept is of limited use to product managers. Instead, in today's fiercely competitive climate, a company's market participation has to be managed proactively in a strategic way. Two principal strategies are available to resourceful product managers in their efforts to overcome impending decline of the sales curve: substitution and extension. Both of them require foresight and careful planning of the firm's actions.

Substitution is a process whereby an old product is replaced by an innovation in the marketplace. It involves a strategy of deliberate displacement of one life cycle by another. A new product is introduced while a recently launched product is still in its growth stage. This is done in order to enable the innovation to build up sufficient

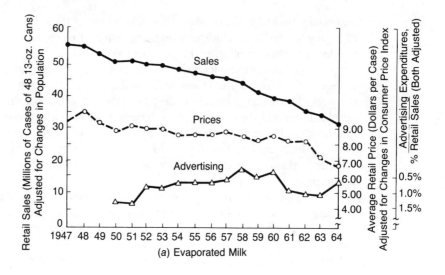

(a) Evaporated Milk

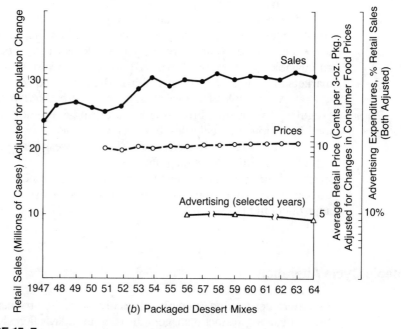

(b) Packaged Dessert Mixes

FIGURE 15–7
Empirical Product Life Cycle Patterns (*Source:* Reprinted with permission from
Robert D. Buzzell, "Competitive Behavior and Product Life Cycles," in *Proceed-*
ings of the 1966 World Congress [Chicago: American Marketing Association,
1966], p. 58)

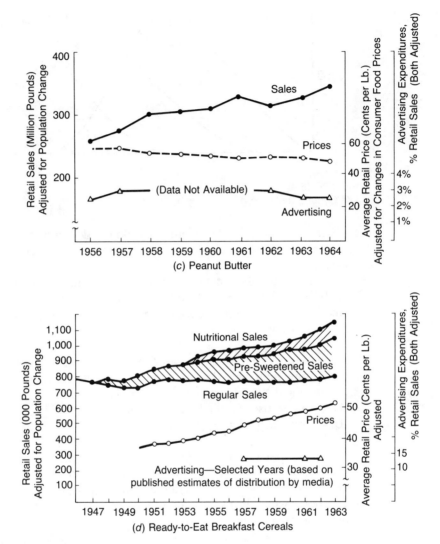

FIGURE 15–7
continued

volume before sales of the established product begin to shrink. At this point, it is essential to excite prospective buyers with an even more advanced and attractive replacement product. This approach overcomes the often slow pace of true technological obsolescence by promoting psychological obsolescence.

With a substitution strategy, sales and profits remain at relatively high levels because old products are withdrawn from the market as soon as new products have picked up enough sales. This pattern is illustrated in Figure 15–8. It requires a substantial ongoing development effort because it takes time to evolve new products properly, and their batting average is not too good. Nonetheless, two industries in particular have espoused this philosophy, the fashion and automobile industries.

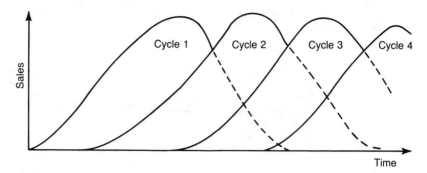

FIGURE 15–8
Life Cycle Substitution

Both are faced with the fact that their products do not wear out fast enough. They make up for this fact by changing styling and/or performance characteristics at least once a year.

As Figure 15–9 demonstrates, *extension* differs significantly from this approach in that it represents the cumulative building of one product life cycle on top of another rather than one replacing the other. This strategy can be implemented in a number of ways:

1. Promoting more frequent usage of the product among its current users
2. Suggesting more varied usage of the product among current users
3. Promoting the product to new user groups
4. Finding new uses for the basic material[20]
5. Developing and offering new product forms

The first two approaches are forms of market expansion. They appeal to current users of the product and suggest to use it more often and/or in more different ways. Because these buyers are already in a using mode, they may welcome such suggestions, which in the case of a food product would probably be presented as mouth-watering recipes.

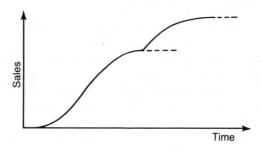

FIGURE 15–9
Life Cycle Extension

Approaches 3 and 4 reach out to new constituencies by addressing new target markets and/or proposing new applications for the technology or material involved. Approach 3 most frequently involves selling the product abroad.[21] Approach 4 can be readily demonstrated by the sales history of nylon, as depicted in Figure 15–10. The dotted lines show the shape that the product life cycle would have taken at any given point in time were it not for the introduction of a new application for this material. Thus, the solid line represents actual sales.

Approach 5 can be exemplified by the marketing of color television sets at a time when black and white sets continue to be available. Creative marketing means discovering and satisfying new needs and wants at a fairly steady clip.

Careful analysis of market conditions and opportunities in accordance with a product's life cycle will help sustain a company's growth. A deeper understanding of the stages of a product's life cycle thus completes the train of thought that started with the internal evolution of a new product and included its diffusion and acceptance by consumers. How this curve ultimately looks and how it affects the company is a reflection of product management's abilities and efforts.

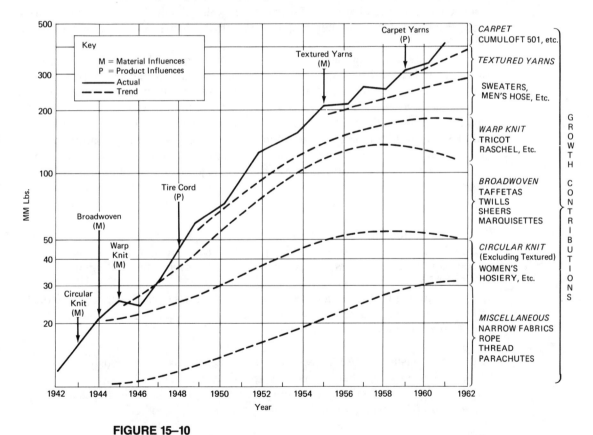

FIGURE 15–10
The Life Cycle of Nylon (*Source:* Reprinted with permission from Jordan P. Yale, "The Strategy of Nylon's Growth: Create New Markets," *Modern Textiles* [Feb. 1964], p. 33. © 1962 by Jordan P. Yale)

SUMMARY

The product life cycle is a model describing the changes in sales volume that a product undergoes during its market life. Sales generally get off to a slow start, explode in a boom, return to a slower pace of growth, and eventually reach a level of virtual stagnation from where they decrease first moderately and then precipitously. This outline of stages can be referred to as the classic product life cycle. Although this model needs some empirical modification, it helps to understand and guide processes and actions throughout a product's market life.

When a radical innovation is introduced by a pioneering company, it usually meets with high market resistance and low demand elasticity. Mostly, indirect channels of distribution are chosen for cost and time reasons. Advertising has to start from scratch in creating primary demand for the new concept. The introductory price is often quite high, only to be lowered substantially under the onslaught of competition from imitators that enter the market in the growth stage. As the early adopters and early majority follow the venturesome innovators, sales expand rapidly and demand elasticity increases. Products are modified only slightly and competitors may even join forces in horizontal cooperative advertising to expand primary demand.

In the maturity stage, demand elasticity increases sharply with the appearance of the late majority as buyers. Thus, prices decline further, accompanied by a marked increase in the size of the product mix. Advertising becomes very competitive and aims to direct demand selectively toward the firm's own brands. Because the market is now well established, some manufacturers will eliminate independent wholesalers and replace them with their own sales organizations. As saturation sets in, the number of competitors and products peaks. Prices bottom out, even though elasticity is still on the rise. The appearance of laggards does not expand sales any more. Decline, finally, means that sellers and buyers are leaving this shrinking market in droves, returning elasticity to virtually zero. More recent products have displaced this now outdated offering.

A combination of three curves is helpful in identifying a product's position on the life cycle—sales volume, profit and loss, and the rate of change of sales volume. Their combination differs for every stage of the cycle, thus aiding in strategy formulation.

Although most product markets follow the classic pattern up to a first peak, there are four alternative ways in which sales volume may develop from this point on. These alternatives look as follows:

Decline—Consumers lose interest and the market shrinks continuously.
Stability—Sales level off and show no signs of lasting decline.
Increase—The product's sales volume continues to grow due to its popularity.
Extension—The company builds one life cycle on top of another.

Each of these alternate patterns is supported by actual case histories.

In its effort to manage proactively a product's life cycle, two principal avenues are available to product management: substitution and extension. Substitution means that a new product deliberately supersedes and replaces an old one. This requires considerable foresight and planning. The development and introduction of a new product have to be initiated before a recently introduced product has had an opportunity to show its full potential in the marketplace. New models in the automobile industry, for example, have to be designed and planned years in advance.

Extension, on the other hand, means the revitalization rather than retirement of a product whose sales have stabilized. More varied or frequent usage, new users or uses, and new product forms help to achieve this objective of continued growth based on a common technology.

NOTES

1. See Nariman K. Dhalla and Sonia Yuspeh, "Forget the Product Life Cycle Concept!" *Harvard Business Review* (Jan.–Feb. 1976): 103–104.
2. See ibid., 103.
3. Robert D. Buzzell, "Competitive Behavior and Product Life Cycles," in *Proceedings of the 1966 World Congress* (Chicago: American Marketing Association, 1966), 50–51.
4. See Al Ries and Jack Trout, *Marketing Warfare* (New York: McGraw-Hill, 1986), 33.
5. See Clare Ansberry, "Simple Cameras Enjoy Rebound in Popularity," *Wall Street Journal,* 4 March 1988.
6. Buzzell, "Competitive Behavior," 51.
7. Lawrence Ingrassia, "Negative Images: Polaroid Faces Tough Sell with Its New Instant while Kodak Confronts Doubts about Its 35-mm," *Wall Street Journal,* 25 March 1986.
8. Ibid.
9. Buzzell, "Competitive Behavior," 51.
10. Philip Kotler, *Marketing Management,* 6th ed. (Englewood Cliffs, NJ: Prentice-Hall, 1988), 362.
11. See William Qualls, Richard W. Olshavsky, and Ronald E. Michaels, "Shortening of the PLC—An Empirical Test," *Journal of Marketing* (Fall 1981): 77.
12. Kotler, *Marketing Management,* 362.
13. See Kathryn Rudie Harrigan, "Strategies for Declining Industries," *Journal of Business Strategy* (Fall 1980): 27.
14. George S. Day, "The Product Life Cycle: Analysis and Applications Issues," *Journal of Marketing* (Fall 1981): 64.

15. Ibid., 65.

16. Ries and Trout, *Marketing Warfare,* 4–5.

17. Assael refers to this phenomenon as "inertia." See Henry Assael, *Consumer Behavior and Marketing Action,* 3rd ed. (Boston: Kent Publishing Co., 1987), 87, 96.

18. The Boston Consulting Group refers to such mature businesses as "cash cows" and emphasizes their vital importance as internal sources of investable funds. See Kotler, *Marketing Management,* 41–42.

19. See Buzzell, Competitive Behavior," 53, 61–64.

20. See Theodore Levitt, "Exploit the Product Life Cycle," *Harvard Business Review* (Nov.–Dec. 1965): 89. Figure 15–9 is similar to exhibit IV in this article but presents the extension strategy concept generically.

21. See Douglas R. Sease, "Selling Abroad: U.S. Exporters Begin to Post Sizable Gains in a Variety of Lines," *Wall Street Journal,* 31 Aug. 1987.

CASE STUDY

FOCUSING ON THE FUTURE

Approximately 80 percent of Eastman Kodak's 1986 revenues of $11.5 billion were derived from the sales of photography equipment, supplies, and services. Although Kodak remained the world's leading photography firm, well ahead of Japan's Fuji, the number two company, Fuji's 1986 sales per employee were $370,000, or nearly four times the figure achieved by Kodak. Kodak also lagged behind Fuji in the use of vibrant but unrealistic film colors that are preferred by camera users. In many ways, therefore, Fuji's product planning strategy was showing the way for Kodak.

Many analysts believed that in spite of Kodak's leading position in the photography market, the firm had significant problems relating to its product planning practices. These difficulties led to Kodak's trailing competitors in such important photographic submarkets as 35mm cameras, instant photography, minilabs, and home video.

Sluggish Giant

After failing to generate meaningful sales for its 35mm cameras, Kodak decided to drop out of this market segment in 1970. Aggressive competitors, such as Canon, Minolta, Olympus, Pentax, and Nikon, quickly took up the lead. These firms revolutionized the industry by introducing easy-to-use, inexpensive, high-quality 35mm cameras. Their attractive product offerings converted many consumers who had previously been using Kodak's

---

This case was contributed by Barry Berman and Joel R. Evans, Professors of Marketing, Hofstra University, Hempstead, New York. The information in this case is drawn from Alex Beam and William B. Glaberson, "Polaroid versus Kodak: The Decisive Round," *Business Week,* 13 Jan. 1986, 37; Leslie Helm, "Why Kodak Is Starting to Click Again," *Business Week,* 23 Feb. 1987, 134–135ff.; Stephen Kindell and Margaret Price, "Storming Mount Fuji," *Financial World,* 22 Sept. 1987, 26–28ff.; *Eastman Kodak Annual Report 1986;* Tom Marinelli and Homer Starr, "Eastman Kodak Builds a Business in 'Life Sciences,' " *Chemical Week,* 16 April 1986, 29–31; Stephen Phillips, "Fiercer Fight to Sell Batteries," *New York Times,* 24 Jan. 1987, 134–135ff.; and Emily T. Smith, "Picture This: Kodak Wants to Be a Biotech Giant, Too," *Business Week,* 26 May 1986, 88ff.

Instamatic cameras. Kodak did not reenter the 35mm camera market until 1985, when it began selling cameras produced by Chinon Industries under the Kodak brand name.

Kodak's fifteen-year absence from this market segment resulted in considerable lost sales, as well as loss of stature and momentum in the photographic equipment market. The company lacked products for increasingly sophisticated and demanding buyers who desired better pictures than those taken by Instamatics. Consequently, it suffered from an excessive reliance on mature photography lines. Kodak's current strategy of selling cameras made by Chinon leaves it vulnerable to currency fluctuations, potential trade restrictions, and the possibility of Chinon terminating its relationship with Kodak after expanding its market share.

In the instant photography field, Kodak did not introduce its first camera until 1976, decades after Polaroid had become solidly entrenched in this market segment. By 1985, Kodak accounted for 20 to 25 percent of the $1 billion instant photography market. From 1976 to 1985, it had sold 16.5 million instant cameras. Nonetheless, Kodak's instant photography business was only marginally profitable.

Then, in 1985, Polaroid Corporation won a lawsuit charging Eastman Kodak with infringing on its instant photography patents. As a result, Kodak was barred from producing, distributing, or selling instant cameras and instant film as of January 9, 1986. Kodak's losses due to its being forced to abandon this business included payments of $50 each to Kodak instant camera owners who could no longer purchase film for these cameras and an operations write-off of about $200 million. It is also threatened by a treble damage legal suit that is still pending, with Polaroid reportedly asking for $1 billion in damages.

Kodak was also late in entering the "60-minute" minilab film processing business. Although Kodak has been selling chemicals and paper to independent instant film labs, these firms have been competing against Kodak in the film processing market. Minilabs now control between 12 and 17 percent of the photo finishing business. Only recently has Kodak begun to market its own minilab system units to retailers and others. One model can process and print seventy-five rolls of film per hour. However, this system was not introduced until many important retailers had already purchased competing units.

In the video camera and recorder market, Kodak was once again a late entrant. Yet video products have the potential to replace such traditional Kodak lines as Super 8 movie cameras, slide projectors, and movie projectors. Kodak's attempt to market an 8mm video camera/recorder made by Matsushita was unsuccessful.

A New Kodak Emerges

Recently, however, the company has been showing signs of renewed vigor and aggressiveness. Kodak's management realizes the importance of efficiency and the need for progressive product planning. Kodak's former employment policy of lifetime employment had earned it the nickname "Great Yellow Father." Today, though, this name no longer applies. In 1987, employment was pared to 121,500 persons, nearly 25,000 less than in 1984. Management also recognizes the importance of the company's foreign operations, which currently account for 40 percent of sales.

Kodak knows that it has to broaden its base beyond photography because this market has been growing at a pace of only 5 percent per year. With a commanding 80 percent market share, the firm has little room to expand in this area. Reaching out into new fields, Kodak has been adding new categories to its portfolio, such as consumer batteries, computer floppy disks, and life sciences products. Exhibit 15–A presents selected financial data for Kodak's established businesses that prompted the company to seek additional avenues for growth.

Kodak entered the consumer battery business in July 1986, using technology developed for the lithium battery powering its disk camera. The battery market is expected to grow about 10 percent per year over the next decade, about twice the rate of photographic products.

EXHIBIT 15–A
Eastman Kodak Company,
Selected Financial Data 1984–1986
($ Million)
Imaging segment[1]

	1986	1985	1984
Sales	9,408	8,531	8,308
Operating earnings	497	378	1,266
Assets	10,309	9,387	7,926
Capital expenditures	1,124	1,244	818

Chemicals segment[2]

	1986	1985	1984
Sales	2,378	2,348	2,464
Operating earnings	227	183	281
Assets	2,266	2,136	2,056
Capital expenditures	314	251	152

[1]The imaging segment includes film, paper, magnetic media, and equipment for photographic imaging and information.
[2]The chemicals segment include fibers, plastics, industrial, and other chemicals.
Source: Eastman Kodak Company Annual Report 1986, p. 45.

The company believes that it has a number of advantages in the battery market: It claims that its alkaline batteries are the longest lasting (each major manufacturer makes a similar claim); its lithium batteries have a shelf life of ten years (versus three years for alkaline batteries); and it estimates that 90 percent of all batteries sold in the United States are distributed through the 200,000 outlets that market other Kodak products.

To differentiate its batteries from competing brands, Kodak uses gold-plated contact tips. While gold is a better conductor for electricity and has more favorable corrosion resistance than other metals, it is used primarily because of its symbolic value in signifying higher quality. In 1986, Kodak achieved a battery market share of 5 percent as compared to 45 percent each for Ralston-Purina's Eveready brand and Kraft's Duracell brand.

Other New Avenues

In 1985, Kodak purchased Verbatim Corporation, a firm that controlled about one-fifth of the floppy disk market in the United States. In 1987, Verbatim had an 18 percent market share and was the fourth largest floppy disk manufacturer, behind Xidex, Maxell, and 3M. Although the current market is highly competitive and mature, Verbatim has been attempting to differentiate its products through significant research and development. For example, a new Teflon-coated floppy disk marketed by Verbatim can protect computer data from being damaged by stains, fingerprints, and even correction ink. Stains can be wiped off the disk with a soft cloth without any loss of data. Preliminary research among 1,235 floppy disk users found that 70 percent said they need disks that are protected from spills and fingerprints.

Kodak has also become involved in the production and marketing of life sciences products, largely through joint ventures with biotechnology companies. The company's Life Sciences Group deals with all areas of human and animal health care (both diagnostic and therapeutic), innovative ways of delivering chemical products to patients, and products for nutrition and agriculture. Among the specific products currently being tested are antiviral drugs, substances that retard aging, and enzymes. These products are an outgrowth of Kodak's expertise in producing and marketing high-quality organic chemicals for more than seventy years. The Life Sciences Group plans to develop lower-cost biological alternatives to making chemicals that are currently being produced synthetically.

Although one forecast states that the Life Sciences Group can grow from $0 sales in 1984 to $1 billion per year by the early 1990s, some analysts are skeptical of Kodak's projections. Among the anticipated problems are high product development and testing costs (they could exceed $100 million per drug product), a ten-year commercialization period from laboratory to market, and a poor market presence (except for a blood analyzer).

Discussion Questions

1. Analyze the data in Exhibit 15–A from the perspective of the product life cycle concept. What strategic direction would you suggest to Kodak's management under these circumstances?
2. Evaluate Kodak's past and present product strategies. What product life cycle strategies are evident in the company's new ventures?
3. Discuss the implications of Kodak's use of Chinon to produce its cameras and of Matsushita to manufacture its batteries.
4. What do you think of Kodak's use of joint ventures with biotech companies in its Life Sciences Group?

CHAPTER 16

New Product Management in Service Firms

The principles for the development and introduction of new tangible goods are equally applicable to service innovations. Even the models used to describe new product processes apply to both types of products.[1] Service firms are just as dependent on a steady stream of new products for their survival and growth as are goods manufacturers. The following quote highlights the importance of an innovative orientation in service industries:

> Service firms must compete in rapidly changing environments with increasing pressures from both well-recognized and nontraditional competitors. Innovations are going to be the principal means for competing, especially for those firms confronted with deregulation. These competitive pressures are impacting the service firm both internally which requires extensive organizational structure changes and externally which focuses new attention on the importance of marketing. Meeting competitive pressures through innovation holds the potential for achieving organizational goals for growth and profitability via new services. Innovation is also instrumental in image development which is extremely important for firms marketing intangibles. Finally, it can provide for a better utilization of physical resources and personnel.[2]

Services differ from goods in several significant ways that pose unique challenges to marketers. These characteristics include intangibility, perishability, simultaneity, inseparability, and heterogeneity. They have important consequences and have to be managed very carefully in the new service development process. Service firms also face an unusual range of competition that encompasses not only other service providers but also buyers' options of self-service or of acquiring a good instead.

The new product typology presented in Chapter 1 is also applicable in the service sector. In contrast to goods manufacturers, however, service firms have a special opportunity to leverage existing customer relationships through the introduction of new services. To make innovation succeed in a service business, care has to be taken to create the proper climate. Formal new product organization in service businesses is, however, still largely in its infancy.

"Most of the factors initiating a need for new goods also apply to services."[3] They include sales, market share and profit growth, product life cycle stagnation or deterioration, technological innovations, and buyer behavior changes, as well as competitive pressure. In addition, there are some forces that are unique to service industries: the desire to utilize facilities, cement relationships, or leverage relationships. A service firm may also have to adapt to deregulation and changes in the service firm life cycle. New opportunities and pressures can also emerge from the growth of franchising.

New product processes in service firms follow essentially the same evolutionary pattern as that outlined in earlier chapters of this book. This reflects the universal applicability of the described model. Unique added steps are process and system design and testing, as well as personnel training. The chapter concludes with a set of guidelines for successful service innovation.

The Nature of Services

As discussed in Chapter 1, *products* are combinations of tangible and intangible benefits that provide satisfaction of buyer needs or wants. Products can be subdivided into goods and services. *Services* differ from goods by being largely intangible in nature. A service can be defined as an activity performed for another person or firm.[4] "Although the performance of most services is supported by tangibles—for instance, the automobile in the case of a taxi service—the essence of what is being bought is a performance rendered by one party for another."[5] It is commonly accepted today that a meal in a fast food restaurant is a borderline case, containing both tangible and intangible elements in equal proportions. In contrast, a meal at a fancy restaurant is considered a service, whereas groceries bought in a self-service supermarket are goods.[6]

Tangibles, in fact, play a role in service production and consumption in two ways: as support goods and as facilitating goods.[7] *Support goods* are used by the service performer in producing the service. They include the aircraft flown by a pilot, the scalpel employed by a surgeon, and the tools used by a mechanic. *Facilitating goods,* on the other hand, are tangible items used by service buyers in consuming a service. They are either consumed in the process or remain in the buyer's possession. Examples include a patient's in-hospital meal, a saver's passbook, and a student's diploma.

Figure 16–1 applies the three-layer concept of a product specifically to a service context. As explained before, the core benefit is the motive that compels a buyer to action in a particular market. It may be the need to establish a banking relationship, to obtain medical advice, or to travel from one point to another. Although the core benefit explains why an individual buyer is in the market for a given type of service, it does not begin to explain the choice of provider. This choice is governed by consideration of the surrounding tangible and intangible benefit bundles.

Tangible benefits relate to the particular kinds of support and facilitating goods used in the delivery of the service. In Figure 16–1, the support goods are subdivided into three categories: facilities, equipment, and uniforms. They all play a role in shaping customers' perceptions and may even influence the actual performance level. And any or all of the four tangible elements could make a difference to a prospective buyer.

Of great importance in the total benefit package comprising a service are the intangible benefits. They include the firm's reputation and the professionalism of

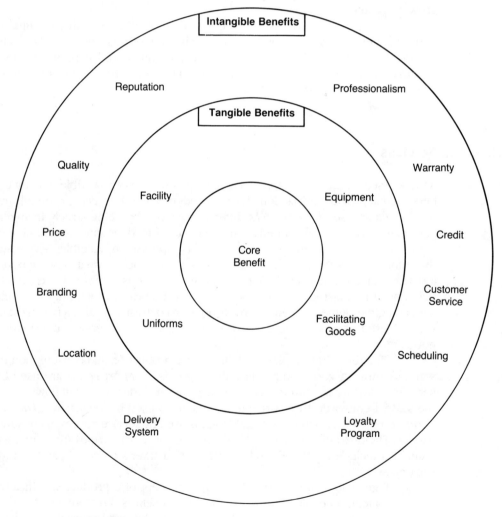

FIGURE 16–1
The Three-Layer Service Concept

its employees, the quality of the service performance, and any warranty offered for it. Intangible benefits also encompass price and credit considerations, service branding, and the level of customer service, and they cover location, as well as scheduling, and the delivery system, as well as any loyalty program.

The reputation or image of a service provider is of utmost importance because it shapes the way people respond to a service firm. Its reputation for budget tourism certainly stood in the way of People Express when it wanted to attract business travelers. In service businesses, the performers are very much part of the product. A sloppily dressed or discourteous employee will not be respected as a professional and may actually drive buyers away. And incompetence is plainly unforgivable.

In a service firm, quality means meeting or exceeding customer expectations and thus creating customer satisfaction.[8] Quality assurance and quality control are just as important as in manufacturing industries.[9] And service warranties can make quite a difference: Respectable car dealers warrant their repair work, Lufthansa guarantees on-time performance (with certain limitations), and Holiday Inns guarantees satisfaction.

Pricing has become considerably more flexible in service industries in recent years. In some industries, periodic price wars have broken out. Perhaps most notorious are the airlines with their perennial fights for market share. Major airlines need vast computer systems to keep track of up to 100,000 different fares that change frequently. Even the staid profession of accounting shows vigorous bidding for audit jobs.

Credit is used somewhat more sparingly as a competitive weapon in service industries. As a whole, major retailers have not fared very well with their own proprietary credit card programs. And house accounts at various other service establishments, such as gambling casinos and restaurants, tend to be restricted to key patrons ("high rollers" in the parlance of the trade) and are not widely promoted.

The power of branding in service businesses has been demonstrated convincingly by numerous chain operations, from Hyatt to McDonald's. Although it is difficult, if not impossible, to obtain a patent on a service concept, brand names can be registered and protected as service marks. Customer service is the function in a business that responds to customer requests, from inquiries to complaints. Its job is to create and maintain customer satisfaction. Because real growth opportunities for most service firms lie in successfully managing relationships with their existing customer bases, customer service offers an intriguing avenue to build business.[10]

Location is considerably more important in a service business than in manufacturing. As a matter of fact, in retailing, the saying goes that the three most important factors are "location, location, and location." Depending on the kind of service offered, a service establishment will be able to draw business only from a limited trading area and will benefit from heavy traffic exposure. This is why fast food outlets are located on main thoroughfares rather than side streets. Similar convenience considerations apply to scheduling or hours of operation. Businesspeople look for frequent flights, and bank depositors for evening and weekend hours. Interest rates are considerably less important than easy accessibility.

The delivery system is the way in which a service is produced and presented. It differs significantly from a roadside Holiday Inn to an inner city Hyatt Regency. The delivery process may even involve electronic means. Many bank customers can choose automated teller machines or even computer-to-computer in-home banking. And loyalty programs are aimed at relationship building by rewarding continued patronage. Frequent flier and frequent guest programs are among the most common of these.[11] They have become so popular, in fact, that several airlines have placed restrictions on eligibility.

Unique Characteristics of Services

Perhaps the most prominent and obvious aspect of services is that they are largely *intangible*. Although they contain tangible elements, services essentially cannot be seen, smelled, touched, held, sensed, or tasted. Because they are basically actions or experiences rather than things, they go out of existence the very moment that they are rendered. The buyer is often left with empty hands and nothing to show for the purchase. Patients consulting a physician, for instance, do not want to be told that there is nothing wrong with them—at a cost of $50 for an office visit. So doctors typically prescribe a drug or regimen to provide the feeling that something is being done for them.

Because of their lack of substance, services cannot be owned and resold. Accordingly, they cannot be distributed through intermediaries. Agents can be employed, however, because they sell only the right to the performance of a service. Travel and insurance agents act in this capacity. And, of course, franchising is widespread in service industries. In this instance, however, the services are produced locally.

Lack of tangibility presents a few other challenges, too. Services that are unsatisfactory cannot be returned. A haircut, for example, that displeases a consumer cannot be undone. Conversely, services cannot be repossessed. A surgeon who is unable to collect on a bill cannot reverse a surgical procedure. Because they are largely intangible, services are difficult to describe, demonstrate, illustrate, promote, differentiate, test, and evaluate. Property insurance provides an example. Viewing it as a necessary evil and unable to understand and distinguish between competitive offerings, consumers tend to choose the lowest-priced coverage they can get.

To overcome the problems associated with intangibility, service marketers should carefully manage the tangible aspects of the service. Where appropriate, tangible elements should be added to reduce the frustration of empty-handedness. Attendee satisfaction at a seminar is likely to increase significantly if the facility is first class, a variety of audiovisual aids are used, and a well-designed workbook helps comprehension, note taking, and continued utilization of the material presented. Celebrities can be used in advertising to assist in developing a distinct corporate identity or image in the buyer's mind. Branding can also be quite helpful in this respect.

An issue closely related to intangibility is *perishability* of services. Because they go out of existence at the very moment that they are created, services cannot be produced in anticipation of demand and stored for ready availability. Rather, they have to be produced on demand, when demand occurs and to the extent that it occurs. This poses considerable problems of capacity and demand management because capacity has to be in place and available to respond when demand occurs. And demand tends to fluctuate heavily throughout the course of a day or year for a variety of service categories. Telephone companies, for instance, experience peak demand during business hours and lagging utilization rates at other times. Utilities face the greatest strains on their systems during hot summer days when air conditioners consume enormous amount of energy. At night and during winter months, electricity supply goes begging.

Compared to goods manufacturers, service marketers thus are at a disadvantage in that they cannot employ the important buffer function of inventories. They may try to cope with these fluctuations by attempting to alter capacity or demand in creative ways. Part-time employees or the sharing of capacity can modify the supply side, and time-of-day pricing can provide a powerful incentive to alter demand patterns. Telephone companies routinely charge less for phone calls made during off-peak hours. Airlines offer a bewildering array of fares to attract business to periods with low load factors.

A third unique characteristic of services is *simultaneity.* This term refers to the fact that services are produced and consumed at the same time. Goods are first produced, then stored, then sold, and later consumed. Services, in contrast, are first sold, then produced and consumed simultaneously. This typically means that the service performer and the customer have to interact and be in the same place at the same time. In other words, the customer is present in the "factory" and actively participates in the production process, significantly affecting its outcome. This fact can make it difficult to control and maintain the integrity of the service production process.

Three arrangements are possible to satisfy the simultaneity requirements:

1. Customer travels to service facility. This is by far the most frequent arrangement. A service facility is centrally located, and service performers deliver the service on the firm's own premises. This is the way in which universities have been delivering education for centuries. Fast food establishments operate in the same way. The major drawback is that a single location will attract patronage only from a very limited area. This suggests opening multiple locations.
2. Performer travels to customer. In this case, the service performer delivers the service on the customer's premises, an arrangement that is more convenient for the buyer. Whereas doctors make few house calls nowadays, certain other professionals do, such as consultants, trainers, and accountants. Increasingly, too, tires and windshields are installed in consumers' driveways by trained crews. And, of course, repair services are usually carried out in this manner.
3. Performer and customer travel together. This rather infrequent arrangement is applicable and appropriate in a limited number of circumstances. This author has

taught graduate classes on the train while the students were traveling to work. Paramedics administer first aid to accident victims in transit to the hospital. Flight attendants serve meals in flight.

Another unique feature of services is that often they cannot be separated from their performers. This phenomenon is referred to as *inseparability.* Customers may even form personal bonds and preferences. Some performers develop a personal following of loyal patrons who will go with them when they change employers or start their own businesses. Such loyalty can be observed in beauty salons where stylists cultivate their own groups of customers. It is also true in the advertising business where recognized talent is followed by account transfers.

The final distinguishing characteristic is *heterogeneity.* This expression describes the fact that a service firm's output varies from location to location, from employee to employee, and even for the same employee from one performance to the next. This variability makes services difficult to standardize. Two professors teaching the same course with the same textbook are likely to teach it quite differently because they bring different backgrounds and perspectives to the task. Under these circumstances, quality control represents a challenge.

To exert some homogenizing influence, thorough education and careful training of service performers are crucial. It is no accident that McDonald's runs extensive training programs at its "Hamburger University." To evaluate performance quality, many service businesses employ "mystery shoppers" who pose as customers and later report on their experiences.

Heterogeneity may, however, be deliberate and strategic, such as in the case of market segmentation where different service levels may be provided for different customer groups. Many hotel chains, for instance, have elite clubs whose members are whisked to their suites by separate elevators and served by concierges as opposed to tourists who are served by the basic hotel staff.

Types of New Services

The new product typology presented in Chapter 1 is equally applicable to goods and services. New services can be brought about by technological changes or marketing changes. A whole new range of services has, for instance, been made possible by the arrival of electronic delivery systems—electronic banking, information, data transmission, diagnostic services. Marketing changes, on the other hand, can alter the presentation of existing service products. Psychotherapists, for instance, are only now beginning to accept the importance of promotion.[12] Once they begin to advertise, their professional services may be seen in a new light or be considered by new customer groups.

Table 16–1 synopotically compares three different schemes for the classification of new services. The most frequent case is *modification,* which involves a change in an existing service. It is designed to update or upgrade the total service package, improving performance and/or appearance. An example of modification is

TABLE 16–1
Types of New Services

Scheuing	Lovelock	Berry
Modification	Style changes Product improvements	Modification of existing services
Differentiation	Product line extensions	Additions to existing service lines
Diversification	New products for currently served market Start-up businesses	New service lines
Market creation	Major innovations	Major innovations
Market expansion		
Market extension		

Source: The first column of this table reflects the classification scheme developed in Chapter 1 of this book. The second column refers to Christopher H. Lovelock, "Developing and Implementing New Services," in *Developing New Services* (Chicago: American Marketing Association, 1984), p. 45, which is, in turn, based on Donald F. Heany, "Degrees of Product Innovation," *Journal of Business Strategy* (Spring 1983): 3–14. The final column reports the breakdown presented by James H. Donnelly, Jr., Leonard L. Berry, and Thomas W. Thompson, *Marketing Financial Services* (Homewood, IL: Dow Jones-Irwin, 1985), pp. 136–137.

the switch from fixed-rate mortgages to adjustable-rate mortgages, or ARMs. This new product proved so popular that in July 1987 it represented 50 percent of all new mortgages written.[13] Another kind of modification could be called a style change. It occurs when a facility's design and decor are altered[14] or when employees are clad in new uniforms.

Another new service type is *differentiation,* otherwise known as line extension. Here, the firm begins to offer more variety in its service mix, usually to appeal to different market segments. Introducing new menu items into the offering of a fast food chain—like McDonald's premixed salads or Burger King's bagel sandwich—falls into this category. Similarly, gold cards issued by member banks of MasterCard or Visa appeal to a more affluent clientele than the standard cards. American Express went one step further with its exclusive platinum card, which elicited an unexpectedly strong response.

Diversification means entering areas of business new to the company. This may involve leveraging the customer relationship to offer different types of services, or a firm may package and deliver available services in innovative ways. Perhaps the firm may find a new way to utilize existing facilities, or it may want to attract a different kind of customer. The following examples show how multifaceted service diversification can be.

Credit card issuers have long promoted insurance, credit card protection, travel clubs, and merchandise catalogs to their customer bases. Charge card issuer American Express is offering its new Optima credit card only to current cardholders. Merrill Lynch's Cash Management Account, introduced in 1977, proved extremely popular: "Never before had a Wall Street firm sought to tie a standard, marginable brokerage account to a money market fund and then grant customers access to that account via either a Visa debit card or traditional checks."[15] It quickly spawned a rash of imitators. In the early 1980s, the major hamburger chains discovered that their facilities were underutilized in the morning and successfully introduced breakfast items. Trying to appeal to the suburban type of business traveler, Marriott developed in painstaking research a new hospitality concept and is now building a chain of Courtyard motels across the United States.

As far as marketing changes are concerned, *market creation* is the most dramatic and thus a rather rare occurrence. It involves building the market for a new type of service from scratch—exactly what the pioneer does in the introduction stage of the product life cycle. This type of innovation also requires a significant change in buyer behavior, which might meet with strong initial resistance. An example is home equity loans. Essentially second mortgages on residences, these products lingered for a long time until aggressive marketing and a boost from tax reform gave them newfound appeal. Freestanding emergency care centers are another case in point. Offering quicker, less expensive medical attention than traditional hospital emergency rooms, they have nevertheless, on the whole, failed to create a response that would lend strong support to this new type of health care delivery system.

Market expansion occurs when a service firm intensifies its efforts to sell more existing services to its current customer base. This may mean running special promotions. Key Bank of southeastern New York, for instance, offered to take 1 percent off the current rate on any fixed-rate consumer loan—for a limited time only. In the packaged goods trade, this is known as a cents-off campaign. Another powerful way to achieve market expansion is to use *cross-selling*. This particular form of personal selling effort, which represents a special type of opportunity in service businesses, involves leveraging existing customer relationships by promoting other services within the firm's mix.[16] A telephone company customer who subscribes to the basic service package may also be interested in a discount calling plan. And car rental companies derive considerable profits from the sale of various types of insurance coverage that well-trained clerks will never fail to mention.

Last, but not least, *market extension* means offering existing services to new markets. This could involve new types of buyers in currently served geographic areas or the pursuit of prospects located in previously unserved geographic areas. The first scenario was present when People Express undertook its ill-fated attempt to woo business travelers to a bargain pleasure traveler airline. The second setting applied when Citibank engaged in a nationwide drive to sign up millions of additional cardholders for its MasterCard and Visa plans. And it holds true, of course, for Household Finance's valiant effort to penetrate the Japanese market for consumer loans.

Prerequisites for Successful Innovation

Innovation in a service business will not happen on a continuous basis unless the proper climate is created and nurtured. Innovativeness involves risk taking. Individuals must be encouraged to venture into uncharted territory. Not all of these ventures can and will be successful. But innovation is the sign of a leader and the fuel of progress.

In contrast to goods manufacturers, however, precious few service firms have formal new product structures. New products thus are all too often the result of whim or happenstance or competitive pressure rather than the outcome of an ongoing, carefully orchestrated effort.

Creating the Proper Climate

The constant updating of a service firm's offering is a necessary prerequisite for its survival and growth in the long run. But innovation is risky, both for individuals in terms of their careers and for the corporation as a whole in terms of financial and image consequences.[17] It involves the possibility of failure and thus requires a daring, entrepreneurial spirit: "Innovation is the specific tool of entrepreneurs, the means by which they exploit change as an opportunity for a different business or a different service."[18]

This entrepreneurial spirit can easily be stifled in large service organizations by inflexible bureaucracies that fail to recognize the merits of innovative approaches. "Now some big companies are fighting back. They are trying to create the spirit, zest and rewards of entrepreneurship right in their corridors, shop floors and laboratories. They are giving employees the resources and freedom to pursue their own ideas, cutting back on traditional red tape, endless meetings and other obstacles that can slow down innovation."[19] This endeavor to free creative people from frustrating restrictions and foster a climate of innovativeness has been called *intrapreneuring.*[20]

Service businesses are very much dependent on, and can greatly benefit from, the presence of an entrepreneurial spirit in their ranks. SAS turned from a bureaucratic, money-losing organization into one of the world's foremost business traveler airlines when a new philosophy authorized and encouraged frontline personnel to take charge of problems and solve them creatively: "By defining clear goals and strategies and then communicating them to his employees and training them to take responsibility for reaching those goals, the leader can create a secure working environment that fosters flexibility and innovation."[21]

Innovativeness tends to flourish in informal settings. Whereas such unstructured situations are feasible in small service firms, larger organizations need some degree of formal structure for their new product efforts. It then takes a deliberate and concerted effort to create, maintain, and nurture the proper *climate*. This concept could be defined as the set of enabling conditions within a firm that facilitates innovation. Besides organizational practices and procedures, this set includes most prominently management attitudes and support. These atttitudes have to combine a concern for employee needs with sensitivity to customer needs:

> When managers in service organizations establish policies and procedures, and otherwise engage in behaviors that show concern for the organization's clients, they are service *enthusiasts.* Service *enthusiasts* engage in activities designed to satisfy the organization's customers. Service *bureaucrats,* on the other hand, are interested in system maintenance, routine, and adherence to uniform operating guidelines and

procedures. The most important difference between these orientations is the service enthusiast's emphasis on the importance of interpersonal relationships at work, concern for the customer, and flexible application of rules as opposed to the bureaucrat's avoidance of interpersonal issues and stress on rules, procedures, and system maintenance.[22]

The proper climate thus will tend to exist where managers are service enthusiasts. They encourage and reward customer responsiveness and a willingness to take risks in developing and implementing new service ideas. "To unleash the innovative spirit, management must *tolerate failure.*"[23] And it must lend its full support to new product endeavors. This support can be demonstrated by means of an innovation fund—"a pool of dollars that is available to support the development and testing of innovative projects."[24]

Another invaluable resource can be franchisees:

> The flow of new ideas from its 1,800 franchisees is one major way McDonald's keeps ahead of its fast-food competition. While McDonald's rivals also tap their franchisees for ideas, McDonald's seems to have had more success with its independent operators, gleaning such winning ideas as the Big Mac, the Egg McMuffin and even Ronald McDonald. Ray Kroc, the chain's legendary founder who died in 1984, encouraged such ideas to percolate from franchisees.[25]

Kroc's successors continue to encourage a few nontraditional outlets to experiment with new ideas and test them on a broader basis if they appear to have merit.

Finally, because people are very much part of the service product, it is essential to involve customer-contact personnel in the innovation process.[26] They are essential to the success of this endeavor in two ways: They may have a better understanding of customer needs than their managers, and their enthusiastic and skillful participation in the ultimate delivery process is crucial to its success.[27]

New Product Organization in Service Businesses

By and large, service firms lack formal structures to drive, direct, and control their new product activities. New products often come about as the result of intuition, personal fancy or inspiration, availability of capacity, or competitive action. Rarely are new product ideas subjected to careful, thorough scrutiny. Not surprisingly, the new services that emerge from this haphazard approach tend to show a lackluster record. Clearly, a formal system and structure are needed for service firms' new product endeavors to ensure continuity of effort and better results.

That is precisely what some leading, highly innovative, and successful service firms have done. Marriott spent three years developing its Courtyard concept. This new type of motel reduces room size and amenities to attract budget-oriented business travelers in suburban locations. This effort was managed by Marriott's vice president for market development.[28] Similarly, the financial services giant Merrill Lynch employs a vice president for new product development, an indication of the importance that this corporation places on this function in retaining its leadership.

The development of its Cash Management Account from concept to operational reality took two years and involved fifty people.[29] Ten years after the initiation of this innovation, the firm's vice president for new product development reported on its success as follows:

> Merrill Lynch's Cash Management Account has been hailed as the most innovative, most revolutionary financial product of our generation. As a measure of its success, more than 20 look-alike central asset accounts have been introduced over the past few years.
>
> We designed CMA to meet the needs of affluent individuals. How have we done? Well, we've signed up more than a million customers and brought in $80 billion worth of assets. Today, we still have more than 75% share of the total market. If CMA were a bank, it would be no. 4 in the U.S. by asset size, right behind Chase Manhattan.[30]

Fast food chains place a similar emphasis on new product management. McDonald's has a vice president of product development, and Wendy's has a substantial research and development staff.[31] This level of commitment is understandable because the fast food industry has reached the maturity stage of the multisite service firm life cycle where "the number of new facilities opened declines substantially and the per facility volumes in real terms level off or in some cases actually decline."[32] To reinvigorate growth, a significant, sustained, well-organized new product effort is essential.

Other firms in a number of service industries show comparable levels of new product commitment and organization. Leading companies use new product proposal forms and guidelines to generate meaningful, adequately substantiated input into the new product process. They employ new product evaluation and review committees of senior executives that can be called into session on short notice to give prompt consideration to new proposals. They then put together systems design teams to create the proper operational framework. They may place ultimate new product authority in a top-level executive committee but leave implementation details to product managers, market managers, and/or venture teams.[33]

New Product Initiative in Service Firms

New product processes in service firms are driven by many of the same forces that energize their counterparts in goods-producing enterprises. These include financial objectives, such as higher sales revenues, market share, and/or profit. New service development may also be triggered by an advanced stage in a product's life cycle. Further, impetus can come from new technologies, changes in buyer behavior, and competitive pressure.[34]

New types of hardware may enable service performers to carry out their tasks faster and/or more accurately. Sophisticated diagnostic equipment can enable a medical professional or an automobile repair shop to offer new kinds of services or shorten production time. Whole new industries have emerged that are based on electronic delivery systems. And human labor may be displaced or customer convenience expanded by the use of service robots.[35]

Changes in buyer behavior create new opportunities for service entrepreneurs. Perhaps the single most significant development has been the growing proportion of working women. This has generated an unprecedented level of need for child day care. It has also contributed to the growth of shopping services and various types of personal financial planning assistance. As the trend toward deinstitutionalization takes hold, the need for home health care and adult day care for the elderly grows.

Competitive pressure is another powerful factor causing new product activities in service businesses. As a matter of fact, it is not uncommon for innovative services to sweep entire industries. Home equity loans have taken the banking industry by storm. "Super Saver" fares put pressure on competing airlines to follow suit. And "same day surgery" is becoming more and more common, sometimes performed in freestanding surgicenters. An idea whose time has come may be so strong that a company has no choice but to jump on the bandwagon.

Some initiating forces, however, are unique to service industries. Among them are the desire to utilize facilities, to cement relationships, or to leverage relationships. Many service providers operate expensive equipment and facilities, regardless of whether they are owned (telephone companies), leased (airlines), or simply managed (hotels). During low-utilization or idle times, this capital earns little or no return. Service businesses, however, tend to be subject to severe fluctuations in demand without the ability to use inventories as buffers. This situation gives rise to new services that result in incremental business during low utilization periods:

> Hamburger chains add breakfast items to their menus, and coffee shops add dinners to theirs. Urban hotels, which cater to the business traveler during the week, develop weekend "mini-vacation" packages for the suburban population in their geographic areas, while resort hotels, jammed with pleasure travellers during school vacations, develop special packages for business groups during off-seasons.[36]

Other examples include alpine slides built by ski resorts, discount calling programs offered by telephone companies, and catering services offered by hospitals.

The desire to strengthen relationships with the existing customer base comes naturally to a service business. After all, long-term relationships with loyal buyers are its stock in trade. This fact is such a truism in the linen rental business that the common way to grow is to buy established routes from competitors or acquire entire existing firms rather than build routes from scratch. In an effort to retain and expand its customer base, a service organization can offer different levels of service at different rates. For instance, in repair contracts, Pitney-Bowes guarantees varying turnaround times for its equipment. A powerful but also expensive way to cement relationships is to reward loyal customers with free travel, accommodations, or merchandise. Such programs are currently offered by airlines, hospitality chains, and credit card issuers.

Having expended considerable effort to establish, build, and maintain strong positive relationships with a carefully selected and cultivated group of buyers, a service firm is well advised to attempt to leverage this valuable asset by offering additional, meaningfully related services. Credit card issuers, for instance, have long marketed insurance, card protection, and travel plans, as well as merchandise catalogs, to their cardholder bases. Newsletter publishers commonly offer seminars and books, perhaps even consulting services, to their subscribers.

Several service industries—banking, telecommunications, transportation, for example—in the past have enjoyed or suffered the heavy hand of regulation by government agencies. In recent years, a number of these industries have been progressively deregulated, allowing their members to enter new fields or offer new types of services. This objective was, in fact, a powerful force behind the breakup of the Bell System. Entry barriers for new players have been lowered (in spite of the thrift crisis, more banks are being founded than closed), and a variety of new services have sprouted on the fertile soil of deregulation. With the shackles of regulation largely or completely shed, competitors become more creative and aggressive.

New Product Processes in Service Firms

In structuring new product processes, service firms need not reinvent the wheel. Rather, currently available models for new product evolution in goods manufacturing firms are definitely applicable to service industries.[37] In fact, the models presented to guide the evolution of new services tend to resemble closely, if not explicitly, the stages outlined by Booz, Allen & Hamilton. Figure 16–2 demonstrates this fact by synoptically comparing three current new service development models with the Booz, Allen & Hamilton outline.

However, to reflect more closely the involvement of service company personnel in the new product process and to illustrate the added steps of process and systems design and testing, as well as personnel training, Figure 16–3 presents a more detailed normative model of new service evolution. The model is shown to consist of a total of fifteen steps. These steps can be grouped into four major stages— direction, design, testing, and introduction. They will now be discussed in some detail.[38]

At the beginning of a process of new service evolution, senior management must chart the course for this effort and give it clear *direction*. This encompasses three sequential steps: the formulation of new service objectives and strategy, idea generation, and idea screening. Thus, the first phase of new service evolution consists of a series of early ideation steps that set the stage and direction for the subsequent effort.

Driven by a sense of urgency and a perceived need for the "quick fix," many service enterprises jump into new service projects by starting with idea generation without first reflecting on strategic issues. This is akin to lifting anchor without first determining the desired destination of a ship. The course of the vessel is then governed by external circumstances. Rather, a well-conceived and implemented new service program begins with the formulation of the objectives and strategy governing the new service effort. Of course, this direction is not conceived in a vacuum. It is

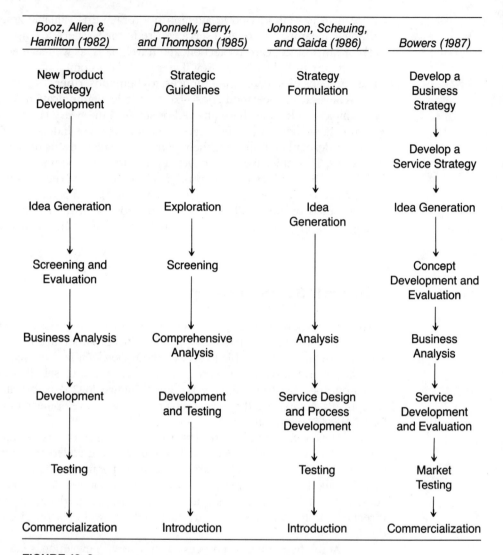

Booz, Allen & Hamilton (1982)	Donnelly, Berry, and Thompson (1985)	Johnson, Scheuing, and Gaida (1986)	Bowers (1987)
New Product Strategy Development	Strategic Guidelines	Strategy Formulation	Develop a Business Strategy
			Develop a Service Strategy
Idea Generation	Exploration	Idea Generation	Idea Generation
Screening and Evaluation	Screening		Concept Development and Evaluation
Business Analysis	Comprehensive Analysis	Analysis	Business Analysis
Development	Development and Testing	Service Design and Process Development	Service Development and Evaluation
Testing		Testing	Market Testing
Commercialization	Introduction	Introduction	Commercialization

FIGURE 16–2

Comparison of New Service Development Models (*Source:* The four models are reprinted with permission from Booz, Allen & Hamilton, Inc., *New Products Management for the 1980s* [New York: Booz, Allen & Hamilton, Inc., 1982], p. 11; James H. Donnelly, Jr., Leonard L. Berry, and Thomas W. Thompson, *Marketing Financial Services* [Homewood, IL: Dow Jones-Irwin, 1985], p. 147; Eugene M. Johnson, Eberhard E. Scheuing, and Kathleen A. Gaida, *Profitable Service Marketing* [Homewood, IL: Dow Jones-Irwin, 1986], p. 167; and Michael R. Bowers, "The New Service Development Process: Suggestions for Improvement," in *The Services Challenge: Integrating for Competitive Advantage,* edited by John A. Czepiel, Carol A. Congram, and James Shanahan [Chicago: American Marketing Association, 1987], p. 70)

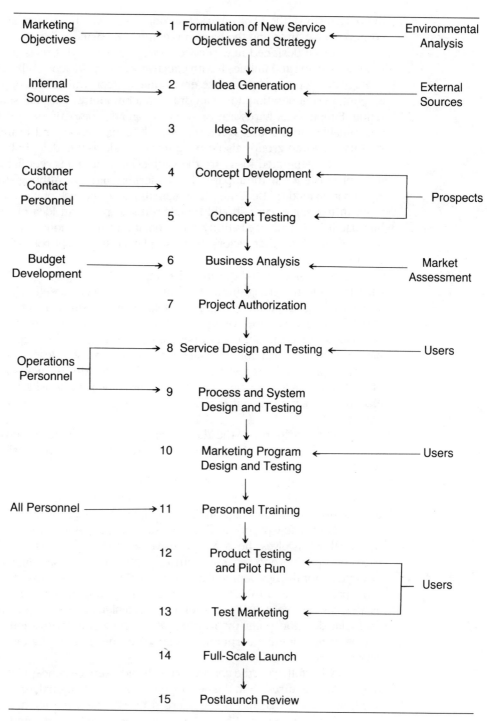

FIGURE 16–3
Normative Model of New Service Evolution

the outgrowth of the firm's marketing objectives, which, in turn, are derived from corporate objectives and the basic mission of the business.

A well-designed new service strategy drives and directs the entire service innovation effort and imbues it with effectiveness and efficiency. Whereas new service strategy development has to take environmental constraints and opportunities into account, idea generation, too, can draw on a number of external sources for inspiration. Suppliers of hardware or services, agents, competitors, and service buyers are valuable input sources. Internal search, consultation, and brainstorming with various employee groups also can significantly add to the idea pool.

The generated ideas are then subjected to a first screening to separate the more promising from the apparently less meritorious ideas. Although this preliminary examination tends to be largely judgmental, due to the lack of hard data at this early point in the game, care should be taken not to reject an idea out of hand simply because it is unusual. Feasibility and profitability are obvious key considerations at this juncture, but other factors may also play an important role, depending on the circumstances.

Steps 4 to 11 of the model comprise the *design* stage. This core phase essentially involves designing and refining a new service, as well as its delivery system and marketing program. In concept development, the surviving ideas are fleshed out into full-fledged service concepts with the help of input from prospects and the company's own customer contact personnel. A *concept* is a description of a potential new service. A typical concept statement would include a description of a problem that a prospect might experience, the rationale for offering the new service, an outline of its features and benefits, and an encouragement to consider its purchase. An example of such a concept statement for a potential new service was presented in Figure 7–2.

Buyer response to the alternative concepts is then examined during concept testing. "A concept test of a new service is a research technique designed to evaluate whether a prospective user (1) understands the idea of the proposed service, (2) reacts favorably to it and (3) feels it offers benefits that answer unmet needs."[39] This research step helps eliminate ideas that find little favor with buyers and simultaneously assists in shaping the feature and benefit bundles of attractive concepts.

For the few proposals that have successfully passed prior checkpoints, business analysis involves the comprehensive scrutiny of the business implications of each concept. This encompasses both a complete market assessment and the drafting of a budget for the development and introduction of each proposed new service. The principal purpose of this step is to develop recommendations for top management as to which new service ideas deserve to be implemented and look most promising. A crucial decision point then occurs at the project authorization step where top management commits corporate resources to the implementation of a single new service idea.

What follows is the conversion of the new service concept into an operational reality. This requires, first, the development of the operational aspects of the service itself, an activity that has been referred to as "blueprinting" a service.[40] Service design should incorporate both the input of prospective users and the active cooperation of operations people, who will ultimately be delivering the new service.

Intimately interwoven with the design of the service itself is the design of its delivery process and system. All of these components have to be developed and tested in concert with each other. The process and system design step, however, is internal in nature and does not involve user input. The delivery mechanism that is very much part of the intangible benefits component of a service has to be installed, refined, and debugged in order to ensure smooth delivery upon introduction. The introductory marketing program has to be formulated and tested in conjunction with prospective users. And all employees have to be familiarized with the nature and operational details of the new service, thus completing the design phase of the process. This last step is, however, critical. All too often, a new service fails because the firm's personnel have not been properly trained to sell and deliver the service.

The next stage of *testing* is broken down into two steps: product testing and pilot run and test marketing. Product testing is used to ascertain potential customers' acceptance of the new service, whereas a pilot run ensures its smooth functioning. Such an operating test represents a dry run that enables the firm to improve and fine-tune the service delivery process. Unfortunately,

> few companies are willing to invest the considerable sums required to prototype a functioning service, because they perceive little difference between the costs in labor, systems and set-up of going "live," and the costs of limited trial. Such logic is, of course, completely fallacious.
>
> Instead of a pilot test, actual market introduction is often the first real test of functionality and market acceptance. By that point, mistakes in design are harder to correct and service modifications needed in order to improve acceptance or operating efficiency are more laborious to implement. There is simply no substitute for a proper rehearsal.[41]

A first round of product testing can offer the new service to the firm's own employees. After subsequent refinements, the service can be retested with a limited group of customers or at a limited number of outlets. Once the service and its delivery system have been fine-tuned and the process has achieved stability, the service marketer can move on to test-market the innovation.

Test marketing examines the salability of the new service and field-tests its marketing program in a few branches of the organization or with a limited sample of buyers. In addition to testing further market reaction to the service (which may be offered in different configurations), test marketing allows management to evaluate alternative marketing mixes. For example, different prices may be charged to assess the impact of price on service demand. Completion of test marketing is followed by a review and final changes in the marketing effort.

As the following quote indicates, however, the results of test marketing are not always clear-cut. And even successful outcomes can produce logistical headaches for national fast food chains.

> One barrier that keeps a lot of promising items from making it to the big time is the policy most chains follow—mainly for cost reasons—of sticking to a standard menu across the country. If one region doesn't like something, that generally means the rest of the nation won't get it, either. A gourmet hamburger Wendy's was developing

ran into trouble in West Virginia where, a spokesman says, "people didn't seem to know what alfalfa sprouts and guacamole are." Burger King has had great success with a mustard burger in Texas—but can't seem to get non-Texans to eat it.

The logistics of national distribution also present a problem. McDonald's had to line up enough supplies of chicken to sell five million pounds of its McNuggets a week. And with more than 6,200 of its restaurants in the U.S., the company can't afford to risk selling items whose ingredients can be affected by droughts or sharp swings in price.[42]

With the delivery system and marketing program in place and thoroughly tested, the company now initiates the full-scale launch of the new service in the *introduction* phase. The innovation is introduced with all the attendant media fanfare to the company's entire marketing area or all its affiliated outlets for systemwide availability. This step is followed by a postlaunch review aimed at determining whether the new service objectives are being achieved, thus closing the loop to step 1 of the evolutionary process. Whether or not adjustments in the marketing program are called for in this control procedure, the management team will learn from this experience and benefit from it for future innovative endeavors.

SUMMARY

New product management in service firms simply represents a special application of the basic principles and methods presented in this book. As a vital sector of the economy, however, service industries, by and large, lack the new product sophistication found in packaged goods firms. Exceptions do, of course, exist. They tend to be confined, though, to industry leaders—large national or international firms that are well-known for their innovativeness.

Services are combinations of core, tangible, and intangible benefits. People, systems, and goods are very much part of the total product experience sought by customers. Several unique characteristics set services apart from goods and make their marketing more challenging. They include intangibility, perishability, simultaneity, inseparability, and heterogeneity.

As far as types of new services are concerned, the typology outlined in Chapter 1 of this book is equally applicable to services. It ranges from modification, differentiation, and diversification to market creation, market expansion, and market extension.

To ensure successful new products in service businesses, creating the proper climate for innovation is essential. This means fostering an entrepreneurial spirit and creating a comfort level in interpersonal relations that encourages risk taking and tolerates failure. Besides climate, however, a sustained innovative effort needs structure. Only a limited number of large service providers show adequate structure, using product managers, committees, and design teams.

New product processes in service firms are energized by many of the same forces that motivate their counterparts in manufacturing firms. They include financial objectives, the product life cycle, new technologies, changes in buyer behavior, and competitive pressure. The factors that are unique to service industries include the desire to utilize facilities, to cement relationships, and to leverage relationships.

A normative model is proposed that outlines the steps appropriate in service firms for evolutionary processes. It builds on earlier material and incorporates the added steps of process and systems design and testing and personnel training.

NOTES

1. See C. Robert Clements, Ronald Stiff, and John A. Czepiel, "Participant Perspectives on New Services Development Systems," in *Developing New Services,* edited by William R. George and Claudia E. Marshall (Chicago: American Marketing Association, 1984), 65.
2. Bernard H. Booms, Duane Davis, and Dennis Guseman, "Participant Perspectives on Developing a Climate for Innovation of New Services," in *Developing New Services,* edited by William R. George and Claudia E. Marshall (Chicago: American Marketing Association, 1984), 23.
3. Christopher H. Lovelock, "Developing and Implementing New Services," in *Developing New Services,* edited by William R. George and Claudia E. Marshall (Chicago: American Marketing Association, 1984), 57.
4. See Eugene M. Johnson, Eberhard E. Scheuing, and Kathleen A. Gaida, *Profitable Service Marketing* (Homewood, IL: Dow Jones-Irwin, 1986), 12.
5. Leonard L. Berry, "Services Marketing Is Different," in *Services Marketing,* edited by Christopher H. Lovelock (Englewood Cliffs, NJ: Prentice-Hall, 1984), 30.
6. See W. Earl Sasser, R. Paul Olsen, and D. Daryl Wyckoff, *Management of Service Operations* (Boston: Allyn & Bacon, 1978), 11.
7. This distinction was first suggested by Rathmell. See John M. Rathmell, *Marketing in the Service Sector* (Cambridge, MA: Winthrop Publishers, 1974), 7.
8. See A. Parasuraman, Valarie A. Zeithaml, and Leonard L. Berry, "A Conceptual Model of Service Quality and Its Implications for Future Research," *Journal of Marketing* (Fall 1985): 42. See also Patrick L. Townsend, *Commit to Quality* (New York: John Wiley & Sons, 1986), 4.
9. See Anthony DiPrimio, *Quality Assurance in Service Organizations* (Radnor, PA: Chilton Book Co., 1987), and A.C. Rosander, *Applications of Quality Control in the Service Industries* (New York: Marcel Dekker, 1985).
10. See the section on "relationship management" in Theodore Levitt, *The Marketing Imagination* (New York: Free Press, 1986), 111–126. See also Robert L. Desatnick, *Managing to Keep the Customer* (San Francisco: Jossey-Bass, 1987).
11. See Constanza Montana, "Hotels Offer 'Frequent-Stay' Plans to Lure Repeat Business Travelers," *Wall Street Journal,* 6 Jan. 1987, and Russell D. Levitt, *Loyalty Marketing* (New York: Loyalty Marketing Co., 1986).
12. See Rifka Rosenwein, "Psychotherapists Begin to Lose Reluctance to Self-Promotion," *Wall Street Journal,* 27 Aug. 1987.
13. See "Up in ARMs," *Poughkeepsie Journal,* 23 Aug. 1987, 1G.
14. See, for instance, Trish Hall, "At Fast-Food Restaurants, Plastic Is Out, and Marble, Brass and Greenhouses Are In," *Wall Street Journal,* 3 Dec. 1985.
15. Ellen S. Perelman, "The Story of CMA," *Transition* (April 1984): 21.

16. See Johnson, Scheuing, and Gaida, *Profitable Service Marketing,* 224–226.

17. See Ann Monroe, "Financial Creations: New-Securities Ideas Are Often Hatched, but Most Are Flops," *Wall Street Journal,* 25 March 1986.

18. Peter F. Drucker, *Innovation and Entrepreneurship* (New York: Harper & Row, 1986), 19.

19. John S. DeMott, "Here Come the Intrapreneurs," *Time,* 4 Feb. 1985, 36.

20. See Gifford Pinchot III, *Intrapreneuring: Why You Don't Have to Leave the Corporation to Become an Entrepreneur* (New York: Harper & Row, 1985).

21. Jan Carlzon, *Moments of Truth* (Cambridge, MA: Ballinger Publishing Co., 1987), 35.

22. Benjamin Schneider, "The Service Organization: Climate Is Crucial," *Organizational Dynamics* (Autumn 1980): 53–54.

23. James H. Donnelly, Jr., Leonard L. Berry, and Thomas W. Thompson, *Marketing Financial Services* (Homewood, IL: Dow Jones-Irwin, 1985), 142.

24. Ibid.

25. Robert Johnson, "McDonald's Franchisee Shakes Things Up," *Wall Street Journal,* 25 Aug. 1987.

26. See Booms, Davis, and Guseman, "Participant Perspectives," 25.

27. See Benjamin Schneider and David E. Bowen, "New Service Design, Development and Implementation and the Employee," in *Developing New Services,* edited by William R. George and Claudia E. Marshall (Chicago: American Marketing Association, 1984), 86–96.

28. See Steve Swartz, "How Marriott Changes Hotel Designs to Tap Midpriced Market," *Wall Street Journal,* 18 Sept. 1985.

29. See Perelman, "The Story of CMA," 22.

30. Brant Wansley, "Innovation at Merrill Lynch," paper presented at *Conference on Personal Financial Planning,* Virginia Beach, VA, 17 May 1985, 1.

31. See John Koten, "Fast-Food Firms' New Items Undergo Exhaustive Testing," *Wall Street Journal,* 5 Jan. 1984.

32. Sasser, Olsen, and Wyckoff, *Management of Service Operations,* 545.

33. See Donnelly, Berry, and Thompson, *Marketing Financial Services,* 143–145.

34. See Lovelock, "Developing and Implementing New Services," 58.

35. See Gene Bylinsky, "Invasion of the Service Robots," *Fortune,* 14 Sept. 1987, 81–88.

36. Sasser, Olsen, and Wyckoff, *Management of Service Operations,* 306.

37. See Clements, Stiff, and Czepiel, "Participant Perspectives," 65.

38. This discussion is based on Eberhard E. Scheuing and Eugene M. Johnson, "A Normative Model of New Service Developoment," paper presented at the 1987 Annual Meeting of the Atlantic Marketing Association, New Orleans, 1–3 Oct. 1987.

39. Patrick E. Murphy and Richard K. Robinson, "Concept Testing for Services," in *Marketing of Services,* edited by James H. Donnelly and William R. George (Chicago: American Marketing Association, 1981), 218.

40. See G. Lynn Shostack, "Service Design in the Operating Environment," in *Developing New Services,* edited by William R. George and Claudia E. Marshall (Chicago: American Marketing Association, 1984), 27–43.

41. Ibid., 35.

42. Koten, "Fast-Food Firms," 25.

CASE STUDY

CHAMPION BANKCARD PROCESSING

The Champion Bankcard Processing Company was formed in 1968 to provide credit card processing and accounting services for financial institutions (credit card issuers). Owned by some 400 member banks of varying size, Champion is a not-for-profit organization and one of the largest bank card processors in the United States. With annual revenues of approximately $80 million and more than 1,000 employees in Long Island, New York, and Cranford, New Jersey, the company has grown to a position of leadership in the bank card industry.

For its members, Champion serves as an alternative to an in-house credit card processing center by providing all of the back-office functions necessary to operate a bank card plan. These include purchase authorizations in response to merchant inquiries, processing and clearing of individual charge slips, preparation, stuffing, and mailing of monthly account statements, card embossing, merchant accounting, and issuance of management reports. As a key player in the bank card industry, Champion is committed to providing leadership, direction, and support to its members by identifying, developing, and implementing the automated financial and processing products and systems required to keep them competitive in the marketplace and help them achieve their goals.

New Product Organization

At Champion, the function of research, development, and implementation of new products intended to increase members' efficiency and profitability is part of corporate development. This function is headed by a vice president, who, in turn, reports to the executive vice president for finance and corporate development. It is responsible for carrying out the following activities involved in the evolution of new financial products:

This case was prepared for instructional purposes. Although based on an actual business situation, names, places, and other data have been disguised.

- Assess the needs of target groups
- Generate new product ideas and enhancements
- Evaluate the organization's strengths and resources
- Project cost savings or profit potential
- Design the product and its promotion for maximum acceptance
- Implement the product into mainstream processing

As Exhibit 16–A illustrates, the genesis of a new product at Champion begins with the emergence of a new product idea. This initial idea is then evaluated by product analysts and a market research study is undertaken to examine the level of potential demand for this kind of offering. A new product manager is assigned the role of product champion. This individual, who works for the vice president for corporate development, faces three decision-making options: conduct further analysis, modify the concept, or reject the proposal and abandon the project.

Provided that the new product manager decides to proceed, a preliminary product description and overview is then prepared for senior management review. Champion maintains a Product Evaluation and Review Committee (PERC), which is composed of four executive vice presidents representing operations, finance and corporate development, marketing, and document processing. This group serves essentially as a screening committee for all new product ideas percolating throughout the organization. If PERC gives its approval to a new concept, further marketing research is undertaken.

During the product research stage, the projected profitability of the proposed new service is determined. Cost estimates are developed, using a number of different assumptions, and various scenarios are analyzed with the help of computer modeling and spreadsheet matrix technology. Costs are then related to forecasted sales volumes to arrive at profit measures and a competitive pricing strategy. If the economic projections do not meet the organization's financial requirements (for instance, break-even point, present value, and profit margin), the

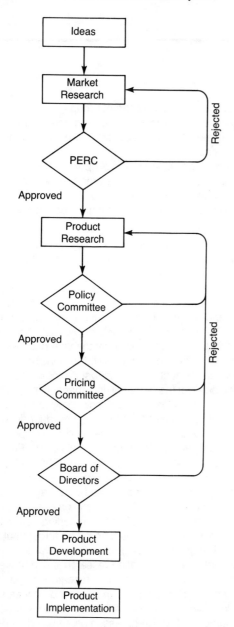

EXHIBIT 16–A
The New Product Development Process at Champion

new product manager can reconfigure the concept or, if this is not feasible, terminate the project.

If the economics of the situation look good, corporate development prepares an appropriation request to document the proposed product and requests the funds necessary to support the proposal. The appropriation request is routed to sponsoring management for approval and subsequently submitted to Champion's Policy Committee for review and approval. This key group is composed of all sixteen of Champion's officers whose ranks start from the vice-presidential level on up. Appropriation requests for new products are presented to the committee by the corporate development officer. The new product concept, operations support, member interest, and marketing and economics are discussed in detail with the committee. If approved by a majority vote, the recommended product pricing is then forwarded for evaluation to Champion's Pricing Committee.

The Pricing Committee consists of Champion's eight senior officers (senior vice presidents and executive vice presidents) and is chaired by a senior executive vice president. In determining prices, the committee conducts a thorough cost and competitive analysis, taking into account the desired overhead recovery level. After approval of the recommended pricing by the committee, the appropriation request and approved pricing are forwarded to Champion's board of directors for final approval. Constituted of fifteen member bank representatives, the board has the final new product decision-making authority.

With the board's approval, a new product moves into the final phase of product development. Here, computer applications are programmed, forms designed, documentation prepared, systems tested, support staff trained, and pilot implementation undertaken. Before full-scale introduction, new products are often test-marketed. If the results are satisfactory, the innovation is launched in the marketplace.

Adding a New Product to the Mix

Champion is committed to providing high-quality, cost-effective, and innovative electronic communications and data base management services to its member institutions. In accordance with this commitment, it recently applied its intricate new product evolution process to a new service package entitled Card Registration and Enhancement Services. The purpose of this package is to assist member banks in obtaining, activating, and retaining cardholders while reducing fraud losses. Although comparable service packages are available from third-party providers, several members had expressed an interest in obtaining these services from Champion.

A Card Registration and Enhancement Services package is a natural extension of Champion's present financial services mix and will enable the organization to be more competitive in its industry. One aspect of the card registration service lets the cardholder list all outstanding credit cards in one computerized file, thus providing an efficient means to report lost or stolen cards. The enhancement services menu enables member banks to offer their cardholders an array of valuable services that increase card activity. The package can be used to differentiate a member's card from those of its competitors and increase the member's market share. The menu includes:

Lost key retrieval
Name/address changes
Lost luggage locator
Car rental discounts
Emergency airline ticketing
Emergency cash
Travelers message center
Twenty-four hour travel reservations
Travel discounts
Air/common carrier travel accident insurance
Automobile rental collision deductible insurance
Hotel burglary insurance
Lost luggage reimbursement insurance

By participating in Champion's Card Registration and Enhancement Services program, members can realize per account savings averaging 60 percent vis-à-vis third parties offering comparable programs. The package is price and feature competitive and offers members the opportunity to increase cardholder outstandings (unpaid account balances, subject to interest charges), promote account activity, and curtail losses on lost/stolen cards.

The idea for the new service package emanated from several members (that is, owners/customers) who felt that their previous vendors' prices were high based on what was required to provide the service. This expression of interest caused corporate development to determine that preliminary member demand existed. Early investigation also indicated that such a package could be provided at a reasonable cost. Although the package included several travel and insurance protection services, Champion perceived the product as a natural extension of its members' credit card services offerings that warranted further research on this concept.

The preliminary product description received prompt approval from PERC. Corporate development then proceeded with further research. Costs were verified through market and competitor analysis, member bank interviews, communications with in-house operations/support staff, examination of trade journals, review of legal and contractual issues, and investigation of other information sources. These costs were then compared with projected sales volumes. It appeared that Champion could offer the package considerably cheaper than the competition.

The appropriation request and recommended pricing were approved in due course. Presented to the board, both received its enthusiastic imprimatur. Product development then moved into high gear. Like most other new products offered by the company, the new package was test-marketed before full-scale launch. Product complexity and competitive factors, testing costs, potential risks involved, and overall strategic considerations determined the level of effort.

Champion utilized a variety of testing techniques, involving its product support staff, member banks, and consumers. Initially, each service in the package was individually tested by systems technicians. Data entry of member bank and consumer test data was thoroughly tested to ensure system conformity. The internal processing of each service application was reviewed in conjunction with the corresponding output deliverables. Automated system interfaces to other accounting systems were examined for accuracy and efficiency. After completion of unit testing, Champion initiated the system testing phase, employing a minimal number of member and cardholder test accounts. During this phase, Champion tested all manual and automated system applications and was assured that all aspects would perform to specifications in a live production environment. Affected outside vendors, internal operations/support staff, a pilot test bank, and consumers participated. Internal operations/support staff were trained to administer the product's delivery process. And the consumer activities employing the enhancement services were closely monitored for error. After three months of pilot bank testing, Champion's corporate development management considered the test results satisfactory and launched the new product full scale in the marketplace.

Marketing the Card Registration and Enhancement Services package included the preparation of product advertisements and of various types of sales literature for distribution to prospects. Champion continues to monitor system performance and maintains the required ongoing system support. Predictably, corporate development is pursuing the addition of additional card enhancement services to expand the service offering further and remain competitive.

Counterstrike!

Only six weeks after Champion began marketing its new service package, ABC Processing struck back. This company had been providing card registration and enhancement services to about one dozen of Champion's member banks for the past three or four years. In an aggressive counterattack, it offered these banks a new Processor Group Discount Program that resulted in prices 10 to 15 percent below Champion's prices. This move was obviously designed to retain the business in the wake of Champion's entry into this field.

Discussion Questions

1. In your opinion, was it prudent for Champion to enter this competitive field at this point and in this manner? Why, or why not?
2. Outline and defend courses of action available to Champion after ABC's counterattack.
3. Should at some time Champion determine that operating expenses were increasing at a faster rate than revenues, what alternatives would be available to Champion's management to correct this situation?
4. After examining Champion's process of new product evolution, do you feel that the company is optimally organized to evaluate new product ideas and turn them into successful operating entities? Why, or why not? If you feel that improvement is possible and desirable, please outline your suggestions in detail.

BIBLIOGRAPHY

Abrams, Bill, "Exploiting Proven Brand Names Can Cut Risk of New Products." *Wall Street Journal,* 22 Jan. 1981.

Abrams, Bill, "Minnesota Mining and Manufacturing Co." *Wall Street Journal,* 9 June 1983.

Abrams, Bill, "Packaging Often Irks Buyers but Firms Are Slow to Change." *Wall Street Journal,* 28 Jan. 1982.

Abrams, Bill, and Janet Guyon, "Ten Ways to Restore Vitality to Old, Worn-Out Products." *Wall Street Journal,* 18 Feb. 1982.

"Advances in Scanner-Based Research System Yield Fast, Accurate New Product Test Results." *Marketing News,* 18 Sept. 1981, 20.

Alsop, Ronald, "Color Grows More Important in Catching Consumers' Eyes." *Wall Street Journal,* 29 Nov. 1984.

Alsop, Ronald, "For More Men, Old Gray Hair Ain't What It Appears to Be." *Wall Street Journal,* 30 July 1987.

Alsop, Ronald, "U.S. Concerns Seek Inspiration for Products from Overseas." *Wall Street Journal,* 3 Jan. 1985.

Alsop, Ronald, "What's a Nissan? New TV Ads Give Car Brand a Personality." *Wall Street Journal,* 15 Oct. 1987.

"AMA Board Approves New Marketing Definition." *Marketing News,* 1 March 1985.

Anders, George, "Ad Agencies and Big Concerns Debate World Brands' Value." *Wall Street Journal,* 14 June 1984.

Anderson, Rolph E., and Joseph F. Hair, Jr., *Sales Management: Text with Cases.* New York: Random House, 1983.

Andreasen, Alan R., "Attitudes and Customer Behavior: A Decision Model," in *Perspectives in Consumer Behavior,* edited by Harold H. Kassarjian and Thomas S. Robertson. Glenview, IL: Scott, Foresman, 1968.

Ansberry, Clare, "Simple Cameras Enjoy Rebound in Popularity." *Wall Street Journal,* 4 March 1988.

Ansberry, Clare, "When Employees Work at Home, Management Problems Often Arise." *Wall Street Journal,* 20 April 1987.

Arndt, Johan, "Word-of-Mouth Advertising and Perceived Risk," in *Perspectives in Consumer Behavior,* edited by Harold H. Kassarjian and Thomas S. Robertson. Glenview, IL: Scott, Foresman, 1968.

Assael, Henry, *Consumer Behavior and Marketing Action,* 3rd ed. Boston: Kent Publishing Co., 1987.

Bacon, Kenneth H., "Higher Quality Helps Boost U.S. Products." *Wall Street Journal* 11 Jan. 1988.

Bailey, Earl L., ed., *Product-Line Strategies.* New York: The Conference Board, 1982.

Bauer, Raymond A., "Consumer Behavior as Risk Taking," in *Perspectives in Consumer Behavior,* edited by Harold H. Kassarjian and Thomas S. Robertson. Glenview, IL: Scott, Foresman, 1968.

Baum, Laurie, "A Powerful Tonic for Warner-Lambert." *Business Week,* 30 Nov. 1987, 144–146.

Berman, Barry, and Joel R. Evans, "Marketing Warfare: A Scenario for the Next Ten Years." *Review of Business* (Summer 1984): 5–8.

Bernstein, Aaron, "How IBM Cut 16,200 Employees—Without an Ax." *Business Week,* 15 Feb. 1988, 98.

Berry, Leonard L., "Services Marketing Is Different," in *Services Marketing,* 29–37, edited by Christopher H. Lovelock. Englewood Cliffs, NJ: Prentice-Hall, 1984.

Blattberg, Robert, and John Golanty, "Tracker: An Early Test Market Forecasting and Diagnostic Model for New Product Planning." *Journal of Marketing Research* (May 1978).

Bonoma, Thomas V., "Get More Out Of Your Trade Shows." *Harvard Business Review* (Jan.–Feb. 1983): 75–83.

Booms, Bernard H., Duane Davis, and Dennis Guseman, "Participant Perspectives on Developing a Climate for Innovation of New Services," in *Developing New Services,* 23–26, edited by William R. George and Claudia E. Marshall. Chicago: American Marketing Association, 1984.

Booz, Allen & Hamilton, Inc., *New Products Management for the 1980s.* New York: Booz, Allen & Hamilton, Inc., 1982.

Boraiko, Allen A., "A Splendid Light: Lasers." *National Geographic,* March 1984, 335ff.

Bowers, Michael R., "The New Service Development Process: Suggestions for Improvement," in *The Services Challenge: Integrating for Competitive Advantage,* 67–71, edited by John A. Czepiel, Carole A. Congram, and James Shanahan. Chicago: American Marketing Association, 1987.

Buggie, Frederick D., *New Product Development Strategies.* New York: AMACOM, 1981.

Bussey, John, and Douglas R. Sease, "Speeding Up: Manufacturers Strive to Slice Time Needed to Develop Products." *Wall Street Journal,* 23 Feb. 1988.

Buzzell, Robert D., "Competitive Behavior and Product Life Cycles," in *Proceedings of the 1966 World Congress,* 50–64. Chicago: American Management Association, 1966.

Buzzell, Robert D., and Bradley T. Gale, *The PIMS Principles.* New York: Free Press, 1987.

Buzzell, Robert D., and Frederik D. Wiersema, "Successful Share-Building Strategies." *Harvard Business Review* (Jan.–Feb. 1981): 135–144.

Bylinsky, Gene, "Invasion of the Service Robots." *Fortune,* 14 Sept. 1987, 81–88.

Bylinsky, Gene, "The New Look at America's Top Lab." *Fortune,* 1 Feb. 1988, 60–64.

Cafarelli, Eugene J., *Developing New Products and Repositioning Mature Brands.* New York: John Wiley & Sons, 1980.

Capon, Noel, and Rashi Glazer, "Marketing and Technology: A Strategic Coalignment." *Journal of Marketing* (July 1987): 1–14.

Carlzon, Jan, *Moments of Truth.* Cambridge, MA: Ballinger Publishing Co., 1987.

Carroad, Paul A., and Connie A. Carroad, "Strategic Interfacing of R&D and Marketing." *Research Management* (Jan. 1982): 28–33.

"Changing a Corporate Culture—Can Johnson & Johnson Go from Band-Aids to High-Tech?" *Business Week,* 14 May 1984, 130ff.

Clements, C. Robert, Ronald Stiff, and John A. Czepiel, "Participant Perspectives on New Services Development Systems," in *Developing New Services,* 65–67, edited by William R. George and Claudia E. Marshall. Chicago: American Marketing Association, 1984.

"Color Needs to Be Integrated in Marketing Plans." *Marketing News,* 11 Nov. 1983, 3.

Cooper, Robert G., *Winning at New Products.* Reading, MA: Addison-Wesley Publishing Co., 1986.

"Copycat Stuff? Hardly!" *Business Week,* Sept. 14, 1987, 112.

Crawford, C. Merle, *New Products Management.* Homewood, IL: Irwin, 1983.

Crawford, C. Merle, *New Products Management,* 2nd ed. Homewood, IL: Irwin, 1987.

Crawford, C. Merle, "Unsolicited New Product Ideas: Handle with Care." *Research Management* (Jan. 1975), 20–25.

Crissy, William, and Robert Boewadt, "Pricing in Perspective." *Sales Management,* 15 June 1971, 44.

Crosby, Philip B., *Quality is Free.* New York: McGraw-Hill, 1979.

Danger, E.P., *Selecting Colour for Packaging.* Brookfield, VT: Gower Publishing Co., 1987.

Day, George S., "The Product Life Cycle: Analysis and Applications Issues." *Journal of Marketing* (Fall 1981): 60–67.

Dean, Joel, "Pricing Policies for New Products." *Harvard Business Review* (Nov.–Dec. 1976).

DeMott, John S., "Here Come the Intrapreneurs." *Time,* 4 Feb. 1985, 36–37.

Desatnick, Robert L., *Managing to Keep the Customer.* San Francisco: Jossey-Bass, 1987.

Dhalla, Nariman K., and Sonia Yuspeh, "Forget the Product Life Cycle Concept!" *Harvard Business Review* (Jan.–Feb. 1976), 103–104.

DiPrimio, Anthony, *Quality Assurance in Service Organizations.* Radnor, PA: Chilton Book Co., 1987.

Donnelly, James H., Jr., Leonard L. Berry, and Thomas W. Thompson, *Marketing Financial Services.* Homewood, IL: Dow Jones-Irwin, 1985.

Dreyfack, Kenneth, "The Big Brands Are Back in Style." *Business Week,* 12 Jan. 1987, 74.

Drucker, Peter F., *Innovation and Entrepreneurship.* New York: Harper & Row, 1986.

Due, Tananarive, "We the People Speak: Give Us Square Kix, Flying Beauty Parlors." *Wall Street Journal,* 14 Sept. 1987.

Duerr, Michael G., *The Commercial Development of New Products.* New York: The Conference Board, 1986.

Dugas, Christine, "Marketing's New Look." *Business Week,* 26 Jan. 1987, 64–69.

Dumaine, Brian, "Designer Bones." *Fortune,* 18 Feb. 1985, 109–110.

Endicott, Craig, "Rating the Soaps in the Quad Cities." *Advertising Age,* 22 Feb. 1982.

Engelmayer, Paul A., "Campbell Plans to Drop Its Tin Soup Can, Reflecting New Emphasis on Convenience." *Wall Street Journal,* 28 March 1984, 35.

Engstrom, Theresa, "Polaroid Pegs Its Future on Electronics." *Wall Street Journal,* 16 Aug. 1984.

" 'Excellence, Inc.': Lectures, Spinoffs, and a TV Special." *Business Week,* 5 Nov. 1984, 88.

Flax, Steven, "How to Snoop on Your Competitors." *Fortune,* 14 May 1984, 28ff.

Flint, Jerry, "Best Car Wins." *Forbes,* 27 Jan. 1986, 73–77.

Foster, Richard N., *Innovation: The Attacker's Advantage.* New York: Summit Books, 1986.

Fox, Robert A., "Putting Marketing on a 'Business' Basis." Presentation to 1982 Marketing Conference, sponsored by The Conference Board, New York, 20 Oct. 1982.

Freedman, Alix M., "National Firms Find That Selling to Local Tastes Is Costly, Complex." *Wall Street Journal,* 9 Feb. 1987.

Freedman, Alix M., "Space-Age Savor: Flavor Specialists Strive for Better Microwave Foods." *Wall Street Journal,* 29 July 1987.

Frey, John B., "Pricing and Product Life Cycle." *Chemtech* (Jan. 1985): 40–43.

Gannes, Stuart, "The Good News about U.S. R&D." *Fortune,* 1 Feb. 1988, 48–56.

"Grand Union: Jimmy Goldsmith's Maverick Plan to Restore Profitability." *Business Week,* 14 May 1984.

Gurnee, Robert F., "Revolution in the Financial Services Industry." Remarks delivered at the 23rd Annual Business Conference of St. John's University, New York, 5 April 1984.

Guyon, Janet, "Fixing a Snack: The Public Doesn't Get a Better Potato Chip without a Bit of Pain." *Wall Street Journal,* 25 March 1983.

Haas, Alan D., "The Kindest Cut of All." *American Way* (Aug. 1984): 99ff.

Hafner, Katherine M., "Bright Smiles, Sweaty Palms." *Business Week,* 1 Feb. 1988, 22–23.

Hall, Trish, "At Fast-Food Restaurants, Plastic Is Out, and Marble, Brass and Greenhouses Are In." *Wall Street Journal,* 3 Dec. 1985.

Hamilton, Joan O'C., "Birth of a Blockbuster: How Genentech Delivered the Goods." *Business Week,* 30 Nov. 1987, 138–142.

Hamilton, Joan O'C., "Old-Time Seltzer in New-Fangled Bottles." *Business Week,* 14 Sept. 1987, 164.

Hampton, William J., and James R. Norman, "General Motors: What Went Wrong." *Business Week,* 16 March 1987, 102–110.

Harrigan, Kathryn Rudie, "Strategies for Declining Industries." *The Journal of Business Strategy* (Fall 1980), 24–30.

Harris, John S., "The New Product Profile Chart: Selecting and Appraising New Projects." *Chemical and Engineering News* 39 (17 April 1961).

Heany, Donald F., "Degrees of Product Innovation." *Journal of Business Strategy* (Spring 1983): 3–14.

Hisrich, Robert D., and Michael P. Peters. *Marketing Decisions for New and Mature Products.* Columbus, OH: Charles E. Merrill, 1984.

"The Hollow Corporation." *Business Week,* Special Report, 3 March 1986, 56–85.

Hopkins, David S., *Options in New-Product Organization.* New York: The Conference Board, 1974.

How to Create Advertising That Sells. New York: Ogilvy & Mather.

"How Xerox Speeds Up the Birth of New Products." *Business Week,* 19 March 1984, 58–59.

Ingrassia, Lawrence, "A Matter of Taste: There's No Way to Tell if a New Food Product Will Please the Public." *Wall Street Journal,* 26 Feb. 1980.

Ingrassia, Lawrence, "Negative Images: Polaroid Faces Tough Sell with Its New Instant while Kodak Confronts Doubts about Its 35-mm." *Wall Street Journal,* 25 March 1986.

"Invention Rejected 20 Times: Copier Revolutionized Work." *Sunday Freeman,* 29 Sept. 1985, 53–54.

"It's Rush Hour for 'Telecommuting,' " *Business Week,* 23 Jan. 1984, 99.

Jain, Subhash C., *Marketing Planning & Strategy.* Cincinnati: South-Western Publishing Co., 1981.

Johnson, Eugene M., David L. Kurtz, and Eberhard E. Scheuing, *Sales Management: Concepts, Practices, and Cases.* New York: McGraw-Hill, 1986.

Johnson, Eugene M., Eberhard E. Scheuing, and Kathleen A. Gaida, *Profitable Service Marketing.* Homewood, IL: Dow Jones-Irwin, 1986.

Johnson, Robert, "McDonald's Franchisee Shakes Things Up." *Wall Street Journal,* 25 Aug. 1987.

Johnson, Ross H., and Richard T. Weber, *Buying Quality.* New York: Franklin Watts, 1985.

Johnson Tracy, Eleanor, "Here Come Brand-Name Fruit and Veggies." *Fortune,* 18 Feb. 1985, 105.

Katz, Elihu, "The Two-Step Flow of Communication," in *Perspectives in Consumer Behavior,* edited by Harold H. Kassarjian and Thomas S. Robertson. Glenview, IL: Scott, Foresman, 1968.

Katz, Elihu, and Paul F. Lazarsfeld, *Personal Influence.* New York: Free Press, 1955.

Khost, Henry P., "Pretesting to Avoid Product Postmortems: Simulated Test Marketing Delivers on Its Promises." *Advertising Age,* 22 Feb. 1982, M-10–M-11.

King, Charles W., "Fashion Adoption: A Rebuttal to the 'Trickle Down' Theory," in *Dimensions of Consumer Behavior,* 2nd ed., edited by James U. McNeal. New York: Appleton-Century-Crofts, 1969.

Klein, Robert L., "Right Price on New Product Boosts Profit Potential." *Marketing Review* (Sept.–Oct. 1985): 24–25.

Koten, John, "Car Makers Use 'Image' Map as Tool to Position Products." *Wall Street Journal,* 22 March 1984.

Koten, John, "Fast-Food Firms' New Items Undergo Exhaustive Testing." *Wall Street Journal,* 5 Jan. 1984.

Kotler, Philip, *Marketing Management.* Englewood Cliffs, NJ: Prentice-Hall, 1967.

Kotler, Philip, *Marketing Management,* 6th ed. Englewood Cliffs, NJ: Prentice-Hall, 1988.

Kotler, Philip, *Principles of Marketing,* 2nd ed. Englewood Cliffs, NJ: Prentice Hall, 1983.

Krogh, Lester C., "Can the Entrepreneurial Spirit Exist within a Large Company?" Paper delivered at the 1984 Research & Development Conference of the Conference Board, New York, 25 April 1984.

Kuczmarski, Thomas D., and Steven J. Silver, "Strategy: The Key to Successful New Product Development." *Management Review* (July 1982).

Kurtz, David L., and Louis E. Boone, *Marketing,* 2nd ed. Hinsdale, IL: Dryden Press, 1984.

Labich, Kenneth, "Monsanto's Brave New World." *Fortune,* 30 April 1984, 57ff.

Larson, Erik, "Many Top Secrets in the Silicon Valley Are Spilled at Tables." *Wall Street Journal,* 29 June 1984.

Levitt, Russell D., *Loyalty Marketing.* New York: Loyalty Marketing Co., 1986.

Levitt, Theodore, "Exploit the Product Life Cycle." *Harvard Business Review* (Nov.–Dec. 1965): 81–94.

Levitt, Theodore, *The Marketing Imagination.* New York: Free Press, 1986.

Levoy, Gregg, "Up in Smoke." *American Way* (1 Oct. 1987).

Lewis, Geoff, "Big Changes at Big Blue." *Business Week,* 15 Feb. 1988, 92–98.

"Life in the Electronic Playpen." *Time,* 28 May, 1984, 70–71.

Loeb, Margaret, "Testers of Cigarettes Find On-Job Puffing Isn't a Drag." *Wall Street Journal,* 22 Aug. 1984.

Lovelock, Christopher H., "Developing and Implementing New Services," in *Developing New Services,* 44–64, edited by William R. George and Claudia E. Marshall. Chicago: American Marketing Association, 1984.

Management of the New Product Function. New York: Association of National Advertisers, 1980.

Market Testing Consumer Products. New York: National Industrial Conference Board, 1967.

McDaniel, Carl, and David A. Gray, "The Product Manager." *California Management Review* (Fall 1980).

McGuire, E. Patrick, *Generating New-Product Ideas.* New York: The Conference Board, 1972.

Miller, James P., "Search for New Drugs Focuses on Organisms under the Sea." *Wall Street Journal,* 24 July 1987.

Monroe, Ann, "Financial Creations: New-Securities Ideas Are Often Hatched, but Most Are Flops." *Wall Street Journal,* 25 March 1986.

Montana, Constanza, "Hotels Offer 'Frequent-Stay' Plans to Lure Repeat Business Travelers." *Wall Street Journal,* 6 Jan. 1987.

More, Roger A., "Risk Factors in Accepted and Rejected New Industrial Products." *Industrial Marketing Management* (Nov. 1982): 9–15.

Morris, Betsy, "Placing Products: Marketing Firm Slices U.S. into 240,000 Parts to Spur Clients' Sales." *Wall Street Journal,* Nov. 3, 1986.

"Most New Products Start with a Bang, End up as a Bomb." *Marketing News,* 27 March 1987, 36.

Murphy, John M., "Developing New Brand Names," in *Branding: A Key Marketing Tool,* 86–97, edited by John M. Murphy. New York: McGraw-Hill, 1987.

Murphy, John M., "What is Branding?" in *Branding: A Key Marketing Tool,* 1–12, edited by John M. Murphy. New York: McGraw-Hill, 1987.

Murphy, Patrick E., and Richard K. Robinson, "Concept Testing for Services," in *Marketing of Services,* 217–220, edited by James H. Donnelly and William R. George. Chicago: American Marketing Association, 1981.

Naisbitt, John, *Megatrends.* New York: Warner Books, 1984.

Nauck, Hasso G., "Mit Markentechnik gegen 'No-Names,' " *Marketing Journal* 1 (1984): 8–12.

"New Products Museum Favors Good Ideas Gone Wrong." *Sunday Freeman,* 23 Sept. 1984, 49.

"The New Sears: Unable to Grow in Retailing, It Turns to Financial Services." *Business Week,* 16 Nov. 1981.

"No Smoking." *Business Week,* 27 July 1987, 40–52.

Opatow, Lorna, "Packaging Is Most Effective When It Works in Harmony with the Positioning of a Brand." *Marketing News,* 3 Feb. 1984.

Parasuraman, A., Valarie A. Zeithaml, and Leonard L. Berry, "A Conceptual Model of Service Quality and Its Implications for Future Research. *Journal of Marketing* (Fall 1985): 41–50.

Perelman, Ellen S., "The Story of CMA." *Transition* (April 1984): 21–27.

Peters, Thomas J., "A Skunkworks Tale." *Best of Business* (Spring 1984): 80–88.

Peters, Thomas J., and Robert H. Waterman, Jr., *In Search of Excellence.* New York: Harper & Row, 1982.

Peters, Thomas J., and Robert H. Waterman, Jr., *In Search of Excellence.* Reprint. New York: Warner Books, 1984.

Pinchot, Gifford, III, *Intrapreneuring: Why You Don't Have to Leave the Corporation to Become an Entrepreneur.* New York: Harper & Row, 1985.

Pitzer, Mary J., "Hey, Ma, What's in the Microwave?" *Business Week,* 30 Nov. 1987, 68, 70.

Port, Otis, "The Push for Quality." *Business Week,* 8 June 1987, 130–135.

"Quaker State Expects Sales Gains with New Packaging System for Oil." *Marketing News,* 3 Feb. 1984, 7.

Qualls, William, Richard W. Olshavsky, and Ronald E. Michaels, "Shortening of the PLC—An Empirical Test." *Journal of Marketing* (Fall 1981): 76–80.

Rathmell, John M., *Marketing in the Service Sector.* Cambridge, MA: Winthrop Publishers, 1974.

"Repositioned Buitoni Foods Tests Marketing Campaign in N.Y., Eyes National Distribution." *Marketing News,* 30 Oct. 1981, 1, 8.

"Research and Development." *Economic Roadmaps* (Oct. 1986): 1–4.

"Research Methodology Detailed for Repositioning Mature Brands." *Marketing News,* 24 June 1983.

Richman, Barry M., "A Rating Scale for Product Innovation." *Business Horizons* (Summer 1962): 37–44.

Ricks, David A., *Big Business Blunders: Mistakes in Multinational Marketing.* Homewood, IL: Dow Jones-Irwin, 1983.

Ries, Al, and Jack Trout, *Marketing Warfare.* New York: McGraw-Hill, 1986.

Ries, Al, and Jack Trout, *Positioning: The Battle for Your Mind.* New York: McGraw-Hill, 1981.

"R.J. Reynolds: The Consumer Is King Again," *Business Week,* 4 June 1984.

Robertson, Dan H., and Danny N. Bellenger, *Sales Management.* New York: Macmillan, 1980.

Rogers, Everett M., *Diffusion of Innovations,* 1st ed. New York: Free Press, 1962.

Rogers, Everett M., *Diffusion of Innovations,* 3rd ed. New York: Free Press, 1983.

Rosander, A.C., *Applications of Quality Control in the Service Industries.* New York, Marcel Dekker, 1985.

Rosenwein, Rifka, "Psychotherapists Begin to Lose Reluctance to Self-Promotion." *Wall Street Journal,* 27 Aug. 1987.

Salmans, Sandra, "New Trials in Test Marketing." *New York Times,* 11 April 1982.

Sasser, W. Earl, R. Paul Olsen, and D. Daryl Wyckoff, *Management of Service Operations.* Boston: Allyn & Bacon, 1978.

Scheuing, Eberhard E., "Focus Group Interviews—A Hot Line to Your Customers," in *Marketing Update.* New York: Alexander-Norton Publishers, 1977.

Scheuing, Eberhard E., "Pricing New Products," in *Marketing Update.* New York: Alexander-Norton Publishers, 1977.

Scheuing, Eberhard E., *Purchasing Management.* Englewood Cliffs, NJ: Prentice-Hall, 1989.

Scheuing, Eberhard E., and Eugene M. Johnson, "A Normative Model of New Service Development." Paper presented at the 1987 Annual Meeting of the Atlantic Marketing Association, New Orleans, 1–3 Oct. 1987.

Schiffman, Leon G., and Leslie Lazar Kanuk, *Consumer Behavior,* 3rd ed. Englewood Cliffs, NJ: Prentice-Hall, 1987.

Schneider, Benjamin, "The Service Organization: Climate Is Crucial." *Organizational Dynamics* (Autumn 1980): 52–65.

Schneider, Benjamin, and David E. Bowen, "New Service Design, Development and Implementation and the Employee," in *Developing New Services,* 82–101, edited by William R. George and Claudia E. Marshall. Chicago: American Marketing Association, 1984.

Sease, Douglas R., "Selling Abroad: U.S. Exporters Begin to Post Sizable Gains in a Variety of Lines." *Wall Street Journal,* 31 Aug. 1987.

Selecting an Advertising Agency. New York: Association of National Advertisers, 1977.

Seligman, Daniel, "Don't Bet against Cigarette Makers." *Fortune,* 17 Aug. 1987, 70–77.

"The Serpentine Path to New Product Success." *Quaker Quarterly* (31 March 1984).

Shelton, Dwight J., "Regional Marketing Works and Is Here to Stay." *Marketing News,* 6 Nov. 1987, 1, 25.

Shostack, G. Lynn, "Service Design in the Operating Environment," in *Developing New Services,* 27–43, edited by William R. George and Claudia E. Marshall. Chicago: American Marketing Association, 1984.

Staw, Barry M., and Jerry Ross, "Knowing When to Pull the Plug." *Harvard Business Review* (March–April 1987): 68–74.

Stein, Jerome W., "How to Develop a Successful Advertising Campaign," in *Marketing Update.* New York: Alexander-Norton Publishers, 1979.

Stein, Jerome W., "How to Select the Right Advertising Agency," in *Marketing Update.* New York: Alexander-Norton Publishers, 1977.

Stricharchuk, Gregory, "Smokestack Industries Adopt Sophisticated Sales Approach." *Wall Street Journal,* 15 March 1984, 33.

Stundza, Tom, "Scrap Scrapes against the Environment." *Purchasing,* 9 April 1987, 64A4–64A11.

"Supermarket Format Propels Bookstop." *Chain Store Age,* Dec. 1987, 57–60.

Swartz, Steve, "How Marriott Changes Hotel Designs to Tap Midpriced Market." *Wall Street Journal,* 18 Sept. 1985.

Tauber, Edward M., "Brand Franchise Extension: New Product Benefits from Existing Brand Names." *Business Horizons,* March–April 1981, 36–41.

Taylor, Alex, III, "Who's Ahead in the World Auto War." *Fortune,* 9 Nov. 1987, 74–88.

Terpstra, Vern, *International Marketing,* 4th ed. Hinsdale, IL: Dryden Press, 1987.

Toffler, Alvin, *The Third Wave.* New York: William Morrow & Co., 1980.

Tottis, Kevin, "Auto Makers Look for Ideas in Rivals' Cars." *Wall Street Journal,* 20 July 1982.

Townsend, Patrick L., *Commit to Quality.* New York: John Wiley & Sons, 1986.

Treece, James B., "Can Ford Stay on Top?" *Business Week,* 28 Sept. 1987, 78–86.

Udell, Gerald G., and Del I. Hawkins, "Corporate Policies and Procedures for Evaluating Unsolicited Product Ideas." *Research Management* (Nov. 1978), 24ff.

"Up in ARMs." *Poughkeepsie Journal,* 23 Aug. 1987, 1G.

von Hippel, Eric, "Get New Products from Customers." *Harvard Business Review* (March–April 1982): 117–122.

Wansley, Brant, "Innovation at Merrill Lynch." Paper presented at Conference on Personal Financial Planning. Virginia Beach, VA, 17 May 1985, 1–24.

Wells, Ken, "How 500 Cats Play Guinea Pig in Pursuit of the Purrfect Food." *Wall Street Journal,* 20 April 1984.

What Advertising Agencies Are: What They Do and How They Do It. New York: American Association of Advertising Agencies, 1976.

Wind, Yoram, "A Framework for Classifying New-Product Forecasting Models," in *New Product Forecasting,* 3–42, edited by Yoram Wind, Vijay Mahajan, and Richard N. Cardozo. Lexington, MA: D.C. Heath Co., 1981.

Wind, Yoram J., *Product Policy: Concepts, Methods, and Strategy.* Reading, MA: Addison-Wesley Publishing Co., 1982.

INDEX

WE VALUE YOUR OPINION—PLEASE SHARE IT WITH US

Merrill Publishing and our authors are most interested in your reactions to this textbook. Did it serve you well in the course? If it did, what aspects of the text were most helpful? If not, what didn't you like about it? Your comments will help us to write and develop better textbooks. We value your opinions and thank you for your help.

Text Title _____ Edition _____

Author(s) _____

Your Name (optional) _____

Address _____

City _____ State _____ Zip _____

School _____

Course Title _____

Instructor's Name _____

Your Major _____

Your Class Rank _____ Freshman _____ Sophomore _____ Junior _____ Senior

_____ Graduate Student

Were you required to take this course? _____ Required _____ Elective

Length of Course? _____ Quarter _____ Semester

1. Overall, how does this text compare to other texts you've used?

_____ Superior _____ Better Than Most _____ Average _____ Poor

2. Please rate the text in the following areas:

	Superior	Better Than Most	Average	Poor
Author's Writing Style	_____	_____	_____	_____
Readability	_____	_____	_____	_____
Organization	_____	_____	_____	_____
Accuracy	_____	_____	_____	_____
Layout and Design	_____	_____	_____	_____
Illustrations/Photos/Tables	_____	_____	_____	_____
Examples	_____	_____	_____	_____
Problems/Exercises	_____	_____	_____	_____
Topic Selection	_____	_____	_____	_____
Currentness of Coverage	_____	_____	_____	_____
Explanation of Difficult Concepts	_____	_____	_____	_____
Match-up with Course Coverage	_____	_____	_____	_____
Applications to Real Life	_____	_____	_____	_____

3. Circle those chapters you especially liked:

   1   2   3   4   5   6   7   8   9   10   11   12   13   14   15   16   17   18   19   20

   What was your favorite chapter? _____

   Comments:

4. Circle those chapters you liked least:

   1   2   3   4   5   6   7   8   9   10   11   12   13   14   15   16   17   18   19   20

   What was your least favorite chapter? _____

   Comments:

5. List any chapters your instructor did not assign. _____

6. What topics did your instructor discuss that were not covered in the text?_____

   _____

7. Were you required to buy this book? _____ Yes   _____ No

   Did you buy this book new or used? _____ New   _____ Used

   If used, how much did you pay? _____

   Do you plan to keep or sell this book? _____ Keep   _____ Sell

   If you plan to sell the book, how much do you expect to receive? _____

   Should the instructor continue to assign this book? _____ Yes   _____ No

8. Please list any other learning materials you purchased to help you in this course (e.g., study guide, lab manual).

   _____

9. What did you like most about this text? _____

   _____

10. What did you like least about this text? _____

    _____

11. General comments:

    May we quote you in our advertising? _____ Yes   _____ No

    Please mail to: Boyd Lane
    College Division, Research Department
    Box 508
    1300 Alum Creek Drive
    Columbus, Ohio 43216

    Thank you!